The Body and the Symbol: Where Desire Takes Form

by

Deivede Eder Ferreira

The Body and the Symbol: Where Desire Takes Form

Psychoanalysis Series, Volume 3

Deivede Eder Ferreira Psychoanalyst

Published by ABRAFP, 2025.

THE BODY AND THE SYMBOL: WHERE DESIRE TAKES FORM

First edition. November 3, 2025.

ISBN: 979-8230987000

Written by Deivede Eder Ferreira Psychoanalyst.

Also by Deivede Eder Ferreira Psychoanalyst

Psychoanalysis Series
Psychoanalysis: The Hidden Architecture of the Mind
Dreams and the Language of the Unconscious
The Body and the Symbol: Where Desire Takes Form
The Mirror of Desire: How the Unconscious Shapes Love

The Philosophers We Loved: A Fictional Collection by ABRAFP
When Plato Loved: The Tragedy of the Man Who Tried to Show the Sun
Schopenhauer, Nietzsche and La Mettrie: The Last Banquet

Standalone
Psychoanalysis

Watch for more at www.abrafp.org.

Table of Contents

Front Matter

Aos cartógrafos silenciosos da alma, aqueles que navegam incansavelmente pelas paisagens labirínticas da psique e cujos instrumentos de compreensão muitas vezes traçam os contornos dos tremores mais profundos do corpo. Este trabalho é oferecido como um humilde testemunho de suas percepções profundas e muitas vezes não ditas. É para os analistas que ouvem não apenas as palavras, mas também os sussurros da carne, para os psicólogos que testemunham a linguagem eloqüente do sofrimento somático e para os psicoterapeutas que guiam seus pacientes através das raízes emaranhadas da experiência psicossomática. É para os alunos que começam sua jornada com uma curiosidade ardente pela condição humana em sua forma mais visceral, ousando questionar como o peso intangível da emoção pode se manifestar na realidade tangível de um músculo tenso, uma dor persistente ou uma sensação fantasma. É para os estudiosos literários que encontram na prosa de Woolf e Mann ecos do mundo interior, e para os filósofos que lidam com a existência em seu nível mais fundamental, corpóreo. Para todos aqueles que entendem que a história humana não está meramente escrita na mente, mas inscrita, do primeiro ao último suspiro, na própria substância do nosso ser, este livro é amorosamente dedicado. Que sirva como um companheiro em suas explorações, uma faísca para uma investigação mais aprofundada e um lembrete do diálogo requintado e duradouro entre a carne e o espírito.

Chapter 1: The Body's Silent Narrative

A forma humana, tão prontamente percebida como um mero vaso biológico, um edifício robusto de ossos, músculos e tendões que nos transporta pelo mundo, é na verdade um instrumento muito mais profundo e intrincado. Não é uma testemunha silenciosa de nossas vidas, mas um participante ativo, na verdade, essencial, no grande, muitas vezes turbulento, desdobramento de nossas mentes inconscientes. Dentro de sua carne, sua própria substância, estão inscritos os dramas de nossas vidas psíquicas mais profundas, um testemunho da conexão indelével entre o que sentimos, o que reprimimos e como nos manifestamos no mundo tangível. Este livro embarca em uma exploração dessa potente simbiose, postulando o corpo como uma tela viva sobre a qual os aspectos mais profundos e muitas vezes ocultos da psique são gravados. Começamos com a premissa de que nossa existência física está longe de ser um pano de fundo passivo; em vez disso, é um colaborador ativo na construção e expressão de nossas narrativas inconscientes.

Considere por um momento a linguagem sutil de nossa fisicalidade. Um tremor na mão ao enfrentar uma verdade difícil, um aperto repentino no peito com a menção de uma memória esquecida, uma dor persistente na parte inferior das costas que parece ancorar um fardo não expresso. Estas não são meras falhas biológicas, disfunções arbitrárias em um sistema previsível. São, de fato, formas potentes de comunicação, enunciados de uma parte de nós mesmos que muitas vezes escapa à expressão linguística direta. O corpo, em sua miríade de sensações, seus gestos involuntários, suas próprias posturas, torna-se um texto rico e em camadas, falando em um dialeto antigo e profundamente pessoal. É o terreno fértil onde as correntes etéreas de nossos pensamentos mais profundos, nossos desejos mais submersos e nossos traumas mais cuidadosamente guardados encontram a realidade inegável e tangível de nossa existência corporal. Essa interseção não é uma preocupação periférica, mas o próprio coração de nossa experiência incorporada, carregando consigo profundas implicações sobre como entendemos a nós mesmos, nosso sofrimento e nosso potencial de cura.

O inconsciente, muitas vezes conceituado como um abismo oculto, um reino subterrâneo de desejos reprimidos e impulsos primitivos, não existe isolado de nosso ser físico. Em vez disso, encontra sua voz, sua expressão, sua própria manifestação, através do corpo. Os sintomas, longe de serem meros incômodos ou erros biológicos, podem ser entendidos como formas de comunicação altamente sofisticadas. Eles são a maneira eloqüente, embora muitas vezes angustiante, do corpo de testemunhar conflitos psíquicos que não podem ser contidos dentro dos limites da consciência. Uma erupção cutânea que surge em momentos de intensa ansiedade social, uma fadiga crônica que suga energia durante períodos de pressão emocional avassaladora, um tique repetitivo que pontua momentos de turbulência interna – essas não são ocorrências aleatórias. São, antes, mensagens codificadas, despachos somáticos do mundo interior, carregando um significado que, uma vez decifrado, pode desbloquear insights profundos sobre o eu.

Essa perspectiva desafia um dualismo cartesiano que há muito domina, separando a mente do corpo como se fossem duas entidades distintas envolvidas em uma dança precária. A psicanálise, em suas explorações mais profundas, revelou consistentemente a inadequação de tal divisão. O corpo não é um mero passageiro no navio da mente; É parte integrante do próprio vaso, sua própria estrutura e funcionamento inextricavelmente ligados às correntes psíquicas que o impulsionam. O inconsciente, portanto, não sussurra no ouvido; Ele vibra nas artérias, aperta no diafragma, dói nas articulações. É uma realidade física palpável, tanto parte do nosso ser quanto de nossos pensamentos e emoções.

Para entender verdadeiramente a psique humana, devemos, portanto, voltar nossa atenção para essa narrativa silenciosa, mas profundamente articulada, inscrita em nossa carne. Devemos aprender a ler a linguagem do corpo, não como uma coleção de funções biológicas, mas como um testemunho vivo de nossas vidas interiores. Isso envolve abordar sensações físicas, dores, prazeres e até gestos cotidianos não como meros epifenômenos, mas como significantes potentes, expressões significativas de processos inconscientes. A tensão sutil em uma mandíbula, o rubor que sobe no pescoço, a maneira como a pessoa habitualmente cruza os braços - esses não são detalhes insignificantes. São os sinais de pontuação, as inflexões sutis, a própria gramática de uma linguagem que fala muito sobre nossos medos mais profundos, nossos desejos mais fervorosos e nossas histórias não resolvidas.

As implicações dessa perspectiva são vastas, particularmente na arena clínica. Quando um paciente apresenta uma constelação de queixas somáticas, não basta descartá-las como psicossomáticas em sentido redutor, implicando uma forma secundária ou menos real de sofrimento. Em vez disso, o analista ou terapeuta deve reconhecer que essas manifestações físicas são expressões primárias de sofrimento psíquico. O corpo, em seu próprio sofrimento, está tentando comunicar algo essencial sobre o mundo interno do paciente, algo que pode ser muito ameaçador, muito complexo ou muito profundamente enterrado para articular diretamente. O sintoma é, sob essa luz, um compromisso, uma maneira de o inconsciente falar, ser ouvido, embora através de um véu de sensação física.

Considere o fenômeno da dissociação. Quando o trauma sobrecarrega a capacidade de processamento simbólico, a mente e o corpo podem se fragmentar. O senso de identidade se torna fraturado e o corpo pode parecer estranho, desconectado ou até mesmo entorpecido. Este não é um colapso do sistema biológico, mas uma profunda resposta psíquica decretada sobre a forma física. O corpo, em sua fragmentação, está espelhando a psique despedaçada. Da mesma forma, a experiência generalizada de ansiedade, com suas manifestações físicas marcantes, como coração acelerado, falta de ar e sensação de desgraça iminente, é um testemunho visceral do envolvimento imediato do corpo com a ameaça psíquica. Os sintomas físicos não são um efeito colateral infeliz da ansiedade; eles são a própria ansiedade, experimentada em sua forma mais crua e corpórea.

This inherent interconnectedness suggests that true self-understanding, and indeed healing, cannot be achieved by addressing the mind in isolation from the body. Psychotherapy, from this perspective, must encompass a recognition and interpretation of the body's narrative. It involves paying attention not only to what is said, but also to how it is said, to the hesitations, the sighs, the shifts in posture, the very way the patient occupies space within the consulting room. The body's presence is a constant, silent commentary on the spoken word, offering a richness and depth that complements and often corrects our conscious accounts of ourselves.

The body, then, is not merely a container for the psyche, but an active interpreter, a translator, and an originator of our deepest experiences. It is a dynamic interface between our internal world and the external reality, a site where abstract psychic forces take on tangible form. The unconscious is not an abstract concept divorced from our physical being; it is woven into the very fabric of our flesh, its pulsations echoing in our heartbeats, its hidden currents flowing through our blood. To engage with the unconscious is, therefore, to engage with the body in all its complexity and mystery.

This exploration will delve into the various ways the body participates in the unconscious drama. We will examine how early bodily experiences shape our sense of self, how trauma leaves indelible somatic imprints, and how desire finds its most potent expression through our physical being. We will consider the body as a text to be read, a language to be deciphered, and a canvas upon which our deepest psychic truths are continually being painted. This is an invitation to listen to the body's silent narrative, to recognize its profound wisdom, and to understand its role as an active, vibrant participant in the ongoing unfolding of who we are. The physical form, far from being a passive recipient of psychic experience, emerges as a co-author of our stories, its language etched in sensation, movement, and symptom, waiting to be heard. This journey into the embodied unconscious promises a richer, more integrated understanding of the human condition, one that embraces the entirety of our being – mind, body, and the ineffable space in between.

The intellectual currents of late 19th and early 20th century Vienna were a fertile ground for nascent ideas about the human psyche, a period when the very nature of consciousness and its discontents was being probed with unprecedented intensity. It was within this milieu that Sigmund Freud, a physician with a neurologist's keen observation and a philosopher's speculative bent, began to articulate a revolutionary understanding of human suffering, an understanding that, even in its nascent stages, implicitly acknowledged the profound interconnectedness of the mind and body. While the prevailing medical discourse often sought purely biological explanations for ailments, Freud, through his work with patients and his theoretical innovations, began to peel back the layers, revealing the intricate ways in which psychological distress could manifest as tangible physical disturbances. This was not a deliberate, pre-planned theorization of "psychoanalytic embodiment" as we might understand it today, but rather an emergent understanding born from clinical necessity and a refusal to dismiss the seemingly inexplicable physical complaints of his patients.

Freud's early encounters with what was then termed "hysteria" proved to be a crucial starting point. The patients he observed, predominantly women, presented with a bewildering array of physical symptoms – paralysis, tremors, sensory disturbances, fainting spells, and even mutism – that defied any clear organic cause. These were not simply the imagined ailments of the idle or the malingering; they were real, debilitating experiences that profoundly impacted the lives of those afflicted. Freud, along with Josef Breuer, his collaborator on early studies of hysteria, began to notice a recurring pattern: these physical symptoms often seemed to be linked to specific, emotionally charged memories or experiences that the patient had either repressed or was unable to fully process. The idea began to take root that the body was not merely a passive recipient of these psychological traumas but an active participant in their manifestation. The repressed emotion, unable to find an outlet through conscious thought or speech, seemed to find a way to express itself through the physical organism.

In their seminal work,

Studies on Hysteria (1895), Freud and Breuer described the concept of "conversion" – the process by which repressed psychic energy, particularly that associated with traumatic experiences, is transformed into physical symptoms. This was a radical departure from the purely somatic models of disease. It posited that the body could, in essence, become a language for the unspeakable. The physical symptom, in this view, was not the disease itself but a symbolic representation of a repressed conflict, a compromise formation that allowed the underlying psychic tension to be partially expressed while also serving as a defense against its full conscious awareness. For instance, a patient experiencing a hysterical paralysis of the arm might be symbolically acting out a forbidden desire or a deeply resented obligation connected to that limb. The physical symptom, therefore, was a coded message, an embodied manifestation of an unresolved psychological drama.

Freud's conceptualization of the libido, his theory of psychosexual development, and his exploration of defense mechanisms further solidified the link between the psychic and the somatic. He proposed that psychic energy, the libido, was fundamentally instinctual and had a physical basis, even if its precise biological underpinnings remained elusive. This energy, he argued, could become "bound" to certain psychic structures or objects and, when thwarted or repressed, could lead to the development of neurotic symptoms, many of which had clear physical manifestations. The oral, anal, and phallic stages of psychosexual development, with their emphasis on bodily erogenous zones and their associated pleasures and conflicts, highlighted the body as the primary site of early psychic development and the locus of potential future neurotic formations. Fixations or traumas occurring during these stages could, Freud suggested, lead to characteristic somatic symptoms later in life.

The concept of the unconscious, central to Freudian theory, also played a pivotal role in understanding the body's narrative. Freud posited that a vast portion of our mental life – our desires, fears, memories, and impulses – exists outside of conscious awareness. This unconscious material, often deeply disturbing or socially unacceptable, is actively repressed, pushed out of consciousness. However, repression is not a complete eradication. These repressed contents continue to exert influence, seeking expression in disguised forms. The body, with its capacity for sensation, movement, and involuntary reaction, provided a potent avenue for this unconscious material to surface. Symptoms were seen as the "return of the repressed," a compromise between the unconscious drive and the forces of repression. The physicality of these symptoms made them particularly compelling evidence for the dynamic interplay between the conscious and unconscious mind.

Consider, for example, the phenomenon of psychosomatic illness, a term that, while sometimes used reductively, has its roots in these early psychoanalytic observations. Freud's work suggested that chronic stress, unresolved emotional conflicts, and repressed trauma could indeed lead to physical pathology. While he might not have delved into the precise neurobiological mechanisms as modern psychosomatic research does, his foundational insight was that the psyche and soma were not separate entities but intimately intertwined. The stress response, the impact of cortisol on bodily systems, the ways in which anxiety can manifest as digestive distress or cardiovascular changes – these are all modern elaborations of the fundamental principle that psychological states have profound and measurable effects on the physical body. Early psychoanalytic theory laid the groundwork for this understanding by positing that the psychic "pressure" of repressed material could find somatic "release."

The intellectual landscape of early 20th-century Vienna, with its emphasis on scientific inquiry alongside a burgeoning interest in subjective experience, provided the perfect backdrop for Freud's revolutionary ideas. He was working in a city that had recently witnessed the artistic and intellectual ferment of figures like Gustav Klimt and Egon Schiele, artists who were exploring the visceral, often unsettling, aspects of the human form and psyche. The scientific establishment, while often resistant, was also grappling with new discoveries in physics and biology that were challenging established certainties. Freud's work, in this context, can be seen as a parallel revolution, one that sought to map the internal landscape of the human mind and to understand how this internal world inevitably expressed itself through the physical being. His meticulous case studies, while focusing on the spoken word and the patient's associations, were always grounded in the observable reality of the patient's suffering, much of which was expressed somatically.

Freud's early writings often grappled with the challenge of articulating the link between the subjective experience of psychic conflict and the objective reality of physical symptoms. He recognized that translating the abstract language of the unconscious into the tangible language of the body was a complex endeavor. The symptom, in his view, was a somatic "language" that required interpretation, much like dreams or slips of the tongue. The body, therefore, was not just a site of manifestation but an active agent in the psychic economy, capable of producing meaning through its distress. The subtle nuances of bodily expression, the involuntary gestures, the patterns of muscle tension, even the rhythm of breathing during a session – these were all considered potential clues to the underlying unconscious processes.

Furthermore, Freud's exploration of the Oedipus complex, while primarily focused on psychological dynamics, inherently involved the body. The intense emotions associated with these early developmental conflicts – desire, rivalry, guilt, fear – were experienced and expressed through bodily sensations and actions. The phallic stage, for instance, is directly tied to the awareness and exploration of the genitals, highlighting the body as the primary arena for these foundational psychic struggles. Later, the concept of the superego, the internalized moral censor, often manifested as guilt that could lead to physical symptoms such as self-punishment or somatic complaints that reflected a sense of unworthiness. The very notion of bodily integrity and the psychological impact of its violation, particularly in the context of sexual trauma, was an implicit element within his broader theoretical framework, even if it was not always explicitly articulated as "embodiment."

The intellectual lineage tracing back to Freud is crucial for understanding how the field of psychoanalysis evolved to embrace the body more explicitly. His initial focus on conversion hysteria and the symbolic meaning of physical symptoms laid the essential groundwork. While he did not develop a fully articulated theory of the embodied psyche in the way that later theorists would, his work undeniably established a critical connection. He demonstrated that psychological distress could cause physical symptoms, and that these symptoms were not arbitrary but held meaning related to repressed conflicts and desires. This was a profound insight that challenged the prevailing Cartesian dualism and began the long process of integrating the mind and body within the framework of psychological understanding. The whispers of the unconscious, Freud observed, were often heard most clearly in the body's cries of distress, in its involuntary expressions of a reality too painful to acknowledge consciously. These early observations, born from the clinical encounter in the consulting rooms of Vienna, were the seeds from which a more profound understanding of the body's silent narrative would eventually blossom.

The spectral presence of the body, as it emerges from the shadows of biological imperative and into the stark light of human consciousness, finds its most potent articulation in the work of Jacques Lacan. Where Freud had illuminated the body as a site of repressed drives and converted symptoms, Lacan, building upon and radically reinterpreting Freudian thought, posited that the very constitution of the corporeal subject is inextricably bound to the advent of language, to the vast and intricate lattice of the Symbolic order. It is not simply that the body *expresses* psychic states; rather, the body, as we come to know and experience it, is *constituted* by the Symbolic. This is a profound shift, moving from an understanding of the body as a passive recipient of psychic inscription to an active participant in its own linguistic and social construction. The body, in Lacanian terms, is not a pre-given biological facticity that then acquires meaning, but rather a phenomenon that emerges *through* the intervention of the Symbolic.

Lacan's assertion that the body is "spoken" by language rather than being a mere biological entity is central to this perspective. We are born, as Lacan famously put it, into a world already pregnant with meaning, a world governed by the laws and structures of the Symbolic order. This order, established through the acquisition of language, social norms, and cultural signifiers, precedes our individual existence and fundamentally shapes our perception of ourselves and the world. Our first entry into this order is through the maternal voice, the maternal gaze, and the maternal body – not as a purely biological entity, but as already mediated by language and social expectation. The infant's cries, its gestures, its nascent bodily functions, are interpreted and given meaning by the Other (primarily the mother, but encompassing the broader social and linguistic network). These interpretations are not neutral; they are imbued with the desires, anxieties, and expectations of the Symbolic order. Thus, the infant's body becomes a site upon which the first linguistic and social inscriptions are made.

This process of being "spoken" has profound implications for bodily alienation. The biological body, with its raw drives and immediate sensations, is a foreign territory that we must navigate through the lens of the Symbolic. We learn to name our body parts, to understand their functions (or supposed functions) according to cultural norms, and to relate to them through socially sanctioned gestures and expressions. This mediation, while necessary for integration into human society, inevitably creates a distance between the lived, raw experience of the body and the conceptual, linguistic representation of it. The body becomes an object of representation, an object that is perceived and understood through the filter of language and social codes. This can lead to a pervasive sense of alienation, where the individual feels estranged from their own physical being, as if inhabiting a form that has been imposed or prescribed rather than organically owned. The body, which should be the most intimate aspect of our being, can become a source of discomfort, a stranger within our own skin, because its perceived reality is largely a product of external linguistic and social forces.

Desire, too, is fundamentally shaped and distorted by the Symbolic order in its relationship to the corporeal subject. Our desires are not simply instinctual urges but are articulated and mediated through the language and social structures we inhabit. Lacan distinguishes between need, demand, and desire. Needs are biological imperatives, but they are quickly translated into demands directed towards the Other. It is in the space between demand and satisfaction that desire emerges – a desire that is not for a specific object but for the recognition of the Other, for the acknowledgement of our being within the Symbolic. This desire is inherently tied to the body, but not in a direct, unproblematic way. The body becomes the site through which we attempt to solicit this recognition, but it is also the site where our desires are fragmented and reified by the Symbolic. The social injunctions about how bodies "should" look, how they should behave, and what pleasures are permissible, all shape our desires, often leading us to pursue phantasms that are products of the Symbolic rather than authentic expressions of our corporeal being. The body becomes a canvas upon which these socially constructed desires are projected, often leading to endless striving and a perpetual sense of lack, as the ultimate object of Symbolic desire – complete recognition – remains perpetually elusive.

The implications for the subject's sense of self are equally profound. Lacan argues that the subject is not a pre-existing, unified entity but is rather formed through its inscription within the Symbolic order. The "I" that we perceive ourselves to be is a linguistic construct, an effect of language and its social functions. This subject is inherently fragmented, split between its conscious awareness and the unconscious forces that shape it, and crucially, between the biological body and its Symbolic representation. The body, in this context, is not a stable foundation for identity but a site where identity is both constructed and fragmented. We are spoken by the Symbolic, and this speaking objectifies us, categorizes us, and assigns us a place within the social fabric. Our bodily characteristics – gender, race, physical abilities – become signifiers that are imbued with social meaning and used to position us within the Symbolic order. These signifiers, while seemingly tied to the corporeal, are ultimately products of the Symbolic, and our identification with them can lead to both a sense of belonging and a profound sense of internal division. The subject, therefore, is not so much an agent inhabiting a body as an effect of the Symbolic order speaking

through the body, creating a sense of self that is perpetually in flux, a mosaic of linguistic and social imprints.

Lacan's concept of the "Imaginary" order, which precedes and interweaves with the Symbolic, offers a crucial bridge to understanding the corporeal subject. The Imaginary is the realm of images, identifications, and the illusion of wholeness, most famously illustrated by the mirror stage. In this crucial moment, the infant, before it has fully mastered its motor control, recognizes itself as a unified whole in the mirror. This image, however, is an external one, a specular identification that offers a premature sense of mastery and completeness. This imagined wholeness is seductive, a stable form that contrasts with the fragmented, chaotic experience of the infant's own body. This Imaginary identification with an external image becomes foundational to the ego, but it also establishes a fundamental duality: the self as perceived and the self as felt. The body, in this early stage, is already being experienced as something that can be seen, an object that can be identified with from the outside.

When the Symbolic order intervenes, it does not erase the Imaginary but rather works upon it, inscribing it with meaning and social value. The unified image of the self in the mirror is now subject to the dictates of language and social norms. The body is no longer just a source of sensation and movement but becomes a signifier, a carrier of meaning within the social order. This is where the paradox of bodily embodiment truly takes root. We are given a linguistic and social framework through which to understand our bodies, but this framework is always mediated, always a representation. The raw, unmediated experience of the body – its pains, its pleasures, its sheer biological presence – is often pushed into the background, deemed less significant than its social and symbolic value. This can lead to a situation where individuals become acutely aware of their bodies as objects to be presented, judged, and managed according to the standards of the Symbolic, while simultaneously feeling disconnected from the visceral reality of their physical being. The body, therefore, becomes a battleground between the imagined wholeness and the fragmented reality imposed by language and social expectation.

The concept of the "signifier" is paramount here. In Lacanian theory, the signifier is the element that represents the subject for another signifier. It is not the word itself, nor the concept it represents, but the linguistic unit that stands for something else within a system of differences. Our bodies, and aspects of our bodies, become signifiers within the Symbolic order. Gender, for instance, is not merely a biological fact but a complex interplay of signifiers – names, pronouns, clothing, social roles – that are assigned and interpreted within the Symbolic. These signifiers, while ostensibly tied to the corporeal, are fluid and socially constructed. An individual's body, with its particular biological attributes, is then positioned within this system of signifiers. This can lead to profound psychological distress when there is a perceived or actual mismatch between the biological body and the Symbolic signifiers that are assigned or that the individual identifies with. The Symbolic order, in its attempt to categorize and make sense of bodies, often imposes rigid structures that can feel alienating and oppressive to the lived experience of the corporeal subject.

This fragmentation of the corporeal subject is not necessarily a pathological state in itself; it is, for Lacan, an inherent condition of being human. We are, by definition, split subjects, constituted by the irreducible gap between the biological and the Symbolic. The challenge lies in how this split is negotiated. When the Symbolic order is too rigid, too demanding, or when there is a significant disruption in the process of identification, the corporeal subject can experience profound alienation and distress. The body can become a site of intense anxiety, a locus of shame, or a source of physical symptoms that are manifestations of this fundamental split. The pressure to conform to Symbolic ideals of beauty, health, and functionality can lead to obsessive behaviors, eating disorders, and a constant sense of inadequacy, all of which underscore the body's capitulation to the demands of the Symbolic.

Furthermore, Lacan's concept of the "real" offers a glimpse into that which resists symbolization, that which lies beyond language and the Symbolic order. The biological body, in its raw, unmediated state – its suffering, its inevitable decay, its fundamental vulnerability – can be seen as a point of contact with the Real. However, our conscious awareness of this Real is always filtered through the Symbolic. We can only speak of our bodily experiences through the language available to us, and this language, by its very nature, transforms and distorts the raw experience. The Real of bodily pain, for example, is mediated by our cultural understanding of illness, our individual histories of suffering, and the linguistic terms we use to describe it. This creates a perpetual tension between the ineffable reality of our corporeal existence and the symbolic representations we use to grasp it. The body, then, is not just a passive receptacle of Symbolic inscription but a dynamic site where the struggles between the Real, the Imaginary, and the Symbolic are played out, shaping our very sense of self.

The Lacanian gaze, distinct from the Freudian objective observation, is crucial in this process. The gaze, for Lacan, is not simply the act of seeing but a fundamental aspect of the Symbolic order that constitutes us as objects. When we are seen, we are placed within a frame of signification. The maternal gaze, as mentioned, is the infant's first encounter with being acknowledged and interpreted. As we grow, we are subjected to countless gazes – parental, peer, societal – each of which confers meaning upon our bodies and our being. This external gaze, imbued with the values and judgments of the Symbolic, becomes internalized, shaping our self-perception and our relationship with our own bodies. We learn to see ourselves through the eyes of the Other, internalizing their expectations and judgments. This can lead to a constant self-monitoring, a perpetual attempt to align our embodied experience with the demands of the external gaze. The body becomes an object on display, scrutinized for its conformity to Symbolic ideals, leading to a sense of being constantly observed and evaluated.

The implications of this for desire are particularly potent. Desire, in Lacanian terms, is often desire for the desire of the Other. We desire what we perceive others to desire, and we often use our bodies as instruments to elicit this desire. The body becomes a tool for performance, for attracting the gaze of the Other, for soliciting recognition and validation within the Symbolic order. This can lead to a disembodied pursuit of an idealized self, where the authentic needs and sensations of the body are sacrificed in the quest to embody a particular image or to fulfill a socially prescribed role. The body is thus mobilized in the service of an often unattainable phantasm, a product of the Symbolic and Imaginary projections that govern our understanding of desire and self-worth. The corporeal subject, in this scenario, is alienated from its own desires, which have been shaped and distorted by the external gaze and the dictates of the Symbolic.

This constant negotiation with the Symbolic order means that the corporeal subject is never fully present to itself in a simple, unmediated way. Our embodiment is always already linguistic, always already socially situated. The feeling of being "in" one's body is not a straightforward biological fact but a complex psychological and linguistic achievement, constantly being negotiated and re-negotiated. When this process is disrupted, or when the demands of the Symbolic become overwhelming, the body can become a site of profound distress, a place where the fragmented self struggles to find coherence. Symptoms, whether physical or psychological, can be understood as an attempt by the subject to articulate this fundamental split, to express that which cannot be fully contained within the Symbolic order. The body, in its silent narrative, bears witness to the ongoing struggle between the biological imperative and the linguistic inscription, between the Real of existence and the Symbolic demands of being human. The corporeal subject, therefore, is not a fixed entity but a dynamic process, a constant becoming shaped by the very forces that seek to define and contain it. It is a subject perpetually spoken, perpetually gazed upon, and perpetually struggling to find its own voice within the labyrinthine structures of language and social law. The body, in this Lacanian framework, becomes not just a biological vessel but a potent locus of meaning, a canvas upon which the intricate dramas of identity, desire, and alienation are endlessly performed.

The spectral presence of the body, as it emerges from the shadows of biological imperative and into the stark light of human consciousness, finds its most potent articulation in the work of Jacques Lacan. Where Freud had illuminated the body as a site of repressed drives and converted symptoms, Lacan, building upon and radically reinterpreting Freudian thought, posited that the very constitution of the corporeal subject is inextricably bound to the advent of language, to the vast and intricate lattice of the Symbolic order. It is not simply that the body *expresses* psychic states; rather, the body, as we come to know and experience it, is *constituted* by the Symbolic. This is a profound shift, moving from an understanding of the body as a passive recipient of psychic inscription to an active participant in its own linguistic and social construction. The body, in Lacanian terms, is not a pre-given biological facticity that then acquires meaning, but rather a phenomenon that emerges *through* the intervention of the Symbolic.

Lacan's assertion that the body is "spoken" by language rather than being a mere biological entity is central to this perspective. We are born, as Lacan famously put it, into a world already pregnant with meaning, a world governed by the laws and structures of the Symbolic order. This order, established through the acquisition of language, social norms, and cultural signifiers, precedes our individual existence and fundamentally shapes our perception of ourselves and the world. Our first entry into this order is through the maternal voice, the maternal gaze, and the maternal body – not as a purely biological entity, but as already mediated by language and social expectation. The infant's cries, its gestures, its nascent bodily functions, are interpreted and given meaning by the Other (primarily the mother, but encompassing the broader social and linguistic network). These interpretations are not neutral; they are imbued with the desires, anxieties, and expectations of the Symbolic order. Thus, the infant's body becomes a site upon which the first linguistic and social inscriptions are made.

This process of being "spoken" has profound implications for bodily alienation. The biological body, with its raw drives and immediate sensations, is a foreign territory that we must navigate through the lens of the Symbolic. We learn to name our body parts, to understand their functions (or supposed functions) according to cultural norms, and to relate to them through socially sanctioned gestures and expressions. This mediation, while necessary for integration into human society, inevitably creates a distance between the lived, raw experience of the body and the conceptual, linguistic representation of it. The body becomes an object of representation, an object that is perceived and understood through the filter of language and social codes. This can lead to a pervasive sense of alienation, where the individual feels estranged from their own physical being, as if inhabiting a form that has been imposed or prescribed rather than organically owned. The body, which should be the most intimate aspect of our being, can become a source of discomfort, a stranger within our own skin, because its perceived reality is largely a product of external linguistic and social forces.

Desire, too, is fundamentally shaped and distorted by the Symbolic order in its relationship to the corporeal subject. Our desires are not simply instinctual urges but are articulated and mediated through the language and social structures we inhabit. Lacan distinguishes between need, demand, and desire. Needs are biological imperatives, but they are quickly translated into demands directed towards the Other. It is in the space between demand and satisfaction that desire emerges – a desire that is not for a specific object but for the recognition of the Other, for the acknowledgement of our being within the Symbolic. This desire is inherently tied to the body, but not in a direct, unproblematic way. The body becomes the site through which we attempt to solicit this recognition, but it is also the site where our desires are fragmented and reified by the Symbolic. The social injunctions about how bodies "should" look, how they should behave, and what pleasures are permissible, all shape our desires, often leading us to pursue phantasms that are products of the Symbolic rather than authentic expressions of our corporeal being. The body becomes a canvas upon which these socially constructed desires are projected, often leading to endless striving and a perpetual sense of lack, as the ultimate object of Symbolic desire – complete recognition – remains perpetually elusive.

The implications for the subject's sense of self are equally profound. Lacan argues that the subject is not a pre-existing, unified entity but is rather formed through its inscription within the Symbolic order. The "I" that we perceive ourselves to be is a linguistic construct, an effect of language and its social functions. This subject is inherently fragmented, split between its conscious awareness and the unconscious forces that shape it, and crucially, between the biological body and its Symbolic representation. The body, in this context, is not a stable foundation for identity but a site where identity is both constructed and fragmented. We are spoken by the Symbolic, and this speaking objectifies us, categorizes us, and assigns us a place within the social fabric. Our bodily characteristics – gender, race, physical abilities – become signifiers that are imbued with social meaning and used to position us within the Symbolic order. These signifiers, while seemingly tied to the corporeal, are ultimately products of the Symbolic, and our identification with them can lead to both a sense of belonging and a profound sense of internal division. The subject, therefore, is not so much an agent inhabiting a body as an effect of the Symbolic order speaking

through the body, creating a sense of self that is perpetually in flux, a mosaic of linguistic and social imprints.

Lacan's concept of the "Imaginary" order, which precedes and interweaves with the Symbolic, offers a crucial bridge to understanding the corporeal subject. The Imaginary is the realm of images, identifications, and the illusion of wholeness, most famously illustrated by the mirror stage. In this crucial moment, the infant, before it has fully mastered its motor control, recognizes itself as a unified whole in the mirror. This image, however, is an external one, a specular identification that offers a premature sense of mastery and completeness. This imagined wholeness is seductive, a stable form that contrasts with the fragmented, chaotic experience of the infant's own body. This Imaginary identification with an external image becomes foundational to the ego, but it also establishes a fundamental duality: the self as perceived and the self as felt. The body, in this early stage, is already being experienced as something that can be seen, an object that can be identified with from the outside.

When the Symbolic order intervenes, it does not erase the Imaginary but rather works upon it, inscribing it with meaning and social value. The unified image of the self in the mirror is now subject to the dictates of language and social norms. The body is no longer just a source of sensation and movement but becomes a signifier, a carrier of meaning within the social order. This is where the paradox of bodily embodiment truly takes root. We are given a linguistic and social framework through which to understand our bodies, but this framework is always mediated, always a representation. The raw, unmediated experience of the body – its pains, its pleasures, its sheer biological presence – is often pushed into the background, deemed less significant than its social and symbolic value. This can lead to a situation where individuals become acutely aware of their bodies as objects to be presented, judged, and managed according to the standards of the Symbolic, while simultaneously feeling disconnected from the visceral reality of their physical being. The body, therefore, becomes a battleground between the imagined wholeness and the fragmented reality imposed by language and social expectation.

The concept of the "signifier" is paramount here. In Lacanian theory, the signifier is the element that represents the subject for another signifier. It is not the word itself, nor the concept it represents, but the linguistic unit that stands for something else within a system of differences. Our bodies, and aspects of our bodies, become signifiers within the Symbolic order. Gender, for instance, is not merely a biological fact but a complex interplay of signifiers – names, pronouns, clothing, social roles – that are assigned and interpreted within the Symbolic. These signifiers, while ostensibly tied to the corporeal, are fluid and socially constructed. An individual's body, with its particular biological attributes, is then positioned within this system of signifiers. This can lead to profound psychological distress when there is a perceived or actual mismatch between the biological body and the Symbolic signifiers that are assigned or that the individual identifies with. The Symbolic order, in its attempt to categorize and make sense of bodies, often imposes rigid structures that can feel alienating and oppressive to the lived experience of the corporeal subject.

This fragmentation of the corporeal subject is not necessarily a pathological state in itself; it is, for Lacan, an inherent condition of being human. We are, by definition, split subjects, constituted by the irreducible gap between the biological and the Symbolic. The challenge lies in how this split is negotiated. When the Symbolic order is too rigid, too demanding, or when there is a significant disruption in the process of identification, the corporeal subject can experience profound alienation and distress. The body can become a site of intense anxiety, a locus of shame, or a source of physical symptoms that are manifestations of this fundamental split. The pressure to conform to Symbolic ideals of beauty, health, and functionality can lead to obsessive behaviors, eating disorders, and a constant sense of inadequacy, all of which underscore the body's capitulation to the demands of the Symbolic.

Furthermore, Lacan's concept of the "real" offers a glimpse into that which resists symbolization, that which lies beyond language and the Symbolic order. The biological body, in its raw, unmediated state – its suffering, its inevitable decay, its fundamental vulnerability – can be seen as a point of contact with the Real. However, our conscious awareness of this Real is always filtered through the Symbolic. We can only speak of our bodily experiences through the language available to us, and this language, by its very nature, transforms and distorts the raw experience. The Real of bodily pain, for example, is mediated by our cultural understanding of illness, our individual histories of suffering, and the linguistic terms we use to describe it. This creates a perpetual tension between the ineffable reality of our corporeal existence and the symbolic representations we use to grasp it. The body, then, is not just a passive receptacle of Symbolic inscription but a dynamic site where the struggles between the Real, the Imaginary, and the Symbolic are played out, shaping our very sense of self.

The Lacanian gaze, distinct from the Freudian objective observation, is crucial in this process. The gaze, for Lacan, is not simply the act of seeing but a fundamental aspect of the Symbolic order that constitutes us as objects. When we are seen, we are placed within a frame of signification. The maternal gaze, as mentioned, is the infant's first encounter with being acknowledged and interpreted. As we grow, we are subjected to countless gazes – parental, peer, societal – each of which confers meaning upon our bodies and our being. This external gaze, imbued with the values and judgments of the Symbolic, becomes internalized, shaping our self-perception and our relationship with our own bodies. We learn to see ourselves through the eyes of the Other, internalizing their expectations and judgments. This can lead to a constant self-monitoring, a perpetual attempt to align our embodied experience with the demands of the external gaze. The body becomes an object on display, scrutinized for its conformity to Symbolic ideals, leading to a sense of being constantly observed and evaluated.

The implications of this for desire are particularly potent. Desire, in Lacanian terms, is often desire for the desire of the Other. We desire what we perceive others to desire, and we often use our bodies as instruments to elicit this desire. The body becomes a tool for performance, for attracting the gaze of the Other, for soliciting recognition and validation within the Symbolic order. This can lead to a disembodied pursuit of an idealized self, where the authentic needs and sensations of the body are sacrificed in the quest to embody a particular image or to fulfill a socially prescribed role. The body is thus mobilized in the service of an often unattainable phantasm, a product of the Symbolic and Imaginary projections that govern our understanding of desire and self-worth. The corporeal subject, in this scenario, is alienated from its own desires, which have been shaped and distorted by the external gaze and the dictates of the Symbolic.

This constant negotiation with the Symbolic order means that the corporeal subject is never fully present to itself in a simple, unmediated way. Our embodiment is always already linguistic, always already socially situated. The feeling of being "in" one's body is not a straightforward biological fact but a complex psychological and linguistic achievement, constantly being negotiated and re-negotiated. When this process is disrupted, or when the demands of the Symbolic become overwhelming, the body can become a site of profound distress, a place where the fragmented self struggles to find coherence. Symptoms, whether physical or psychological, can be understood as an attempt by the subject to articulate this fundamental split, to express that which cannot be fully contained within the Symbolic order. The body, in its silent narrative, bears witness to the ongoing struggle between the biological imperative and the linguistic inscription, between the Real of existence and the Symbolic demands of being human. The corporeal subject, therefore, is not a fixed entity but a dynamic process, a constant becoming shaped by the very forces that seek to define and contain it. It is a subject perpetually spoken, perpetually gazed upon, and perpetually struggling to find its own voice within the labyrinthine structures of language and social law. The body, in this Lacanian framework, becomes not just a biological vessel but a potent locus of meaning, a canvas upon which the intricate dramas of identity, desire, and alienation are endlessly performed.

Merleau-Ponty's Touch: Phenomenology of Lived Experience

While Lacan's schema offers a compelling account of the body as a construct of language and the social order, it is Maurice Merleau-Ponty's phenomenological exploration that brings us back to the immediate, unmediated reality of our corporeal existence. Merleau-Ponty diverged from the Cartesian mind-body dualism, which posits a distinct separation between the thinking subject and the material body, arguing instead for the body as the primary vehicle of our engagement with the world. For Merleau-Ponty, the body is not merely an object that we possess or an instrument that we use; it is the very condition of possibility for our experience. It is through our lived body, with its senses, its movements, and its capacity for feeling, that we are fundamentally "in-the-world." This concept of the "lived body" (corps propre) is central to his philosophy, emphasizing that our embodiment is not a passive state but an active, dynamic relationship with our surroundings.

Merleau-Ponty contended that our most fundamental understanding of the world is not derived from abstract thought or intellectual reasoning, but from pre-reflective, embodied experience. Our perception, our sensations, and our movements are not isolated inputs fed into a cognitive processor; they are intertwined elements that constitute our being-in-the-world. Consider the simple act of reaching for a cup of coffee. Before any conscious deliberation, our body already anticipates the weight, the texture, and the temperature. Our hand extends, guided by an implicit understanding of space and our own corporeal capabilities. This is not a calculated decision, but an immediate, embodied response. The hand reaching out is not a detached limb acting upon command; it is an extension of our intentionality, an expression of our desire to interact with the world. The flesh of our hand, the warmth of the ceramic, the scent of the coffee – these are not merely data points but fused elements of a unified, embodied experience.

The richness of this phenomenological perspective lies in its meticulous attention to the qualitative details of sensory experience. Merleau-Ponty invites us to move beyond intellectual descriptions and to engage with the "texture" of our lived reality. The world, as experienced through the body, is not a collection of discrete objects with inherent properties, but a field of potential actions and meaningful interactions. The rough bark of a tree is not just a surface texture but an invitation to touch, to feel the contours, perhaps to sense its age and resilience. The coolness of water on a hot day is not merely a temperature reading but a palpable sensation of relief and rejuvenation. These sensory experiences are not merely passive registrations of external stimuli; they are active processes of engaging with the world, shaping our understanding and our being. The light filtering through leaves is not just lumens and wavelengths; it is a dappled dance of warmth and shadow that paints the world with a specific mood. The sound of rain is not just decibels; it is a percussive symphony that can evoke feelings of melancholy or cozy introspection.

Touch, in particular, holds a privileged position in Merleau-Ponty's philosophy. It is the most primordial sense, the one through which we first establish our presence in the world and our separateness from it. When we touch something, we simultaneously feel the object and feel ourselves touching it. There is a reciprocity, a mutual intertwining. My hand, as it touches the smooth surface of a table, is also aware of its own pressure, its own texture, its own warmth. This inherent reflexivity of touch means that it is never purely external. The world presses in on us, and we press back. This dynamic exchange is crucial to our understanding of self and other, of inside and outside. Imagine running your fingers along the edge of a worn book. You feel the paper, the embossed title, the subtle nicks and tears accumulated over time. Simultaneously, you are aware of the slight friction against your fingertips, the pressure exerted, the subtle contours of your own skin mapping the contours of the book. It is a feedback loop, a constant dialogue between the self and the object, mediated by the very flesh of your being.

This embodied perception extends to our understanding of space and movement. We do not navigate the world by calculating distances and angles; we do so through our kinesthetic sense, our internal awareness of our body's position and potential for movement. We have a "body schema," an implicit, unconscious understanding of our body's dimensions and capabilities, which allows us to move through space with fluidity and grace. Stepping over an obstacle requires not a precise measurement of its height, but an intuitive grasp of how our legs need to move. Reaching for a distant object involves a subtle adjustment of posture, a rebalancing of our weight, all orchestrated by this innate bodily intelligence. The world is not a neutral, objective space that we passively inhabit; it is a "lived space," imbued with meaning and shaped by our potential for action. A familiar room is not just a collection of dimensions and furniture but a landscape of accessible pathways and comfortable nooks, understood through the body's habitual engagement with it.

Merleau-Ponty's emphasis on the "thickness" of experience is vital here. Unlike a purely intellectual apprehension of an object, our embodied encounter is characterized by a certain depth, a richness of interwoven sensations and possibilities. When we see a chair, we don't just register its visual form; we also have an implicit understanding of its function – it is for sitting. We might feel the coolness of its surface if we touch it, the slight creak it makes when weight is applied, the way its form invites our body to recline. These multiple dimensions of experience are not layered on top of one another but are simultaneously present, creating a dense, meaningful encounter. This "thickness" is what distinguishes lived experience from a mere intellectual dissection of reality. It is the felt reality of the world, the world as it presents itself to our embodied consciousness, pregnant with potential and laden with meaning.

The implications of this phenomenological understanding are far-reaching, particularly when we consider how it challenges the notion of a disembodied consciousness or a purely linguistic construction of the self. While language and social structures undeniably shape our perception, Merleau-Ponty reminds us that they do not wholly determine it. Our primary mode of being in the world is through our body, and our body's immediate, unmediated engagement with its environment forms the bedrock of our experience. The world is not merely an abstract concept that we then seek to map onto our physical form. Rather, our physical form is already oriented towards the world, already engaged in a continuous dialogue with it. The rustle of leaves is not just a sound wave; it is a sensory event that evokes a sense of place, of nature, of quietude, all before language intervenes to categorize it as "wind" or "trees."

Consider the experience of learning a new physical skill, such as riding a bicycle or playing a musical instrument. Initially, we might try to intellectualize the process, consciously focusing on each movement, each instruction. But true mastery comes not from conscious deliberation, but from the body's developing "feel" for the activity. The muscle memory, the intuitive adjustments, the seamless integration of sensory feedback and motor response – these emerge from practice and embodied engagement. The body learns its own language, a language of movement, balance, and coordination that transcends explicit verbal instruction. The feeling of effortless gliding on a bike, or the fluid transition between chords on a guitar, is a testament to this embodied knowledge. It is the lived body, not the abstract mind, that truly learns and masters these skills.

Furthermore, Merleau-Ponty's focus on the lived body highlights the irreducibility of our corporeal existence. Our bodies are not simply vessels that contain our consciousness; they are the very means by which we experience consciousness. Pain, for instance, is not an abstract concept of damage; it is a visceral, embodied reality. The sharp sting of a cut, the dull ache of a strained muscle, the throbbing intensity of a headache – these are sensations that are deeply personal and profoundly influential on our state of being. They are not simply signals to be processed by the brain; they are felt experiences that shape our perception, our mood, and our actions. The body, in its capacity for both pleasure and suffering, grounds us in the tangible reality of existence, providing a constant reminder of our finitude and our vulnerability.

This perspective also offers a powerful counterpoint to the alienation often described in post-structuralist thought. While acknowledging the influence of social and linguistic forces, Merleau-Ponty's phenomenology reasserts the primacy of our embodied connection to the world. We are not merely alienated subjects adrift in a sea of signifiers; we are embodied beings, inherently connected to the physical reality around us. This connection is not always seamless or unproblematic, but it is fundamental. The experience of a warm embrace, the taste of a shared meal, the rhythm of walking with a loved one – these are profound, embodied experiences that speak to our innate capacity for connection and our deep-seated embeddedness in the world.

The subtle nuances of our sensory world, often overlooked in our rush towards intellectualization, are brought to the fore by phenomenology. The way light plays on surfaces, creating depth and texture; the subtle variations in scent that indicate ripeness or decay; the felt resistance of air against our skin as we move – these are not trivial details. They are the constituent elements of our lived experience, the raw material from which our understanding of the world is forged. The world, when viewed through the lens of the lived body, is not a sterile, objective landscape, but a vibrant, dynamic tapestry of sensory impressions and potential interactions. It is a world that speaks to us not just through language, but through its very physicality, its textures, its smells, its resistances, and its invitations.

Therefore, while Lacan's framework illuminates how the Symbolic order inscribes itself upon the body, Merleau-Ponty's phenomenology reminds us of the primordial reality of the body itself, as the ground and medium of all experience. The body is not merely a canvas for linguistic and social meaning; it is the active, sensing, moving agent through which meaning is not only received but also generated. It is in this rich, embodied interplay that our narrative of existence truly begins, a narrative written not just in words, but in the very felt substance of our being. The silent narrative of the body, thus, finds its voice not only in the pronouncements of the Symbolic, but in the immediate, felt reality of its engagement with the world.

The spectral presence of the body, as it emerges from the shadows of biological imperative and into the stark light of human consciousness, finds its most potent articulation in the work of Jacques Lacan. Where Freud had illuminated the body as a site of repressed drives and converted symptoms, Lacan, building upon and radically reinterpreting Freudian thought, posited that the very constitution of the corporeal subject is inextricably bound to the advent of language, to the vast and intricate lattice of the Symbolic order. It is not simply that the body *expresses* psychic states; rather, the body, as we come to know and experience it, is *constituted* by the Symbolic. This is a profound shift, moving from an understanding of the body as a passive recipient of psychic inscription to an active participant in its own linguistic and social construction. The body, in Lacanian terms, is not a pre-given biological facticity that then acquires meaning, but rather a phenomenon that emerges *through* the intervention of the Symbolic.

Lacan's assertion that the body is "spoken" by language rather than being a mere biological entity is central to this perspective. We are born, as Lacan famously put it, into a world already pregnant with meaning, a world governed by the laws and structures of the Symbolic order. This order, established through the acquisition of language, social norms, and cultural signifiers, precedes our individual existence and fundamentally shapes our perception of ourselves and the world. Our first entry into this order is through the maternal voice, the maternal gaze, and the maternal body – not as a purely biological entity, but as already mediated by language and social expectation. The infant's cries, its gestures, its nascent bodily functions, are interpreted and given meaning by the Other (primarily the mother, but encompassing the broader social and linguistic network). These interpretations are not neutral; they are imbued with the desires, anxieties, and expectations of the Symbolic order. Thus, the infant's body becomes a site upon which the first linguistic and social inscriptions are made.

This process of being "spoken" has profound implications for bodily alienation. The biological body, with its raw drives and immediate sensations, is a foreign territory that we must navigate through the lens of the Symbolic. We learn to name our body parts, to understand their functions (or supposed functions) according to cultural norms, and to relate to them through socially sanctioned gestures and expressions. This mediation, while necessary for integration into human society, inevitably creates a distance between the lived, raw experience of the body and the conceptual, linguistic representation of it. The body becomes an object of representation, an object that is perceived and understood through the filter of language and social codes. This can lead to a pervasive sense of alienation, where the individual feels estranged from their own physical being, as if inhabiting a form that has been imposed or prescribed rather than organically owned. The body, which should be the most intimate aspect of our being, can become a source of discomfort, a stranger within our own skin, because its perceived reality is largely a product of external linguistic and social forces.

Desire, too, is fundamentally shaped and distorted by the Symbolic order in its relationship to the corporeal subject. Our desires are not simply instinctual urges but are articulated and mediated through the language and social structures we inhabit. Lacan distinguishes between need, demand, and desire. Needs are biological imperatives, but they are quickly translated into demands directed towards the Other. It is in the space between demand and satisfaction that desire emerges – a desire that is not for a specific object but for the recognition of the Other, for the acknowledgement of our being within the Symbolic. This desire is inherently tied to the body, but not in a direct, unproblematic way. The body becomes the site through which we attempt to solicit this recognition, but it is also the site where our desires are fragmented and reified by the Symbolic. The social injunctions about how bodies "should" look, how they should behave, and what pleasures are permissible, all shape our desires, often leading us to pursue phantasms that are products of the Symbolic rather than authentic expressions of our corporeal being. The body becomes a canvas upon which these socially constructed desires are projected, often leading to endless striving and a perpetual sense of lack, as the ultimate object of Symbolic desire – complete recognition – remains perpetually elusive.

The implications for the subject's sense of self are equally profound. Lacan argues that the subject is not a pre-existing, unified entity but is rather formed through its inscription within the Symbolic order. The "I" that we perceive ourselves to be is a linguistic construct, an effect of language and its social functions. This subject is inherently fragmented, split between its conscious awareness and the unconscious processes that shape it, and crucially, between the biological body and its Symbolic representation. The body, in this context, is not a stable foundation for identity but a site where identity is both constructed and fragmented. We are spoken by the Symbolic, and this speaking objectifies us, categorizes us, and assigns us a place within the social fabric. Our bodily characteristics – gender, race, physical abilities – become signifiers that are imbued with social meaning and used to position us within the Symbolic order. These signifiers, while seemingly tied to the corporeal, are ultimately products of the Symbolic, and our identification with them can lead to both a sense of belonging and a profound sense of internal division. The subject, therefore, is not so much an agent inhabiting a body as an effect of the Symbolic order speaking

through the body, creating a sense of self that is perpetually in flux, a mosaic of linguistic and social imprints.

Lacan's concept of the "Imaginary" order, which precedes and interweaves with the Symbolic, offers a crucial bridge to understanding the corporeal subject. The Imaginary is the realm of images, identifications, and the illusion of wholeness, most famously illustrated by the mirror stage. In this crucial moment, the infant, before it has fully mastered its motor control, recognizes itself as a unified whole in the mirror. This image, however, is an external one, a specular identification that offers a premature sense of mastery and completeness. This imagined wholeness is seductive, a stable form that contrasts with the fragmented, chaotic experience of the infant's own body. This Imaginary identification with an external image becomes foundational to the ego, but it also establishes a fundamental duality: the self as perceived and the self as felt. The body, in this early stage, is already being experienced as something that can be seen, an object that can be identified with from the outside.

When the Symbolic order intervenes, it does not erase the Imaginary but rather works upon it, inscribing it with meaning and social value. The unified image of the self in the mirror is now subject to the dictates of language and social norms. The body is no longer just a source of sensation and movement but becomes a signifier, a carrier of meaning within the social order. This is where the paradox of bodily embodiment truly takes root. We are given a linguistic and social framework through which to understand our bodies, but this framework is always mediated, always a representation. The raw, unmediated experience of the body – its pains, its pleasures, its sheer biological presence – is often pushed into the background, deemed less significant than its social and symbolic value. This can lead to a situation where individuals become acutely aware of their bodies as objects to be presented, judged, and managed according to the standards of the Symbolic, while simultaneously feeling disconnected from the visceral reality of their physical being. The body, therefore, becomes a battleground between the imagined wholeness and the fragmented reality imposed by language and social expectation.

The concept of the "signifier" is paramount here. In Lacanian theory, the signifier is the element that represents the subject for another signifier. It is not the word itself, nor the concept it represents, but the linguistic unit that stands for something else within a system of differences. Our bodies, and aspects of our bodies, become signifiers within the Symbolic order. Gender, for instance, is not merely a biological fact but a complex interplay of signifiers – names, pronouns, clothing, social roles – that are assigned and interpreted within the Symbolic. These signifiers, while ostensibly tied to the corporeal, are fluid and socially constructed. An individual's body, with its particular biological attributes, is then positioned within this system of signifiers. This can lead to profound psychological distress when there is a perceived or actual mismatch between the biological body and the Symbolic signifiers that are assigned or that the individual identifies with. The Symbolic order, in its attempt to categorize and make sense of bodies, often imposes rigid structures that can feel alienating and oppressive to the lived experience of the corporeal subject.

This fragmentation of the corporeal subject is not necessarily a pathological state in itself; it is, for Lacan, an inherent condition of being human. We are, by definition, split subjects, constituted by the irreducible gap between the biological and the Symbolic. The challenge lies in how this split is negotiated. When the Symbolic order is too rigid, too demanding, or when there is a significant disruption in the process of identification, the corporeal subject can experience profound alienation and distress. The body can become a site of intense anxiety, a locus of shame, or a source of physical symptoms that are manifestations of this fundamental split. The pressure to conform to Symbolic ideals of beauty, health, and functionality can lead to obsessive behaviors, eating disorders, and a constant sense of inadequacy, all of which underscore the body's capitulation to the demands of the Symbolic.

Furthermore, Lacan's concept of the "real" offers a glimpse into that which resists symbolization, that which lies beyond language and the Symbolic order. The biological body, in its raw, unmediated state – its suffering, its inevitable decay, its fundamental vulnerability – can be seen as a point of contact with the Real. However, our conscious awareness of this Real is always filtered through the Symbolic. We can only speak of our bodily experiences through the language available to us, and this language, by its very nature, transforms and distorts the raw experience. The Real of bodily pain, for example, is mediated by our cultural understanding of illness, our individual histories of suffering, and the linguistic terms we use to describe it. This creates a perpetual tension between the ineffable reality of our corporeal existence and the symbolic representations we use to grasp it. The body, then, is not just a passive receptacle of Symbolic inscription but a dynamic site where the struggles between the Real, the Imaginary, and the Symbolic are played out, shaping our very sense of self.

The Lacanian gaze, distinct from the Freudian objective observation, is crucial in this process. The gaze, for Lacan, is not simply the act of seeing but a fundamental aspect of the Symbolic order that constitutes us as objects. When we are seen, we are placed within a frame of signification. The maternal gaze, as mentioned, is the infant's first encounter with being acknowledged and interpreted. As we grow, we are subjected to countless gazes – parental, peer, societal – each of which confers meaning upon our bodies and our being. This external gaze, imbued with the values and judgments of the Symbolic, becomes internalized, shaping our self-perception and our relationship with our own bodies. We learn to see ourselves through the eyes of the Other, internalizing their expectations and judgments. This can lead to a constant self-monitoring, a perpetual attempt to align our embodied experience with the demands of the external gaze. The body becomes an object on display, scrutinized for its conformity to Symbolic ideals, leading to a sense of being constantly observed and evaluated.

The implications of this for desire are particularly potent. Desire, in Lacanian terms, is often desire for the desire of the Other. We desire what we perceive others to desire, and we often use our bodies as instruments to elicit this desire. The body becomes a tool for performance, for attracting the gaze of the Other, for soliciting recognition and validation within the Symbolic order. This can lead to a disembodied pursuit of an idealized self, where the authentic needs and sensations of the body are sacrificed in the quest to embody a particular image or to fulfill a socially prescribed role. The body is thus mobilized in the service of an often unattainable phantasm, a product of the Symbolic and Imaginary projections that govern our understanding of desire and self-worth. The corporeal subject, in this scenario, is alienated from its own desires, which have been shaped and distorted by the external gaze and the dictates of the Symbolic.

This constant negotiation with the Symbolic order means that the corporeal subject is never fully present to itself in a simple, unmediated way. Our embodiment is always already linguistic, always already socially situated. The feeling of being "in" one's body is not a straightforward biological fact but a complex psychological and linguistic achievement, constantly being negotiated and re-negotiated. When this process is disrupted, or when the demands of the Symbolic become overwhelming, the body can become a site of profound distress, a place where the fragmented self struggles to find coherence. Symptoms, whether physical or psychological, can be understood as an attempt by the subject to articulate this fundamental split, to express that which cannot be fully contained within the Symbolic order. The body, in its silent narrative, bears witness to the ongoing struggle between the biological imperative and the linguistic inscription, between the Real of existence and the Symbolic demands of being human. The corporeal subject, therefore, is not a fixed entity but a dynamic process, a constant becoming shaped by the very forces that seek to define and contain it. It is a subject perpetually spoken, perpetually gazed upon, and perpetually struggling to find its own voice within the labyrinthine structures of language and social law. The body, in this Lacanian framework, becomes not just a biological vessel but a potent locus of meaning, a canvas upon which the intricate dramas of identity, desire, and alienation are endlessly performed.

While Lacan's schema offers a compelling account of the body as a construct of language and the social order, it is Maurice Merleau-Ponty's phenomenological exploration that brings us back to the immediate, unmediated reality of our corporeal existence. Merleau-Ponty diverged from the Cartesian mind-body dualism, which posits a distinct separation between the thinking subject and the material body, arguing instead for the body as the primary vehicle of our engagement with the world. For Merleau-Ponty, the body is not merely an object that we possess or an instrument that we use; it is the very condition of possibility for our experience. It is through our lived body, with its senses, its movements, and its capacity for feeling, that we are fundamentally "in-the-world." This concept of the "lived body" (corps propre) is central to his philosophy, emphasizing that our embodiment is not a passive state but an active, dynamic relationship with our surroundings.

Merleau-Ponty contended that our most fundamental understanding of the world is not derived from abstract thought or intellectual reasoning, but from pre-reflective, embodied experience. Our perception, our sensations, and our movements are not isolated inputs fed into a cognitive processor; they are intertwined elements that constitute our being-in-the-world.

Consider the simple act of reaching for a cup of coffee. Before any conscious deliberation, our body already anticipates the weight, the texture, and the temperature. Our hand extends, guided by an implicit understanding of space and our own corporeal capabilities. This is not a calculated decision, but an immediate, embodied response. The hand reaching out is not a detached limb acting upon command; it is an extension of our intentionality, an expression of our desire to interact with the world. The flesh of our hand, the warmth of the ceramic, the scent of the coffee – these are not merely data points but fused elements of a unified, embodied experience.

The richness of this phenomenological perspective lies in its meticulous attention to the qualitative details of sensory experience. Merleau-Ponty invites us to move beyond intellectual descriptions and to engage with the "texture" of our lived reality. The world, as experienced through the body, is not a collection of discrete objects with inherent properties, but a field of potential actions and meaningful interactions. The rough bark of a tree is not just a surface texture but an invitation to touch, to feel the contours, perhaps to sense its age and resilience. The coolness of water on a hot day is not merely a temperature reading but a palpable sensation of relief and rejuvenation. These sensory experiences are not merely passive registrations of external stimuli; they are active processes of engaging with the world, shaping our understanding and our being. The light filtering through leaves is not just lumens and wavelengths; it is a dappled dance of warmth and shadow that paints the world with a specific mood. The sound of rain is not just decibels; it is a percussive symphony that can evoke feelings of melancholy or cozy introspection.

Touch, in particular, holds a privileged position in Merleau-Ponty's philosophy. It is the most primordial sense, the one through which we first establish our presence in the world and our separateness from it. When we touch something, we simultaneously feel the object and feel ourselves touching it. There is a reciprocity, a mutual intertwining. My hand, as it touches the smooth surface of a table, is also aware of its own pressure, its own texture, its own warmth. This inherent reflexivity of touch means that it is never purely external. The world presses in on us, and we press back. This dynamic exchange is crucial to our understanding of self and other, of inside and outside. Imagine running your fingers along the edge of a worn book. You feel the paper, the embossed title, the subtle nicks and tears accumulated over time. Simultaneously, you are aware of the slight friction against your fingertips, the pressure exerted, the subtle contours of your own skin mapping the contours of the book. It is a feedback loop, a constant dialogue between the self and the object, mediated by the very flesh of your being.

This embodied perception extends to our understanding of space and movement. We do not navigate the world by calculating distances and angles; we do so through our kinesthetic sense, our internal awareness of our body's position and potential for movement. We have a "body schema," an implicit, unconscious understanding of our body's dimensions and capabilities, which allows us to move through space with fluidity and grace. Stepping over an obstacle requires not a precise measurement of its height, but an intuitive grasp of how our legs need to move. Reaching for a distant object involves a subtle adjustment of posture, a rebalancing of our weight, all orchestrated by this innate bodily intelligence. The world is not a neutral, objective space that we passively inhabit;

it is a "lived space," imbued with meaning and shaped by our potential for action. A familiar room is not just a collection of dimensions and furniture but a landscape of accessible pathways and comfortable nooks, understood through the body's habitual engagement with it.

Merleau-Ponty's emphasis on the "thickness" of experience is vital here. Unlike a purely intellectual apprehension of an object, our embodied encounter is characterized by a certain depth, a richness of interwoven sensations and possibilities. When we see a chair, we don't just register its visual form; we also have an implicit understanding of its function – it is for sitting. We might feel the coolness of its surface if we touch it, the slight creak it makes when weight is applied, the way its form invites our body to recline. These multiple dimensions of experience are not layered on top of one another but are simultaneously present, creating a dense, meaningful encounter. This "thickness" is what distinguishes lived experience from a mere intellectual dissection of reality. It is the felt reality of the world, the world as it presents itself to our embodied consciousness, pregnant with potential and laden with meaning.

The implications of this phenomenological understanding are far-reaching, particularly when we consider how it challenges the notion of a disembodied consciousness or a purely linguistic construction of the self. While language and social structures undeniably shape our perception, Merleau-Ponty reminds us that they do not wholly determine it. Our primary mode of being in the world is through our body, and our body's immediate, unmediated engagement with its environment forms the bedrock of our experience. The world is not merely an abstract concept that we then seek to map onto our physical form. Rather, our physical form is already oriented towards the world, already engaged in a continuous dialogue with it. The rustle of leaves is not just a sound wave; it is a sensory event that evokes a sense of place, of nature, of quietude, all before language intervenes to categorize it as "wind" or "trees."

Consider the experience of learning a new physical skill, such as riding a bicycle or playing a musical instrument. Initially, we might try to intellectualize the process, consciously focusing on each movement, each instruction. But true mastery comes not from conscious deliberation, but from the body's developing "feel" for the activity. The muscle memory, the intuitive adjustments, the seamless integration of sensory feedback and motor response – these emerge from practice and embodied engagement. The body learns its own language, a language of movement, balance, and coordination that transcends explicit verbal instruction. The feeling of effortless gliding on a bike, or the fluid transition between chords on a guitar, is a testament to this embodied knowledge. It is the lived body, not the abstract mind, that truly learns and masters these skills.

Furthermore, Merleau-Ponty's focus on the lived body highlights the irreducibility of our corporeal existence. Our bodies are not simply vessels that contain our consciousness; they are the very means by which we experience consciousness. Pain, for instance, is not an abstract concept of damage; it is a visceral, embodied reality. The sharp sting of a cut, the dull ache of a strained muscle, the throbbing intensity of a headache – these are sensations that are deeply personal and profoundly influential on our state of being.

They are not simply signals to be processed by the brain; they are felt experiences that shape our perception, our mood, and our actions. The body, in its capacity for both pleasure and suffering, grounds us in the tangible reality of existence, providing a constant reminder of our finitude and our vulnerability.

This perspective also offers a powerful counterpoint to the alienation often described in post-structuralist thought. While acknowledging the influence of social and linguistic forces, Merleau-Ponty's phenomenology reasserts the primacy of our embodied connection to the world. We are not merely alienated subjects adrift in a sea of signifiers; we are embodied beings, inherently connected to the physical reality around us. This connection is not always seamless or unproblematic, but it is fundamental. The experience of a warm embrace, the taste of a shared meal, the rhythm of walking with a loved one – these are profound, embodied experiences that speak to our innate capacity for connection and our deep-seated embeddedness in the world.

The subtle nuances of our sensory world, often overlooked in our rush towards intellectualization, are brought to the fore by phenomenology. The way light plays on surfaces, creating depth and texture; the subtle variations in scent that indicate ripeness or decay; the felt resistance of air against our skin as we move – these are not trivial details. They are the constituent elements of our lived experience, the raw material from which our understanding of the world is forged. The world, when viewed through the lens of the lived body, is not a sterile, objective landscape, but a vibrant, dynamic tapestry of sensory impressions and potential interactions. It is a world that speaks to us not just through language, but through its very physicality, its textures, its smells, its resistances, and its invitations.

Therefore, while Lacan's framework illuminates how the Symbolic order inscribes itself upon the body, Merleau-Ponty's phenomenology reminds us of the primordial reality of the body itself, as the ground and medium of all experience. The body is not merely a canvas for linguistic and social meaning; it is the active, sensing, moving agent through which meaning is not only received but also generated. It is in this rich, embodied interplay that our narrative of existence truly begins, a narrative written not just in words, but in the very felt substance of our being. The silent narrative of the body, thus, finds its voice not only in the pronouncements of the Symbolic, but in the immediate, felt reality of its engagement with the world.

This chapter has embarked on a journey to understand the body not as a mere biological vessel, but as a profound locus of meaning, a text inscribed with the history of our inner lives and our interactions with the world. We have moved from the foundational insights of Freud, which located psychic dramas within the corporeal form, to the intricate philosophical architectures of Lacan, where the body is understood as fundamentally constituted by language and the Symbolic order. Lacan's assertion that the body is "spoken," rather than merely expressing, forces us to reconsider our most basic assumptions about selfhood and embodiment. The body, in this light, is not a stable, pre-existing entity, but a dynamic, fragmented subject, perpetually negotiated between the biological Real, the Imaginary identifications, and the overarching structures of the Symbolic. The profound implications of this perspective are evident in how our desires, our sense of self, and our very experience of alienation are woven into the fabric of our corporeal existence, shaped by the language and social norms that precede and surround us.

Yet, to solely focus on the symbolic inscription would be to overlook the undeniable immediacy of our embodied reality. Merleau-Ponty's phenomenological approach offers a vital counterpoint, bringing us back to the lived experience of the body as the primary mode of our engagement with the world. Through his concept of the "lived body," we grasp how our perceptions, movements, and sensations are not mere inputs but constitutive elements of our being-in-the-world. The richness of sensory experience, particularly the profound reciprocity of touch, reveals a pre-reflective understanding of ourselves and our surroundings that precedes and informs linguistic interpretation. The body, for Merleau-Ponty, is not a passive object but an active agent, an embodied consciousness that actively shapes and is shaped by its environment. This perspective underscores the irreducibility of our corporeal existence, grounding us in a tangible reality that offers both connection and vulnerability.

It is the synthesis of these perspectives that lays the groundwork for the entire exploration that follows in this book. The central thesis we will continue to unravel is that the body speaks a symbolic language. Every ache, every tremor, every surge of pleasure, every averted gaze, every unconscious gesture – these are not random biological occurrences. They are, in fact, expressions, coded communications from the unconscious mind, mediated by the structures of language and social understanding. Physical sensations, often dismissed as mere bodily complaints, can be seen as potent metaphors, symbolic representations of deeper psychological processes. A persistent pain in the shoulder might, for instance, symbolize an unwillingness to bear a certain emotional burden, while a sudden flush of heat could signify a repressed desire or an overwhelming emotion breaking through the Symbolic dam.

This book invites you, the reader, to embark on a journey of interpretation. To approach your own bodily experiences, and indeed the bodily experiences of those around you, not as mere biological facts, but as texts waiting to be read. We will delve into the rich tapestry of symbolic language that the body employs, exploring how unconscious conflicts manifest in physical form, how repressed desires find their expression in somatic symptoms, and how our deepest psychological truths are often communicated in the silent, eloquent language of the flesh. By unpacking these symbolic expressions, we can begin to understand the hidden dialogue between our conscious awareness and the vast, often elusive, landscape of the unconscious. This exploration promises not only a deeper understanding of ourselves but also a more profound and compassionate engagement with the embodied narratives of others. The body, in its intricate and often perplexing manifestations, holds the key to unlocking some of the most fundamental aspects of the human psyche, offering a pathway to integration, healing, and a more complete understanding of what it means to be truly alive.

Chapter 2: The Psyche's Topography and Structure

Freud, in his pioneering explorations of the human mind, offered a conceptual architecture that continues to resonate through psychodynamic thought: the topographical model of the psyche. This model, a cornerstone of his early work, divides the mind into three distinct provinces: the conscious, the preconscious, and the unconscious. While seemingly abstract, this framework provides a crucial lens through which to understand the enigmatic relationship between our inner world and our physical manifestations. It suggests that much of what we experience, particularly our most baffling somatic symptoms, does not originate from the rational, accessible layers of our awareness, but from the murky, often turbulent depths of the unconscious.

The conscious mind, as its name suggests, is the realm of our immediate awareness. It is the theatre of our current thoughts, perceptions, and feelings – the part of us that is fully awake and engaged with the external world at any given moment. This is the part of us that reads these words, that processes the information, that forms judgments and makes decisions based on what is directly available to it. It is a limited space, however, a sliver of illumination in a vast expanse of mental darkness. Our conscious capacity for processing information is finite; we can only hold so much in our immediate attention before it slips away or is pushed aside by newer stimuli. This limited scope is precisely why the other provinces of the mind become so significant, acting as vast reservoirs of mental content that are not currently in our direct awareness but are nonetheless profoundly influential.

Beneath the surface of the conscious lies the preconscious. This can be thought of as a mental waiting room, a transitional space where thoughts, memories, and feelings reside that are not currently active in consciousness but can be readily retrieved. It is the repository of information that we are not actively thinking about but can easily bring to mind if prompted. For instance, your childhood phone number, the name of your first pet, or the details of a conversation you had yesterday – these are all likely residing in your preconscious. They are not occupying your conscious attention right now, but with a little effort, you can summon them forth. The preconscious acts as a gatekeeper of sorts, filtering information from the unconscious, allowing certain elements to pass into consciousness while keeping others suppressed. It is a crucial intermediary, bridging the gap between the accessible and the utterly hidden.

The most profound and influential, yet the most elusive, of Freud's topographical divisions is the unconscious. This is the vast, submerged continent of the psyche, a realm of instinctual drives, repressed memories, unresolved conflicts, and deeply buried desires. It is a domain that operates according to its own logic, a logic that is often irrational, timeless, and driven by the relentless pursuit of pleasure. The contents of the unconscious are not readily accessible to conscious awareness. They are often too threatening, too painful, or too socially unacceptable to be allowed into the light of day. Instead, they are banished, repressed, and hidden away, yet they do not disappear. Like a powerful undercurrent, they continue to shape our thoughts, feelings, and behaviors, often in ways that we do not consciously understand. This hidden reservoir of mental energy is the wellspring from which many of our psychological struggles, including somatic symptoms, are thought to arise.

The metaphor of a hidden landscape is particularly apt when trying to grasp the nature of the unconscious. Imagine a vast ocean, with the tip of an iceberg breaking the surface – that visible tip represents our conscious mind. The much larger, submerged portion of the iceberg, hidden beneath the waves, is the unconscious. We only see a fraction of what lies beneath, and yet that submerged mass profoundly influences the iceberg's movement, its direction, and its stability. Similarly, the unconscious, though unseen, dictates the course of our mental lives. The ocean itself, with its shifting currents and hidden depths, can be likened to the dynamic processes of the psyche. The currents are the flow of psychic energy, the drives and desires that propel us forward, sometimes in predictable ways, sometimes in unpredictable surges. The hidden depths represent the truly inaccessible regions, the primeval fears and urges that lie at the very core of our being.

Within this submerged landscape, Freud posited the existence of repressed material. These are thoughts, memories, or desires that were once in consciousness but were deemed too disturbing or unacceptable, and were therefore actively pushed down into the unconscious. This repression is a defense mechanism, a way for the ego to protect itself from overwhelming anxiety or psychic pain. However, this material does not cease to exist simply because it is no longer conscious. It remains active, seeking expression, and exerting influence from its hidden vantage point. The energy associated with these repressed elements can find outlets in various ways, often through indirect means. It is in this dynamic interplay between the repressed and the forces that seek to keep it suppressed that much of psychological distress, including the manifestation of physical symptoms, is believed to originate.

When the pressure from the unconscious becomes too great, or when the defenses that hold it at bay begin to weaken, the repressed material can find its way into consciousness, albeit in a distorted or disguised form. This can manifest as dreams, parapraxes (slips of the tongue or memory lapses), or, most significantly for our discussion, as somatic symptoms. The body, in this Freudian view, becomes a canvas upon which the dramas of the unconscious are played out. Physical ailments, unexplained pains, and functional disorders can be understood as the symbolic language of the repressed, a way for the unconscious to communicate its presence and its demands. The symptom, therefore, is not merely a physical malfunction; it is a coded message, a compromise formation that allows a portion of the repressed material to find expression while still maintaining a degree of disguise from conscious awareness.

Consider, for instance, a person who, in their conscious life, presents as impeccably controlled and rational, outwardly exhibiting no sign of emotional turmoil. Yet, they might suffer from chronic headaches or digestive problems that have no clear medical explanation. According to the topographical model, these symptoms could be the somatic manifestation of repressed anger or anxiety. The unconscious rage, unable to be expressed directly due to social conditioning or personal history, finds an outlet in physical discomfort. The headache becomes a stand-in for the unspoken frustration, the churning stomach a physical representation of internal turmoil. The energy of the repressed emotion is converted into physical pain or dysfunction, a process that Freud termed "conversion." The body, in essence, "speaks" the language of the unconscious when words fail or are forbidden.

The concept of psychic energy, or libido, is also central to understanding how unconscious material can manifest somatically. Freud believed that this psychic energy, largely driven by instinctual urges, seeks expression and discharge. When its direct expression is blocked by repression, this energy can become dammed up, building pressure within the unconscious. This pent-up energy can then be redirected, transformed, and ultimately find an outlet in physical symptoms. The energy of a repressed sexual desire, for example, might be converted into a phobia or a compulsive behavior that, while seemingly unrelated, serves to contain and manage the underlying anxiety. The body, in its physical susceptibility, becomes the ultimate recipient of this redirected psychic energy. The intensity of the unconscious drive dictates the intensity of the somatic manifestation.

The vastness of the unconscious also explains why these symptoms can appear so baffling and resistant to conscious control. Because their roots lie in a realm that is beyond our direct access, conscious willpower or rational explanation often proves insufficient to alleviate them. One cannot simply "will away" a repressed trauma that is manifesting as chronic pain. The underlying unconscious conflict must be addressed, the repressed material brought into awareness (or at least understood in its dynamic), and the psychic energy that is being bound up in the symptom must be released or redirected. This is where therapeutic interventions, such as psychoanalysis, aim to explore the hidden landscape of the unconscious, to uncover the repressed material, and to facilitate its integration into the conscious mind.

Furthermore, the dynamic nature of the unconscious, with its constant interplay of drives, defenses, and repressions, means that somatic symptoms can evolve and change over time. As circumstances shift, as new conflicts arise, or as defenses are modified, the ways in which the unconscious expresses itself can also transform. A symptom that once served to contain a particular repressed fear might, in a new context, become insufficient, leading to the emergence of a new symptom or a modification of the existing one. This fluidity underscores the living, evolving nature of the psyche and its powerful influence over the physical body. The landscape of the unconscious is not static; it is a perpetually shifting terrain, with new territories being submerged and old ones resurfacing in altered forms.

The journey into the unconscious, as Freud envisioned it, is not merely an academic exercise; it is a deeply personal and often challenging exploration. It requires a willingness to confront the hidden aspects of oneself, to acknowledge the power of repressed drives, and to understand that our physical experiences are often deeply intertwined with our psychological histories. The topographical model, despite its age, offers a powerful framework for appreciating this intricate connection. It suggests that within the depths of our being lie forces that, when unacknowledged or unintegrated, can erupt into the physical realm, shaping our health, our well-being, and our overall experience of life. The body, in its capacity to manifest these hidden dramas, becomes a profound, if sometimes painful, testament to the enduring power of the unconscious mind.

In the intricate cartography of the psyche, Sigmund Freud proposed not only distinct topographical regions but also a dynamic structural framework, a tripartite system that governs our inner landscape and, crucially, our embodied experience. Where the topographical model mapped the territories of the conscious, preconscious, and unconscious, the structural model – comprising the Id, Ego, and Superego – delineates the agencies that inhabit and contend within these realms. This is not merely an abstract division; it is a vibrant, often turbulent, ecosystem where primal urges clash with societal imprints, and a mediating force attempts to maintain a semblance of order. The body, far from being a passive vessel, becomes the ultimate stage upon which the dramas of these psychic agencies are enacted, the tangible canvas for the intangible conflicts that define our existence.

The Id, the most primitive and primal of these psychic structures, is the bedrock of our being, the reservoir of raw instinctual drives and desires. Born from the unconscious, it operates on the pleasure principle, a relentless pursuit of immediate gratification. The Id knows no morality, no logic, no time; it simply demands. Its energy, the libido, is the fundamental psychic force that fuels all mental activity. Imagine the Id as a newborn infant, crying out for nourishment, for comfort, for the cessation of discomfort, utterly unconcerned with the conditions or consequences of its demands. It is the embodiment of "I want," an unbridled force seeking an outlet. These drives are not necessarily malicious, but they are powerful and often disruptive to the ordered functioning of life. They represent our fundamental biological and instinctual needs – hunger, thirst, sex, aggression – and their ceaseless urge for expression.

The Id's relentless pursuit of pleasure, its refusal to acknowledge reality's constraints, creates a constant pressure within the psyche. This pressure is not merely metaphorical; it is the engine of psychic energy, a force that seeks discharge. When these primal demands are thwarted, when the Id's desires are blocked by external reality or internal prohibitions, a tension arises. This tension is the very stuff of psychic conflict, and it is this conflict that often finds its most palpable expression in the physical body. Consider the intense hunger pangs that can grip someone deprived of food; this is the Id's demand for sustenance asserting itself physically. Or the surge of adrenaline and the tightening in the chest that accompanies overwhelming anger; this is the Id's aggressive drive manifesting somatically. The Id, in its pure, unadulterated form, seeks immediate somatic release for its urges, pushing for direct physical expression whenever possible.

Emerging from the Id, and in constant negotiation with it, is the Ego. The Ego represents the reality principle, the part of the psyche that understands the constraints of the external world and seeks to mediate between the Id's desires and the demands of reality. It is the executive branch of the personality, responsible for decision-making, problem-solving, and navigating the complexities of social interaction. The Ego does not negate the Id's drives but seeks to satisfy them in socially acceptable and realistic ways. It is the voice of reason, the planner, the strategist. While the Id screams, "I want it now!", the Ego whispers, "Perhaps later, and maybe in a different way." The Ego develops through our experiences, learning from the consequences of our actions and developing defense mechanisms to manage the anxieties that arise from the clash between the Id and external reality.

The Ego's crucial role in managing the Id's impulses is where the connection to embodiment becomes particularly profound. The Ego must often find indirect routes for the Id's urges, channeling them into activities that are less immediately gratifying but ultimately more sustainable and acceptable. For instance, the aggressive impulses of the Id might be channeled into competitive sports, professional ambition, or even rigorous intellectual debate. The sexual drives of the Id might be sublimated into artistic creation, scientific inquiry, or deep interpersonal relationships. These are not mere diversions; they are sophisticated transformations of raw psychic energy. However, this constant mediation requires immense psychic effort, a continuous expenditure of energy to contain, redirect, and manage the Id's powerful demands. This effort itself can have a physical toll. The chronic tension of the Ego striving to maintain control, to suppress unacceptable urges, can manifest as muscle tension, headaches, or digestive disturbances – the body literally bearing the strain of psychic management.

The Ego's primary tools for managing the Id and reality are its defense mechanisms. These are largely unconscious psychological strategies employed to protect the Ego from anxiety arising from unacceptable thoughts or feelings. Repression, denial, projection, displacement, rationalization – these are just a few of the Ego's arsenal. Each defense mechanism represents a specific way the Ego attempts to resolve internal conflict and prevent the Id's desires from breaching conscious awareness. For example, if the Id harbors a forbidden desire, the Ego might employ repression to push it back into the unconscious. If this fails, it might resort to displacement, redirecting the impulse onto a less threatening target. These mechanisms, while serving a protective function, often involve a significant investment of psychic energy and can lead to the symptomatic expression of the repressed material. The very act of psychological defense can create a somatic manifestation. Imagine a person who, under extreme stress, experiences a sudden loss of voice – a form of conversion disorder where anxiety about speaking forbidden truths manifests as a physical inability to speak. This is the Ego's defense strategy playing out on the physical stage.

The third pillar of Freud's structural model is the Superego. This is the internalized moral compass, the embodiment of societal and parental values, prohibitions, and ideals. The Superego develops through identification with parents and other authority figures, internalizing their rules and judgments. It is divided into two parts: the conscience, which punishes wrongdoing with guilt and shame, and the ego ideal, which sets standards for behavior and strives for perfection. The Superego acts as a harsh, critical judge, constantly monitoring the Ego and condemning any deviation from its rigid moral code. It represents the "shoulds" and "should nots" of our lives, the internalized voice of authority that can be both a source of guidance and a relentless tormentor.

The Superego's impact on embodiment is often felt through the pervasive presence of guilt and shame. When the Ego fails to satisfy the Id's impulses in a way that meets the Superego's exacting standards, the Superego unleashes its punitive arsenal, inducing feelings of unworthiness, self-blame, and anxiety. This psychic punishment can be intensely felt in the body. The gnawing sensation of guilt can manifest as a knot in the stomach, while the shame of perceived failure can lead to a sinking feeling, slumped posture, or social withdrawal. The Superego's moralizing function can also lead to an overemphasis on self-control and restraint, further exacerbating the tension between the Id's desires and the Ego's struggle to manage them. This can result in a body that is constantly held in a state of tension, a physical manifestation of the Superego's perpetual vigilance and condemnation.

The inherent tension between the Id, Ego, and Superego creates a dynamic and often precarious balance within the psyche. The Id relentlessly pushes for immediate gratification, the Superego imposes strict moral limitations, and the Ego struggles to navigate the treacherous path between them, all while attempting to maintain contact with external reality. This ongoing internal drama is the source of a significant portion of our psychic energy, a constant ebb and flow of desire, inhibition, and negotiation. When this equilibrium is disturbed – when the Id's drives become too powerful, the Superego's demands too harsh, or the Ego's defenses too weak – the psychic energy that is bound up in these conflicts can find an outlet in the physical body.

This is where the concept of psychic energy, or libido, plays a pivotal role in understanding somatic manifestations. Freud posited that this energy is constantly seeking expression and discharge. When the normal channels of expression are blocked by repression (the Ego's work) or condemnation (the Superego's influence), the energy becomes dammed up, building pressure. This pent-up psychic energy can then be converted, transformed, and ultimately expressed through physical symptoms. This process, often referred to as conversion, is a hallmark of certain psychoneurotic disorders. A repressed emotional conflict, unable to find conscious expression, is literally converted into a bodily symptom. For example, an individual experiencing intense, unexpressed rage might develop a chronic cough, the explosive nature of the cough mirroring the suppressed outburst of anger. The body becomes the site of this psychic energy's frustrated attempts at discharge.

The body, in this structural dynamic, is not merely a passive recipient of psychic distress; it is an active participant, a canvas upon which the internal battles are painted. The physical symptoms that arise are often not random but are symbolic representations of the underlying unconscious conflict. A paralysis of a limb, for instance, might symbolically represent an unconscious desire to flee from a situation or an inability to act on a forbidden impulse. A psychosomatic pain might serve to keep an individual from engaging in an activity that triggers unconscious anxiety. These symptoms, while distressing, can also be seen as a compromise formation – a way for the unconscious to express itself while still being partially disguised from conscious awareness and, crucially, from the Superego's judgment. The symptom, in this sense, is a solution, albeit a maladaptive one, to an unbearable psychic conflict.

Consider the pervasive anxiety that many individuals experience. This anxiety is often a manifestation of the Ego's struggle to manage the competing demands of the Id and the Superego. The Id might be pushing for an impulsive, potentially destructive action, while the Superego is vehemently condemning any such thought. The Ego, caught in the middle, experiences an overwhelming sense of dread and apprehension. This anxiety, if not consciously processed, can manifest physically. It can lead to a racing heart, shortness of breath, muscle tension, or gastrointestinal distress. The body's physiological alarm system is activated, reflecting the internal psychic alarm that is constantly sounding. The intensity of the somatic symptoms often correlates with the intensity of the underlying psychic conflict.

The structural model also sheds light on the phenomenon of guilt and its somatic expressions. The Superego's punitive function can lead to profound feelings of guilt, even for thoughts or desires that have never been acted upon. This internalized guilt can be a heavy burden, and the body may bear witness to it. Somatic symptoms such as fatigue, apathy, or even physical ailments like ulcers can be seen as a form of self-punishment, a physical manifestation of the Superego's relentless condemnation. The individual might unconsciously feel they "deserve" to suffer physically because of their perceived transgressions. This can create a vicious cycle, where the physical suffering reinforces the guilt, which in turn intensifies the Superego's accusations, leading to further somatic distress.

Furthermore, the Ego's defense mechanisms, while protecting against overwhelming anxiety, can also contribute to somatic manifestations. For example, if an individual repeatedly represses forbidden desires, the energy associated with these desires does not disappear; it remains potent in the unconscious. This dammed-up energy can find its way into the body. Repressed sexual energy, for instance, has been theorized to manifest in various somatic complaints, from headaches to sexual dysfunction. The body becomes a substitute for the direct expression of these primal urges. Similarly, the defense of denial, where an individual refuses to acknowledge a painful reality, can lead to the physical symptoms of the denied condition eventually becoming undeniable.

The interplay between the Id, Ego, and Superego is not a static arrangement but a dynamic process that unfolds throughout an individual's life. Early childhood experiences, particularly the development of the Ego and Superego in relation to parental figures and societal norms, lay the groundwork for how these psychic agencies will interact. Traumatic experiences, unresolved conflicts, and significant life stressors can all disrupt this delicate balance, leading to an amplification of psychic tension and an increased likelihood of somatic symptom formation. The body, in its inherent sensitivity, becomes a highly attuned barometer of these internal psychic fluctuations.

The concept of embodiment, therefore, is inextricably linked to the structural dynamics of the psyche. It is not simply about the physical body housing the mind, but about the body being an integral part of the psychic apparatus, a site of expression, conflict, and resolution. The primal drives of the Id, the reality-testing of the Ego, and the moralistic pronouncements of the Superego are not abstract concepts confined to the mental realm; they are forces that shape our physical experiences, our health, and our very sense of self. The body, in its capacity to experience pain, pleasure, tension, and release, offers a tangible language for the often-invisible dramas unfolding within our psychic structure. To understand the body is, in many ways, to understand the embodied struggle of the Id, Ego, and Superego, a perpetual dance between instinct, reality, and morality that defines the human condition. The somatic symptom, in this light, is not an anomaly but a profound expression of this fundamental psychic architecture, a testament to the intricate and often inseparable relationship between our inner world and our physical being.

The body, then, becomes more than just a recipient of psychic distress; it transforms into an active participant, a sophisticated arena where the warring factions of the psyche forge their truces and wage their silent battles. This is the realm of the compromise formation, a concept that lies at the very heart of understanding how internal psychic conflicts manifest in physical symptoms. A bodily symptom, in this psychoanalytic view, is rarely a simple, straightforward indication of a pathological process. Instead, it is a complex, often ingenious, negotiated settlement – a compromise arrived at when opposing psychic forces find themselves in an untenable impasse.

Imagine the psychic landscape as a densely populated city, with its various districts representing the Id, Ego, and Superego, each with its own peculiar laws and demands. The Id, in its lower districts, seethes with primal urges, a constant thrum of desire and aggression demanding immediate release. The Superego, perched in its austere, judgment-laden towers, imposes rigid moral codes and pronounces severe penalties for any transgression. Caught between these forces is the Ego, the harried administrator, constantly striving to maintain order, to appease both the insatiable Id and the unforgiving Superego, all while attempting to navigate the external reality. When the Ego finds itself unable to resolve a particularly potent conflict – when a forbidden wish from the Id cannot be directly gratified due to the Superego's condemnation, and yet cannot be entirely suppressed without causing overwhelming anxiety – it must find another way.

This is where the body steps in, becoming the site of a complex, often unconscious, negotiation. A compromise formation allows a repressed wish, a forbidden desire, or an unacknowledged emotion to achieve a partial, disguised expression. The symptom, therefore, serves a dual purpose: it provides a circuitous route for the prohibited psychic content to gain some form of discharge, thereby alleviating some of the unbearable psychic tension, and simultaneously, it conceals the true nature of that content from conscious awareness and, crucially, from the Superego's relentless scrutiny. The symptom acts as a coded message, a hieroglyph of the unconscious, conveying a truth that cannot be spoken directly.

Consider the case of a woman who harbors a deep-seated, unconscious rage towards a domineering figure in her life. This rage, originating from the Id, is too powerful and too socially unacceptable to be expressed directly. The Superego would vehemently condemn any overt display of anger, flooding her with guilt and shame. The Ego, tasked with managing this dangerous impulse, cannot simply repress it entirely, as the pent-up energy would create unbearable anxiety. Instead, the Ego might facilitate a compromise formation where this repressed rage is converted into a chronic, debilitating migraine. The throbbing pain of the migraine offers a palpable, physical outlet for the dammed-up aggressive energy. The intensity of the headache can mirror the intensity of the suppressed rage, and the incapacitating nature of the symptom can effectively immobilize the individual, preventing her from engaging with the person who triggers her anger – a form of unconscious protection. The migraine is a symptom, yes, but it is also a compromise: the rage is not fully expressed, but its energy finds a physical vent, offering a partial release from the unbearable psychic pressure. The body, in this instance, has become the silent spokesperson for an unspeakable emotion.

Another potent example can be observed in the realm of sexual repression. Imagine an individual whose upbringing instilled profound guilt and shame around any expression of sexual desire. The Id, with its inherent drive for sexual gratification, remains active, but the Superego's prohibitions are absolute. The Ego, caught in this bind, might find a compromise in the development of a psychogenic skin condition, such as eczema or psoriasis, characterized by intense itching and discomfort. The itching, a constant, irritating, and deeply physical sensation, can be understood as a somatic manifestation of repressed sexual arousal or a forbidden sexual fantasy. The discomfort serves to distract from the underlying sexual tension, and the physical manifestation itself becomes a form of punishment that appeases the Superego, while simultaneously offering a substitute for the unfulfilled sexual drive. The skin, the boundary between the self and the world, becomes the locus of this internal conflict, erupting with the suppressed energy. The symptom, again, is a compromise: the forbidden pleasure is not experienced directly, but the associated energy and guilt find a somatic outlet, a coded expression of the repressed desire.

The concept of conversion, central to understanding these compromise formations, highlights how psychic energy, when blocked from its normal routes of expression, can be transformed and discharged through physical symptoms. This transformation is not a mystical process, but rather a complex psychological mechanism where an emotional conflict is literally converted into a bodily symptom. The symptom often carries symbolic meaning related to the underlying conflict. For instance, a paralysis of a limb might represent an unconscious desire to escape a situation or an inability to take a forbidden action. The limb, unable to perform the forbidden act or facilitate escape, becomes physically incapacitated – a somatic enactment of the psychic prohibition.

The internal psychic economy is a ceaseless marketplace of competing forces, and the body is the ultimate trading floor where these negotiations are finalized. Each symptom represents a unique bargain struck between the repressed wish and the forces of repression. The intensity of the symptom often reflects the strength of the underlying conflict. A mild discomfort might signify a less potent or more effectively disguised conflict, while a severe, debilitating symptom suggests a more profound and difficult-to-manage psychic struggle. The symptom, in this light, is a testament to the psyche's desperate, often ingenious, attempts to maintain a semblance of balance and avoid psychic disintegration.

This idea of the body as a site of compromise also sheds light on how symptoms can fluctuate and change over time. As the dynamics between the Id, Ego, and Superego shift, as new experiences challenge existing defenses, or as external circumstances change, the nature of the compromise formation may also evolve. A symptom that once served its purpose effectively might become obsolete, or new conflicts might arise, necessitating the formation of new symptoms. This fluidity underscores the dynamic and living nature of the psychic apparatus and its constant engagement with the physical self.

Furthermore, the very nature of the symptom can be influenced by cultural and societal factors, as well as an individual's personal history and the specific ways in which their psychic agencies have developed. What might be expressed somatically in one culture might be verbalized or acted out in another. The body, while a universal aspect of human experience, becomes imbued with personal and cultural meanings that shape the expression of internal conflict. For example, anxieties related to social standing or performance might manifest differently in individuals with varying levels of internalized societal expectations, as dictated by their Superego.

The compromise formation is not merely an intellectual abstraction; it is a living, breathing aspect of human psychology that profoundly impacts our physical well-being. It explains why individuals can suffer from physical ailments with no clear organic cause, and why the alleviation of psychic distress can sometimes lead to the disappearance of long-standing bodily complaints. The symptom is, in essence, a distorted echo of an unexpressed truth, a physical manifestation of a psychic wound that demands acknowledgement, even if it is only through the language of the body. The body, in its suffering, is not simply broken; it is communicating a complex story of internal negotiation, a testament to the intricate and often fraught relationship between our inner world and our embodied existence. Each ache, each pain, each functional disturbance can be seen as a chapter in this ongoing narrative of psychic compromise, a whispered testament to the enduring power of the unconscious to shape our physical reality.

The intricate machinery of the psyche, as Freud so meticulously began to unravel, is not powered by a single, monolithic force, but by a complex interplay of energies. Within this dynamic system, a critical distinction emerges, one that illuminates the very engine of bodily expression: the difference between 'drive' (Trieb) and 'instinct' (Instinkt). While often used interchangeably in casual discourse, their psychoanalytic meanings diverge significantly, and understanding this divergence is paramount to grasping how our inner world manifests in the physical. Instinct, in its biological sense, is a fixed, inherited pattern of behavior, a pre-programmed response to specific stimuli, observable in the animal kingdom with predictable regularity. A bird building a nest, a salmon swimming upstream – these are instincts. They are teleological in their biological purpose, serving survival and propagation.

Psychoanalytic drives, however, are a more fluid, more human phenomenon. They are indeed rooted in bodily needs, in the irreducible biological demands of the organism – hunger, thirst, the need for sleep, the imperative of sexual release. These are the raw materials, the primal surges that originate from the somatic realm. Yet, a drive is not merely a biological imperative; it is imbued with a psychic aim, a psychological object, and a force that propels it towards discharge. It is this psychic component, this inherent directionality and variability, that distinguishes it from the rigid blueprint of an instinct. A drive, therefore, is not simply a bodily need; it is a need that has been cathected with psychic energy, endowed with a purpose that transcends mere biological survival and enters the complex arena of desire, pleasure, and indeed, conflict.

Consider the drive for nourishment. Biologically, it is the need for sustenance to maintain bodily function. Psychically, however, it becomes entwined with experiences of comfort, security, and early maternal gratification. The aim is not just to fill the stomach but to achieve a state of satisfaction that has profound emotional resonance. Similarly, the sexual drive, while rooted in biological imperatives, is a vast and convoluted landscape of psychic aims, object choices, and fantasies that extend far beyond simple procreation. It is this infusion of psychic energy and aim that transforms a mere bodily tension into a powerful, often turbulent, psychic drive. These drives are the fundamental energies that compel bodily expression, shaping our physical experiences in ways that are both profound and often confounding. They are the unseen currents that surge beneath the surface of our conscious awareness, dictating the ebb and flow of our physical and emotional lives.

The inherent tension and paradoxes within these drives are not incidental features; they are, in fact, the very crucible from which psychic and somatic conflict is forged. Freud's groundbreaking concept of the drives' dualistic nature – the life instincts (Eros) and the death instincts (Thanatos) – encapsulates this fundamental paradox. Eros, encompassing all that is constructive, unifying, and creative, strives to build, to preserve, and to love. It is the force behind our desires for connection, for growth, for the perpetuation of life itself. Yet, intertwined with this life-affirming impulse is the relentless, inexorable force of Thanatos, the drive towards dissolution, destruction, and a return to the inorganic. This death instinct is not simply a passive state of decay but an active, albeit often masked, tendency towards aggression, self-destruction, and the undoing of life's complex arrangements.

This inherent duality creates a constant, internal dialectic. The energy of Eros seeks expression, seeking to forge connections, build structures, and create pleasurable experiences. But Thanatos, in its ceaseless urge towards entropy and disintegration, acts as a counterforce, generating friction, resistance, and ultimately, conflict. The psychic apparatus is perpetually engaged in the arduous task of mediating these opposing forces, attempting to harness the creative potential of Eros while simultaneously defending against the destructive impulse of Thanatos. This internal struggle is not a theoretical construct confined to the abstract realms of psychoanalytic thought; it is a lived reality, a constant negotiation that plays out, in myriad ways, within the physical body.

The body, then, becomes the ultimate arena for these dynamic forces. It is where the life-affirming energies of Eros manifest as vitality, passion, and the desire for physical connection. It is also the site where the destructive currents of Thanatos can find their expression, not always as overt self-harm, but as somatic symptoms that embody a turning inward of aggression, a disintegration of well-being, or a profound weariness that seems to pull the organism towards stillness and cessation. The relentless pressure of these drives, originating in the visceral reality of the body but imbued with the complex aims and fantasies of the psyche, creates a continuous tension. When these drives are thwarted, when their aims cannot be met, or when their opposing natures create an unbearable internal pressure, the resulting psychic conflict spills over, demanding a physical outlet.

The body's capacity to serve as a stage for this internal drama is remarkable. It is not merely a passive recipient of psychic distress; it becomes an active participant, a canvas upon which the unseen battles of the psyche are painted. The force of a drive, when dammed up by internal prohibitions or external frustrations, does not simply dissipate. Instead, it seeks an alternative route for discharge, and often, this route leads to the somatic realm. This can manifest as an excess of energy that finds release in restless activity or agitation, or conversely, as a profound depletion that leads to fatigue and lethargy. The intensity of our physical sensations – the throbbing ache of a headache, the tightness in the chest, the churning in the stomach – can be understood as direct correlates of the energy generated by these fundamental drives, and the conflicts they engender.

Consider the drive for aggression, a manifestation of Thanatos. In its pure, instinctual form, it might be directed outward towards a perceived threat. However, within the psychic landscape, it becomes far more complex. If this aggression is directed towards someone with whom the individual has a deeply ambivalent relationship, or if its expression is severely inhibited by internalized social norms and moral codes (the Superego), the psychic energy associated with it cannot be directly discharged. The Ego, tasked with managing this volatile force, finds itself in a bind. To suppress it entirely would be to risk a buildup of dangerous tension. To express it directly might lead to catastrophic consequences, both internally (guilt, shame) and externally (punishment, ostracization).

In such a scenario, the body becomes the ingeniously negotiated compromise. The aggressive energy, unable to find its intended target, may be turned inward, manifesting as self-punishing symptoms. This could take the form of chronic pain, where the body is metaphorically "punished" for aggressive impulses. Alternatively, the repressed aggression might fuel psychosomatic conditions. The clenched jaw of bruxism, the tension headaches, the digestive disturbances – these can all be seen as physical manifestations of a drive that is both potent and deeply conflicted. The body, in these instances, is not merely suffering from a physical ailment; it is enacting a drama of repressed aggression, a testament to the powerful forces at play within the psyche. The sheer force of the drive, its inherent tension, finds a physical idiom for expression, a language of pain and discomfort that bypasses conscious awareness and the censoring gaze of the Superego.

The creative potential of Eros also finds its expression in the body, though not always in ways that are immediately apparent or conventionally understood. The drive for connection, for love, for intimacy, fuels our desire for physical closeness, for touch, for sexual expression. When these desires are frustrated, repressed, or distorted by internal conflicts, the psychic energy associated with Eros can also become a source of somatic disturbance. The longing for connection might manifest as a phantom pain, an ache that speaks of a yearning for presence, for touch, for a relationship that is missing. The unfulfilled sexual drive, as discussed in the previous context, can find expression in a myriad of somatic symptoms, from itching to chronic fatigue, demonstrating that even the most creative and life-affirming drives can, when blocked, lead to suffering.

The paradox of the drives lies in their dual capacity. The same force that drives us towards creation, towards building relationships, towards experiencing pleasure, also carries within it the potential for destruction and dissolution. This is not a flaw in the system but an intrinsic characteristic. The drive for sexual release, for instance, while inherently pleasurable and conducive to the continuation of the species, can also be a source of immense conflict, guilt, and anxiety when it clashes with internalized moral codes. The energy associated with this drive, when its direct expression is forbidden, can be diverted into other channels, leading to a range of somatic expressions, from nervous habits to more serious psychosomatic illnesses.

The force of these drives is immense. They are not simply fleeting impulses but deep-seated biological and psychic energies that propel us through life. Their origin in the body imbues them with a visceral power that cannot be easily ignored or dismissed. When these powerful forces are engaged in conflict, when Eros and Thanatos are locked in their eternal struggle, or when the aims of a drive are constantly thwarted, the tension generated is immense. The body, as the tangible reality of our existence, becomes the inevitable battleground where this tension is discharged, transformed, and ultimately, expressed. The language of the body, therefore, is a language of drives: of hunger and satiation, of desire and frustration, of connection and isolation, of creation and dissolution. Understanding the nature of these drives, their origins in bodily needs and their complex psychic aims, is to begin to decipher the profound and often mysterious ways in which our inner world shapes our embodied experience. The body is not a separate entity from the psyche; it is the very ground upon which the drama of the drives is played out, the ultimate expression of our most fundamental energies and their ceaseless, often paradoxical, journey.

The human body, often perceived as a mere vessel for the mind, is in fact a profoundly active participant in the drama of our psychic lives. It is not a silent, passive recipient of the pressures and conflicts brewing within the unconscious, but a vibrant, dynamic agent capable of articulating what words often fail to capture. This intricate relationship between mind and body underscores a crucial understanding: that our physical being is not merely a consequence of our psychological state, but a potent force in its own right, capable of manifesting the deepest, most hidden aspects of ourselves. The clandestine messages carried by our physical being, often veiled in metaphor and symbolism, are the focus of our ongoing investigation, revealing a language of symptoms, sensations, and states of being that speak volumes about the unseen currents of our inner world.

Consider the subtle, yet undeniable, ways in which the unconscious exerts its influence through the body. These are not always dramatic or catastrophic events, but can be as seemingly innocuous as a persistent fidget, an involuntary tic, or a sudden, inexplicable wave of fatigue. A hand that unconsciously drums a restless rhythm on a table can be more than just a sign of boredom; it might be an echo of an unexpressed impatience, a kinetic expression of an internal tension that cannot be verbalized. The tightening of shoulders, a common response to stress, can escalate into a chronic state of muscular tension, a physical manifestation of a mind perpetually on guard, bracing against perceived threats. These are not random occurrences, but rather sophisticated, albeit often painful, expressions of the deepest parts of ourselves, a somatic language communicating what remains locked away in the realm of the unspoken.

The phenomenon of psychosomatic illness stands as a powerful testament to this agency of the body. Here, the physical realm becomes a canvas upon which psychic conflict is painted with the brushstrokes of disease. A recurring headache, for instance, may not simply be a biological malfunction, but a physical echo of a deeply repressed anger, an internal storm that finds no other outlet. The stomach churns, not just from indigestible food, but from the anxiety of an impending confrontation or a gnawing sense of guilt. The skin erupts in rashes, not from an allergen, but from an unbearable emotional pressure that seeks to manifest externally. In these instances, the body is not merely suffering from a physical ailment; it is enacting a drama of the psyche, a visceral narrative of internal struggles that have found a physical idiom for expression. The body, in its very suffering, asserts its agency, transforming unspeakable psychic pain into tangible, physical discomfort.

This bodily agency extends even to the seemingly neutral states of health and illness. Our overall vitality, our susceptibility to certain diseases, and even our capacity for healing can be profoundly influenced by our unconscious states. A persistent feeling of low energy, a pervasive weariness that no amount of rest can alleviate, can be more than a simple physical depletion. It can be a sign of a psychic disinvestment, a profound lack of motivation stemming from a sense of hopelessness or a deeply buried despair. Conversely, a robust sense of well-being, a vibrant energy that seems to bubble up from within, can reflect a psychic equilibrium, a harmonious integration of our inner world, even if that harmony is not consciously recognized. The body, in its very capacity for thriving or languishing, becomes a barometer of our psychic landscape.

The body's capacity to express the unconscious is also evident in the realm of involuntary movements and behaviors. A person who habitually bites their nails might be unconsciously attempting to soothe an internal anxiety. A tremor that appears during moments of heightened emotional arousal can be a physical manifestation of an overwhelming affect that the conscious mind cannot contain. These actions, occurring without conscious intent, are direct emanations from the unconscious, a way for the psyche to release pent-up energy or to communicate a state of distress that cannot be articulated through language. They are physical dialogues, enacted by the body on behalf of a psyche struggling to express itself.

Furthermore, the body's architecture and its very functioning can become imbued with unconscious meaning. A constricted posture, for example, might signify a holding back of emotions, a defensive stance against vulnerability. A tendency towards obesity can, in some cases, be understood as an unconscious attempt to create a protective barrier, a physical manifestation of a desire for self-envelopment against perceived external threats or internal emptiness. Conversely, a lean, wiry physique might, in other contexts, reflect a frantic energy, a perpetual state of unease that manifests as a restless, almost ascetic physicality. These are not deterministic pronouncements, but rather possibilities within the complex tapestry of bodily expression, where the physical form itself becomes a repository of unconscious narratives.

The realm of sexual expression, a primary domain of drives and their psychic aims, further illuminates the body's agency. When sexual desires are repressed, conflicted, or unmet, the psychic energy associated with them does not simply vanish. It is often transmuted and redirected, finding expression in a myriad of somatic phenomena. This can range from an overwhelming, generalized sexual frustration that manifests as agitation or irritability, to more specific physical symptoms such as chronic pain, fatigue, or even dermatological issues. The body, in these instances, becomes a surrogate for the unfulfilled or forbidden sexual impulse, a substitute organ for a desire that cannot be directly acknowledged or expressed. The very intensity of physical sensations, whether pleasurable or painful, can be seen as a testament to the potent energy of these drives, and the body's capacity to translate their psychic momentum into tangible experience.

The experience of illness, particularly chronic or seemingly inexplicable conditions, can also serve as a form of unconscious communication. When individuals are unable to articulate their emotional pain, their grief, or their frustration, the body may take over the burden of expression. A persistent cough that resists medical treatment might be a physical manifestation of an unexpressed sob, a deep sadness that cannot be released. A chronic fatigue that medical science struggles to diagnose could be a somatic representation of a profound psychic exhaustion, a bodily protest against an overwhelming burden of responsibility or a lack of meaning. In such cases, the illness itself becomes a message, a desperate plea from the unconscious for recognition and understanding. The body, in its very affliction, asserts its agency, demanding attention to the underlying psychic distress.

The body's role as an agent of the unconscious also highlights the limitations of purely biomedical approaches to understanding human suffering. While physical symptoms require medical attention, a complete understanding often necessitates delving into the psychological roots of the distress. By recognizing the body as a dynamic communicator, we open ourselves to a richer, more nuanced understanding of what it means to be unwell. This perspective moves beyond a simple cause-and-effect model of disease, acknowledging the intricate interplay between our inner world and our physical reality. The body, in this light, is not a malfunctioning machine, but a living, breathing testament to the complex and often hidden landscape of the human psyche.

The capacity of the body to manifest the unconscious is not limited to states of distress or illness. Even in moments of apparent well-being, the unconscious can subtly shape our physical experiences. The subtle gestures of affection, the unconscious mirroring of another's posture, the physical expressions of joy and excitement – these are all ways in which the unconscious finds a physical outlet. These manifestations of Eros, the life-affirming drives, demonstrate that the body's agency is not solely about expressing pain or conflict, but also about celebrating connection, vitality, and the myriad forms of human flourishing that originate in the depths of our psyche. The physical expression of love, the energetic embrace, the shared laughter that shakes the body – these are all potent affirmations of the psyche's capacity to animate and enrich our embodied existence.

The body, therefore, is not a mere spectator in the theatre of the mind. It is a principal actor, an essential medium through which the unconscious communicates its truths, its desires, and its discontents. The language of the body, though often oblique and symbolic, is a rich and profound form of expression that can reveal what remains hidden from conscious awareness. To truly understand ourselves, we must learn to listen to this physical discourse, to decipher the silent pronouncements of our embodied selves. The symptoms we experience, the sensations we feel, and the very state of our physical health are all part of an ongoing dialogue between our conscious and unconscious minds, a dialogue in which the body plays an active, and often indispensable, role. This acknowledgment of the body's agency is not merely an intellectual exercise; it is a crucial step towards a more holistic and compassionate understanding of human experience, recognizing that our physical being is an inextricable and eloquent expression of our deepest psychic reality. The hidden messages carried by our physical being are not merely the vestiges of past traumas or unresolved conflicts; they are the dynamic, living expressions of our most fundamental selves, constantly striving for recognition, integration, and ultimately, a form of wholeness that transcends the mere sum of our physical and mental parts.

Chapter 3: The Imaginary Envelope and Self-Perception

The journey into the self, into the very construction of what we perceive as "I," begins not with an internal spark of self-awareness, but with an external gaze. This is the paradox at the heart of Jacques Lacan's concept of the Imaginary order, a fundamental phase in psychic development where the subject is constituted through images, through identifications that are, by their very nature, external to the nascent self. It is in this realm of the Imaginary that the ego, that seemingly solid and unified sense of self, first begins to coalesce, not as a product of introspection, but as a reflection.

Central to this understanding is Lacan's pivotal notion of the "mirror stage." Imagine a pre-linguistic infant, a swirling vortex of uncoordinated impulses and fragmented sensations. This infant has no coherent sense of a unified body, no clear distinction between itself and its environment. Its experience is one of disarray, a dismemberment of sensation where limbs move independently and the boundaries of the self are fluid and indistinct. Then, an encounter occurs. Perhaps it's the infant's own reflection in a polished surface, or the benevolent gaze of a caregiver who mirrors back an image of a complete, coherent being. In this moment of recognition, a profound transformation takes place. The infant, for the first time, sees itself as a whole, as a distinct entity separate from the chaotic flux of its internal experience and the surrounding world. This external image, this unified reflection, is grasped as "me."

This "mirror stage," typically occurring around six to eighteen months of age, is not simply about recognizing one's face. It is an act of identification with an external image that the infant experiences as superior, as more complete and integrated than its own fragmented internal state. Lacan famously described this as a "jubilation," a moment of joyous recognition of a gestalt, a unified form that promises an end to the internal discord. This image becomes the template for the ego, the ideal that the subject will perpetually strive to embody. It is the first "imaginary envelope" that the nascent self wraps itself in, a protective, albeit illusory, shell of wholeness.

This imaginary envelope is crucial because it provides a sense of containment and coherence to an otherwise bewildering existence. Before the mirror stage, the infant's body is experienced as a collection of disconnected parts, prone to involuntary spasms and unfelt sensations. There is no sense of ownership, no unified spatial awareness. The mirror, however, presents a singular, stable image. The infant sees its limbs moving in concert, its features forming a recognizable whole. This external image is then internalized, becoming the foundational blueprint for the ego. The "I" is thus born, not from within, but by capturing and identifying with an external representation.

However, this identification is inherently illusory. The image in the mirror is a static, idealized representation. It does not capture the messy, fluctuating reality of the infant's lived experience, the constant internal shifts, the feelings of hunger, discomfort, and confusion. Yet, it is this idealized image that the ego clings to, an anchor in the turbulent sea of infantile experience. This is the essence of the Imaginary order: a realm of images, identifications, and specular relationships where the self is constructed through a fascination with its own likeness, an externalized ideal. The ego, in this sense, is fundamentally an imaginary construct, a misrecognition of the self as the image it has adopted.

The consequences of this fundamental misrecognition are far-reaching. Because the ego is formed through identification with an idealized external image, it is inherently alienated from the subject's true, lived experience. The "I" that we believe ourselves to be is, in large part, a fiction, a carefully constructed façade built upon borrowed images. This creates a fundamental split within the subject, a tension between the idealized self of the Imaginary and the fragmented, messy reality of the lived self. This split fuels the human drive for completeness, the perpetual pursuit of an ideal that is always just out of reach, because the very foundation of that ideal is rooted in an external, and therefore unattainable, image.

The Imaginary order is characterized by this specular identification, this fascination with the image of oneself and others. It is the realm of resemblance, of likeness, where the subject seeks to find itself in the other and to be recognized by the other. This plays out not only in the infant's relationship with its reflection but also in its interactions with caregivers. The caregiver's loving gaze, the way they hold and speak to the infant, all provide images of the infant that contribute to its nascent ego formation. The infant seeks to conform to these images, to become the "good baby" it perceives itself to be in the eyes of the other.

This process of identification is not passive. The subject actively chooses which images to embrace and which to reject, though these choices are often unconscious and heavily influenced by the social and cultural milieu. The media, for example, bombards us with idealized images of beauty, success, and happiness, creating a constant stream of potential identifications. We are encouraged to aspire to these images, to mold ourselves in their likeness, further entrenching the Imaginary construction of the ego. The more we strive to embody these external ideals, the further we move from our own authentic selves, creating a sense of alienation and discontent.

The imaginary envelope, therefore, acts as both a shield and a prison. It protects the fragile self from the overwhelming chaos of raw experience, providing a sense of unity and stability. However, it also traps the subject within a world of appearances, of superficial identifications. We become so invested in the image we project that we may lose touch with our inner feelings, our true desires, and our authentic needs. The pursuit of this idealized image can lead to a relentless striving for perfection, a fear of exposing any perceived flaws or imperfections, and a constant anxiety about not measuring up.

Consider the adolescent grappling with identity. This is a period marked by intense Imaginary activity, as the adolescent attempts to forge a coherent sense of self by experimenting with different images and identifications. They may adopt the style, the mannerisms, and even the beliefs of admired figures – musicians, actors, friends – seeking to find a self that feels solid and complete. This is the adolescent trying on different imaginary envelopes, searching for the one that best fits, the one that offers a sense of belonging and self-worth. While this exploration is a necessary part of development, it can also be a source of immense anxiety and insecurity, as the adolescent fears being exposed as an impostor, as someone who is merely mimicking rather than genuinely being.

The Imaginary order is also the site of much of our social interaction. We engage with others primarily through their images, through the roles they play and the appearances they present. We form judgments and make assumptions based on these external representations, often without truly understanding the complex inner lives of others. This can lead to miscommunication, prejudice, and a general superficiality in our relationships. We relate to the image of the other, rather than to the other as a complex, multifaceted subject.

Furthermore, the Imaginary order is deeply intertwined with the development of narcissism. The initial jubilation of the mirror stage, the fascination with the perfect, idealized image, can become a dominant mode of relating to oneself and the world. The narcissistic individual is perpetually in love with their own image, their own reflection, and seeks constant admiration and validation from others. They are trapped within the Imaginary, unable to move beyond the specular relationship to a more authentic connection with themselves and others. This can manifest as a profound fear of criticism, a hypersensitivity to perceived slights, and a relentless need to maintain the illusion of perfection.

The Imaginary is also the domain of fantasy. Our daydreams, our aspirations, our idealized notions of love and happiness are all products of the Imaginary order. These fantasies provide a temporary escape from the often harsh realities of life, offering a glimpse of a more perfect world, a more complete self. However, if we become too attached to these fantasies, if we allow them to dictate our expectations of reality, they can become a source of disappointment and disillusionment. We may find ourselves constantly comparing our lived experiences to our imagined ideals, leading to a persistent sense of dissatisfaction.

Lacan's concept of the Imaginary highlights the fundamental social and relational nature of human subjectivity. We are not born with a pre-formed self; we are made through our interactions with the world, through the images we absorb and the identifications we make. The "I" is not a fixed entity but a fluid, ever-changing construct, perpetually shaped by the Imaginary. This realization can be disorienting, challenging our deeply held beliefs about our autonomy and self-sufficiency. It suggests that our sense of self is, to a significant degree, a social and linguistic construct, woven from the threads of external images and societal expectations.

The development of language plays a crucial role in solidifying the Imaginary. Once the subject begins to acquire language, it can begin to label and categorize its identifications. The word "I" becomes associated with the idealized image, further reinforcing the ego's construction. However, language also introduces the Symbolic order, which begins to challenge the purely Imaginary realm, creating a more complex psychic landscape.

Despite its illusory nature, the Imaginary order is an essential stage in psychic development. It provides the necessary foundation for the formation of the ego, allowing the subject to navigate the world with a sense of coherence and continuity. Without the Imaginary envelope, the subject would remain fragmented and disoriented. The challenge lies not in eradicating the Imaginary, but in recognizing its limitations, in understanding that the idealized image is not the totality of the self. It is about learning to distinguish between the image we project and the reality of our lived experience, between the performance of self and the authentic self. This is a lifelong process of negotiation, of striving to integrate the fragmented experiences of the self within the illusory framework of the Imaginary, moving towards a more nuanced and authentic understanding of who we are. The ongoing dialogue between the Imaginary, the Symbolic, and the Real will continue to shape this understanding, making the formation of the "I" a dynamic and ever-evolving project.

The infant's jubilant recognition in the mirror, that initial grasp of a unified self, is merely the first step in a lifelong process of incorporating external ideals. The "imaginary envelope" that Lacan described is not a static garment donned once and for all, but a dynamic, permeable membrane constantly absorbing and reflecting the images that surround us. As we move beyond the solitary contemplation of our own reflection, we enter a world teeming with other gazes, other expectations, and a vast array of meticulously curated images that begin to shape not just our sense of self, but specifically, the way we perceive and inhabit our own bodies. This is where the body itself becomes a canvas, painted with the brushstrokes of external appraisals and societal dictates.

The internalization of these external images is a complex psychological dance, a continuous negotiation between the lived, felt reality of our physical being and the idealized, often unattainable representations that bombard us daily. We are not born with a fully formed body image; rather, it is constructed, layer by painstaking layer, through a series of identifications. Think of the child observing their parents, absorbing their postures, their self-deprecating remarks about a perceived imperfection, or their pride in a particular physical attribute. These early observations, often absorbed unconsciously, begin to lay the groundwork for what is considered a "good" or "bad" body. The way a mother smooths her hair or a father flexes his arm can become imprinted, unconsciously, as desirable or unremarkable.

As we mature, this process expands exponentially, particularly with the advent of mass media and, more recently, digital platforms. We are inundated with images that present a narrow, often distorted, ideal of physical perfection. These are not just abstract notions; they are concrete representations of bodies that are deemed attractive, healthy, successful, and worthy of admiration. Advertisements for fitness products showcase impossibly sculpted physiques; fashion magazines present models whose proportions defy biological reality; social media feeds overflow with filtered, posed, and meticulously edited portrayals of individuals seemingly living flawless, photogenic lives. Each of these images acts as a potential template, an external blueprint that whispers, "This is how you
should look."

The psychological mechanism through which these external images are integrated is primarily one of identification, but it is a complex form of identification, often tinged with envy and a desire for aspiration. We don't always consciously choose to emulate these images; rather, they seep into our consciousness, shaping our desires and influencing our self-evaluation. We begin to compare our own bodies – the body that feels hunger pangs, experiences fatigue, bears the marks of age or life's accidents – with these polished, external representations. This comparison is rarely favorable. The lived body, with its inherent messiness and imperfection, inevitably falls short of the idealized image.

This discrepancy between the lived body and the internalized ideal is the fertile ground for discontent. It creates a fundamental disconnect, a schism between the physical reality we inhabit and the phantom body we strive to embody. The imaginary envelope, which initially promised wholeness, now becomes a cage, trapping us in a perpetual state of self-criticism. Every perceived flaw – a wrinkle, a few extra pounds, a scar, a less-than-perfect smile – becomes a source of shame, a deviation from the idealized norm. We internalize the societal judgment that these imperfections render us less worthy, less attractive, and ultimately, less complete.

Consider the pervasive influence of beauty standards. These are not universal truths but culturally constructed ideals that shift and change over time, yet they exert immense pressure on individuals. For decades, a slender physique was paramount in Western cultures, leading to widespread body dissatisfaction and the proliferation of restrictive diets and extreme exercise regimes. More recently, there has been a shift towards a more curvaceous ideal in some circles, but even this carries its own set of pressures and expectations. The point is not the specific standard, but the very existence of a rigid, external standard against which individuals feel compelled to measure themselves. The body becomes an object of constant scrutiny, a project to be perfected rather than a vessel to be inhabited.

This internalization process is often exacerbated by the phenomenon of social comparison. We are wired to compare ourselves to others, and in the age of social media, this comparison is constant and often skewed. We are presented with the highlight reels of other people's lives, their most flattering photos, their most impressive achievements. When we compare our own behind-the-scenes reality to their curated public image, the perceived gap can be devastating to our self-esteem. This is particularly true when it comes to body image. Scrolling through Instagram, one might see an endless stream of seemingly flawless bodies, leading to the unconscious internalization of the belief that one's own body is inherently inadequate.

The disconnect between the lived body and the idealized body can manifest in various psychological and behavioral patterns. It can lead to disordered eating, where the pursuit of the ideal body overrides the body's natural hunger cues and nutritional needs. It can result in excessive exercise, driven not by a desire for health and well-being, but by a punishing regime aimed at eradicating perceived flaws. It can fuel a constant need for external validation, a desperate search for compliments and reassurance that we are "enough," that we are meeting the internalized ideal.

Furthermore, the language we use to describe our bodies often reflects this internalization of external judgments. We might speak of "bad" body parts, of needing to "fix" or "change" aspects of ourselves. This language frames the body as something to be conquered or modified, rather than accepted and nurtured. The very act of labeling certain body parts as "problem areas" is a direct result of internalizing societal narratives about what constitutes an undesirable physique. These narratives, often originating from industries that profit from insecurity, become deeply embedded in our self-perception.

The concept of the "imaginary envelope" thus takes on a more specific and often problematic dimension when applied to body image. It is no longer just about a general sense of self-coherence, but about a specific, often gendered and culturally influenced, idealized body. This imagined body becomes the ultimate aspiration, the benchmark against which our actual physical selves are perpetually measured and found wanting. This can create a profound sense of alienation from our own bodies, feeling like strangers inhabiting a physical form that does not align with the image we have internalized.

The impact of this internalization can be particularly acute during adolescence, a period already fraught with identity formation and heightened self-consciousness. Teenagers are bombarded with images of their peers and media personalities, creating intense pressure to conform to evolving trends and beauty standards. The body is undergoing rapid and often unpredictable changes, making it a focal point of anxiety and self-doubt. The external images of idealized bodies become powerful anchors for their developing sense of self, and deviations from these images can be experienced as profound personal failures.

This pressure extends beyond mere physical appearance. The idealized body is often associated with qualities like strength, vitality, discipline, and even moral virtue. A "healthy" body is often equated with a "good" person, while a body that deviates from the norm might be implicitly or explicitly associated with laziness, indulgence, or a lack of self-control. These moral judgments, deeply ingrained in societal discourse, further fuel the shame and anxiety surrounding body image. We don't just dislike our perceived physical flaws; we internalize the belief that these flaws reflect poorly on our character.

The integration of external bodily ideals is also deeply intertwined with our experiences of trauma and vulnerability. For individuals who have experienced abuse or neglect, their bodies may become sites of shame and disconnection. External images, even those that promote health and well-being, can feel inaccessible or even threatening if they do not align with a deeply ingrained sense of bodily brokenness. The imaginary envelope, in such cases, might be a fragile shield, perpetually threatened by the echoes of past trauma that have fundamentally altered the relationship with the physical self.

Furthermore, the pursuit of the idealized body can become a form of displacement for other unmet needs or unresolved psychological issues. When individuals feel powerless in other areas of their lives, controlling their diet or their physical appearance can offer a superficial sense of agency. The body becomes a project that can, in theory, be perfected, providing a tangible outcome for effort and dedication, even if this outcome is an illusion. This can perpetuate a cycle of self-improvement that is never truly satisfying, as the underlying issues remain unaddressed.

The pervasiveness of these internalized images means that even in our most intimate moments, we may be subject to an internal critic shaped by external standards. The desire for connection and intimacy can be hampered by a fear of being truly seen, of having our physical imperfections exposed. We might engage in behaviors designed to conceal or disguise aspects of our bodies, perpetuating the illusion of the idealized self even in the presence of trusted others. This creates a barrier to authentic connection, as we are presenting a carefully constructed image rather than our lived reality.

Ultimately, the body as a mirror, reflecting internalized external images, highlights a fundamental tension in human experience. We are embodied beings, experiencing the world through our physical senses, yet our perception of these bodies is heavily mediated by a cultural landscape that often promotes unrealistic and damaging ideals. The imaginary envelope, in this context, becomes a source of both comfort and profound distress. It offers a seductive promise of belonging and acceptance, but at the cost of alienating us from the very physical reality we inhabit. Recognizing this dynamic is a crucial step towards reclaiming a more grounded, accepting, and authentic relationship with our bodies, moving beyond the tyranny of external images to embrace the complex, imperfect, and ultimately, real physicality of our existence. It is a call to dismantle the internalized judgments, to challenge the relentless comparisons, and to begin the arduous but liberating process of seeing our bodies not as reflections of external ideals, but as the unique, irreplaceable vessels of our lived experience.

The initial exhilaration of self-recognition, the nascent feeling of being a cohesive entity, is a foundational moment, but it is also an illusion. Lacan's concept of the imaginary order, while essential for constructing a unified self, is built upon a shimmering edifice of borrowed images and identifications. This inherent illusory nature, the very fabric of the "imaginary envelope," sets the stage for a lifelong dance between aspiration and dissatisfaction. The self, once perceived as whole in the mirror's reflection, becomes a project, a constant negotiation with ideals that are perpetually just out of reach. This striving is not merely a quest for self-improvement; it is often a desperate attempt to bridge the widening chasm between the imagined self and the felt reality of our existence, a chasm that breeds a persistent hum of disquiet.

This tension arises from the fundamental paradox of identification. We coalesce around images, around projections of what it means to be complete, integrated, and worthy. Yet, these images are never truly our own, nor are they ever fully attainable. They are external blueprints, meticulously crafted and often impossibly perfect. The imaginary envelope, therefore, can become a gilded cage, offering the comfort of a defined boundary but simultaneously limiting our capacity to embrace the fluid, messy, and imperfect nature of our actual selves. The desire for wholeness, initially a protective shell, transforms into a relentless engine of self-scrutiny. Every perceived deviation from the internalized ideal becomes a source of profound discomfort, a signifier of incompleteness. This is not a passive discontent; it is an active, often painful, process of self-critique, fueled by the constant comparison between the lived, embodied experience and the spectral perfection of the imaginary.

Consider the pervasive influence of aspirational narratives. We are inundated with stories, both personal and public, that celebrate mastery, effortless achievement, and an unwavering sense of self-possession. These narratives, amplified by social media, often present a curated version of reality, where struggles are smoothed over and imperfections are either hidden or reframed as charming eccentricities. When we internalize these narratives, we begin to expect the same frictionless progression in our own lives. Any stumble, any moment of doubt, any deviation from a planned trajectory can feel like a catastrophic failure. The imaginary envelope, designed to provide a stable sense of self, instead becomes a canvas onto which we project these unattainable standards, leading to a gnawing feeling of inadequacy when our lived experiences inevitably fall short.

The trap of the imaginary lies in its seductive promise of control. In a world that often feels unpredictable and chaotic, the ability to construct and adhere to an idealized self-image offers a potent, albeit illusory, sense of agency. We believe that by meticulously curating our external presentation – our appearance, our accomplishments, our social interactions – we can somehow dictate the outcome of our lives, ensuring acceptance and admiration. This pursuit of an idealized persona, however, comes at a significant cost. It requires constant vigilance, a perpetual effort to maintain the facade, and a deep-seated fear of exposure. The energy expended in this effort could otherwise be directed towards genuine self-discovery and authentic connection, but it is instead consumed by the Sisyphean task of maintaining an illusion.

The discontents of this illusory wholeness are not merely personal; they are deeply social. The idealized self we project is often designed to elicit approval and validation from others. We internalize societal expectations about success, attractiveness, and social desirability, and we strive to embody these ideals to gain a sense of belonging. However, this reliance on external validation creates a precarious foundation for self-esteem. When the feedback we receive does not align with our internalized ideals, or when we perceive that others are achieving these ideals more effortlessly, a sense of envy and bitterness can arise. This envy is not simply a desire for what another possesses; it is often a reflection of our own perceived deficiencies, a painful reminder of the gap between our lived reality and the imaginary ideal we cling to.

Furthermore, the very act of identifying with external ideals can lead to a profound sense of alienation from our own authentic desires and experiences. When we are constantly striving to fit a mold, we risk silencing the inner voice that speaks to what truly nourishes us, what brings us genuine joy, and what makes us feel alive. The body, in particular, becomes a battleground. The idealized body, often presented as the ultimate symbol of success and self-discipline, can overshadow the body's natural wisdom – its signals of fatigue, hunger, and pleasure. We may push ourselves beyond our limits, ignoring the body's pleas for rest, all in the pursuit of an external standard that may not even align with our own well-being. This disconnect between mind and body, fueled by the imaginary envelope, can lead to chronic stress, burnout, and a pervasive sense of unfulfillment.

The allure of the imaginary envelope also manifests in how we construct narratives about our past and future. We tend to embellish our successes and downplay our failures, creating a polished autobiography that conforms to the idealized self we wish to present. This selective memory and forward projection can prevent us from fully integrating our past experiences, including our mistakes and setbacks, which are crucial for growth and learning. The imaginary self, in its quest for perfection, resists the messy, contradictory, and often painful truths of our personal histories. This resistance can lead to a feeling of being perpetually stuck, unable to move forward because the past has been edited into an unconvincing, idealized narrative.

The constant striving, inherent in the illusory nature of the imaginary, can also manifest as a form of existential anxiety. If our sense of wholeness and worth is contingent on achieving an external ideal, then the possibility of failure or falling short becomes a source of deep unease. This anxiety can fuel a perpetual state of hypervigilance, where we are constantly scanning for threats to our carefully constructed self-image. The fear of being "found out" – of being revealed as less accomplished, less attractive, or less perfect than we appear – can be paralyzing. This fear prevents us from taking risks, from embracing vulnerability, and from engaging fully with life.

The cultural emphasis on rapid self-transformation further exacerbates these discontents. We are bombarded with messages that suggest that profound change can be achieved quickly and easily, through the right product, the right technique, or the right mindset. This narrative of instant gratification undermines the value of patience, perseverance, and the slow, organic process of personal growth. When our efforts to align with the imaginary ideal do not yield immediate results, we can become discouraged and abandon our pursuits, reinforcing the feeling of inadequacy. The imaginary envelope, in this context, becomes a treadmill, constantly demanding more, offering no genuine arrival.

Moreover, the illusory nature of the imaginary order can lead to a superficial understanding of happiness. We often equate happiness with the attainment of external goals – a promotion, a new car, a romantic partner – believing that these achievements will finally bring us a sense of lasting contentment. However, once these goals are reached, the happiness is often fleeting, and we find ourselves searching for the next object of desire to fill the void. This relentless pursuit of external markers of success prevents us from cultivating an inner source of joy and satisfaction. The imaginary self, focused on external validation, struggles to connect with the deeper, more enduring sources of well-being.

The tension between the lived body and the idealized self, central to the discontents of the imaginary, can also manifest as a form of self-estrangement. We may feel a disconnect from our physical sensations, our emotional responses, and even our own thoughts, as they do not align with the perfectly composed image we aspire to project. This can lead to a feeling of being an imposter in our own lives, constantly performing a role rather than genuinely inhabiting our experiences. The imaginary envelope, in its attempt to create a unified and desirable self, ironically leads to a profound sense of fragmentation and alienation.

The desire for wholeness, as represented by the imaginary envelope, is a fundamental human aspiration, but when it is built upon the shifting sands of external ideals, it inevitably leads to a terrain of discontents. The gap between the polished facade and the lived reality, between the projected self and the authentic self, becomes a source of perpetual striving, anxiety, and a deep-seated feeling of inadequacy. Recognizing this illusory nature is the first step towards dismantling the trap of the imaginary, towards embracing the complexities and imperfections of our embodied existence, and towards finding a more grounded and authentic sense of self. This journey requires a conscious effort to challenge the internalized ideals, to cultivate self-compassion, and to find contentment not in the unattainable perfection of the imaginary, but in the rich, messy, and profoundly real landscape of our lived experience. The discomfort, the striving, and the persistent feeling of not being enough are the very signs that the imaginary envelope, while providing a temporary illusion of wholeness, is ultimately failing to contain the full, vibrant, and imperfect truth of who we are. It is in acknowledging these discontents, in sitting with the discomfort of this gap, that the possibility for genuine integration and self-acceptance begins to emerge, moving beyond the seductive but ultimately hollow promise of an idealized, imaginary self.

The body, that most intimate and immediate of our realities, becomes a stage upon which the drama of the other's gaze is perpetually performed. From the earliest moments of our existence, we learn to understand ourselves not just through our own nascent sensations, but through the reflections and reactions of those around us. The infant, reaching out to touch a parent's face, is not merely exploring texture and form; they are also calibrating their own presence against the responsive presence of the other. This primal interaction establishes a fundamental truth: our sense of self, and crucially, our sense of our physical self, is woven from threads of external perception. The imaginary envelope, that protective yet constricting shell we construct around our identity, is particularly vulnerable in its corporeal manifestations. It is bombarded by the echoes of what others see, what they deem acceptable, desirable, or even merely *normal.*

This external gaze is not a monolithic entity. It is a complex tapestry woven from individual judgments, societal norms, and pervasive cultural ideals. What is considered beautiful in one era or culture can be seen as unremarkable or even undesirable in another. Yet, within any given context, these ideals exert a powerful, often unconscious, influence on how we apprehend our own bodies. We internalize these external standards, filtering them through the lens of our personal experiences and relationships, and they become the benchmarks against which we measure our own physical selves. The imaginary envelope, therefore, is not merely a static construct; it is a dynamic, perpetually renegotiated boundary, shaped by the constant influx of perceived judgments from the world outside. This internalization process can be insidious. We may not even be aware of the extent to which our self-perception is being dictated by the imagined opinions of others, so deeply embedded have these external dictates become. The very air we breathe, metaphorically speaking, is saturated with these cultural pronouncements on the ideal body.

Consider the pervasive influence of media, a primary conduit for disseminating these idealized images. From glossy magazine covers to fleeting social media feeds, we are relentlessly exposed to bodies that have been sculpted, retouched, and presented as the epitome of physical perfection. These are not merely representations; they are potent signifiers that become internalized blueprints for what our own bodies

should be. The imaginary envelope, in its attempt to create a cohesive and desirable self, readily absorbs these images, transforming them into aspirations that often feel utterly divorced from our lived corporeal reality. This can lead to a gnawing dissatisfaction with our own physical form. The curve of a hip, the texture of skin, the distribution of weight – aspects that are fundamentally natural and individual – become subjects of intense scrutiny when measured against these manufactured ideals.

The consequence of this relentless comparison is often a profound sense of body dissatisfaction. The imaginary envelope, meant to provide a sense of contained selfhood, instead becomes a source of internal conflict. We are no longer simply

inhabiting our bodies; we are critically *judging* them, constantly seeking to mold them into conformity with the external templates we have absorbed. This can manifest in a variety of ways, from obsessive dieting and excessive exercise to a reluctance to be seen or to engage in activities that might draw attention to perceived flaws. The body, which should be a source of grounded presence and sensory experience, becomes a site of anxiety and shame. The 'gaze of the other,' even when it is not actively directed at us, looms large in our internal landscape, dictating what we feel we must achieve or conceal.

This internalization of external judgment is not simply a matter of aesthetic preference; it is deeply intertwined with our sense of worth and belonging. Societal narratives often equate physical attractiveness with desirability, success, and even moral virtue. The attractive individual is often perceived as more competent, more trustworthy, and more deserving of positive attention. This creates a powerful incentive to conform to prevailing beauty standards, as doing so is implicitly linked to gaining social approval and validation. The imaginary envelope, in this context, is shaped not just by what we

want to be, but by what we believe we *need* to be to be accepted and valued by others. This can lead to a painful paradox: the more we try to align our bodies with external ideals to gain acceptance, the more we may alienate ourselves from our authentic physical selves.

The dynamics of social comparison are particularly potent when it comes to body image. We are wired to compare ourselves to others, a mechanism that can be adaptive in many contexts, but which can become a source of considerable distress when applied to our physical appearance. We scan our environment, consciously or unconsciously, for benchmarks against which to measure ourselves. On a crowded street, in a gym, or even scrolling through social media, we are constantly exposed to a diverse range of bodies, and inevitably, we engage in comparative processes. If these comparisons consistently highlight perceived deficiencies relative to internalized ideals, the imaginary envelope becomes a rigid, self-critical structure. We begin to see our bodies not as unique and functional entities, but as collections of perceived imperfections.

This can lead to a profound disconnection from our embodied experience. The signals our bodies send – hunger, fatigue, pleasure, pain – can be ignored or distorted if they do not align with the demands of the idealized self. For instance, an individual might push themselves to exercise beyond their physical limits, ignoring the body's pleas for rest, because they believe that discomfort and exertion are necessary to achieve a certain physique. This suppression of the body's natural wisdom, driven by the pressure to conform to external standards, can have detrimental effects on both physical and mental well-being. The imaginary envelope, in its obsession with the external gaze, effectively silences the internal voice of the body.

The concept of 'beauty standards' itself is a powerful manifestation of the 'gaze of the other.' These standards are not inherent truths; they are social constructs that shift and evolve, reflecting the prevailing values and power dynamics of a given society. What is considered beautiful today might have been deemed unattractive in a previous generation, and vice versa. Yet, the force of these shifting standards is undeniable. They shape our desires, our anxieties, and the very way we inhabit our physical forms. The imaginary envelope, in attempting to create a unified and acceptable self, becomes a vessel for these ever-changing cultural mandates. This can lead to a perpetual state of striving, a never-ending quest to keep pace with a moving target.

Furthermore, the influence of the 'gaze of the other' is not limited to overt judgments or media portrayals. It also operates through subtle social cues, through the unspoken expectations of family, friends, and romantic partners. The casual remark about weight, the lingering glance at a perceived flaw, the comparison to someone else's physique – these seemingly minor interactions can leave lasting imprints on our self-perception. The imaginary envelope absorbs these cues, weaving them into the fabric of our internal dialogue. What might be a fleeting observation from another can become a deeply ingrained belief about our own inadequacy. This highlights the pervasive and often insidious nature of the 'gaze,' demonstrating how it can penetrate the most intimate realms of our self-awareness.

The body, in its raw materiality, is often perceived as something that needs to be perfected, managed, and controlled to meet these external expectations. This creates a fundamental tension between our lived, embodied reality and the idealized, often disembodied, image we are encouraged to pursue. The imaginary envelope, in its quest for a cohesive and socially acceptable self, can thus contribute to a sense of alienation from our own physicality. We may feel like strangers in our own skin, constantly at odds with the body we possess, striving for a version that exists only in the realm of ideals. This disconnect is a significant source of psychological distress, as it undermines the fundamental sense of being at home in one's own being.

The pressure to conform to idealized body types also disproportionately affects certain groups, particularly women and marginalized communities. Historically and culturally, specific aesthetic standards have been imposed, often reinforcing existing power imbalances. For individuals who do not fit these prescribed norms, the 'gaze of the other' can be a source of constant marginalization and discrimination. The imaginary envelope, in such cases, can become a site of deep conflict, as the individual grapples with the pressure to conform to a standard that may feel entirely foreign or even oppressive, while simultaneously experiencing the sting of external disapproval.

The relentless pursuit of an idealized body, driven by the 'gaze of the other,' can also have significant economic implications. The multi-billion dollar beauty and diet industries thrive on this dissatisfaction, offering solutions and products that promise to help individuals achieve the coveted ideal. This creates a feedback loop where the external gaze fuels anxieties, which in turn drive consumption, reinforcing the very standards that created the initial unease. The imaginary envelope, in this context, becomes not just a psychological construct but also a commodity, subject to market forces and consumer pressures.

Moreover, the concept of the 'gaze' extends beyond the visual. It encompasses the ways in which our bodies are perceived and judged through language, through cultural narratives, and through social interactions. A body that is deemed too loud, too quiet, too assertive, or too passive can all be subject to negative judgment, further shaping the individual's self-perception and the boundaries of their imaginary envelope. This underscores the multi-faceted nature of external influence on body image, demonstrating that it is not solely about appearance but also about how our physical presence is interpreted and evaluated within a broader social context.

The impact of the 'gaze of the other' on body image is a powerful testament to the interconnectedness of the self and society. Our internal sense of what is desirable, acceptable, and beautiful is profoundly shaped by external forces. The imaginary envelope, while offering a sense of self-definition, can become a mirror reflecting not our authentic selves, but the often-unrealistic and demanding ideals imposed by the world around us. This can lead to a perpetual cycle of self-criticism and striving, a constant negotiation with an idealized other that ultimately distracts us from embracing and valuing our own unique, embodied existence. The challenge lies in recognizing the influence of this external gaze, in deconstructing the internalized ideals it promotes, and in cultivating a more compassionate and accepting relationship with our own bodies, moving beyond the limitations of the imaginary envelope and into the reality of our lived physicality.

When the very fabric of our perceived self, the carefully constructed imaginary envelope that houses our sense of being, begins to unravel, the consequences can be profound and deeply disorienting. This is not a gentle unraveling, but often a violent tearing, a shattering of the illusion of wholeness that trauma, overwhelming psychic distress, or profound disillusionment can inflict. The smooth, protective boundary that delineates the self from the other, the internal from the external, cracks under the pressure, and through these fissures seeps a disquieting reality of fragmentation and disconnection.

One of the most arresting manifestations of this breakdown is dissociation. It is as if the self, overwhelmed by unbearable reality or a crushing internal conflict, attempts to escape by fragmenting itself, or by detaching from aspects of its own experience. This detachment can manifest in a multitude of ways, but at its core lies a disruption of the continuity of consciousness, memory, identity, or perception. The individual might feel as though they are observing their own life from a distance, as an impartial spectator to events that are nonetheless happening

to them. This sense of 'unreality' is not a mere philosophical pondering; it is a visceral, lived experience. The world can appear muted, dreamlike, or even artificial, a sensation often described as derealization. The solid, tangible reality that others take for granted becomes suspect, shimmering at the edges, lacking its usual weight and significance. It is as though the very light has changed, casting an unfamiliar, alien glow on everything familiar.

This derealization is often accompanied by a parallel sense of depersonalization, where the self, too, becomes estranged. The individual may feel disconnected from their own body, their own thoughts, emotions, or actions. The hands that reach out might feel like someone else's, the voice that speaks may sound alien, the memories of past events might feel like stories they have heard but not experienced. The coherent narrative of a personal history begins to fracture, leaving behind disconnected episodes or a vague sense of continuity that feels hollow. The imaginary envelope, once a container for a unified self, now feels like a sieve, with essential parts of the self leaking out, or like a shattered mirror, reflecting a multitude of fragmented images rather than a single, whole reflection.

In its most severe forms, this fragmentation can lead to profound difficulties in maintaining a sense of personal identity. The boundaries between different states of being, different emotional responses, or even different perceived selves can blur or become distinct and warring factions within the psyche. The cohesiveness that allows us to navigate the world with a stable sense of who we are, where we end and others begin, is compromised. This is particularly evident in conditions like dissociative identity disorder, where distinct personality states, each with its own memories, patterns of behavior, and even physical characteristics, emerge and take control at different times. This represents an extreme form of the imaginary envelope's collapse, where the protective shell has not just cracked, but has fundamentally broken into separate, often uncommunicating, compartments.

The body, that most intimate anchor of our embodied self, often becomes a primary site of this dissociative experience. When the psyche recoils from overwhelming pain, physical or emotional, it can compartmentalize or numb sensations, leading to a profound disconnect from one's physical reality. This can manifest as a lack of awareness of bodily needs, a feeling of the body being alien or unreal, or even physical symptoms that have no apparent medical cause. The body's integrity, a fundamental aspect of the imaginary envelope's containment, is thus compromised. The skin, which should be the boundary between the self and the world, can feel porous, or conversely, like an impenetrable barrier that separates the self from genuine experience.

This leads to conditions like body dysmorphic disorder (BDD), where the individual experiences intense preoccupation with perceived flaws in their appearance. These perceived flaws are often minor or nonexistent to others, but to the individual, they are glaring defects that cause significant distress and impairment. BDD can be understood as a manifestation of a deeply fractured self-perception, where the individual's capacity to integrate external feedback and internal sensations about their body is severely distorted. The imaginary envelope, in this context, is not so much cracked as it is warped, with a hyper-focus on perceived imperfections that dominate the entire psychic landscape. The body becomes the battleground for a self that feels fundamentally unacceptable, an object of constant, agonizing scrutiny.

The shattering of the imaginary envelope can stem from various sources, but severe trauma stands as a particularly potent catalyst. When an individual experiences events that overwhelm their capacity to cope – such as abuse, neglect, accidents, or combat exposure – the psyche may resort to drastic measures to survive. Dissociation is a common adaptive response in the face of unbearable circumstances, a way for the mind to distance itself from the immediate horror. However, this protective mechanism can leave lasting scars. The imagined envelope, fractured during the traumatic event, may never fully reassemble, leaving the individual perpetually feeling vulnerable, disconnected, and fragmented. The world outside, which was the source of the trauma, can become a place of constant threat, while the internal world becomes a chaotic, unpredictable space.

The feeling of fragmentation is not merely an intellectual concept; it is a deeply emotional and sensory experience. It can feel like being pulled in multiple directions at once, like disparate pieces of oneself are incapable of cohering. There is a pervasive sense of not being whole, of being incomplete, and this incompleteness can manifest as anxiety, depression, a pervasive sense of emptiness, or a constant, gnawing fear. The capacity for genuine connection with others can be impaired, as the individual struggles to present a stable, unified self, or to truly feel present and engaged in relationships. The imaginary envelope, meant to facilitate healthy interaction with the world, instead becomes a barrier, a testament to internal disarray.

In some instances, the cracking of the imaginary envelope can lead to a hyper-vigilant state, where the individual is perpetually on edge, anticipating further disintegration or external threats. Every perceived flaw, every perceived rejection, every moment of discomfort can feel like further evidence of their brokenness. This can lead to a vicious cycle, where the fear of fragmentation perpetuates the very feelings of distress that contribute to it. The individual may become intensely self-conscious, hyper-aware of how others might perceive their perceived flaws, leading to avoidance behaviors and further isolation. The imagined gaze of the other, which previously shaped the envelope, now becomes a source of amplified terror, a confirmation of internal disunity.

The integration of fragmented aspects of the self is a slow and often arduous process. It requires creating a safe and stable internal and external environment, where the individual can begin to gently re-explore the shattered pieces of their experience. Therapy, in its various forms, plays a crucial role in this process, providing a container for the fragmented self, a space where the disowned parts can be acknowledged, understood, and gradually reintegrated. This involves not just intellectual understanding, but also emotional processing and the development of new ways of relating to oneself and the world. The goal is not necessarily to erase the cracks, for they may remain as scars, but to weave them into a new tapestry of selfhood, one that acknowledges the fragility and resilience of the human psyche.

The experience of derealization and depersonalization, while terrifying, can also be seen as the psyche's desperate attempt to create distance from overwhelming internal or external stimuli. When the imaginary envelope fails to provide adequate protection, the mind may resort to these extreme measures to preserve itself from complete annihilation. The world, and the self, are rendered less real, less potent, to make them more bearable. This highlights the adaptive, albeit maladaptive in the long term, nature of these dissociative phenomena. They are not arbitrary breakdowns, but rather intricate, though painful, responses to unbearable psychic pressure.

The intensity of body dysmorphia can be understood as a manifestation of the profound shame and self-loathing that can accompany the cracking of the imaginary envelope. When the self feels fundamentally flawed or broken, this feeling is often projected onto the physical form, which becomes the tangible evidence of this perceived inadequacy. The preoccupation with specific body parts or features becomes a way of localizing and externalizing an otherwise diffuse sense of inner turmoil. The desire to correct these perceived flaws becomes a desperate attempt to regain a sense of wholeness and acceptance, both internally and from the imagined gaze of others.

The process of re-experiencing and integrating traumatic memories, often a core component of healing from shattered psychic envelopes, can be intensely challenging. When these memories resurface, they can trigger intense emotional and physical responses, often feeling as if the trauma is happening all over again. This can lead to a resurgence of dissociative symptoms, as the psyche struggles to integrate these overwhelming experiences into its ongoing narrative. The therapeutic relationship becomes a crucial element here, providing a stable and supportive presence that can help the individual navigate these difficult terrain without becoming further fragmented.

Furthermore, the social and cultural context in which these experiences occur can significantly impact their manifestation and the individual's path to recovery. Societies that are more accepting of vulnerability and mental health struggles may offer greater support, while those that emphasize stoicism and perfection can exacerbate feelings of shame and isolation. The constant barrage of idealized images in media can also amplify body dysmorphia and feelings of inadequacy, making the task of reassembling a healthy imaginary envelope even more daunting. The pressure to conform to external standards can, when the internal container is already compromised, feel like an insurmountable burden.

Ultimately, the cracking of the imaginary envelope is a testament to the profound interconnectedness of our internal world and our external reality, and the intricate ways in which our sense of self is constructed and maintained. It reveals the vulnerability inherent in our psychological architecture, but also the remarkable resilience of the human spirit to strive for coherence and healing even in the face of profound fragmentation. The journey through this breakdown is not about returning to an unbroken state, but about learning to live with the scars, to integrate the fragmented pieces, and to build a new, perhaps more complex, but ultimately more authentic and integrated sense of self.

Chapter 4: Jouissance: Pleasure Beyond Pleasure

The human psyche, in its relentless pursuit of satisfaction, often navigates a landscape of pleasure and its myriad gradations. We speak of contentment, of fulfillment, of simple enjoyment, all terms that map onto a spectrum of gratification. Yet, lurking beyond these familiar terrains, in the shadowed recesses of desire and the incandescent peaks of experience, lies a concept that resists easy definition, a force that both draws us in and threatens to consume us: Lacan's *jouissance*. To attempt a straightforward translation is to court futility, for *jouissance* is not merely "pleasure" or "enjoyment" in the common parlance. It is something far more potent, something that dances on the precipice of pain, a forbidden fruit that, once tasted, leaves an indelible mark, a yearning for more even as it saturates. It is an ecstatic surplus, an overflowing of the symbolic order, a return to a primal, pre-linguistic intensity that can be both ecstatic and terrifying.

The very elusiveness of

jouissance is, in a way, its defining characteristic. Lacan himself wrestled with its articulation, acknowledging its resistance to neat categorization. It is a concept that proliferates, mutating and manifesting in ways that often confound our attempts to pin it down. It is the scream that escapes the throat during moments of intense pleasure, the shiver that runs down the spine when confronted with the sublime, the compulsive repetition of a behavior that brings no discernible "good" but feels undeniably necessary. It is the intoxicating rush that accompanies transgression, the dizzying feeling of being simultaneously alive and on the verge of dissolution. This is not the gentle hum of contentment, but a resonant vibration that shakes the very foundations of the self.

To speak of

jouissance is to step outside the reassuring boundaries of the ego's carefully constructed reality. It is to venture into the realm of the Real, that which resists symbolization, the raw, unmediated experience that lies beneath the veneer of language and social convention. This is a realm where pleasure is not simply a reward for appropriate behavior or the satisfaction of a need, but a force that erupts from within, often in defiance of logic or even self-preservation. It is the secret of the symptom, the unconscious drive that compels us towards actions that seem, from a rational perspective, self-defeating. It is the sublime terror of the abyss, the intoxicating allure of the forbidden.

Consider the addict, chasing a high that momentarily obliterates the mundane, the emptiness, the gnawing discomfort of existence. The substance itself is but a vehicle; the true object of pursuit is that fleeting moment of intense, overwhelming sensation – the

jouissance that temporarily suspends the ordinary suffering of being. This is not simple pleasure; it is a rupture, a tearing away from the fabric of everyday life into a state of heightened, often destructive, intensity. The pleasure derived is inextricably linked to the transgression, the defiance of societal norms and personal well-being. The very act of self-destruction, in its extremity, can become a perverse source of this ecstatic surplus.

Similarly, think of the artist or the performer who, in the throes of creation or execution, experiences a state of ecstatic absorption. The hours blur, the self seems to dissolve, and an intense, almost painful, focus takes hold. This is not the calm satisfaction of a job well done, but a fervent channeling of energy, a wrestling with an overwhelming force that demands expression. The resulting work might be hailed as genius, but the process itself was likely fraught with anxiety, obsession, and an almost manic intensity. This is

jouissance – the creative impulse that burns so brightly it risks consuming the artist. It is the point where the pursuit of beauty or truth becomes an all-consuming, potentially dangerous, passion.

Lacan often linked

jouissance to the body, not as a mere biological instrument, but as a site of profound psychic intensity. The body is where this excess, this unsymbolizable jouissance, often makes itself felt. It is in the throes of sexual ecstasy, where the boundaries of the self blur and a primal force takes over, that we glimpse *jouissance*. It is in the inexplicable ache of phantom limbs, the inexplicable pain of psychosomatic ailments, the visceral shudder of fear or delight. These are not simply physiological responses; they are eruptions of a psychic energy that exceeds the symbolic order, a testament to the fact that our bodies are not merely machines, but conduits for an experience that often defies rational explanation. The body, in its capacity to feel intensely, becomes a locus for the reception and expression of this excessive pleasure.

The concept of

jouissance is also deeply intertwined with the idea of the Other, not as a benevolent figure, but as that which holds the key to our desire and our suffering. For Lacan, the Other represents the symbolic order, the realm of language, law, and social norms. Yet, *jouissance* often operates in defiance of this Other. It is the pleasure that we derive from breaking the rules, from transgressing the boundaries set by the Other. It is the secret enjoyment that we keep hidden, the part of ourselves that we refuse to surrender to the symbolic order. This hidden enjoyment, this unspeakable delight, is a powerful force that shapes our desires and our behaviors, often in ways we do not fully understand.

The inherent tension within

jouissance is its dual nature: it is both intensely pleasurable and potentially destructive. It is the siren song that lures us onto the rocks, the intoxicating elixir that can lead to ruin. The pursuit of *jouissance* can lead to obsessive behaviors, to addiction, to a disregard for consequences. Yet, it is also the very engine of our deepest desires, the spark that ignites creativity, passion, and the very drive to live fully. Without this excess, this capacity for transgressive pleasure, life might become a dull, predictable affair, devoid of the intensity that makes it meaningful, even in its suffering.

The difficulty in grasping

jouissance further underscores its profound significance. It is a concept that exists at the limits of our conceptual and linguistic capacities. It points to an experience that lies beyond the reach of ordinary language, an experience that can only be alluded to, hinted at, rather than fully articulated. This is not a failure of language, but a testament to the profound mystery of the human psyche, and the irreducible gap between our subjective experience and our attempts to represent it. *Jouissance* is the ghost in the machine, the unspeakable kernel of jouissance that forever eludes our attempts to capture and contain it.

One can see

jouissance manifest in the almost ritualistic repetition of certain acts, even when they lead to negative consequences. The gambler who, despite mounting losses, continues to play, driven by the phantom possibility of that overwhelming win, that moment of pure, unadulterated ecstasy. The obsession is not with the money, but with the possibility of that singular, annihilating experience of *jouissance*. Similarly, consider the fascination with danger, the thrill-seeker who courts death in extreme sports. The fear is palpable, the risk is undeniable, yet the exhilaration, the feeling of being intensely alive at the very edge of existence, represents a potent form of *jouissance*. It is the body's visceral engagement with the forbidden, the ultimate transgression against the instinct for self-preservation.

This concept also touches upon the uncanny, that sense of something both familiar and deeply unsettling. Think of certain works of art or music that evoke a strange, almost disturbing, sense of pleasure. A melody that is both beautiful and melancholic, a painting that is both captivating and disquieting. These experiences can trigger a

jouissance that is not straightforwardly pleasurable but tinged with a sense of unease, a recognition of something that lies beyond our normal framework of understanding. It is a pleasure that arises from the disruption of our expectations, from the confrontation with something that is both deeply resonant and fundamentally alien.

The paradoxical nature of

jouissance is what makes it so compelling and so challenging. It is the pleasure that hurts, the joy that is laced with sorrow, the fulfillment that leaves one wanting more. It is the experience that transcends the ordinary categories of pleasure and pain, of good and evil, of sanity and madness. It is the wild, untamed energy of the psyche, a force that can be both the source of our greatest joys and our deepest torments. To understand *jouissance* is to begin to grasp the complex and often contradictory nature of human desire and the profound ways in which we seek satisfaction, even at the cost of our own well-being. It is the engine of our obsessions, the wellspring of our passions, and the ultimate enigma of the human condition. The very impossibility of its full articulation in language speaks volumes about its power, a power that resides in its resistance to containment, its perpetual overflow, its ecstatic excess that whispers of a reality just beyond our grasp, yet profoundly felt.

The body, often perceived as the vessel of our everyday existence, a mere instrument for navigating the mundane, becomes, in the realm of *jouissance*, a site of profound and often radical excess. It is here, in the visceral, the tangible, the undeniable reality of flesh and sensation, that the ineffable quality of this beyond-pleasure erupts with an intensity that can shatter our carefully constructed sense of self. We are accustomed to associating pleasure with comfort, with satisfaction, with the gentle easing of tension. But *jouissance* throws a stark light on the darker, more exhilarating, and often more disquieting manifestations of this drive. It is not the quiet hum of contentment that resonates here, but the roaring inferno, the deafening silence, the blinding flash that leaves one both illuminated and utterly undone.

Consider, for a moment, the apex of sexual experience. Beyond the biological imperative, beyond the mutual gratification, lies a precipice. It is a moment where language falters, where conscious thought dissolves, and the body is overtaken by a force that seems to emanate from a primal, pre-linguistic core. In this state of ecstatic union, the boundaries of the individual self blur, merging into a singular, overwhelming sensation. It is not simply the release of tension, nor the achievement of a physiological goal. It is a surplus, an overflowing of energy that can feel both divine and terrifying. The body, in its surrender to this overwhelming tide, becomes a conduit for

jouissance. The spasms, the gasps, the involuntary cries – these are not mere biological responses; they are the sonic manifestations of an excess that cannot be contained by the symbolic order. The sheer intensity, the feeling of being utterly consumed by the moment, is a testament to the body as the stage upon which this ultimate pleasure, this *jouissance*, is enacted. This is a pleasure that borders on pain, a dissolution that verges on annihilation, yet the subject plunges headlong into it, driven by an insatiable yearning for this very extremity. It is in these moments of profound physical and psychic upheaval that the body reveals its capacity to hold and express an experience that transcends the ordinary. The post-coital silence, the lingering tremors, the sense of profound exhaustion coupled with an almost delirious exhilaration – these are the aftershocks of having brushed against the sublime, of having touched that which lies beyond the realm of normal pleasure.

Yet,

jouissance is not confined to the peaks of ecstatic pleasure. It also finds a disturbing resonance in the embrace of suffering, in the deliberate courting of torment. Masochism, in its various forms, offers a stark illustration of this paradox. Here, the body is not merely a passive recipient of pleasure, but an active participant in its own subjugation, in its own infliction of pain. The lacerations, the restraints, the psychological manipulation – these are not experienced as mere suffering but as gateways to a potent form of *jouissance*. The pain, rather than being an antithesis to pleasure, becomes its very catalyst, its amplifier. The transgression of bodily integrity, the defiance of the instinct for self-preservation, the surrender to an external force that dictates experience – these elements combine to create a powerful surge of *jouissance*. The body becomes a canvas upon which this extreme, transgressive pleasure is inscribed. The exquisite agony, the trembling anticipation of the next infliction, the cathartic release that follows the peak of pain – these are all markers of a profound, albeit perverse, engagement with *jouissance*. It is a testament to the fact that pleasure, in its Lacanian sense, is not simply about avoiding pain, but about encountering intensity, about pushing the boundaries of what the body and psyche can endure. The masochist, in their willing submission to pain, is not seeking to negate pleasure but to locate it in its most extreme, most overwhelming form. The body, in its capacity to feel, to register even the most agonizing sensations, becomes the ultimate site for this potent, self-inflicted *jouissance*. It is a testament to the complex and often contradictory ways in which the human psyche seeks out experience, even when that experience is couched in terms of suffering. The pleasure derived is not in the absence of pain, but in the very experience of it, in the profound way it can saturate the senses and momentarily suspend the ordinary anxieties of existence.

The thrill-seeker, the one who courts danger for the sheer exhilaration of it, also taps into this dimension of the body as a site of

jouissance. The climber scaling a sheer cliff face, the skydiver plummeting towards the earth, the race car driver pushing the limits of speed and control – these individuals are not simply seeking to impress others or achieve a physical feat. They are actively seeking out a heightened state of being, a moment where the ordinary world recedes and an intense, visceral reality takes over. The body, under extreme duress, becomes hyper-aware. Every muscle tenses, every nerve ending vibrates with a heightened sensitivity. The fear is palpable, a primal response that is undeniable, yet it is intertwined with an intoxicating rush, a sense of being intensely alive precisely because death is a tangible possibility. This is not the calm satisfaction of achievement; it is a ferocious, almost animalistic, engagement with existence. The body becomes the focal point of an overwhelming experience, where the stakes are ultimate and the sensations are magnified. The drop in the stomach, the racing heart, the surge of adrenaline – these are the physical manifestations of a *jouissance* that arises from the proximity of annihilation. It is the body, in its most fundamental drive for survival, being pushed to its absolute limit, and in that extremity, finding a form of ecstatic release. The transgression here is against the instinct for self-preservation, and the reward is a potent infusion of life force, a feeling of being utterly present and undeniably real. The very risk of losing everything, of dissolving into nothingness, paradoxically intensifies the experience of being.

Beyond these more dramatic examples,

jouissance can manifest in subtler, yet equally profound, ways through heightened sensory experiences. Think of the visceral reaction to certain music, the kind that doesn't just please the ear but vibrates through the very bones, sending shivers down the spine and raising goosebumps. It's a physical response that transcends mere aesthetic appreciation. The music bypasses the rational mind and speaks directly to a deeper, more instinctual part of the self. The crescendo builds, the rhythm intensifies, and the body responds with an involuntary surge of energy. This is *jouissance* – the moment when the sensory input is so overwhelming, so potent, that it exceeds the capacity of ordinary pleasure, creating a surplus of feeling that registers physically. The tears that well up unexpectedly, the sudden urge to move or shout, the feeling of being utterly transported – these are all indications of the body registering an excess of stimulation, an overflow of affect.

Consider also the experience of intense physical exertion, the "runner's high" that athletes often describe. It's not just the satisfaction of completing a grueling workout; it's a profound, almost euphoric, state that can arise from pushing the body to its limits. The release of endorphins plays a role, of course, but the psychological component is equally significant. The mind, temporarily freed from its usual worries and anxieties, experiences a clarity and lightness. The body, though fatigued, feels alive and vibrant. This state of heightened physicality, where the boundaries between effort and pleasure blur, is a prime example of the body facilitating *jouissance*. It's the feeling of being utterly present in one's own physical being, a state of intense, almost ecstatic, self-awareness that arises from the expenditure of energy.

Even in the realm of food and drink, beyond simple nourishment or gustatory pleasure,

jouissance can be found. The slow savoring of a complex flavor, the way it unfolds on the palate, lingering and evolving – this can be more than just enjoyment. It can be a deep, satisfying encounter with the material world, a moment where the body registers a profound fulfillment. Certain intensely flavored or texturally unique foods can elicit a strong, almost primal, response. The burst of sweetness, the satisfying crunch, the creamy richness – these sensations, when experienced with full attention, can lead to a kind of embodied ecstasy. It's a moment where the body is deeply satisfied, a satisfaction that goes beyond the mere alleviation of hunger. It is a testament to the body's capacity to register and appreciate intensity, to find a form of *jouissance* in the very act of consumption. The experience can be so profound that it momentarily eclipses other concerns, drawing the subject into a purely sensory and visceral present.

The concept of the uncanny, that unsettling feeling of something being both familiar and strangely alien, also touches upon the body's encounter with

jouissance. Think of phantom limb sensations, where a person experiences intense pain or sensation in a limb that has been amputated. This is not a delusion; it is a powerfully real experience for the subject. The body, or at least the psychic representation of the body, continues to register sensations even in the absence of the physical organ. This phenomenon points to the idea that the body is not merely a biological machine but a locus of psychic intensity, a site where the symbolic order can break down and a more primal, unmediated experience can emerge. The pain, in its sheer intensity and its inexplicable origin, can become a form of *jouissance* – an overwhelming, undeniable sensation that defies rational explanation. It is a rupture in the usual functioning of the body and mind, a stark reminder of the limits of our understanding and the profound mystery of embodied existence.

Furthermore, the body's capacity for psychosomatic symptoms – physical ailments with no apparent organic cause, but deeply rooted in psychological distress – can also be understood through the lens of

jouissance. The unexplained aches, the persistent fatigue, the digestive issues that plague individuals with high levels of stress or unresolved trauma – these are not simply manifestations of mental anguish. They are the body's way of voicing an unspeakable suffering, of giving physical form to an excess of psychic pain that cannot be articulated through language. In some extreme cases, this bodily manifestation can become a perverse source of *jouissance*. The intense focus on the symptom, the relief it might provide by externalizing internal conflict, the way it can command attention and elicit care – all these elements can contribute to a cycle where the symptom, though painful, becomes strangely compelling. The body, in its suffering, becomes a site of intensified experience, a dark mirror reflecting an unresolvable psychic tension. It is a grim testament to the body's capacity to hold and express that which the conscious mind cannot process, offering a potent, albeit agonizing, form of *jouissance*.

The very notion of the body as a site of excess challenges our everyday assumptions about control and containment. We often strive to regulate our bodies, to keep them within socially acceptable norms, to manage our appetites and our emotions. But

jouissance reminds us that the body is also a wild, untamed territory, a source of energies and intensities that can erupt unexpectedly, defying our attempts at mastery. The involuntary shudder of fear or delight, the sudden flush of anger, the uncontrollable urge to laugh or cry – these are all moments when the body asserts its own agency, when it expresses an affect that transcends our conscious will. These are not necessarily pleasurable experiences in the conventional sense, but they are moments of intense vitality, of being undeniably alive. They are glimpses of the raw, unmediated experience that lies beneath the surface of our carefully constructed selves.

In essence, the body, in its capacity to feel, to suffer, to experience ecstasy and torment, becomes the primary stage for the enactment of

jouissance. It is where the ineffable finds its physical manifestation, where the excess of the psyche breaks through the boundaries of the symbolic order. Whether in the throes of sexual rapture, the embrace of pain, the thrill of danger, or the profound resonance of sensory experience, the body is the conduit through which this overwhelming, transgressive pleasure makes itself known. It is a reminder that our embodied existence is not merely a passive shell but a dynamic field of psychic intensity, a site where the most profound and often most disturbing aspects of our humanity are played out. The body, in its sheer capacity to feel, becomes the ultimate register of *jouissance*, a testament to the fact that pleasure, in its most potent form, often resides on the very edge of experience, where it borders on pain, on dissolution, and on the terrifying, exhilarating unknown.

The Law, that scaffolding of prohibitions and permissions that structures our social reality, is not merely an external constraint upon our actions. It is, in a profound sense, internalized, becoming the very architect of our desire. We learn what to want, and more importantly, what not to want, through the intricate network of societal injunctions. Yet, it is precisely within the shadow of these injunctions, at the very edges of what is deemed permissible, that the tempestuous currents of *jouissance* often find their most potent expression. Desire, after all, is not a simple, straightforward pursuit of satisfaction. It is a fundamentally restless force, one that is often ignited, paradoxically, by the very act of prohibition. The forbidden fruit, as the ancient narrative so vividly illustrates, gains its intoxicating allure not despite its proscribed status, but precisely because of it. The Law erects boundaries, and the human psyche, in its intricate dance with desire and *jouissance*, is perpetually drawn to test the strength of those boundaries, to probe their limits, and sometimes, to shatter them entirely.

This probing is not necessarily a conscious rebellion or a calculated act of defiance. More often, it is an almost elemental compulsion, a yearning for an intensity that the everyday, Law-abiding existence cannot provide. The Law, in its attempt to regulate and civilize, inevitably curtails the raw, untamed energies of human experience. It channels our drives into socially acceptable forms, aiming for a harmonious equilibrium. But this very channeling, this containment, creates a pressure, a buildup of energies that seek release. And when that release occurs, it often does so in ways that exceed the Law's intended boundaries, erupting as

jouissance. This is where the Law becomes not just a set of rules, but a crucible for the emergence of this radical excess. The prohibition itself becomes the very condition for the possibility of its transgression, and in that transgression, the unleashing of a pleasure that is more than pleasure, a *jouissance* that inscribes itself onto the body with an almost violent force.

Consider the complex dynamics of addiction. The addict, caught in a seemingly inescapable cycle, is perpetually in transgression of the Law – the Law of health, the Law of social responsibility, the Law of self-preservation. Yet, for the addict, the substance or behavior in question offers not just a fleeting escape from suffering, but a profound, albeit destructive, encounter with

jouissance. The initial transgression of the Law – taking the first drink, using the first drug – opens a portal to an overwhelming sensory and psychic experience. The body is flooded, the mind is altered, and for a precious, terrifying moment, the everyday anxieties and prohibitions fall away, replaced by an intensity that is both intoxicating and annihilating. This is *jouissance* at its most starkly contradictory: a profound engagement with life, enacted through the deliberate violation of the very principles that sustain it. The Law, in this instance, is not merely broken; it is rendered utterly irrelevant in the face of this overwhelming subjective experience. The cycle of addiction is, in many ways, a relentless pursuit of this forbidden *jouissance*, a desperate attempt to recapture that initial, overwhelming transgression, even as the consequences become increasingly dire. The body, in its physiological and psychological dependence, becomes a battleground where the Law and the yearning for this excessive pleasure wage an unending war.

The realm of sexuality, too, is rife with instances where the Law and

jouissance are inextricably linked through transgression. While most sexual activity falls within the accepted norms of the Law, it is often at the fringes of these norms, in the exploration of desires that push the boundaries of what is considered acceptable, that *jouissance* can erupt with particular intensity. The taboo surrounding certain sexual practices, the fascination with the forbidden, the thrill of engaging in acts that are publicly condemned but privately yearned for – these are all testament to the power of the Law to not only constrain but also to generate desire. When these desires are acted upon, when the Law is transgressed, the resultant experience can be a potent infusion of *jouissance*. This is not simply about the pleasure of orgasm, but about the overwhelming sensation that arises from having defied societal norms, from having touched upon something that is deemed inherently "wrong" or "dirty." The body, in its heightened arousal and its surrender to these transgressive desires, becomes a vessel for this excess. The blush that spreads across the skin, the racing heart, the gasping breath – these are not just physiological responses to sexual stimulation; they are the outward manifestations of a *jouissance* that has been unlocked by the act of transgression. The very act of breaking the Law, in this context, becomes a catalyst for an experience that transcends ordinary pleasure, offering a fleeting but intense moment of being utterly, impossibly alive.

The legal system itself, with its intricate web of statutes and penalties, provides a stark illustration of the Law's relationship with transgression and the potential for

jouissance. The thrill associated with criminal activity, the sense of power and exhilaration that some individuals derive from defying the Law and evading capture, speaks to a complex interplay of desire and prohibition. For the criminal, the Law is not a set of guiding principles but an obstacle to be overcome, a challenge to be met. The act of breaking the Law, of outsmarting the system, can become a source of immense satisfaction, a confirmation of one's own power and cunning. This is a form of *jouissance* that is inextricably linked to the risk of punishment, to the ever-present threat of being caught and subjected to the Law's punitive force. The adrenaline rush, the heightened awareness, the feeling of being at the absolute edge of existence – these are all components of a *jouissance* that is fueled by the very act of transgression. The body, in its readiness for action and its heightened state of alert, becomes the site where this transgressive pleasure is experienced. The courtroom drama, the tense pursuit, the dramatic capture –

these are all narratives that, in their fictionalized forms, tap into this underlying human fascination with the clash between the Law and the defiant individual, a fascination that reveals the potent allure of *jouissance* found in the very act of transgression.

Beyond these more dramatic manifestations, the concept of *jouissance* as a limit-experience of the Law can be seen in subtler, yet equally pervasive, ways. Consider the social pressure to conform, the unspoken rules that govern our everyday interactions. Even seemingly innocuous transgressions – a white lie, a petty act of deception, a moment of rudeness – can, for some, offer a fleeting sense of release, a momentary surge of *jouissance*. These are not acts of grand rebellion, but small, almost imperceptible breaches of the social contract. Yet, in those moments, the individual might experience a peculiar sensation, a surge of self-assertion that is amplified by the very act of deviating from the norm. The Law here is not a codified legal statute, but the unwritten code of social conduct, and its transgression, however minor, can open a space for a localized, personal eruption of *jouissance*. The body might register this in a subtle shift of posture, a knowing smirk, a quickened heartbeat – a small, visceral testament to the pleasure of stepping, however momentarily, outside the prescribed boundaries.

The persistent human fascination with the forbidden, with that which the Law explicitly prohibits, is a powerful testament to its role in shaping desire. This fascination is not simply a matter of curiosity; it is deeply rooted in the understanding that prohibitions often point to powerful, unmanaged energies. The Law, in its attempt to contain these energies, inadvertently highlights their existence and their potency. When we encounter these prohibitions, particularly those that resonate with our deepest, perhaps unacknowledged, desires, a tension arises. This tension is the fertile ground upon which *jouissance* can bloom. The Law, in seeking to maintain order, creates a system of checks and balances, but it also, by its very nature, creates an inverse space, a realm of the outlawed, the undesirable, the illicit. It is into this space that the yearning for *jouissance* often ventures.

Think about the enduring appeal of cautionary tales, of stories that warn against the dangers of stepping outside societal norms. While their explicit purpose is to reinforce the Law, their narrative power often lies in the vivid depiction of the transgressions themselves. We are drawn into the forbidden worlds, captivated by the characters who dare to defy convention, even as we acknowledge the dire consequences they often face. This is not a morbid fascination with suffering, but a recognition of the intense vitality, the raw energy, that can be unleashed when the Law is challenged. The narrative arc of such stories often climaxes not in the reinforcement of the Law, but in the spectacular, and often tragic, display of

jouissance that arises from its transgression. The body, in these narratives, becomes the ultimate stage for this drama, bearing the physical and psychic marks of both the Law's constraints and the unleashed force of *jouissance*.

The very concept of guilt, a cornerstone of many legal and moral systems, is intimately tied to the Law's transgression. Guilt is the affective response to having violated a prohibition, a painful acknowledgment of the boundary crossed. Yet, even in the experience of guilt, there can be a perverse form of

jouissance. The intensity of the feeling, the sheer weight of the transgression, can saturate the subject's entire being. For some, this overwhelming emotional experience, this profound engagement with their own wrongdoing, can become a powerful, albeit self-destructive, source of *jouissance*. The body, in its palpable experience of distress, of anxiety, of self-recrimination, becomes a testament to the power of the Law and the profound impact of its violation. It is a stark reminder that *jouissance* is not always about pleasure in the conventional sense; it is about intensity, about an excess of experience that can be both exhilarating and devastating. The guilt-ridden individual, consumed by their transgression, is in a state of intense affective engagement, a state that, however painful, can represent a radical departure from the mundane, a form of *jouissance* born from the ashes of violated Law.

The Law, therefore, is not a monolithic entity that simply dictates what we can and cannot do. It is a dynamic and complex force that shapes our desires, defines our boundaries, and, paradoxically, creates the very conditions for the emergence of

jouissance. It is in the tension between the Law and our insatiable yearning for something beyond mere satisfaction, something that pushes us to the limits of our being, that we encounter this radical excess. The transgression of the Law, whether overt or subtle, becomes a pathway to an intensity of experience that can both affirm and annihilate us. The body, as the locus of our physical and psychic being, bears the indelible marks of this perpetual struggle, serving as the ultimate register of *jouissance* in its most transgressive and profound forms. This constant negotiation between the Law and desire, between prohibition and the yearning for excess, defines a fundamental aspect of the human condition, a condition perpetually balanced on the precipice of pleasure and annihilation, order and chaos, the permissible and the utterly, intoxicatingly forbidden.

The insistent hum of the body, a constant reminder of its biological imperatives, often finds itself caught in a peculiar eddy, a whirlpool of repetitive action that seems to defy the very logic of pleasure and pain. This is not the straightforward pursuit of satisfaction, the seeking of comfort or the avoidance of discomfort. Instead, it is a far more complex and often bewildering phenomenon, one that speaks to the deeper, more intractable currents of *jouissance*. We speak here of repetition, not as a sign of stagnation, but as a dynamic, almost vital, force that compels the psyche to revisit certain experiences, certain behaviors, not for their eventual fulfillment, but for the very act of their recurring pursuit. This is the realm of the repetition compulsion, a concept that, when viewed through the lens of *jouissance*, reveals itself not as a mere glitch in the system, but as a profound testament to the body's stubborn adherence to a certain, often fraught, intensity.

Consider the smoker, eternally reaching for the next cigarette, even as the acrid smoke burns their lungs and the doctor's grim pronouncements echo in their ears. The pleasure of the nicotine hit is fleeting, often overshadowed by guilt, by the knowledge of impending harm, by the sheer futility of the act. Yet, the hand reaches, the match strikes, the inhale follows. This is not a simple hedonistic calculus gone awry. It is the body's insistent rehearsal of a particular enactment, a physical ritual that seems to hold a singular, irreducible significance. The

jouissance here is not found in the serene contentment of a healthy body, but in the sharp, almost violent punctuation of the act itself, in the brief but potent transgression of self-preservation. The body, in its physical craving and its learned movements, becomes the unwitting conductor of this compulsive symphony, a symphony that plays out the same notes again and again, each repetition reinforcing the underlying rhythm, the underlying compulsion, the underlying, dark allure of a pleasure that insists on its own perpetuation. The suffering is not an incidental byproduct; it is, in a strange and paradoxical way, woven into the very fabric of this *jouissance*. It is the price of admission to this intense, recurring drama, a drama played out on the skin, in the lungs, in the very blood that courses through the veins.

This compulsion to repeat is not limited to overtly self-destructive behaviors. It manifests in subtler, yet equally persistent, ways in our everyday lives. Think of the individual who repeatedly finds themselves in the same toxic relationships, drawn to partners who mirror past betrayals or inflict familiar hurts. Logically, they know better. They have the memory of pain, the scars of past disappointments. Yet, they are compelled to re-enter the fray, to rehearse the familiar script, to seek out the echo of a pain that, in its very familiarity, has become strangely comforting, a perverse form of recognition. The

jouissance here is not in the successful attainment of love or companionship, but in the very act of confronting, and re-confronting, the phantom of past trauma. The body, in its emotional responses, its anxiety, its eventual resignation or heartbreak, becomes the repository of this repeated suffering, each iteration etching itself deeper, becoming a part of the body's somatic memory. The cycle offers a grim sort of validation, a confirmation that the past, with all its attendant intensities, is still very much alive within them. The prohibition – "Do not repeat past mistakes" – is not merely ignored; it is, in a profound sense, made irrelevant by the sheer force of the drive to re-enact.

The stage of the body is crucial in understanding this compulsion. It is not merely a passive recipient of psychic commands, but an active participant, a site where the drive for

jouissance finds its most visceral expression. The repetitive act, whether it be picking at a wound, compulsively checking a locked door, or engaging in an addictive behavior, is often accompanied by a cascade of physical sensations. The quickened pulse, the furrowed brow, the tightened jaw, the shallow breath – these are not just physiological byproducts of anxiety or stress. They are part of the somatic texture of *jouissance*, the bodily inscriptions of a pleasure that insists on its own recurrence, even in the face of demonstrable suffering. The body learns to anticipate these sensations, to even crave them, as they become inextricably linked to the pursuit of this excessive experience. It is as if the body, having once encountered this potent, overwhelming intensity, is forever seeking to recapture it, to recreate the conditions that first unlocked it, even if those conditions are inherently harmful or painful. The repetition becomes a ritual, a way of coaxing the body to relive a specific affective and physiological state, a state that, despite its negative valence, offers a profound departure from the ordinary and the mundane.

Lacan's concept of the "real" offers a useful lens through which to understand this phenomenon. The real is that which resists symbolization, that which lies outside the order of language and meaning.

Jouissance is intimately connected to the real, to that traumatic kernel of experience that cannot be fully integrated into our symbolic universe. The repetition compulsion, in this view, can be seen as a desperate, futile attempt to grapple with this unassimilable element, to repeatedly push against its boundaries, to try to master it through sheer force of enactment. Each repetition is an attempt to grasp what remains elusive, to force the unrepresentable into the realm of the visible and the tangible, even if that realm is one of pain and suffering. The body, in its repetitive actions, becomes the very instrument of this attempt, its movements and sensations the only language available to speak of that which remains stubbornly beyond words. The *jouissance* is in the struggle itself, in the insistent engagement with this intractable core of experience, in the refusal to let it lie dormant.

Consider the subtle, yet pervasive, habit of self-sabotage. The student who procrastinates until the last possible moment, risking academic failure, not out of laziness, but out of an almost unconscious drive to experience the frenetic energy of last-minute panic. The professional who, on the cusp of a significant promotion, finds a way to undermine their own efforts, to create a crisis that distracts from the potential for success. In these instances, the Law of achievement and reward is circumvented, not through external failure, but through an internally orchestrated disruption. The

jouissance is not in the achievement, but in the dramatic oscillation between potential success and the precipice of failure, in the intense, albeit self-inflicted, pressure cooker of anxiety. The body, in its heightened stress response, its racing thoughts, its physical tension, becomes the embodiment of this compulsive oscillation. It is a performance of a particular kind of psychic drama, a drama that, by its very repetition, becomes a form of morbid attachment. The prohibition against self-harm, in its most encompassing sense, is transgressed by this internal, habitual undermining.

This compulsive repetition can also be observed in the way we tell stories about ourselves. We often find ourselves returning to certain narratives, retelling the same traumas, the same triumphs, the same perceived injustices, as if for the first time. These stories, though symbolic, carry with them a powerful affective charge. The repetition of the narrative, the re-enactment of the emotional arc, can become a form of

jouissance, a way of keeping a particular intensity of experience alive. The body remembers the emotions associated with these stories – the fear, the anger, the sorrow, the exhilaration – and the act of recounting them can evoke a phantom echo of those feelings. This is not simply a matter of memory recall; it is a deliberate, often unconscious, re-animation of a past state of being. The *jouissance* is in the prolonged engagement with a potent emotional landscape, a landscape that, once traversed, becomes a familiar territory that the psyche, and the body, feel compelled to revisit. The prohibition against dwelling excessively on the past, against allowing it to dictate the present, is circumvented by the sheer addictive quality of the emotional resonance.

The body's role in repetition compulsion is not merely mechanical; it is deeply entwined with the affective and symbolic dimensions of

jouissance. When an action is repeated, it becomes ingrained. Not just in the neural pathways of the brain, but in the very musculature, in the posture, in the involuntary reflexes. The body learns to perform these actions almost automatically, as if on cue, when certain triggers are present. This automaticity, while seemingly efficient, can also be a sign of the compulsive nature of the drive. The body is executing a program, a program that has been written and rewritten through repeated enactment, a program that leads back, inexorably, to the source of that elusive, intense *jouissance*. The body, in its physical memory and its habitual responses, becomes the archive of these repetitions, a living testament to the enduring power of a pleasure that, however paradoxical, insists on its own return.

Furthermore, the concept of

jouissance as an excess that disrupts the smooth functioning of the pleasure principle is key. The pleasure principle dictates that we seek pleasure and avoid pain. However, *jouissance* operates beyond this, offering an intensity that can be deeply pleasurable even when it involves pain or suffering. The repetition compulsion is a prime example of this. The individual is not simply seeking pleasure in the conventional sense; they are seeking an encounter with a radical excess, an experience that pushes them beyond the limits of ordinary sensation. The repetition of the behavior, therefore, becomes a method for accessing this excess, for ensuring that the body and mind remain attuned to this particular frequency of intense experience. The suffering that accompanies the repetition is not a deterrent, but often an integral part of the *jouissance* itself, a testament to the fact that they are indeed pushing boundaries and engaging with something that lies outside the comfortable and the predictable. The body, in its capacity to endure and even thrive on certain forms of stress and pain, becomes the ultimate site where this transgressive *jouissance* is enacted and perpetuated.

The fascination with the taboo, with that which is forbidden, often fuels the engine of repetition. When a prohibition is particularly potent, when it touches upon a deep-seated, perhaps unacknowledged, desire, it can create a powerful tension. This tension can lead to an obsessive focus on the forbidden object or behavior, and this focus, in turn, can manifest as repetitive thoughts and actions. The

jouissance is derived not only from the act of transgression itself, but from the prolonged engagement with the forbidden, from the constant circling around its allure, from the imagined possibilities it represents. The body, in its internal arousal and anticipation, its heightened sensitivity to cues associated with the forbidden, becomes complicit in this repetitive dance. The prohibition, rather than extinguishing the desire, can amplify it, transforming it into a persistent, almost inescapable, refrain that plays out in the physical and psychic life of the individual. The intensity of this engagement, this sustained focus on the forbidden, is a hallmark of *jouissance*, a sign that the individual is operating in a register of experience that transcends the ordinary pursuit of happiness.

The body, therefore, is not a neutral ground for these psychic dramas. It is an active participant, a willing, or at least compelled, player in the theater of repetition and

jouissance. From the subtle twitch of a hand reaching for a familiar comfort to the profound physical toll of addiction, the body bears witness to the persistent drive for an intensity that lies beyond the Law, a drive that finds its expression in the relentless, and often bewildering, act of repeating. The suffering is not a sign of failure, but a testament to the profound engagement with this excess, a testament to the body's stubborn adherence to a pleasure that defies reason, a pleasure that insists on its own, recurring, and often devastating, enactment.

The insistent hum of the body, a constant reminder of its biological imperatives, often finds itself caught in a peculiar eddy, a whirlpool of repetitive action that seems to defy the very logic of pleasure and pain. This is not the straightforward pursuit of satisfaction, the seeking of comfort or the avoidance of discomfort. Instead, it is a far more complex and often bewildering phenomenon, one that speaks to the deeper, more intractable currents of *jouissance*. We speak here of repetition, not as a sign of stagnation, but as a dynamic, almost vital, force that compels the psyche to revisit certain experiences, certain behaviors, not for their eventual fulfillment, but for the very act of their recurring pursuit. This is the realm of the repetition compulsion, a concept that, when viewed through the lens of *jouissance*, reveals itself not as a mere glitch in the system, but as a profound testament to the body's stubborn adherence to a certain, often fraught, intensity.

Consider the smoker, eternally reaching for the next cigarette, even as the acrid smoke burns their lungs and the doctor's grim pronouncements echo in their ears. The pleasure of the nicotine hit is fleeting, often overshadowed by guilt, by the knowledge of impending harm, by the sheer futility of the act. Yet, the hand reaches, the match strikes, the inhale follows. This is not a simple hedonistic calculus gone awry. It is the body's insistent rehearsal of a particular enactment, a physical ritual that seems to hold a singular, irreducible significance. The

jouissance here is not found in the serene contentment of a healthy body, but in the sharp, almost violent punctuation of the act itself, in the brief but potent transgression of self-preservation. The body, in its physical craving and its learned movements, becomes the unwitting conductor of this compulsive symphony, a symphony that plays out the same notes again and again, each repetition reinforcing the underlying rhythm, the underlying compulsion, the underlying, dark allure of a pleasure that insists on its own perpetuation. The suffering is not an incidental byproduct; it is, in a strange and paradoxical way, woven into the very fabric of this *jouissance*. It is the price of admission to this intense, recurring drama, a drama played out on the skin, in the lungs, in the very blood that courses through the veins.

This compulsion to repeat is not limited to overtly self-destructive behaviors. It manifests in subtler, yet equally persistent, ways in our everyday lives. Think of the individual who repeatedly finds themselves in the same toxic relationships, drawn to partners who mirror past betrayals or inflict familiar hurts. Logically, they know better. They have the memory of pain, the scars of past disappointments. Yet, they are compelled to re-enter the fray, to rehearse the familiar script, to seek out the echo of a pain that, in its very familiarity, has become strangely comforting, a perverse form of recognition. The

jouissance here is not in the successful attainment of love or companionship, but in the very act of confronting, and re-confronting, the phantom of past trauma. The body, in its emotional responses, its anxiety, its eventual resignation or heartbreak, becomes the repository of this repeated suffering, each iteration etching itself deeper, becoming a part of the body's somatic memory. The cycle offers a grim sort of validation, a confirmation that the past, with all its attendant intensities, is still very much alive within them. The prohibition – "Do not repeat past mistakes" – is not merely ignored; it is, in a profound sense, made irrelevant by the sheer force of the drive to re-enact.

The stage of the body is crucial in understanding this compulsion. It is not merely a passive recipient of psychic commands, but an active participant, a site where the drive for

jouissance finds its most visceral expression. The repetitive act, whether it be picking at a wound, compulsively checking a locked door, or engaging in an addictive behavior, is often accompanied by a cascade of physical sensations. The quickened pulse, the furrowed brow, the tightened jaw, the shallow breath – these are not just physiological byproducts of anxiety or stress. They are part of the somatic texture of *jouissance*, the bodily inscriptions of a pleasure that insists on its own recurrence, even in the face of demonstrable suffering. The body learns to anticipate these sensations, to even crave them, as they become inextricably linked to the pursuit of this excessive experience. It is as if the body, having once encountered this potent, overwhelming intensity, is forever seeking to recapture it, to recreate the conditions that first unlocked it, even if those conditions are inherently harmful or painful. The repetition becomes a ritual, a way of coaxing the body to relive a specific affective and physiological state, a state that, despite its negative valence, offers a profound departure from the ordinary and the mundane.

Lacan's concept of the "real" offers a useful lens through which to understand this phenomenon. The real is that which resists symbolization, that which lies outside the order of language and meaning.

Jouissance is intimately connected to the real, to that traumatic kernel of experience that cannot be fully integrated into our symbolic universe. The repetition compulsion, in this view, can be seen as a desperate, futile attempt to grapple with this unassimilable element, to repeatedly push against its boundaries, to try to master it through sheer force of enactment. Each repetition is an attempt to grasp what remains elusive, to force the unrepresentable into the realm of the visible and the tangible, even if that realm is one of pain and suffering. The body, in its repetitive actions, becomes the very instrument of this attempt, its movements and sensations the only language available to speak of that which remains stubbornly beyond words. The *jouissance* is in the struggle itself, in the insistent engagement with this intractable core of experience, in the refusal to let it lie dormant.

Consider the subtle, yet pervasive, habit of self-sabotage. The student who procrastinates until the last possible moment, risking academic failure, not out of laziness, but out of an almost unconscious drive to experience the frenetic energy of last-minute panic. The professional who, on the cusp of a significant promotion, finds a way to undermine their own efforts, to create a crisis that distracts from the potential for success. In these instances, the Law of achievement and reward is circumvented, not through external failure, but through an internally orchestrated disruption. The

jouissance is not in the achievement, but in the dramatic oscillation between potential success and the precipice of failure, in the intense, albeit self-inflicted, pressure cooker of anxiety. The body, in its heightened stress response, its racing thoughts, its physical tension, becomes the embodiment of this compulsive oscillation. It is a performance of a particular kind of psychic drama, a drama that, by its very repetition, becomes a form of morbid attachment. The prohibition against self-harm, in its most encompassing sense, is transgressed by this internal, habitual undermining.

This compulsive repetition can also be observed in the way we tell stories about ourselves. We often find ourselves returning to certain narratives, retelling the same traumas, the same triumphs, the same perceived injustices, as if for the first time. These stories, though symbolic, carry with them a powerful affective charge. The repetition of the narrative, the re-enactment of the emotional arc, can become a form of

jouissance, a way of keeping a particular intensity of experience alive. The body remembers the emotions associated with these stories – the fear, the anger, the sorrow, the exhilaration – and the act of recounting them can evoke a phantom echo of those feelings. This is not simply a matter of memory recall; it is a deliberate, often unconscious, re-animation of a past state of being. The *jouissance* is in the prolonged engagement with a potent emotional landscape, a landscape that, once traversed, becomes a familiar territory that the psyche, and the body, feel compelled to revisit. The prohibition against dwelling excessively on the past, against allowing it to dictate the present, is circumvented by the sheer addictive quality of the emotional resonance.

The body's role in repetition compulsion is not merely mechanical; it is deeply entwined with the affective and symbolic dimensions of

jouissance. When an action is repeated, it becomes ingrained. Not just in the neural pathways of the brain, but in the very musculature, in the posture, in the involuntary reflexes. The body learns to perform these actions almost automatically, as if on cue, when certain triggers are present. This automaticity, while seemingly efficient, can also be a sign of the compulsive nature of the drive. The body is executing a program, a program that has been written and rewritten through repeated enactment, a program that leads back, inexorably, to the source of that elusive, intense *jouissance*. The body, in its physical memory and its habitual responses, becomes the archive of these repetitions, a living testament to the enduring power of a pleasure that, however paradoxical, insists on its own return.

Furthermore, the concept of

jouissance as an excess that disrupts the smooth functioning of the pleasure principle is key. The pleasure principle dictates that we seek pleasure and avoid pain. However, *jouissance* operates beyond this, offering an intensity that can be deeply pleasurable even when it involves pain or suffering. The repetition compulsion is a prime example of this. The individual is not simply seeking pleasure in the conventional sense; they are seeking an encounter with a radical excess, an experience that pushes them beyond the limits of ordinary sensation. The repetition of the behavior, therefore, becomes a method for accessing this excess, for ensuring that the body and mind remain attuned to this particular frequency of intense experience. The suffering that accompanies the repetition is not a deterrent, but often an integral part of the *jouissance* itself, a testament to the fact that they are indeed pushing boundaries and engaging with something that lies outside the comfortable and the predictable. The body, in its capacity to endure and even thrive on certain forms of stress and pain, becomes the ultimate site where this transgressive *jouissance* is enacted and perpetuated.

The fascination with the taboo, with that which is forbidden, often fuels the engine of repetition. When a prohibition is particularly potent, when it touches upon a deep-seated, perhaps unacknowledged, desire, it can create a powerful tension. This tension can lead to an obsessive focus on the forbidden object or behavior, and this focus, in turn, can manifest as repetitive thoughts and actions. The

jouissance is derived not only from the act of transgression itself, but from the prolonged engagement with the forbidden, from the constant circling around its allure, from the imagined possibilities it represents. The body, in its internal arousal and anticipation, its heightened sensitivity to cues associated with the forbidden, becomes complicit in this repetitive dance. The prohibition, rather than extinguishing the desire, can amplify it, transforming it into a persistent, almost inescapable, refrain that plays out in the physical and psychic life of the individual. The intensity of this engagement, this sustained focus on the forbidden, is a hallmark of *jouissance*, a sign that the individual is operating in a register of experience that transcends the ordinary pursuit of happiness.

The body, therefore, is not a neutral ground for these psychic dramas. It is an active participant, a willing, or at least compelled, player in the theater of repetition and

jouissance. From the subtle twitch of a hand reaching for a familiar comfort to the profound physical toll of addiction, the body bears witness to the persistent drive for an intensity that lies beyond the Law, a drive that finds its expression in the relentless, and often bewildering, act of repeating. The suffering is not a sign of failure, but a testament to the profound engagement with this excess, a testament to the body's stubborn adherence to a pleasure that defies reason, a pleasure that insists on its own, recurring, and often devastating, enactment.

From Suffering to Signification: Reclaiming 'Jouissance'

The exploration of

jouissance has, thus far, cast a long shadow, often painting it as an inexorable force that binds us to repetitive suffering. We have witnessed its manifestation in the compulsive rituals of addiction, the recurring patterns of destructive relationships, and the insidious whispers of self-sabotage. In these instances, the pursuit of an excessive, often painful, intensity seems to lead only to further entanglement, a deepening of the very wounds we might unconsciously seek to alleviate. The body becomes a battleground, inscribed with the scars of repeated transgression, its sensations a constant reminder of a pleasure principle that has been fundamentally disrupted. It is a landscape where the Law, the societal and internal dictates of what is acceptable and beneficial, is not merely broken, but rendered almost irrelevant by the sheer force of a drive that compels a return to the precipice, again and again. The suffering, in these contexts, appears not as an unfortunate byproduct, but as an integral component of the experience, the very texture of a pleasure that defies conventional understanding.

Yet, to leave the discussion here would be to succumb to a deterministic view, one that offers little hope for agency or transformation. While the compulsive nature of

jouissance is undeniable, it is not necessarily an immutable sentence. The very intensity that leads to suffering also points to a powerful, vital energy within the human psyche. This energy, when understood and approached with a different intention, can potentially be harnessed, re-directed, and ultimately, transformed. The shift from suffering to signification is not about eradicating *jouissance*, but about re-framing our relationship with it, moving from a position of passive victimhood to one of active engagement and conscious choice. This requires a profound re-evaluation of how we perceive and interact with the excessive, the transgressive, and the intensely felt aspects of our lives.

The first step in this transformative process lies in acknowledging the symbolic language of

jouissance. What we often dismiss as mere "bad habits" or "irrational behaviors" are, in fact, deeply encoded narratives, attempts by the psyche to communicate something that cannot be easily articulated through conventional means. The repetitive act, the craving, the obsession – these are not random occurrences; they are enactments, performances that carry meaning, even if that meaning is obscured by the accompanying pain. The individual who compulsively checks their doors, for instance, is not simply being anxious; they may be attempting to symbolically secure a sense of safety in a world that feels fundamentally precarious, a world where internal boundaries have been breached. The smoker, in their ritualistic act, might be enacting a complex relationship with autonomy, rebellion, or a desperate attempt to self-soothe in the face of overwhelming stress. These are not justifications for the behavior, but rather invitations to decode the underlying messages.

This decoding requires a willingness to listen to the body, not just as a source of unpleasant sensations, but as a repository of history and unconscious desires. The somatic experiences that accompany

jouissance – the racing heart, the flush of heat, the knot in the stomach – are not merely physiological responses; they are signposts, pointing towards the specific affective and psychic states that the individual is compelled to re-experience. When these sensations become familiar, even in their discomfort, they can offer a perverse sense of recognition, a confirmation that a particular psychic drama is being played out. Therapy, in this context, can serve as a crucial space for this symbolic interpretation. Through dialogue, through careful attunement to the nuances of language and bodily expression, the analyst or therapist can help the individual to unravel the threads of these compulsive enactments, to translate the body's repetitive language into a more coherent narrative.

By giving voice to the unspoken, by symbolising the unrepresentable, we begin to reclaim a measure of control. The repetitive act, once an automatic response, can gradually become a conscious choice, or at least a choice that is more readily understood and potentially modified. This is not about achieving a state of perfect rational control, which would be antithetical to the very nature of

jouissance. Rather, it is about introducing a space for deliberation, for questioning the necessity of the repetition, for exploring alternative ways of meeting the underlying psychic need. The aim is not to eliminate the excess, but to integrate it more consciously, to allow it to express itself in ways that are less destructive and more conducive to a sense of meaning and well-being. This process of signification, of finding meaning in what was once experienced as senseless suffering, is where the potential for transformation truly lies.

Consider the individual who has a history of engaging in emotionally volatile relationships. They might repeatedly find themselves drawn to partners who are unpredictable, demanding, and ultimately, hurtful. From the perspective of suffering, this is a cycle of repeated trauma, a testament to the repetition compulsion gone awry. However, if we view this through the lens of signification, we can begin to ask: What does this pattern symbolize? Perhaps it represents a deeply ingrained, albeit unconscious, attempt to re-enact and ultimately master a childhood experience of unpredictability or emotional neglect. The intensity of the volatile relationship, the highs and lows, the dramatic reconciliations and arguments, may mirror the intensity of that early, unresolved trauma. By consciously recognizing this symbolic dimension, the individual can begin to disengage from the destructive pattern, not by simply trying to "choose better," but by addressing the underlying psychic wound that the pattern was attempting to express and, paradoxically, perpetuate.

The body, which was once the site of the suffering, can become an ally in this process of reclaiming *jouissance*. Instead of being an involuntary instrument of compulsion, it can become a source of information, a guide towards understanding the deeper currents of desire and need. Mindfulness practices, somatic therapies, and even the simple act of paying close attention to bodily sensations during moments of intense craving or emotional arousal can provide invaluable insights. These practices help to de-automatize the repetitive act, creating a crucial pause between the impulse and the enactment. In that pause, there is space for conscious awareness, for questioning the automatic response, and for choosing a different path. The body, in its capacity to register subtle shifts in emotion and energy, can become a teacher, guiding us towards a more integrated and less destructive experience of intensity.

This reframing of
jouissance from a source of torment to a realm of potential signification has profound implications for therapeutic work. It moves away from a model that seeks to simply suppress or eliminate problematic behaviors, towards one that aims to understand their underlying symbolic meaning and the psychic needs they are attempting to address. The goal is not to eliminate desire or intensity, but to guide them towards more constructive and fulfilling expressions. This might involve exploring creative outlets, engaging in passionate pursuits that are life-affirming rather than life-denying, or cultivating relationships that offer genuine connection and emotional safety, rather than the familiar, albeit painful, echoes of past trauma.

The concept of "excess" itself can be re-examined. While
jouissance often manifests as a harmful excess, it also points to a fundamental human drive for experiences that transcend the mundane, that touch upon the profound and the sublime. The challenge lies in differentiating between destructive excess and life-affirming intensity. This requires a nuanced understanding of

the body's role, not as a passive victim of compulsive drives, but as an active participant in the creation of meaning. When we learn to listen to its signals, to interpret its language, and to guide its energies, we can begin to reclaim *jouissance* from the realm of suffering and imbue it with significance. The body, in its capacity to feel deeply, to experience intensely, and to move with purpose, becomes the locus of this transformation, a testament to the enduring human quest for a life lived not just adequately, but fully and meaningfully. This is the ultimate reclamation: to move beyond the mere avoidance of pain and towards a conscious, deliberate engagement with the very forces that define our existence, transforming the shadow of suffering into the light of lived significance.

Chapter 5: The Language of Symptoms: Body as Text

The human body, often perceived as a mere biological machine, a collection of organs and systems functioning in a predictable, mechanistic fashion, harbours a far more intricate and eloquent language. It speaks not in the precise syntax of propositional statements, but in a visceral, often enigmatic dialect of sensations, aches, and involuntary reactions. This is the language of symptoms, and to relegate them to the realm of mere biological error is to miss their profound communicative potential. Symptoms are not simply unwelcome disruptions to the body's equilibrium; they are, in fact, eloquent, if often distressing, dispatches from the unconscious, symbolic messages attempting to articulate that which cannot, or will not, be voiced through conventional means.

Psychoanalytic theory, particularly through the groundbreaking work of Freud, has long posited that the unconscious mind is a repository for desires, fears, and memories that are too painful, too socially unacceptable, or too disruptive to be consciously acknowledged. These repressed elements do not simply disappear; they persist, exerting a powerful influence on our mental and emotional lives. When direct verbal expression is blocked, the unconscious finds alternative channels, and the body, in its tangible, undeniable presence, becomes a fertile ground for such expression. Symptoms, therefore, emerge as a form of psychosomatic theatre, a physical enactment of internal turmoil. They are the body's desperate attempt to bypass the censorship of the conscious mind and communicate vital information about underlying psychic distress.

Consider the persistent headache that plagues an individual grappling with a demanding and emotionally suffocating work environment. While a physician might prescribe pain relievers and suggest stress management techniques, a psychoanalytic perspective would look deeper. Is the headache a physical manifestation of an unspoken resentment towards an oppressive boss? Does it symbolize a desperate yearning for release, a feeling of being trapped and unable to escape? The throbbing pain, the pressure behind the eyes, the sensitivity to light – these are not random physiological events. They are the body's visceral translation of an unarticulated scream for autonomy, a physical protest against a situation that violates the individual's sense of self and well-being. The very intensity of the pain can be seen as a measure of the repressed emotion, a powerful testament to the psychic energy invested in keeping that emotion hidden.

Similarly, a recurring skin rash might emerge in someone experiencing significant relationship anxiety. The itching, the redness, the inflammation – these are not simply an allergic reaction to an external irritant. They can be interpreted as the body's way of creating a physical barrier, a visible manifestation of an unconscious desire for distance or separation, or perhaps a reaction to feeling "exposed" or vulnerable in an intimate connection. The discomfort and aesthetic disruption of the rash might serve as a tangible representation of the emotional discomfort and disruption the individual is experiencing in their relationships, a physical manifestation of feeling "uncomfortable in one's own skin." The symptom becomes a visual metaphor for the internal state, a coded message about the fragility of emotional boundaries.

The language of symptoms is not always straightforward; it is often metaphorical, allusive, and deeply personal. What one symptom signifies for one individual may mean something entirely different for another, depending on their unique history, their unconscious associations, and the specific conflicts they are struggling to resolve. This is where the art of psychoanalytic interpretation becomes crucial. It is not a matter of applying a universal symptom-to-meaning dictionary, but of engaging in a collaborative exploration with the individual to unravel the specific narrative their body is trying to tell. This involves attending not only to the symptom itself – its location, its intensity, its timing – but also to the context in which it arises, the emotions that accompany it, and the life events that may have preceded its appearance.

For instance, a persistent cough that resists medical treatment might, for one person, represent an unexpressed anger, a choked-back rage that the body is attempting to expel. For another, it could symbolize a feeling of helplessness, a silent plea for attention or care that has gone unanswered. The cough, in its rasping insistence, can be seen as a physical manifestation of a repressed voice, a voice that is struggling to be heard. The effort involved in coughing, the expulsion of air, can be seen as a desperate attempt to clear the chest of a psychic burden, to release something that is lodged deep within. The body, in its physiological response, is performing a drama of internal conflict, attempting to externalize an internal impasse.

The concept of

jouissance that we explored earlier, the excessive, transgressive enjoyment that often skirts the edges of pain and suffering, also finds its expression through the body's symbolic language. Symptoms can, in a paradoxical way, be a source of this excessive enjoyment, a way of engaging with a potent psychic intensity that transcends the ordinary. The individual who compulsively scratches an itchy rash, for example, might derive a fleeting, albeit destructive, sense of relief or even pleasure from the act, a brief respite from the underlying emotional tension. This fleeting enjoyment, this peculiar form of *jouissance*, is intimately linked to the symbolic meaning of the symptom itself – the relief from the itch may be a stand-in for a deeper, more profound, but ultimately unfulfilled, psychic release.

The body, therefore, becomes a text, a living document inscribed with the history of the psyche. Symptoms are the words, the phrases, the punctuation marks within this text, each carrying a potential meaning that can unlock a deeper understanding of the individual's inner world. When we encounter a symptom, we are not simply faced with a biological problem; we are invited into a dialogue with the unconscious, a conversation that can lead to healing and integration. The challenge, and the art, lies in learning to read this somatic script, to decipher its cryptic verses, and to understand the profound truths it reveals about our deepest desires, our unresolved conflicts, and our most enduring vulnerabilities.

The specificity of symptoms is also a crucial aspect of their symbolic language. It is rarely a case of a vague, generalized malaise. Instead, the unconscious often chooses particular forms of distress that hold a specific, personal resonance. A sharp pain in the left shoulder, for example, might be connected to a feeling of being unsupported or burdened, particularly if the individual associates that side of the body with a particular aspect of their life or identity.

The location, the quality of the sensation – is it a dull ache, a burning sensation, a stabbing pain? – all contribute to the symbolic tapestry. These details are not arbitrary; they are the precise brushstrokes of the unconscious artist, carefully chosen to convey a nuanced message.

Consider the phenomenon of phantom limb pain. For individuals who have undergone amputation, the experience of pain in a limb that is no longer physically present is a powerful testament to the body's capacity to retain a somatic memory of psychic experience. The pain is not generated by damaged tissue, but by the brain's persistent representation of the limb, a representation deeply intertwined with the individual's sense of self and their history of interaction with the world. This phantom pain can be understood as a symbolic communication of loss, of a profound disruption to the body image and the sense of wholeness, a potent reminder of what has been taken away. The intensity of the pain can mirror the intensity of the grief or trauma associated with the loss.

This symbolic articulation through the body is not a conscious choice; it is an unconscious process, a testament to the power of repressed material to find an outlet. The individual suffering from a psychosomatic symptom is not malingering or fabricating their distress. They are genuinely experiencing the physical manifestations of their psychic struggles. The pain is real, the discomfort is palpable, and the impact on their lives can be significant. The difference lies in the origin and the meaning of that suffering. It is not solely a matter of cellular dysfunction but a profound interplay between mind and body, where the psychic realm finds its most urgent and undeniable expression.

The act of understanding symptoms as symbolic messages also involves recognizing their potential to be a form of self-protection, however paradoxical. By externalizing internal conflict into a physical symptom, the individual may be unconsciously attempting to contain and manage psychic energies that would otherwise be overwhelming. The symptom can serve as a focal point for the distress, making it seem more manageable than diffuse anxiety or unarticulated grief. It can also act as a signal, a warning that something is deeply amiss, prompting the individual to seek help or to make changes in their life, even if they are not consciously aware of the underlying cause. The body's distress, in this sense, can be a protective mechanism, a last-ditch effort to maintain psychic equilibrium.

The unconscious mind, in its wisdom, often employs metaphor and allegory in its communication. A feeling of being "choked" by responsibility might manifest as a sore throat or difficulty breathing. A sense of being "weighed down" by guilt could translate into persistent back pain or a feeling of heaviness in the chest. These are not mere coincidences; they are the body's way of speaking in its own rich, metaphorical language, a language that often bypasses the literal and taps into deeper, more evocative truths. The symptom becomes a visceral representation of an abstract emotional state, making the invisible palpable.

For example, consider an individual who experiences frequent bouts of nausea when faced with difficult conversations or social interactions. This nausea can be interpreted as a physical manifestation of an unconscious desire to "throw up" or expel unpleasant emotions or words that are difficult to articulate. It is the body's way of saying, "I cannot stomach this," translating a psychic aversion into a physical one. The sensation of rising bile, the queasiness, the actual vomiting – these are the physical expressions of an internal struggle to digest and process difficult interpersonal experiences. The symptom provides a tangible, albeit unpleasant, way of dealing with that which is emotionally indigestible.

The challenge in deciphering these symbolic messages lies in the fact that the unconscious does not operate with a universal grammar. The meaning of a symptom is deeply embedded in the individual's personal history and their unique symbolic universe. What might represent repressed anger in one person could symbolize unexpressed grief in another. This is why a generic interpretation of symptoms is often insufficient, and why a therapeutic relationship, where trust and openness can flourish, is so vital. In such a space, the individual can begin to explore the associations and feelings that arise in relation to their symptoms, gradually uncovering the hidden narrative.

The body, in its intricate complexity, becomes a canvas upon which the dramas of the psyche are painted. Symptoms are the vivid hues, the sharp lines, the subtle shadings that reveal the underlying emotional landscape. They are not arbitrary disturbances but meaningful expressions of internal states that have found no other avenue for release. To truly understand ourselves, we must learn to listen to this silent, yet eloquent, language of the body, to recognize the profound wisdom embedded within its aches, its pains, and its inexplicable sensations. For within these bodily dispatches lies the key to understanding the deepest, most unspoken truths of our being. The body, in its suffering, is not merely a site of malfunction; it is a locus of profound, symbolic meaning, waiting to be deciphered.

The experience of pain, a universal human affliction, is too often relegated to the realm of the purely physical, a signal of biological damage or dysfunction. Yet, from a psychoanalytic vantage point, pain is far more than a mere physiological alarm. It is a language, a potent and often urgent form of communication from the psyche to the conscious mind, a visceral translation of emotional turmoil that has found no other outlet. When we speak of "decoding pain," we are not suggesting a reduction of suffering, but an exploration of its deeper, symbolic significance. Pain, in its myriad forms, can serve as a powerful, albeit uncomfortable, vessel for psychological states that remain unacknowledged or unarticulated. It is the body's somatic testament to an inner world in distress.

Consider the raw, immediate sensation of acute pain. A sharp, localized stab, like that felt after a sudden injury, can sometimes mirror a sudden, jarring emotional shock. Imagine someone receiving devastating news – a betrayal, a profound loss. The immediate physical reaction can be an almost identical sensation: a chest-clenching ache, a sharp pang in the gut, a searing pain in the head. These are not simply the body's sympathetic response to emotional distress; they are, in many instances, the unconscious mind's way of processing an overwhelming experience by translating it into a physically digestible, albeit painful, format. The sharpness of the pain can reflect the suddenness and intensity of the emotional blow, the localized nature of the pain a way of containing and compartmentalizing an experience that threatens to engulf the entire self. The body, in its primal wisdom, finds a way to experience the unbearable by making it concrete, by giving it a physical locus. This is not to say the pain isn't "real" in a physiological sense, but that its origin and its intensity are deeply intertwined with the psychic landscape. The body becomes the stage for a drama of shock and disorientation that the conscious mind is not yet equipped to process.

Chronic pain, in contrast to its acute counterpart, presents a more complex narrative. It is a persistent, often low-grade, but unyielding thrum of discomfort that can pervade an individual's life. This enduring sensation can often be a somatic manifestation of ongoing psychological burdens. Think of the individual burdened by a pervasive sense of guilt, an unspoken shame that gnaws at their conscience day after day. This internal gnawing can find expression as a dull, persistent ache in the back, a feeling of being constantly "weighed down" by an invisible load. The back, historically and symbolically, represents support and the capacity to carry burdens. Chronic back pain, therefore, can be a powerful physical metaphor for an overwhelming sense of responsibility, a past transgression that cannot be forgiven, or a deep-seated belief in one's own unworthiness. The pain becomes a constant, physical reminder of this inner state, a somatized echo of an unresolved psychic conflict that the individual carries with them relentlessly. It's as if the body is saying, "I cannot bear this weight any longer," even when the conscious mind has pushed the guilt or shame into the shadows.

Similarly, chronic anxiety can manifest as a generalized, pervasive physical discomfort. A constant knot in the stomach, a persistent tension in the shoulders and neck, or a general feeling of unease that permeates the body can all be expressions of an underlying, unaddressed anxiety. This diffuse physical distress mirrors the amorphous nature of anxiety itself – a feeling of dread or worry without a clearly identifiable source. The muscles, in their chronic state of tension, are physically embodying the hypervigilance and unease of an anxious mind. The stomach, the seat of so many visceral emotions, can become a focal point for the internal turmoil, reflecting a feeling of being unable to "digest" or process the stresses of life. This is not a conscious choice; it is the body's involuntary, physical translation of a mind in a state of perpetual alert. The discomfort serves as a constant, physical reminder of this inner state, a somatized echo of an unresolved psychic conflict that the individual carries with them relentlessly.

Consider the specific quality of pain. A burning sensation, for instance, can be deeply evocative. It can represent a suppressed rage, an anger that is simmering beneath the surface, too hot to be consciously expressed. Imagine a situation where an individual has been repeatedly wronged or humiliated, but has been forced to suppress their natural reaction of anger. This pent-up fury can manifest as a burning pain, perhaps in the chest, the throat, or even the skin. The intensity of the burning sensation can be directly proportional to the intensity of the unexpressed rage. The body, unable to vocalize its fury, resorts to a physical metaphor, transforming internal heat into an external, palpable sensation. This burning can be a desperate attempt to purge the system of this toxic emotion, to somehow "burn it out" through physical manifestation. The pain, in this instance, is the visible scar tissue of an emotional inferno that has been denied expression.

Localized pain, as we touched upon earlier, offers a more targeted interpretation. A sharp, shooting pain in the arm might symbolize a feeling of being unable to "reach out" or to act decisively in a particular area of one's life. A persistent ache in the knee could represent a difficulty in "bending" or adapting to circumstances, a stubborn refusal to yield. The right side of the body is often associated with the external world, action, and assertiveness, while the left side is linked to the internal world, intuition, and receptivity. Therefore, pain in the right knee might speak to an issue with asserting oneself in the external world, while pain in the left knee might relate to a more internal struggle with flexibility or yielding to one's own emotions or intuitions. These associations are not absolute, but they offer rich avenues for exploration, suggesting that the body's architecture itself is imbued with symbolic meaning. The specific location of the pain provides clues to the specific area of the psyche that is experiencing distress.

The body's capacity to translate emotional suffering into physical sensation is a testament to the profound interconnectedness of mind and body. This is not a mystical concept but a demonstrable reality observed in clinical practice and explored in depth by psychoanalytic theory. Emotions that are too overwhelming, too shameful, or too threatening to be processed consciously can find a physical home. The symptom becomes a substitute, a tangible representation of an intangible psychological state. This substitution can, paradoxically, offer a form of relief. By externalizing internal pain into a physical symptom, the individual may unconsciously create a sense of containment. The diffuse, overwhelming nature of emotional distress can be channeled into a more specific, and thus seemingly more manageable, physical complaint. The pain, while undoubtedly unpleasant, can become a focal point, a signal that something is wrong and needs attention, even if the conscious mind is unaware of the true source of the problem.

Consider the phenomenon of somatization, where emotional distress is expressed primarily through physical symptoms. An individual might experience a wide range of physical ailments – fatigue, headaches, digestive issues, muscle aches – without a clear medical explanation. These symptoms are not imagined; they are real physical experiences, but their roots lie in unresolved emotional conflicts. The body becomes the primary language through which these unexpressed emotions are communicated. The complexity of the symptom picture can mirror the complexity of the underlying psychological issues. It is as if the unconscious is using every available bodily channel to make its plea heard, to signal the depth of the internal suffering. The more the emotional distress is suppressed, the more insistent and varied the physical manifestations can become.

The interpretation of pain, therefore, requires a nuanced approach. It is not a simple matter of assigning a single meaning to a particular type of pain. Instead, it involves a deep dive into the individual's personal history, their relationships, their cultural background, and their unique symbolic associations. The meaning of a "stabbing" pain in the chest will differ greatly depending on whether it is linked to a recent romantic rejection, a feeling of suffocation in a family dynamic, or a profound sense of loss. The context is paramount. The therapeutic setting provides a crucial space for this exploration. By creating an environment of trust and safety, the individual can begin to unpack the layers of meaning associated with their physical pain, to connect the dots between their bodily sensations and their emotional experiences. This process can be challenging, as it often involves confronting deeply buried emotions and painful memories.

The unconscious mind often employs metaphor and imagery in its communication, and pain is a particularly potent medium for this symbolic language. A deep, aching pain can symbolize a profound sense of loss or grief, a sorrow that has settled deep within the bones. This is not a superficial sadness, but a pervasive emotional wound that has become ingrained in the very fabric of the individual's being. The pain becomes a constant companion, a physical reminder of what has been lost and the enduring impact of that loss. It's as if the body is expressing a lament, a sustained mourning that has no end in sight because the emotional wound has not yet begun to heal.

Furthermore, the specific character of the pain can offer further clues. Is it a dull, throbbing pain, suggesting a persistent, underlying unease? Or is it a sharp, stabbing pain, indicating a sudden, acute emotional wound? Is it a burning pain, hinting at suppressed anger or shame? Is it a cramping pain, perhaps related to a feeling of being constricted or unable to move forward? Each quality of sensation carries its own symbolic weight, contributing to the rich tapestry of the body's language. The unconscious mind, in its intricate workings, selects the most fitting physical metaphor to convey the nature of the psychic distress. It is a masterful artist, using the body as its canvas and pain as its medium, to create a visceral representation of the soul's suffering.

The process of understanding pain as a form of symbolic expression is not about diminishing the reality of the physical experience. The pain is real, and its impact on an individual's life can be profound and debilitating. However, by exploring the potential symbolic meanings behind the pain, individuals can begin to access the underlying emotional issues that are contributing to their suffering. This can open up new pathways for healing, allowing for a more integrated approach that addresses both the physical and psychological dimensions of their distress. The goal is not to eliminate the pain by ignoring its emotional origins, but to understand it, to work through the emotions it represents, and in doing so, to find a more profound and lasting relief. The body's text, inscribed with the language of pain, holds the key to unlocking a deeper understanding of ourselves and our journey toward wholeness.

The symptom, often perceived solely as a burden, a source of suffering to be eradicated, carries a hidden, paradoxical dimension: a form of unconscious reward. This is not to suggest that individuals consciously seek out illness or distress, but rather that, within the intricate economy of the psyche, even the most debilitating symptom can offer a peculiar form of solace or advantage. This phenomenon, known in psychoanalytic circles as the "secondary gain" of the symptom, speaks to the remarkable ingenuity of the unconscious mind in its relentless pursuit of equilibrium, however precarious. The symptom, in its very existence, can serve as a sophisticated defense mechanism, a shield against anxieties and truths that are too formidable to confront directly.

Consider the symptom as a bulwark. For many, the raw, unadulterated confrontation with certain emotional realities can be utterly overwhelming. The unconscious, acting as a vigilant guardian of the psyche, may then seize upon a physical manifestation – a headache, a chronic fatigue, a persistent cough – as a convenient, and often less threatening, substitute. The symptom becomes a diversion, a tangible object upon which to focus the psychic energy that would otherwise be consumed by the unbearable. The pain, the discomfort, the limitations imposed by the symptom, though undeniably real and distressing, can paradoxically serve to ward off a more profound psychic disintegration. The patient might complain of debilitating migraines, which, while incapacitating, effectively preclude them from engaging in a high-pressure work environment that they unconsciously dread or feel incapable of managing. The migraine, in this scenario, functions not merely as a biological event, but as a powerful psychic alibi, a somatic declaration of "I cannot." The dread associated with the potential failure or the unbearable stress of the work situation is effectively contained, or at least transmuted, into the more manageable, albeit agonizing, reality of the headache. The pleasure, therefore, is not in the pain itself, but in the avoidance of a greater, more existential psychic suffering.

This defensive function extends to the realm of interpersonal relationships as well. Symptoms can become a powerful, albeit unconscious, tool for influencing the behavior of others. The ailing individual, by virtue of their infirmity, can elicit sympathy, care, and attention that might otherwise be withheld or overlooked. This is the realm of the secondary gain derived from the social sphere. A child's persistent cough might, for instance, ensure that a parent's undivided attention is focused on them, providing a sense of security and importance that is difficult to attain through other means. In adulthood, a chronic illness can become a means of avoiding responsibilities, of eliciting a sense of duty from partners or family members, or even of punishing them indirectly through the burden of care. The symptom, in these instances, becomes a form of non-verbal communication, a plea for connection, a demand for recognition, or a subtle assertion of power within a relationship dynamic. The "pleasure" here lies in the fulfillment of these unconscious needs, the establishment of a particular relational pattern, however unhealthy it may appear from an external perspective. The individual, without conscious awareness, may be deriving a sense of being needed, of being important, or of exercising a form of control that their more assertive selves are incapable of achieving.

The symptom can also serve as a potent defense against guilt and responsibility. By externalizing internal conflict into a physical ailment, the individual can, in a sense, abdicate their agency. The failure to act, the transgression committed, or the uncomfortable truth acknowledged can be conveniently attributed to the illness. "I could not attend the meeting because of my back pain," or "I did not call my mother because I was feeling so unwell." These statements, while potentially factually accurate regarding the immediate physical experience, can also serve as unconscious attempts to deflect blame and avoid confronting the underlying emotional reasons for the inaction. The symptom becomes a scapegoat, a physical manifestation that conveniently absorbs the psychic burden of guilt. The relief derived from this deflection, the easing of conscience, can be a powerful, albeit unconscious, motivator for maintaining the symptom. The individual is not necessarily consciously choosing to be sick to avoid guilt; rather, the symptom arises as a psychic compromise, a way for the unconscious to manage an unbearable level of self-condemnation. The physical pain becomes a form of psychic penance, a way to "pay for" perceived transgressions without having to consciously acknowledge them.

Furthermore, the symptom can serve as a form of identity, a defining characteristic that provides a sense of coherence, however distorted, to an otherwise fragmented self. For individuals who feel lost, uncertain of their place in the world, or lacking a strong sense of self-worth, the symptom can become a fixed point of reference. "I am the one with the chronic fatigue," or "I am the one who suffers from anxiety." This identification can provide a sense of predictability and belonging, even if that belonging is to a community of the unwell. The unconscious mind may cling to the symptom as a way of anchoring the self, of defining who one is in the absence of other, more positive identifications. The struggle to overcome such a symptom can therefore be deeply complex, not just because of the physical discomfort it entails, but because it represents a potential dissolution of a deeply ingrained, albeit maladaptive, sense of self. The pleasure, in this case, is not active enjoyment but the passive comfort of familiarity, the avoidance of the terrifying void of non-identity.

The interplay between the expression of psychic distress and its defensive function is a delicate and intricate dance. While the symptom undeniably serves to communicate an inner turmoil, it simultaneously erects barriers against deeper exploration and resolution. The very act of somaticizing an emotion can, paradoxically, render that emotion less accessible to conscious awareness and therapeutic intervention. By translating an abstract anxiety into a concrete bodily sensation, the unconscious has, in a sense, "contained" the anxiety. The patient might be experiencing significant stomach pain, which, upon deeper exploration, is linked to unresolved fears about their financial security. While the stomach pain is a real symptom, it has effectively transformed the diffuse, nebulous anxiety about money into a localized, physical discomfort. This containment, while offering a degree of respite from the overwhelming nature of the anxiety, can also make it more challenging to address the root cause. The patient might become focused on alleviating the stomach pain through medication or physical therapies, inadvertently avoiding the deeper psychological work required to confront their financial anxieties.

This highlights the strategic, almost intelligent, nature of the unconscious. It is not a chaotic entity but one that operates with a logic all its own, a logic driven by the imperative of self-preservation, even if that preservation comes at the cost of suffering. The symptom is a compromise formation, a solution that is both problematic and, in its own way, functional. It allows the individual to continue functioning, to maintain a semblance of psychic order, by managing intolerable conflicts and anxieties. The "pleasure" in the symptom, therefore, is rarely overt or consciously recognized. It is a subtle, often unconscious, satisfaction derived from the successful deflection of pain, the fulfillment of unmet needs, or the maintenance of a precarious internal balance.

Consider the case of an individual experiencing a persistent cough that intensifies whenever they are in the presence of a particular family member. The cough, while physically bothersome, may serve to create distance, to signal discomfort, and to interrupt potentially conflictual interactions. The unconscious motivation might be to avoid a confrontation or to express unspoken resentment without the risk of overt aggression. The relief experienced from avoiding the confrontation, or from subtly asserting boundaries through the cough, can be interpreted as a form of secondary gain. The cough becomes a shield, a conversational stopper, and a non-verbal expression of distress that allows the individual to navigate a difficult interpersonal situation without direct engagement. The physical discomfort of the cough is, in this instance, a price paid for the psychic relief of avoiding a more potent, and potentially damaging, emotional encounter.

The deceptive nature of these unconscious gains lies in their subtlety. They are not always dramatic or obvious. Often, they manifest as a quiet avoidance of something perceived as worse, or a passive fulfillment of a deep-seated need. The individual might not consciously realize they are deriving benefit from their symptom, but the symptom persists because, on some level, it is serving a vital purpose within their psychic economy. It is a testament to the body's profound capacity to act as a canvas for the mind's deepest conflicts and most ingenious defense mechanisms. The symptom is a language, as we have explored, but it is a language that speaks in riddles, offering solace and defense under the guise of suffering. To truly understand the body's text, one must learn to read not only the explicit narrative of pain and discomfort, but also the implicit, often unconscious, benefits that the symptom provides, thereby revealing its complex and paradoxical role in maintaining psychic equilibrium.

The therapeutic process, therefore, often involves carefully deconstructing the symptom, not to simply eliminate it, but to understand the psychic work it is performing. By bringing the unconscious motivations and defensive functions of the symptom into conscious awareness, the individual can begin to develop more adaptive and direct ways of meeting their needs and managing their conflicts. This involves a careful exploration of the individual's history, their relationships, and their internal world, seeking to understand what unbearable truths the symptom is protecting them from, what unmet needs it is fulfilling, and what anxieties it is warding off. Only by understanding the "pleasure" or the gain, however unconscious, can the symptom be truly understood and, ultimately, transformed. The symptom is not merely a sign of illness; it is a complex psychic maneuver, a testament to the mind's enduring struggle for survival and stability in the face of overwhelming emotional challenges. It is a painful, yet often effective, strategy for navigating the treacherous terrain of the human psyche.

The body, in its eloquent silence and often startling expressiveness, becomes a living text, a repository of unspoken narratives. The language of symptoms is not a coded cipher meant to confound, but rather a deeply personal lexicon, forged in the crucible of individual experience. To truly understand this language, we must move beyond a purely biological interpretation and engage with the rich tapestry of unconscious meaning that imbues each ache, each tremor, each phantom sensation. It is within the clinical encounter, where vulnerability is met with careful attunement, that these hidden narratives begin to unfurl. Through anonymized case examples, we can illuminate how these seemingly inexplicable bodily manifestations serve as profound expressions of underlying psychic distress and unconscious conflict.

Consider, for instance, the case of Mr. Abernathy, a man in his late fifties who presented with a persistent, hacking cough that defied all medical explanation. His lungs were clear, his airways unobstructed, and no allergen or irritant could be identified. Yet, the cough was relentless, particularly pronounced during his weekly visits to his aging mother. He described it as an involuntary spasm, a sudden expulsion of air that left him breathless and embarrassed. Medically, it was a non-event, a ghost in the machine. Psychologically, however, it was a powerful utterance. Mr. Abernathy harbored a deep-seated resentment towards his mother, a woman who had, throughout his life, maintained a suffocating grip on his autonomy, often through passive-aggressive tactics and thinly veiled criticisms. His cough, we began to understand, was not merely a reflex; it was a physical manifestation of his struggle to speak his truth, to assert his boundaries, and to expel the toxic emotional atmosphere that permeated his interactions with her. The act of coughing, a forceful expulsion, mirrored his unconscious desire to eject the suffocating influence of his mother, to create a physical barrier between himself and the verbal barbs that he could not, or would not, directly confront. Each cough was a protest, a plea for air in a suffocating emotional space. It was his body's way of saying, "I cannot breathe in this environment." The secondary gain here was not one of comfort or avoidance of a more significant threat, but rather a desperate, somatic attempt at self-preservation, a way to reclaim a measure of control over his own respiratory system when his psychological autonomy felt constantly under siege. The therapeutic task involved helping Mr. Abernathy to translate this bodily language into verbal expression, to find a more direct and less physically costly way to articulate his feelings of suffocation and resentment, and to build the internal fortitude to withstand the emotional storms that his mother's presence often evoked.

Then there was Ms. Bellweather, a vibrant artist in her early thirties, who began to experience a phantom limb sensation in her right arm, the very arm she used to bring her canvases to life. The sensation was described as a persistent, gnawing emptiness, as if her arm had been amputated, yet she could see it, move it, and feel it. It was a visceral contradiction that baffled both her and her physicians. This phenomenon, occurring against a backdrop of immense creative pressure and a burgeoning fear of professional obsolescence, began to reveal its symbolic weight. Ms. Bellweather had recently received significant critical acclaim, leading to an overwhelming schedule of commissions and exhibitions. While on the surface, this was the realization of her lifelong dreams, beneath the surface, a profound anxiety brewed. She felt an imposter, convinced that her recent success was a fluke, and that her true creative wellspring had run dry. The phantom limb, in this context, became a poignant metaphor for her perceived loss of artistic vitality. Her dominant arm, the instrument of her creative power, felt as if it had been severed, rendering her incapable of producing the work that was now expected of her. The emptiness was the void she feared would consume her if her creative muse abandoned her. The phantom sensation was a visceral embodiment of her fear of professional impotence, a somatic manifestation of an artist who felt she had lost her most vital tool. The unconscious message was clear: "My ability to create, my very artistic identity, feels lost to me." The therapeutic work focused on exploring these anxieties of inadequacy, of helping Ms. Bellweather to understand that her creative wellspring was not a finite resource that could be severed, but rather a dynamic process that could be nurtured and replenished, even in the face of external pressures. The goal was to help her reclaim her arm, not as a physical appendage, but as a symbol of her integrated creative self, a self she could trust to continue to produce, even when the fear of failure loomed large. The phantom sensation, in its startlingly vivid reality for Ms. Bellweather, served as a stark, embodied warning from her unconscious, prompting her to confront the fragility of her self-worth when it was so tightly yoked to external validation and creative output.

Another compelling example is that of Mr. Croft, a middle-aged accountant who developed a chronic, intensely itchy rash that spread across his chest and arms, resisting all topical treatments. The itching was maddening, a constant, unbearable torment that disrupted his sleep and his concentration at work. Mr. Croft was a man who prided himself on his meticulousness and his emotional restraint. He had recently discovered evidence of significant financial irregularities within his firm, implicating senior partners. His internal struggle was immense: his loyalty to the company and his fear of repercussions warred with his innate sense of integrity and his desire to expose the wrongdoing. The rash, we came to understand, was a physical manifestation of this unbearable internal conflict, a skin that could not contain the itching, burning truth he was trying to suppress. The itching was the outward projection of his inner agitation, the insistent, maddening urge to reveal what he knew, to scratch away the deceit that had infested his professional life. His meticulous nature, which usually kept his emotions tightly contained, was failing him, and his body was taking over the expression of his inner turmoil. The rash was the outward sign of his internal discomfort, a physical eruption mirroring the ethical dilemma he faced. The sensation of being unable to scratch enough to find relief symbolized his inability to truly resolve the situation; the truth was there, palpable and irritating, but he could not find a way to truly expunge it. The unconscious message was a desperate cry: "This is unbearable! I am being eaten alive by this secret!" The secondary gain, though not consciously sought, was a form of self-punishment and a way to externalize the guilt and anxiety associated with his knowledge. By suffering physically, he was, in a sense, "paying" for his complicity through inaction. The therapeutic journey for Mr. Croft involved helping him to differentiate between the physical sensation and the underlying emotional and ethical conflict. It was about empowering him to find a voice for his integrity, to understand that the physical agony was a symptom of his psychic distress, and that the resolution lay not in scratching his skin, but in confronting the truth and taking decisive action, whatever the personal cost. The rash served as a visceral alarm bell, a physical representation of the ethical contagion he was experiencing, forcing him to acknowledge the severity of his internal conflict.

These vignettes, though brief, underscore a fundamental principle: the body is not merely a passive recipient of psychic distress; it is an active participant in its expression and, at times, its management. The cough that signifies unspoken resentment, the phantom limb that embodies a feared loss of identity, the incessant rash that betrays a suppressed truth – these are not isolated anomalies. They are powerful illustrations of the body's capacity to translate the abstract language of the unconscious into the concrete language of sensation and symptom. The therapeutic process, in this light, becomes an act of translation, a careful deciphering of this somatic text, allowing the individual to understand the hidden narratives their body has been weaving, and to ultimately rewrite them with words. The unconscious, in its relentless drive for equilibrium, will find a way to communicate, often through the most intimate and undeniable channels available to us – our own physical being. Understanding these signals requires a willingness to look beyond the surface, to listen not just to what is said, but to what is felt, to what aches, and to what itches, for within these bodily disturbances lie the profoundest truths of our inner lives. The body, when it speaks in symptoms, offers not just a diagnosis of illness, but a deeply personal testament to the human condition, a testament that, when read with understanding and compassion, can lead to healing and integration.

From Suffering to Signification: The Therapeutic Goal

The journey through the landscape of psychosomatic symptoms, as we have begun to explore, is often a deeply arduous one, marked by confusion, distress, and a profound sense of alienation. The body, in its eloquent, often urgent, communication, has presented its grievances. We have seen how an ache, a tremor, a phantom sensation, or an inexplicable eruption can serve as potent, albeit painful, messengers from the unconscious. These manifestations are not random occurrences; they are, as our previous explorations have illustrated, deeply personal and symbolically charged expressions of internal conflict, unarticulated emotions, and unresolved psychic dramas. The therapeutic endeavor, therefore, is not simply about silencing these bodily outcries, but about embarking on a transformative process: the transmutation of raw, discomfiting suffering into meaningful signification. This is the central aim of our clinical work, the ultimate horizon towards which we guide our patients.

To achieve this transformation, the initial and paramount task is to foster an environment where the patient can begin to perceive their symptoms not as alien invaders or inexplicable malfunctions, but as integral parts of their own narrative, albeit a narrative written in a language previously unknown or ignored. This requires a fundamental shift in perspective, moving away from a purely reductionist, biomedical model that often isolates the symptom from the person experiencing it. Instead, we embrace a holistic view, recognizing the intricate interplay between mind, body, and experience. The body, in its wisdom, has found a way to externalize what the psyche could not bear to contain or articulate. Our role, as clinicians, is to become skilled translators, sensitive listeners to this profound, non-verbal dialogue. We assist the patient in discerning the underlying psychic material that the symptom is attempting to convey. This is not about intellectual dissection alone, but about cultivating an emotional and somatic attunement to the deeper currents of the self.

Consider the case of Eleanor, a woman in her late forties who presented with a persistent, debilitating vertigo. The world would spin and lurch, rendering her incapable of walking a straight line or maintaining her balance. Medical investigations revealed no inner ear abnormalities, no neurological deficits, and no clear physiological cause. Eleanor, a woman who had always prided herself on her stability and control, found herself utterly disoriented, both physically and existentially. She described her life as having been "turned upside down" after a recent, acrimonious divorce, which had left her feeling adrift and powerless. Her vertigo, we began to explore, was not merely an inconvenience; it was a visceral embodiment of her shattered sense of groundedness and her profound disorientation in the wake of this life-altering event. The sensation of the world spinning mirrored her internal chaos, her inability to find stable footing in her new reality. The loss of physical balance was a direct reflection of her loss of emotional and relational equilibrium.

In our sessions, we didn't immediately seek to "cure" the vertigo. Instead, we focused on the feeling of instability itself. We explored the fear that accompanied each dizzying episode, the terror of losing control, of falling into an abyss. We invited Eleanor to imagine her life before the divorce, a life she perceived as stable, and then to contrast it with her current state of profound imbalance. Through careful inquiry, we began to connect the physical sensation of spinning with the emotional upheaval of her divorce. The symptom became a vivid, undeniable representation of her psychic distress. It was her body's way of screaming, "I don't know where I am! My foundation has crumbled!" The secondary gain was not one of conscious avoidance, but rather a desperate, somatic attempt to process an overwhelming loss of control by physically embodying that very loss. By feeling the instability so acutely, she was, in a sense, forced to acknowledge the depth of her internal disarray.

The therapeutic work then involved helping Eleanor to articulate, in words, the feelings of powerlessness, grief, and anger that the vertigo had so vividly expressed. We worked on identifying specific aspects of her divorce that contributed to this sense of imbalance – the betrayal, the loss of shared future, the sudden solitude. As she began to verbalize these previously inchoate emotions, to give them shape and form through language, a curious phenomenon began to occur. The intensity of the vertigo started to diminish. It wasn't a sudden disappearance, but a gradual receding, like a tide slowly going out. As Eleanor gained a more robust understanding of the emotional roots of her physical distress, as she began to integrate the experience of her divorce into her conscious narrative, her body found less urgent need to express it through such a dramatic somatic protest. The meaning had begun to be found, and in that finding, a degree of resolution was initiated. The vertigo, once a terrifying symptom, began to transform into a poignant, albeit painful, chapter in her life story, a testament to her resilience and capacity for emotional processing.

This process of finding meaning is not a simple decoding, but an active co-creation between the patient and the therapist. It involves a willingness to sit with discomfort, to explore the shadowy corners of the psyche, and to trust in the body's innate capacity for healing once its messages are heard. The ultimate goal, therefore, transcends mere symptom alleviation. While the reduction of physical suffering is undeniably a crucial and often immediate aim, it is the deeper integration and understanding of the self that constitutes the true therapeutic victory. When a symptom is simply suppressed or eradicated without understanding its genesis, it often resurfaces in another form, or lies dormant, ready to erupt again under different pressures. True healing, in the psychosomatic realm, lies in transforming the suffering into a pathway for psychic growth and self-awareness.

This transformation is akin to alchemy, where base metals are transmuted into gold. The raw, unrefined ore of bodily symptom is transformed into the precious metal of self-knowledge. The pain, the confusion, the fear associated with the symptom becomes the crucible in which new understanding is forged. For instance, consider the persistent headaches that plagued Marcus, a young man who struggled with perfectionism and an overwhelming fear of failure. His headaches would intensify during periods of high academic or professional pressure, often leaving him incapacitated and unable to perform the very tasks he dreaded failing. Medically, these were diagnosed as tension headaches, but the intensity and predictability suggested a deeper origin.

In therapy, we explored the intricate link between his drive for flawlessness and his physical agony. The headaches, we hypothesized, were not merely a consequence of muscle tension, but a physical manifestation of his internal pressure cooker. His unconscious mind, unable to tolerate the unbearable stress of his perfectionistic demands, found a way to incapacitate him, thereby offering a paradoxical form of "relief" from the performance anxiety. The headache, in this context, became a somatic protest against the self-imposed tyranny of perfection. It was the body's way of saying, "This is too much. I must stop. I cannot bear this pressure any longer." The secondary gain here was a complex form of self-protection, a physical shutdown that, while painful, served to interrupt the cycle of unbearable anxiety and self-criticism.

Our work with Marcus focused on helping him to recognize the symptom not as a personal failing, but as a signal from a part of himself that was overwhelmed. We explored the origins of his perfectionism, tracing it back to early experiences of conditional love and approval. As he began to understand the roots of his fear, and as he learned to challenge the rigid, all-or-nothing thinking that fueled his anxiety, the headaches began to lose their tyrannical grip. He started to experiment with setting more realistic goals, with allowing himself to make mistakes without catastrophic self-condemnation. He learned to recognize the early signs of increasing tension and to implement strategies for stress management

before the debilitating headache would strike.

The shift for Marcus was profound. The headaches, once a source of shame and incapacitation, became a marker of his internal state, a reliable indicator of when he was pushing himself too hard.

They transformed from an enemy to be vanquished into a wise, albeit demanding, messenger. He learned to listen to its warnings, not with fear, but with a growing understanding of his own vulnerabilities and limits. This allowed him to approach his work and his life with a greater sense of balance and self-compassion. The physical suffering had, indeed, been transmuted into a catalyst for profound personal growth and a more integrated sense of self. He was no longer merely an individual battling painful symptoms, but a person who had learned to understand and respond to his body's intricate language, thereby forging a more resilient and authentic existence.

This journey from suffering to signification is not always linear, nor is it always complete. The unconscious is a vast and complex territory, and the body's language can be nuanced and multifaceted. There may be relapses, periods of increased symptom intensity, or the emergence of new manifestations as old conflicts are revisited or new ones arise. However, the foundation of understanding that is laid through this process provides the individual with a powerful toolkit for navigating future challenges. They learn to approach their bodily experiences with curiosity rather than dread, with a sense of agency rather than helplessness.

The therapeutic goal, therefore, is not to achieve a state of perpetual symptom-free bliss, but to cultivate a resilient and integrated self that can engage with life's inevitable challenges without succumbing to overwhelming somatic distress. It is about fostering a capacity for meaning-making, for finding purpose even in pain, and for recognizing that the body's complaints, when understood, can illuminate the path towards a richer, more authentic, and ultimately, more vital life. The symptom, in its most profound therapeutic potential, ceases to be a mere aberration or a sign of weakness, and becomes instead a testament to the human spirit's indomitable drive towards wholeness and understanding, a profound invitation to know oneself more deeply. The very intensity of the suffering often points to the immense psychic energy that is being bound up in the symptom, energy that, once released and understood, can be redirected towards growth, creativity, and a more profound connection with oneself and the world. It is in this intricate dance between physical expression and psychic exploration that the deepest forms of healing and self-discovery are found. The language of symptoms, once deciphered, becomes a roadmap to the self, guiding us towards a more integrated and meaningful existence.

Chapter 6: Repression and Defense: The Body's Fortifications

The unconscious mind, a vast and often turbulent ocean beneath the placid surface of our awareness, is not a quiescent realm. It is a dynamic arena where primal drives, unspeakable desires, and painful experiences, deemed too volatile for conscious embrace, are relegated. This relegation is not a passive eviction; it is an active, often forceful, expulsion. This is the essence of repression, a fundamental defense mechanism that serves to protect the ego from overwhelming anxiety and psychic fragmentation. It is a psychological janitor, diligently sweeping away anything that threatens the carefully constructed facade of our conscious selves. Yet, this meticulously maintained tidiness comes at a cost. The repressed material does not simply vanish; it lingers, a potent force yearning for expression, like a dammed-up river straining against its barriers.

Repression, in its psychoanalytic conception, is far from a singular, decisive act. It is not a one-time burial of a forbidden thought or a traumatic memory. Rather, it is a continuous, ongoing process, a vigilant guard at the gates of consciousness. Imagine a tireless sentry, perpetually scanning the horizon of the psyche, ready to intercept any thought, feeling, or impulse that dares to approach the conscious mind with the scent of the forbidden. This ceaseless activity requires a significant expenditure of psychic energy, a constant effort to keep the unwanted material sequestered in the depths of the unconscious. This is the psychological equivalent of holding your breath; it is sustainable for a time, but the pressure to exhale, to release, is ever-present. The more vehemently we attempt to suppress a thought, the more insistent its return often becomes. This is the paradox of repression: in its effort to erase, it often inadvertently inscribes a more indelible mark.

The ego, in its relentless pursuit of stability and social acceptability, employs repression as its primary tool for self-preservation. Thoughts that are socially unacceptable, desires that violate moral codes, or memories that are too traumatic to bear are summarily dismissed from conscious awareness. Consider the young child, perhaps exposed to early sexual curiosity or witnessing a disturbing event. The sheer overwhelming nature of such experiences, coupled with the societal injunctions against their expression, can lead to a powerful act of repression. The memory, the associated feelings, the very impulses are pushed beyond the threshold of awareness, sealed away in the unconscious. This act, while seemingly protective in the short term, lays the groundwork for future psychological complexities. The energy invested in maintaining this repression, in keeping these buried secrets, is considerable. It is like maintaining a vast underground vault, requiring constant surveillance and reinforcement to prevent any breach.

This psychic barrier, erected by repression, is not an impenetrable fortress. The unconscious, by its very nature, is a fluid and dynamic entity. The repressed material, though banished from direct sight, continues to exert its influence. It may manifest indirectly, in subtle shifts in mood, in peculiar anxieties, or in the seemingly irrational choices we make. The boundary between the conscious and the unconscious is not a rigid wall, but a permeable membrane, susceptible to leakage and seepage. When the conscious mind is weakened, perhaps through fatigue, stress, or illness, these breaches can become more pronounced. The carefully guarded secrets can begin to whisper, to exert a pressure that the ego finds increasingly difficult to resist.

The body, often perceived as a purely physical entity, can become an unwitting stage upon which this internal drama plays out. When the psychological defenses are strained, when the psychic energy dedicated to repression becomes overwhelming, the body can offer a potent, albeit involuntary, outlet for the repressed material. This is where the concept of the "body's fortifications" takes on a profound significance. The physical organism becomes an extension of the ego's defensive strategy, a locus where the unconscious attempts to communicate what the conscious mind refuses to acknowledge. The repressed thoughts, desires, and memories, denied direct access to consciousness, can find an alternative route, a somatic pathway that bypasses the conscious censorship.

This process is not necessarily conscious or deliberate. The individual is not actively choosing to manifest a symptom to express a repressed fear. Instead, it is a more primitive, instinctual form of expression. The body, in its wisdom, seeks to externalize internal distress when verbal or emotional expression is too fraught or impossible. The dammed-up emotional energy, unable to find a conscious channel, builds pressure until it finds an outlet, often through physiological means. This can manifest in a myriad of ways, from vague physical discomfort to the emergence of distinct psychosomatic symptoms. The body becomes the canvas upon which the repressed narrative is painted in somatic hues.

Consider the individual who, in childhood, experienced a profound betrayal by a trusted caregiver, a betrayal so deeply wounding that acknowledging it would have shattered their sense of safety and security. The memory of the event, along with the accompanying feelings of anger, fear, and disgust, may be thoroughly repressed. Yet, this repressed material does not cease to exist. It continues to churn within the unconscious, seeking a way to be acknowledged. This repressed energy might then find its expression through a chronic skin condition, perhaps an itchy rash that flares up during times of stress, a constant, irritating reminder of a buried hurt. The itching sensation, while physically experienced, can be understood as a somatic echo of the buried emotional discomfort, a physical manifestation of an unacknowledged transgression. The skin, the very boundary of the self, becomes the site of this struggle, a porous barrier mirroring the permeable boundary between the conscious and the unconscious. The individual experiences the itching, the discomfort, the irritation, but may struggle to connect it to the buried memory of betrayal. The symptom serves as a constant, albeit confusing, presence, a somatic signal that something is deeply amiss, even if the conscious mind remains oblivious to the source.

Another example might be the person who harbors intense, repressed rage towards a demanding or critical parent. The conscious mind has learned to suppress this anger, to maintain an outward appearance of compliance and filial piety. The very thought of expressing such anger might be accompanied by overwhelming guilt or fear of abandonment. However, this pent-up aggression must find an outlet. It might then manifest as persistent, debilitating migraines. The throbbing pain, the feeling of pressure building within the skull, can be seen as a visceral representation of the unexpressed, contained rage. The head, the seat of thought and reason, becomes the battleground for this internal conflict. The migraine, in this instance, is not simply a physiological event; it is a somatic scream, a physical eruption of a suppressed emotional storm. The individual experiences the searing pain, the nausea, the sensitivity to light, but the underlying cause – the unacknowledged, repressed anger – remains hidden from conscious awareness. The symptom is a stand-in for the forbidden emotion, a physical proxy for a psychic reality that the ego cannot afford to confront.

Repression, therefore, is not merely the act of "forgetting" in the ordinary sense of the word. It is an active, dynamic process of psychic censorship, a vital but often costly defense mechanism. The energy required to maintain this repression can be substantial, and when these psychic fortifications are breached, the repressed material can find its way to expression through the body. The psychosomatic symptom, in this light, becomes a complex signifier, a somatic manifestation of a psychic struggle, a body speaking the language of the unconscious when the conscious mind remains stubbornly silent. It is a testament to the body's enduring capacity to communicate, even when all other channels are seemingly closed. The symptom is a message, albeit a coded one, from the depths of the self, demanding attention and understanding.

The operation of repression is not a simple on/off switch; it exists on a continuum, with varying degrees of intensity and success. Some repressed material might be so deeply buried, so thoroughly shielded by layers of defense, that it has minimal direct impact on conscious life, manifesting only in subtle, easily dismissible ways.

Other material, however, might be more volatile, pushing against the boundaries of the unconscious with greater force. These more insistent impulses or memories, though still outside of conscious awareness, can exert a more powerful influence on an individual's thoughts, feelings, and behaviors, often leading to more prominent somatic manifestations. The more insistent the repressed material, the greater the psychic energy required to keep it at bay, and the more likely it is that this energy will find an outlet through bodily channels.

Consider the individual who, due to early childhood experiences of neglect and emotional starvation, developed an intense, repressed longing for love and connection. This longing, deemed too vulnerable and too painful to be consciously acknowledged, is pushed into the unconscious. The conscious ego, in its attempt to compensate and to avoid the pain of this unmet need, might develop an obsessive focus on achievement and external validation. This can lead to a relentless pursuit of success, a constant striving for recognition. However, the repressed longing continues to exert its influence. It might manifest as a chronic sense of emptiness or a vague, persistent fatigue, a physical weariness that belies the individual's outward achievements. This fatigue, while seemingly physical, can be understood as a somatic representation of the soul's exhaustion, a physical symptom of a deeply buried emotional deficit. The body, in its profound connection to the emotional state, signals the weariness of a spirit that has been denied its most fundamental need for connection and love. The individual might attribute this fatigue to overwork or lack of sleep, failing to recognize its deeper roots in a repressed emotional hunger.

The very nature of what is deemed "unacceptable" by the ego is, of course, shaped by individual history, cultural norms, and societal expectations. What is repressed in one individual might be openly expressed by another. However, the fundamental mechanism remains the same: the exclusion of material that threatens the ego's sense of integrity, safety, and self-esteem. This can include not only traumatic memories but also forbidden desires, aggressive impulses, or even deeply felt emotions that were never validated in early life. For instance, a person who was consistently told that it was "unladylike" to express anger might repress their aggressive impulses, only to find them manifesting as chronic digestive issues, a somatic expression of the internal turmoil and suppressed aggression that cannot find a voice. The gut, often referred to as the "second brain," becomes a site where this unexpressed emotional energy churns, leading to physical symptoms that can range from indigestion and bloating to more severe gastrointestinal disorders. The symptom becomes a substitute for the unexpressed emotion, a physical manifestation of internal conflict.

The maintenance of these psychic fortifications is a dynamic, ongoing process. It is not as if the repressed material is locked away in a static vault. Rather, it is in a constant state of subtle agitation, of seeking to regain access to conscious awareness. This constant pressure necessitates a continuous expenditure of psychic energy. This energy, if it were to be consciously directed, could be used for growth, creativity, or healthy emotional processing. However, when bound up in the service of repression, it becomes a force that can, in its unmanaged intensity, overwhelm the very defenses designed to contain it. The body, in its close and intimate connection to the psyche, becomes an accessible channel for this displaced energy.

The concept of the body as a site of repression's breach is crucial for understanding psychosomatic illness. It highlights how the physical symptoms are not mere coincidences or random bodily dysfunctions. Instead, they are often deeply symbolic, serving as a somatic translation of the repressed psychic material. The symptom becomes a form of communication, a desperate attempt by the unconscious to draw attention to that which has been consciously ignored or denied. It is as if the body is saying, "You will not listen to my emotional cries, so I will make you feel my pain." The specific nature of the symptom can often offer clues to the underlying repressed material. For example, a feeling of being choked or suffocated might be linked to repressed emotions of powerlessness or a fear of being overwhelmed. A tremor might be a manifestation of repressed anxiety or a suppressed urge to flee.

The continuous struggle to keep repressed material out of awareness is an exhausting endeavor. The ego's defenses, while effective to a degree, are not infallible. External stressors, life transitions, or even internal shifts in psychic equilibrium can weaken these defenses, allowing the repressed content to exert a more potent influence. When this happens, the body often becomes the first line of defense, or rather, the first point of symptomatic manifestation. The individual might experience a sudden onset of a physical ailment that seems to have no clear medical cause, baffling both the patient and their physicians. This is often the point at which the psychosomatic perspective becomes particularly relevant, suggesting that the roots of the physical distress lie in the unresolved conflicts of the unconscious.

The "wall of forgetting," as it were, is not a smooth, impenetrable barrier. It is a complex structure, riddled with cracks, weaknesses, and hidden passages. Repression, though a powerful defense, is not a perfect solution. The repressed material, like water seeping through a dam, will eventually find a way to express itself. And when it does, the body, in its profound interconnectedness with the psyche, is often the first to bear witness. The ongoing nature of repression means that this is not a static situation, but a dynamic tension, a constant interplay between the forces of containment and the impulses of expression. The body, in its vulnerability, becomes the ultimate confidante of the unconscious, a silent witness to the profound struggles waged within the depths of the psyche.

The body, far from being a mere passive recipient of psychological distress, actively participates in the intricate dance of defense. It is not simply a vessel for repressed emotions but a dynamic stage upon which unconscious strategies unfold, a vital component in the ego's ongoing battle to maintain equilibrium and protect itself from unbearable truths. When direct confrontation with forbidden desires or painful realities is too threatening, the psyche enlists the physical organism in a complex, often unwitting, network of protective maneuvers. This engagement is not a conscious decision but an automatic, instinctual recalibration designed to preserve the fragile sense of self.

One of the most fundamental ways the body becomes a site of defense is through denial, a mechanism that operates with particular potency when confronted with physical sensations or the stark reality of illness. The ego, in its desperate attempt to avoid the anxiety and vulnerability associated with physical suffering, can simply refuse to acknowledge its presence. This is not mere stoicism or bravery; it is a profound unconscious erasure of sensory input or diagnostic evidence. Imagine an individual experiencing persistent, gnawing pain in their chest, a pain that radiates down their arm. The conscious mind, terrified of the implications – a heart attack, a life-altering condition – may unconsciously suppress these signals. The sensation is there, a physical reality, but it is perceived not as a symptom of grave illness, but as a fleeting discomfort, perhaps indigestion or muscle strain. The body's own alarm bells are silenced by a powerful psychological override. The individual might dismiss their spouse's concerns, insist they are merely tired, or even alter their behavior to avoid situations that might trigger a more intense awareness of the discomfort. They are, in essence, engaged in a somatic form of willful ignorance, a refusal to let the physical reality penetrate the ego's carefully constructed bubble of well-being. This denial can have dire consequences, leading to delayed diagnosis and treatment, as the body's organic plea for attention is systematically ignored by the mind. The language of the body, in such cases, becomes a foreign tongue, unread and unheeded.

Consider the athlete who, despite a searing pain in their knee during a crucial game, pushes through, attributing the agony to a minor sprain. The roar of the crowd, the adrenaline, and the intense desire to win all contribute to a powerful psychological environment that facilitates this denial. The body is screaming out a warning, but the ego's demand for victory overrides it. The physical sensation is minimized, distorted, or entirely disregarded. This is not about feigning strength; it is a genuine unconscious act of self-deception aimed at preserving a desired self-image and avoiding the immediate threat of injury and its consequences. The pain is real, a physiological event, but its perceived significance is drastically reduced by the defensive posture of the mind. The athlete might continue to compete, further damaging the joint, all while their conscious awareness remains focused on the score and the performance, not the escalating physical distress. The body, in its capacity for enduring pain, becomes a tool for the ego's denial, a testament to the mind's ability to reshape even the most undeniable physical realities.

Beyond denial, the body becomes a canvas for projection, another potent defense mechanism where unacceptable bodily impulses or desires are unconsciously attributed to others. These are often drives that are too primitive, too socially deviant, or too guilt-inducing for the ego to acknowledge as its own. Imagine an individual harboring a deep, unconscious envy of a colleague's success. This envy, if consciously recognized, might be perceived as malicious or indicative of personal inadequacy. Instead of confronting these feelings, the individual might project them onto the colleague, perceiving

them as envious. This projection can manifest in a variety of ways related to the body. The individual might interpret the colleague's innocent actions – a casual glance, a friendly gesture – as laden with hostility or ill will, fueled by this imputed envy. They might become hyper-vigilant, constantly scrutinizing the colleague's body language, searching for signs of this projected animosity. A colleague's flushed face might be interpreted not as a sign of exertion or embarrassment, but as a physical manifestation of their burning envy. The individual's own internal discomfort is thus externalized, made manifest in their perception of another's physical being.

This projection can also extend to more primal bodily drives. An individual with strong, repressed aggressive impulses might perceive others as inherently hostile and prone to violence. They might feel that everyone around them is constantly looking for a fight, their own suppressed aggression re-attributed to the external world. The tension in a stranger's shoulders, the sharpness of another person's tone of voice – these are all filtered through the lens of the projected aggression, seen as overt threats. The individual's own physical body might even become a site of heightened tension, constantly anticipating conflict, its muscles braced for an attack that exists primarily within their own unconscious. This creates a self-fulfilling prophecy, where the perceived threat from others can elicit defensive or aggressive responses from the individual, thereby confirming their distorted perception. The body, in its readiness for combat, becomes a physical echo of the projected internal battle.

Displacement offers another fascinating way the body becomes involved in defensive strategies. This mechanism involves redirecting a drive or emotion from its original, more threatening target to a safer, more acceptable one. The primal urges of aggression or sexuality, often powerful and potentially destructive, are prime candidates for displacement. Consider a person who experiences intense, unexpressed rage towards their boss but feels powerless to confront them. The aggression, unable to be discharged directly, might be displaced onto a less threatening target, such as a family member or even a pet. This displacement can manifest physically. The individual might find themselves becoming unusually irritable and quick to anger with their spouse, snapping at minor infractions or engaging in disproportionate arguments. Their physical body might betray this pent-up rage through clenched fists, a tense jaw, or a general feeling of agitated energy that needs an outlet. The intensity of the emotion is real, and it finds a physical expression, but its target has been shifted.

The realm of sexual drives also frequently involves displacement. An individual struggling with forbidden sexual desires, perhaps due to societal taboos or personal moral conflicts, might displace these urges onto less direct or acceptable outlets. This could manifest as an excessive focus on sexually charged media, an obsessive pursuit of romantic entanglements that remain superficial, or even a heightened interest in discussing sexual matters in a detached, clinical way. The physical arousal or the underlying drive remains, but it is channeled into activities or conversations that are removed from the direct, forbidden object of desire. The body's capacity for arousal or its underlying drive for connection is thus engaged, but in a way that the ego deems less risky. This can lead to a sense of frustration or dissatisfaction, as the displaced drive never truly finds its intended fulfillment. The physical energy remains, a restless current seeking a conduit, but the chosen channels offer only partial, and often ultimately unfulfilling, release. The body, in its very physiological responses, can become a conduit for these displaced energies, its urges channeled and re-routed in complex unconscious stratagems.

Furthermore, the body can serve as a repository for trauma, manifesting symptoms that are not direct expressions of conscious memory but rather somatic echoes of overwhelming experiences. When traumatic events are too shattering for the psyche to process consciously, they can become lodged in the body, bypassing verbal articulation. This phenomenon is often observed in conditions like Post-Traumatic Stress Disorder (PTSD), where individuals may experience physical symptoms such as hypervigilance, trembling, or unexplained aches and pains that are directly linked to past trauma. The body, in its intricate network of nerves and tissues, can hold onto the physiological charge of the traumatic experience, even when conscious memory is fragmented or absent. The act of remembering might be repressed, but the body retains a visceral imprint. A sudden noise might trigger a full-blown physiological stress response – rapid heartbeat, shallow breathing, muscle tension – not because the individual consciously recalls the traumatic event, but because the body itself remembers the threat. The physical reaction becomes a defense against re-experiencing the overwhelming emotional and psychological impact of the trauma, a somatic reenactment that keeps the original horror at bay, yet still causes profound distress.

The skin, the outermost boundary of the self, is a particularly sensitive site for these bodily defenses. Its role as a physical barrier between the internal and external world makes it a natural location for the ego to enact its strategies of containment and projection. Conditions like eczema, psoriasis, or chronic itching can sometimes be understood as somatic manifestations of repressed emotional turmoil or unresolved interpersonal conflicts. The itching, for instance, can represent an unacknowledged yearning for attention or connection, a physical manifestation of a deep-seated need that cannot be consciously articulated or met. The discomfort is real, a tangible physical sensation that demands notice, but its psychological root may remain hidden. Similarly, rashes or lesions could be seen as a physical eruption of suppressed anger or shame, the skin becoming a literal battleground for internal conflict. The body is expressing what the mind cannot, or will not, acknowledge. The skin, in its vulnerability and sensitivity, becomes a surface upon which the unconscious drama of defense is enacted.

The gastrointestinal system, often referred to as the "second brain" due to its complex nervous system and its intimate connection to emotional states, also serves as a prominent site for bodily defenses. Issues such as irritable bowel syndrome (IBS), ulcers, or persistent indigestion can be linked to repressed stress, anxiety, or unresolved emotional conflicts. The gut's sensitivity to emotional distress makes it a prime candidate for psychosomatic manifestations. A person who is constantly suppressing their anger or anxiety might experience chronic stomach pain or digestive upset. The physical symptoms become a way for the body to react to the internal pressure that the conscious mind is attempting to ignore. The clenched jaw of suppressed rage can manifest as a churning stomach; the racing thoughts of anxiety can translate into a frantic, upset gut. This is not to say that all gastrointestinal issues are psychosomatic, but in cases where medical explanations are insufficient, exploring the body's role in defense becomes crucial. The gut, in its capacity to absorb and process, can also become a site where unassimilated emotional experiences are physically manifested.

Even muscular tension and chronic pain can be understood as somatic defenses. A person holding onto significant amounts of stress or unexpressed grief might develop persistent muscle aches and pains, particularly in the neck, shoulders, and back. These areas are often associated with carrying burdens or holding oneself rigidly against emotional impact. The body's muscles, in their state of perpetual readiness or contraction, can become a physical manifestation of the ego's ongoing effort to brace itself against overwhelming emotions or external pressures. The physical pain serves as a constant, albeit often unhelpful, reminder of the underlying emotional strain. It is as if the body is physically trying to hold itself together, to prevent the eruption of something that the conscious mind cannot manage. This muscular bracing, while a form of defense, can become debilitating in its own right, further impacting an individual's quality of life.

The concept of the body as a site of defense underscores the profound interconnectedness of the mind and body. It challenges a purely Cartesian dualism, suggesting instead that our physical selves are deeply interwoven with our psychological processes. When the ego employs defenses like denial, projection, and displacement, it is not merely manipulating abstract thoughts; it is engaging the biological reality of the organism. The body, in its capacity to feel, to react, and to manifest symptoms, becomes an active participant in this intricate web of self-protection. Understanding these bodily fortifications is not about blaming the individual for their physical ailments but about recognizing the complex, often unconscious, ways in which the organism strives for a precarious balance. The body, in its silence and its suffering, can speak volumes about the battles waged within the unseen landscape of the psyche. It is a testament to the resilience of the human organism, but also a poignant reminder of the significant toll that repression and defense can take on our physical well-being. The unconscious, when denied its rightful expression through conscious processing, invariably finds a way to make itself known, and the body, in its undeniable reality, often bears the brunt of this subterranean struggle, transforming psychic tension into palpable physical sensation.

When the psyche finds itself unable to articulate its internal turmoil through the conventional channels of language and conscious thought, it often resorts to a more ancient and primal form of communication: the body. Somatization, in this context, is not merely a symptom; it is a desperate, often unconscious, plea for recognition, a translation of unbearable emotional pain into the undeniable language of physical sensation. It is the body, in its profound capacity for experiencing and expressing distress, becoming the primary, and sometimes sole, interpreter of a psyche under siege. When emotional expression is blocked, whether by ingrained defense mechanisms, the overwhelming nature of trauma, or a learned inability to identify and verbalize feelings, the body steps in, taking on the burden of the unexpressed. This is not a conscious choice, nor is it an act of malingering; it is a deep-seated, instinctual recalibration of how distress is managed, a shift from the psychological to the somatic. The body, in its intricate network of nerves, muscles, and organs, becomes the stage upon which the drama of the repressed plays out, manifesting as a constellation of physical symptoms that often defy straightforward medical explanation.

The phenomenology of somatization is as varied as the human experience itself. It is characterized by the presence of significant physical symptoms that cause distress or impairment in daily functioning, but for which no adequate medical or physiological explanation can be found after thorough investigation. These symptoms can range from chronic pain syndromes—headaches, backaches, abdominal pain—to gastrointestinal disturbances, fatigue, dizziness, and even more complex neurological complaints. The crucial element is that these physical manifestations are not simulated; they are genuinely experienced by the individual. The pain is real, the fatigue is debilitating, the nausea is intense. However, the underlying cause is not a disease of the organ system in question, but rather an overflow of emotional or psychological tension that the individual cannot otherwise discharge. The body becomes the canvas, and the symptoms are the brushstrokes of an internal, unarticulated narrative.

Consider the individual who presents with a persistent, unremitting headache that has plagued them for months, or even years. Medical examinations, including neurological scans and detailed blood work, reveal no underlying pathology. Yet, the pain is a constant companion, a dull throb or a searing intensity that disrupts sleep, concentration, and social interaction. This headache might be the body's way of shouting a silent scream of overwhelming anxiety that the individual cannot consciously acknowledge. Perhaps they are grappling with a demanding and emotionally abusive relationship, or they are burdened by a secret shame they cannot bear to reveal. The headache, in this scenario, becomes a physical manifestation of this unbearable psychic pressure, a tangible symptom that forces a certain level of attention, even if it redirects the focus away from the emotional wound itself. The body's protest is undeniable, yet the root cause remains elusive when viewed solely through a medical lens.

Another common presentation is chronic fatigue, a pervasive exhaustion that cannot be alleviated by rest. This fatigue might accompany a deep sense of depression or a feeling of hopelessness that the individual struggles to express. They may feel trapped in their circumstances, lacking the energy or the will to initiate change. The somatic symptom of fatigue serves as a powerful, albeit unhelpful, way to enact this feeling of helplessness. It can also function as an unconscious escape from responsibilities or expectations that feel too overwhelming. The body, by succumbing to exhaustion, signals a limit, a point beyond which the individual feels they can no longer function. This is not a conscious decision to be inactive, but a profound physical manifestation of an internal state of depletion and despair.

Gastrointestinal complaints are also frequently encountered in the realm of somatization. Individuals may experience chronic nausea, vomiting, diarrhea, constipation, or abdominal pain that doesn't align with any specific digestive disorder. These symptoms can be particularly potent in expressing repressed anger, anxiety, or a feeling of being overwhelmed by external circumstances – the literal "sick feeling" that many describe when facing something deeply unsettling. The gut, with its dense network of nerves and its intimate connection to emotional states, is a prime candidate for translating psychological distress into physical symptoms. A person who feels powerless to express their anger might find their stomach churning, their digestion disrupted, as their body literally rebels against the pent-up fury. The "gut feeling" takes on a terrifyingly literal dimension.

The language of the body in somatization is rich and often metaphorical. Symptoms can represent unconscious desires, fears, or conflicts in symbolic ways. A persistent cough might symbolize an unexpressed cry for attention or a desire to expel something noxious from within. Dizziness or vertigo can represent a feeling of disorientation, a loss of grounding, or a fear of falling into something unbearable. Skin conditions, such as eczema or psoriasis, can manifest as a physical eruption of repressed emotions, the skin, our boundary with the world, becoming inflamed by internal conflict. These bodily expressions are not random; they often carry a specific, albeit unconscious, meaning for the individual, reflecting the unique nature of their internal struggles.

The challenge for both the patient and the clinician lies in deciphering this bodily language. Patients experiencing somatization often feel frustrated and misunderstood. They are in physical pain, experiencing genuine distress, yet they are told that "nothing is wrong." This can lead to a cycle of seeking medical opinions, undergoing numerous tests, and feeling increasingly alienated and invalidated. The physician, faced with persistent physical symptoms and the absence of a clear organic cause, may feel perplexed, frustrated, and even suspicious. There can be an unconscious tendency to dismiss the patient's complaints as "all in their head," a phrase that, while sometimes accurate in identifying a psychological component, often carries a dismissive and invalidating tone.

The diagnostic process for somatization is, therefore, a complex puzzle. It requires a thorough medical evaluation to rule out any underlying organic pathology, followed by a careful exploration of the patient's psychological and emotional landscape. This often involves eliciting the patient's history in a way that allows for the emergence of emotional themes and life stressors. Clinicians must be attuned to the subtle cues that might indicate a psychological origin for physical symptoms. This might involve observing the patient's affect, their narrative style, their interpersonal interactions, and the temporal relationship between their physical symptoms and life events.

The act of somatization itself can be understood as a form of defense, a way for the ego to protect itself from overwhelming emotional pain. By converting psychological distress into physical symptoms, the individual can distance themselves from the unbearable emotional content. The focus shifts from the terrifying internal world to the tangible reality of physical discomfort. This can provide a temporary reprieve from overwhelming anxiety, depression, or trauma. However, this is a double-edged sword. While it may protect the psyche in the short term, it often leads to chronic physical suffering, functional impairment, and a perpetuation of the underlying emotional issues, which remain unaddressed.

Furthermore, the body's capacity for somatization can be amplified by cultural factors and learned behaviors. In some cultures, overt emotional expression may be discouraged, leading individuals to internalize their distress and express it through physical means. Similarly, individuals who have not been taught to identify or articulate their emotions may be more prone to somatizing. The family environment can also play a significant role, with children who grow up in families where illness is used as a means of gaining attention or expressing distress being more likely to develop somatization patterns later in life.

The somatic experience in somatization is not simply a passive manifestation of distress; it is an active process of embodying unresolved psychological conflict. The body, in its complex biological and neurological systems, becomes an arena where the unresolvable finds a form of expression. It is a testament to the profound interconnectedness of mind and body, highlighting how deeply entwined our psychological and physical states truly are. When words fail, and the conscious mind is unable to process or articulate its pain, the body often takes up the mantle, speaking a language of symptoms that, while often baffling, carries a profound and urgent message from the depths of the self. Recognizing this somatic language is the first crucial step in helping individuals to bridge the gap between their internal suffering and their external reality, leading them towards a more integrated and holistic path of healing. The body, in its unwavering commitment to communicate, offers a pathway, however arduous, back to the reintegrated self.

Anxiety, at its core, is a signal of psychic danger, a tempest warning that the ego perceives itself to be under threat, its integrity compromised. Yet, this internal alarm system does not solely operate in the abstract realm of thought and emotion. Instead, it frequently erupts into the tangible, physical landscape of the body, transforming an internal, often unarticulated, psychic threat into a visceral, undeniable somatic experience. This section delves into the intricate dance between the anxious psyche and the corporeal form, exploring how the body becomes both the battleground and the messenger of this pervasive internal distress. The physiological manifestations of anxiety are not mere epiphenomena, the incidental byproducts of an agitated mind. Rather, they are an intrinsic and fundamental component of the anxious experience, representing the body's immediate and often primal reaction to what the psyche construes as a formidable danger.

Consider the sudden, often startling, onset of a racing heart. The palpitations are not simply a curious bodily sensation; they are the body's urgent biological response, the cardiovascular system accelerating its rhythm in anticipation of a perceived threat. This is the heart, that tireless engine of life, attempting to pump blood with increased vigor, preparing the organism for fight or flight, even when the perceived danger is purely psychological. The chest may feel tight, constricted, as if an invisible hand is squeezing the very breath from one's lungs. This shortness of breath, this desperate gasp for air, is a direct corollary of the heart's frantic pace and the body's heightened state of arousal. It is the respiratory system striving to meet the demands of an emergency that exists, at least initially, within the confines of the mind. The breath becomes shallow, rapid, often leading to a sensation of suffocation, a terrifying physical manifestation of an overwhelming psychic burden.

Sweating, too, is a common hallmark of anxiety, often appearing as a cold, clammy sheen on the skin, or a profuse, drenching perspiration that can occur even in cool environments. This is the body's thermoregulatory system, activated by the stress response, attempting to cool the organism down in anticipation of exertion, or perhaps as a primitive means of shedding a perceived contaminant. The sweat glands, under the command of the sympathetic nervous system, become hyperactive, mirroring the heightened state of alert that permeates the entire system. Alongside these manifestations, trembling and shaking are frequently observed. The hands may tremble uncontrollably, the legs may feel weak and unsteady, and in more severe cases, the entire body may be wracked with tremors. This is the muscular system, primed for action but often held in a state of tense anticipation, its fine motor control disrupted by the surge of adrenaline and the pervasive physiological agitation. It is as if the body is vibrating with the unexpressed fear, the energy of the threatened ego seeking an outlet.

These physical symptoms – the pounding heart, the constricted chest, the clammy sweat, the trembling limbs – are not merely passive indicators of inner turmoil. They are active, dynamic components of the anxious experience, imbuing it with a visceral, embodied quality. When an individual experiences anxiety, it is not just their thoughts that are disturbed; their entire being is engulfed. The sensation is often described as a physical seizing, a feeling of being trapped within one's own body, a body that feels alien and uncontrollable. This visceral nature of anxiety underscores the fundamental interconnectedness of mind and body. The psychic threat, however abstract it may seem, is processed by the limbic system and other primitive brain structures that are intimately connected to the autonomic nervous system, which governs these involuntary bodily responses.

The ego's defensive maneuvers, while aimed at protecting psychic integrity, often serve to amplify these physical manifestations. When repression is employed to push threatening thoughts or impulses out of conscious awareness, the associated anxiety does not simply vanish. Instead, it is often displaced onto the body, finding its expression in these somatic complaints. The energy that would have been engaged in conscious processing or emotional expression is instead channeled into physiological arousal. This is why anxiety can feel so overwhelming; it is not just a mental state but a full-bodied physiological storm. The body becomes the stage upon which the battle for psychic equilibrium is waged, and the symptoms are the visible, palpable evidence of the ongoing conflict.

Consider the individual who experiences a sudden, intense panic attack. In such instances, the physical symptoms can be so alarming that they are often mistaken for a serious medical emergency, such as a heart attack or a stroke. The heart races, the chest pain intensifies, breathing becomes erratic, and a sense of impending doom washes over them. This is the body, in its extreme reaction to perceived psychic annihilation, enacting a full-blown physiological crisis. The individual may feel as though they are dying, a testament to the sheer power and terror of these bodily responses. Yet, upon medical examination, no underlying organic cause is found. This is because the threat, in this moment, is not a physical invasion but a psychological one – a sudden, overwhelming surge of anxiety that the ego, for a fleeting moment, cannot contain.

The phenomenology of these physical manifestations is highly individual, yet common threads emerge. For some, it is the relentless pounding of their heart, a constant reminder of their internal disquiet. For others, it is the pervasive sense of unease in their stomach, the "butterflies" that never seem to settle, or the gnawing sensation that portends a more severe digestive disturbance. The muscles may tense and ache, leading to chronic headaches, back pain, or a general feeling of bodily stiffness and discomfort. The skin might become hypersensitive, prone to flushing, itching, or even developing rashes. These are all bodily translations of psychic tension, the physical correlates of a mind in a state of hypervigilance and distress.

The defensive function of these somatic responses is multifaceted. Firstly, as previously alluded to, they serve to displace the anxiety from its original psychic source. By focusing on the physical symptom – the pain, the breathlessness, the trembling – the individual can, in a way, distance themselves from the unbearable emotional or cognitive content that triggers the anxiety. The symptom becomes a tangible, albeit unpleasant, object of concern, a surrogate for the more abstract and potentially overwhelming psychological threat. This allows for a certain degree of emotional regulation, as the ego's limited capacity is now directed towards managing the physical discomfort rather than confronting the full extent of the psychic danger.

Secondly, these physical manifestations can act as a form of communication, albeit an unconscious one. When an individual is unable to articulate their distress verbally, or when their internal state is too overwhelming to be processed consciously, the body speaks. The pain, the fatigue, the nausea – these are all ways the body communicates that something is deeply wrong. They can be cries for help, pleas for attention, or signals of profound internal distress. This is particularly evident in cases where individuals have experienced trauma or have grown up in environments where emotional expression was discouraged or punished. In such contexts, the body often becomes the primary language for expressing suffering.

Furthermore, these somatic responses can serve a defensive purpose by creating distance in interpersonal relationships. An individual experiencing intense anxiety might withdraw from social situations due to their physical symptoms, or they might elicit care and concern from others through their visible distress. This can, in some instances, provide a buffer against perceived interpersonal threats or fulfill unconscious needs for attention or reassurance. However, this defensive strategy is often a double-edged sword, as it can also lead to social isolation and further exacerbate feelings of helplessness and distress.

The visceral nature of anxiety means that it is not something that can be easily reasoned away. When the body is experiencing these powerful physiological responses, the individual feels physically ill, physically threatened. This is why attempts to simply "think positively" or "calm down" can be so ineffective for someone experiencing significant anxiety. The command to stop the racing heart or to cease the trembling is often impossible to obey because the underlying mechanisms are rooted in primal physiological responses, not in conscious volition. The body, in these moments, is operating on a level that bypasses rational thought.

The interplay between psychic threat and bodily fortification is a continuous cycle. A perceived threat leads to anxiety, which triggers physiological arousal. This arousal, in turn, can be experienced as a threat in itself, leading to a feedback loop of escalating anxiety and intensified physical symptoms. For example, the fear of having a panic attack can, in itself, trigger the physiological sensations that are characteristic of a panic attack, creating a self-fulfilling prophecy of distress. The body's readiness for danger becomes the very source of its perceived danger.

The language of the body in anxiety is rich and varied. A tightness in the chest can represent the crushing weight of an unacknowledged responsibility or the constriction of repressed emotions. A churning stomach can symbolize the unease of an unresolved conflict or the revulsion towards a situation that cannot be escaped. Dizziness and lightheadedness can reflect a feeling of disorientation or a fear of losing one's footing in life. Even seemingly minor physical discomforts, such as a dry mouth or a knot in the throat, can be potent expressions of suppressed fear or an inability to speak one's truth. These are not arbitrary symptoms;

they are deeply symbolic, carrying the imprint of the individual's unique psychic landscape.

Understanding these physical manifestations as integral to the experience of anxiety, rather than simply as its side effects, is crucial for effective therapeutic intervention. When the body is seen as speaking a language of distress, the focus shifts from merely suppressing symptoms to understanding the underlying psychic threats that they represent. This involves creating a space where the individual can begin to make sense of their bodily sensations, to connect them to their thoughts, feelings, and experiences, and ultimately, to find more adaptive ways of managing psychic danger. It is about helping the individual to interpret the body's signals not as signs of impending doom, but as messages from the self, requiring attention and understanding. The body's fortifications, in this light, are not merely prisons but potential pathways to deeper self-awareness and healing.

The journey through the labyrinth of repression and defense, particularly as it manifests in the body, inevitably leads us to the threshold of transformation. We have explored how the ego erects fortifications, intricate systems of denial, distortion, and avoidance, to shield itself from unbearable psychic pain. We have witnessed how this internal siege often spills over into the physical realm, transforming abstract anxieties into tangible, often distressing, somatic experiences. Yet, the narrative does not end with the description of these bodily defenses. Our focus now shifts to the therapeutic imperative: how do we, as individuals and as those who guide others, move beyond merely understanding these fortifications to actively working through them? The aim is not to dismantle the walls entirely, for they were erected for a reason, a testament to the psyche's urgent need for self-preservation. Instead, the goal is to understand the blueprints of these defenses, to recognize their patterns, and ultimately, to integrate the guarded material in a way that fosters greater psychic freedom and a more harmonious existence within one's own skin.

Reclaiming embodiment, in this context, is not about eradicating the body's protective responses but about liberating them from their rigid, often counterproductive, patterns. It involves a profound re-education of the self, a process of becoming more intimately acquainted with the subtle language of the body and understanding the historical and emotional narratives it carries. The body, having been enlisted as a silent sentinel against psychic threat, can be re-envisioned as a source of wisdom, a guide towards wholeness. This reclamation begins with the courageous act of turning towards, rather than away from, the somatic experiences that have been relegated to the periphery of conscious awareness. It necessitates a willingness to tolerate the discomfort, the initial surge of anxiety that often accompanies the breaching of these long-established defenses.

Consider the individual who has historically experienced crippling digestive issues, a perpetually churning stomach that has been attributed to stress or poor diet. Through careful therapeutic exploration, it may emerge that this somatic discomfort is intimately linked to an unresolved childhood conflict, a deeply buried shame, or a suppressed rage that was deemed too dangerous to express. The stomach, in this instance, has become a vessel for containing these overwhelming emotions, a physical manifestation of an internal pressure cooker. The therapeutic work involves gently probing the origins of these feelings, allowing them to be acknowledged and, in time, processed. This might involve recalling forgotten memories, articulating long-held grievances, or simply bearing witness to the raw emotional pain without the immediate need to suppress it. As these repressed elements are gradually brought into the light of conscious awareness, the body's defensive hold can begin to loosen. The churning may not disappear overnight, but its intensity may diminish, its frequency may lessen, and its perceived terror may abate as the underlying psychic material finds a more appropriate outlet for expression and resolution.

This process is akin to tending to a garden that has been left untended for too long. The weeds of repression have grown thick, choking out the more delicate plants of authentic emotion and embodied experience. The work of reclaiming embodiment involves carefully identifying and removing these weeds, not with brute force, but with precision and care. Each weed pulled represents a defense mechanism understood, a repressed memory unearthed, or a forbidden emotion acknowledged. As the garden is cleared, the sunlight of awareness can begin to reach the soil, allowing the original, healthy plants to flourish. This flourishing is the essence of reclaiming embodiment – a return to a more vibrant, integrated, and responsive way of being in one's physical self.

The therapeutic relationship itself becomes a crucial crucible for this work. In the safe and containing space of the therapeutic encounter, individuals can begin to experiment with relinquishing some of their habitual defenses. The therapist acts as a co-explorer, providing a mirror to the individual's internal world and offering a steady presence as they navigate unfamiliar emotional terrain. The therapist's attunement to the client's bodily expressions – the subtle shifts in posture, the unconscious gestures, the tone of voice

– can be invaluable in highlighting the somatic dimensions of their psychic struggles. When a client describes feeling "stuck," the therapist might notice a rigidity in their shoulders or a clenching of their jaw, offering a gentle invitation to explore the physical sensation alongside the emotional narrative. This integrated approach, acknowledging both the psychological and somatic dimensions, is fundamental to effective therapeutic change.

One of the most significant challenges in working through defenses is the inherent resistance they present. Defenses, by their very nature, are designed to keep certain experiences out of awareness, and their persistence is a testament to their perceived necessity. Therefore, the therapeutic process is rarely linear. There will be moments of breakthrough, followed by periods of regression as the ego scrambles to reinforce its familiar boundaries. The therapist must possess a deep understanding of these ebb and flow, offering encouragement during times of difficulty and celebrating moments of progress, however small. The client, too, must cultivate patience and self-compassion, recognizing that profound transformation takes time and sustained effort.

Consider the defense of intellectualization, where an individual might discuss traumatic events in a detached, analytical manner, devoid of emotional affect. While this can provide a temporary shield, it prevents the integration of the emotional impact of the experience. Therapeutic work might involve gently challenging this intellectual distance, inviting the client to connect with the feelings that lie beneath the surface. This could be facilitated by asking questions that encourage sensory awareness: "What did that feel like in your body at the time?" or "If that experience had a color, what would it be?" By shifting the focus from abstract cognition to embodied sensation, the therapist can help the client access the buried emotions that have been walled off. As these emotions are slowly brought into conscious experience, the intellectual defenses can begin to yield, allowing for a more complete and integrated processing of the trauma.

Similarly, the defense of dissociation, where an individual may feel detached from their body or their surroundings, often serves to numb overwhelming psychic pain. Reclaiming embodiment in such cases involves painstakingly rebuilding the connection between the mind and the body. This might begin with simple grounding exercises, such as focusing on the sensation of one's feet on the floor, the feeling of the chair beneath them, or the rhythm of their own breath. Over time, through consistent practice and guided exploration, the individual can learn to inhabit their body more fully, to experience the richness of sensory input without being overwhelmed by it. The goal is to cultivate a sense of presence and safety within the physical self, transforming the body from a source of alienation into a sanctuary of being.

The concept of "working through" defenses is not about judgment or condemnation. It is about understanding the benevolent intention behind these mechanisms, even when their current manifestations are causing distress. Defenses are often born out of necessity, a child's ingenious solution to an intolerable situation. As adults, with greater resources and a more developed ego, we can revisit these early strategies and find more adaptive ways of coping. This is where the therapeutic alliance is paramount. The therapist, by offering an unconditional positive regard, creates an environment where the individual can explore the origins of their defenses without fear of shame or rejection. This allows for a profound loosening of the grip that these defenses hold.

Furthermore, the therapeutic process of working through defenses often involves a conscious re-engagement with the repressed material itself. This is not about forcing oneself to relive traumatic experiences, but about gradually and safely exploring the thoughts, feelings, and memories that have been pushed out of awareness. This might involve dream analysis, where repressed material often finds symbolic expression, or guided imagery, where the individual can safely explore inner landscapes. As the repressed content emerges, it can be understood and integrated into the individual's life narrative. This integration is key to reducing the need for the body to continue its role as a fortress. When the psychic threat is understood and processed, the physical fortifications can begin to dissolve.

The impact of this work extends beyond the individual. As a person becomes more integrated and less reliant on problematic defenses, their capacity for authentic connection with others deepens. They are more able to be present, to communicate their needs and feelings directly, and to engage in relationships without the interference of unconscious defensive maneuvers. This leads to a richer, more fulfilling social life and a greater sense of belonging. The body, once a site of conflict and distress, becomes a source of vitality and presence, a vehicle for experiencing the world with greater clarity and joy.

Ultimately, reclaiming embodiment through the process of working through defenses signifies a profound movement towards psychic freedom. It is the liberation from the tyranny of unconscious processes, the breaking of the chains that bind the individual to repetitive patterns of suffering. It is the discovery that one's own body, rather than being a source of betrayal or discomfort, can be a trusted ally, a source of wisdom, and a pathway to deeper self-understanding and authentic living. This is not a destination but a continuous process, a lifelong journey of exploration, integration, and unfolding. Each step taken towards understanding and working through defenses is a step towards a more embodied, authentic, and free self. The body's fortifications, once seen as rigid prisons, can indeed become the gateways to a more expansive and liberated existence.

Chapter 7: The Imaginary, Symbolic, and Real Dimensions

The intricate landscape of human subjectivity, particularly as it is experienced and expressed through the body, can be illuminated by a theoretical framework that moves beyond simple dualisms. Jacques Lacan, a pivotal figure in psychoanalytic thought, offered such a framework through his conceptualization of three orders: the Imaginary, the Symbolic, and the Real. These are not discrete territories one enters and exits, but rather interwoven dimensions that constantly shape and are shaped by one another, forming the very fabric of our existence. Understanding these orders provides a powerful lens through which to examine how our corporeal selves are constructed, how they interact with the world, and how psychic distress can manifest somatically.

The Imaginary order is perhaps the most intuitive, as it deals with the realm of images, identifications, and the formation of the ego. It is the world of appearances, of self-perception, and of our relationship with others as mirrored beings. In the Imaginary, we encounter ourselves as distinct entities, separate from the world and from others. This is the stage of the mirror phase, a critical developmental moment where the infant, hitherto experiencing a fragmented and uncoordinated body, recognizes itself in its totality within the specular reflection. This recognition is a jubilant, albeit illusory, moment of mastery. The image of the unified body, however, is an external one, projected onto the mirror, and therefore fundamentally an identification with an

other's image. This foundational identification with an image is what establishes the ego, a construct built upon a fundamental misrecognition. The ego, in this sense, is an imaginary formation, a cohesive self-image that masks the underlying fragmentation and the chaotic reality of bodily drives. On a bodily level, the Imaginary is where we develop our sense of bodily schema, the internal representation of our body and its parts, and how we project an idealized or distorted image of ourselves onto others. It is the domain of narcissistic admiration and envy, the desire to be the perfect image we perceive in the mirror, or the painful realization of our perceived inadequacy when compared to the idealized images of others. This can manifest somatically through preoccupations with appearance, the pursuit of a certain body type, or the distress caused by perceived flaws. For instance, someone who experiences chronic body dysmorphia is deeply enmeshed in the Imaginary, caught in a perpetual struggle with their perceived bodily image, unable to reconcile their internal representation with their actual physical form, often projecting an image of defectiveness that is not objectively present. This constant striving for an unattainable ideal, born from the Imaginary, can lead to significant somatic suffering, from eating disorders to self-harm, all driven by the desperate attempt to align the physical self with an imagined perfection.

The Symbolic order, in stark contrast to the fluid and visual nature of the Imaginary, is the realm of language, law, and structure. It is the world of the signifier, of words and symbols that represent something else, creating meaning and order within the chaos of experience. This order is fundamentally social and intersubjective; it is through language that we are integrated into a community, that we learn the rules and prohibitions that govern our desires and actions. The Symbolic is the network of shared meanings, the cultural and familial codes that pre-exist us and into which we are born. It is through the Symbolic that the raw, unmediated impulses of the body are given form and significance, but also, crucially, are subjected to prohibition and constraint. The acquisition of language is the entry into the Symbolic, and with it comes the recognition of lack, of the inherent incompleteness that arises from the fact that no signifier can ever fully capture the totality of a lived experience. The Law of the Father, a key Lacanian concept within the Symbolic, represents the overarching prohibitions and structures that shape our desires and guide our behavior, dictating what is permissible and what is forbidden. On a bodily level, the Symbolic dictates how our bodies are perceived, categorized, and treated within society. Our names, our gender designations, our social roles – all are inscribed through the Symbolic. It is the realm where bodily functions are imbued with cultural meaning, where purity and pollution, health and sickness, are defined by shared symbolic systems. Consider the societal taboos surrounding menstruation or defecation; these are not inherent qualities of the bodily functions themselves but are constructed through the Symbolic order, shaping our individual experiences and emotional responses to these aspects of our physicality. The experience of shame related to certain bodily functions is a prime example of the Symbolic order's impact. A person might feel profound shame about their body odor, for instance, not because of any inherent biological harm it causes, but because the Symbolic order has assigned it a negative value, associating it with uncleanliness and social ostracization. This internalized symbolic judgment can lead to obsessive cleaning rituals, social withdrawal, and a pervasive sense of bodily contamination, illustrating how the Symbolic directly influences our somatic self-perception and the anxieties we attach to our physical being. The unconscious itself, for Lacan, is structured like a language, a web of signifiers where meaning is constantly deferred and where repressed desires find their indirect expression through slips of the tongue, dreams, and bodily symptoms.

The Real, the third order, is perhaps the most elusive and challenging to grasp. It is that which resists symbolization, the raw, unmediated aspect of existence that cannot be fully captured or contained by the Imaginary or the Symbolic. The Real is the unspeakable, the traumatic, the encounter with brute facticity that shatters our carefully constructed sense of reality. It is the domain of jouissance, an excessive enjoyment that exceeds the pleasure principle and can be both ecstatic and terrifying. On a bodily level, the Real is the raw sensation, the undifferentiated flux of physiological experience, the brute fact of our embodiment that precedes and underlies our identifications and symbolic meanings. It is the pain that cannot be articulated, the anxiety that has no name, the ultimate encounter with mortality. Trauma, in its most profound sense, is an irruption of the Real, a moment where the Symbolic and Imaginary orders are overwhelmed, leaving an indelible mark on the psyche and the body. This can manifest as unexplainable physical symptoms, chronic pain, or a pervasive sense of dread. For example, a deeply traumatic event, particularly one experienced before the full development of language, may not be amenable to symbolic processing. The individual might be left with a visceral, somatic response to triggers that seem innocuous to others. The body remembers what the mind cannot articulate. A sudden, inexplicable panic attack, occurring in a seemingly safe environment, can be understood as an eruption of the Real – a moment where the Symbolic order fails to contain an underlying, unrepresentable anxiety. The physical symptoms – the racing heart, shortness of breath, dizziness – are direct manifestations of this overwhelming encounter. The individual struggles to find words to explain their experience, because the experience itself transcends the available symbolic lexicon. The Real is also the fundamental lack that underlies our being, the awareness of our finitude and the ultimate unknowability of ourselves and the world. This can manifest as existential anxiety, a vague but persistent sense of unease that no amount of symbolic reassurance or Imaginary identification can fully quell. The body, in its raw, unmediated presence, is the closest we can come to this Real, yet it also remains perpetually beyond our full comprehension and control. The persistent ache in a limb without a clear medical diagnosis, the feeling of being fundamentally "off" in one's own skin, can be traced to these encounters with the Real, moments where the protective veils of the Imaginary and Symbolic momentarily falter, exposing us to the unvarnished, sometimes terrifying, truth of our being.

These three orders are not mutually exclusive but are in constant interplay, each profoundly influencing the others. The Imaginary depends on the Symbolic for its structure and meaning, and the Symbolic is, in turn, shaped by the Imaginary identifications that humans form. Both the Imaginary and the Symbolic grapple with the Real, attempting to contain, represent, and make sense of it, but ultimately failing to fully master its disruptive force. For instance, our sense of self (Imaginary) is constructed through language and social norms (Symbolic), but the raw, unbidden urges and sensations of the body (Real) constantly threaten to disrupt this constructed identity. A person who has undergone a significant bodily trauma, such as a serious accident, might find their Imaginary sense of self shattered. They might struggle to reconcile their pre-accident self-image with their current physical reality, and their ability to use language (Symbolic) to describe their experience might be limited by the sheer overwhelming nature of the event. The persistent physical pain that follows, even after the wound has healed, can be seen as a somatic echo of the Real, a reminder of the brutal materiality that transcended their usual defenses.

In the context of understanding bodily experience, this tripartite framework offers a sophisticated approach. The Imaginary dimension helps us understand the subjective experience of our body as an image, how we perceive ourselves and how we project that image onto others. This is crucial for understanding issues related to body image, self-esteem, and the role of aesthetics in our lives. The Symbolic order illuminates how our bodies are inscribed with social and cultural meanings, how language shapes our understanding of health, illness, and embodiment, and how societal expectations influence our relationship with our physical selves. This is vital for understanding the social construction of illness, the impact of stigma, and the power of narrative in shaping our embodied realities. Finally, the Real reminds us of the irreducible materiality of our existence, the raw, unmediated experiences of pain, pleasure, and finitude that lie beneath the veneer of our identifications and symbolic representations. It accounts for the aspects of bodily experience that resist easy explanation, the traumatic residues, and the existential dimensions of embodiment.

Throughout this chapter, we will utilize this Lacanian triad to unpack the complex relationship between the mind and the body. We will explore how the Imaginary can lead to a distorted perception of the body, how the Symbolic can impose oppressive norms and meanings onto our physicality, and how the Real, in its persistent intrusion, can manifest as somatic distress that defies easy categorization. By navigating these three orders, we can begin to appreciate the profound ways in which our psychic lives are enacted and experienced through our bodies, moving towards a more integrated and nuanced understanding of embodied existence. The somatic symptoms we experience are not merely biological events; they are deeply intertwined with the Imaginary constructions of our self, the Symbolic meanings we have internalized, and the persistent, often disruptive, presence of the Real.

The very essence of our embodied existence, the corporeal reality we inhabit, is deeply and irrevocably intertwined with the Imaginary order. This dimension, as we have begun to sketch, is the realm of images, of visual perception, and crucially, of identification. It is the fertile ground upon which our sense of self, our ego, first takes root, nurtured by the specular reflections that grant us the illusion of unity. This is not merely a theoretical construct but a palpable experience, a constant negotiation with the visual presentation of ourselves and the world. The body, within the Imaginary, is less a lived, visceral entity and more an object to be seen, an image to be managed.

Consider, for a moment, the concept of the "imaginary envelope." This is not a physical casing, but a psychic membrane, a construct woven from visual impressions and identifications that surrounds and contains our nascent sense of self. It begins, as Lacan famously described, with the mirror phase. The infant, adrift in a sea of fragmented bodily sensations, experiencing its limbs as uncoordinated and alien, encounters its reflection. In that moment of recognition, a miraculous, albeit illusory, coherence emerges. The infant grasps a unified image of itself, an image that is external, complete, and distinct from the disarray of its internal sensations. This external, perceived wholeness becomes the template for the developing ego. The ego, therefore, is fundamentally an imaginary formation, a solidified image that masks the underlying disunity and the constant flux of biological drives. It is the idealized, static portrait that we carry within us, a crucial but ultimately deceptive representation of who we are.

This process of identification is not a one-time event but a continuous operation. We are constantly bombarded by images – in the media, in social interactions, in our own internal dialogues. These images become fodder for our imaginary identifications, shaping our perception of what constitutes a desirable or acceptable body. The allure of the perfect image is a powerful force within the Imaginary. It is the sculpted physique of a film star, the impossibly smooth skin of a magazine model, the seemingly effortless grace of an athlete. These are not simply visual stimuli; they are potent signifiers that invite identification, urging us to mold ourselves, our bodies, into their likeness. This drive towards an idealized image can be a source of motivation, pushing us to engage in healthy behaviors, but it can also become a consuming obsession, leading to a profound disconnect between our actual lived body and the perfect image we aspire to embody.

The body, within the Imaginary, becomes a canvas upon which we paint our desires and insecurities. We project onto our bodies the ideals we have internalized, and we scrutinize them through the lens of these idealized images. A wrinkle is not just a sign of aging; it is a perceived imperfection that deviates from the timeless image of youth. A few extra pounds are not merely a variation in weight; they are a failure to achieve the slender ideal. This constant comparison, this striving to align our physical reality with an imagined perfection, is a hallmark of the Imaginary order's influence on our embodied experience. The body, in this sense, is experienced as an object of scrutiny, a site of potential shame or admiration, rather than a lived, dynamic entity.

This disconnect between the lived body and the imagined body is a fertile ground for somatic distress. When the gap between who we believe we should be, based on the idealized images we have internalized, and who we perceive ourselves to be becomes too vast, the psychic tension can manifest physically. The individual struggling with body dysmorphia, for instance, is profoundly trapped within the Imaginary. Their perception of their own body is distorted by an internal, hyper-critical gaze, fixated on perceived flaws that are often invisible to others. The imaginary perfect body, etched into their psyche, becomes an unattainable standard, leading to immense suffering and a profound alienation from their own physical form. They are, in essence, at war with the image they hold of themselves, a war waged on the terrain of their physical being.

The allure of the perfect image extends beyond individual aspirations. It permeates our culture, creating a societal pressure cooker where the emphasis on appearance can be overwhelming. The proliferation of filtered images on social media platforms, the ubiquity of cosmetic surgery advertisements, and the constant barrage of celebrity endorsements for beauty products all contribute to a cultural landscape that prioritizes a manufactured, idealized version of the body. This collective obsession with a narrow definition of beauty can lead to widespread body dissatisfaction, eating disorders, and a general sense of inadequacy that is projected onto our own physical selves. We are encouraged to see our bodies not as sites of lived experience, vitality, and connection, but as projects to be perfected, as images to be endlessly refined.

Furthermore, the Imaginary order's emphasis on visual perception can lead to a sense of detachment from the body's internal states. The raw sensations of hunger, fatigue, or pain can be suppressed or ignored if they do not align with the desired image of a constantly energetic, perfectly functioning individual. This can lead to a paradoxical situation where individuals are hyper-vigilant about their outward appearance but profoundly out of touch with their internal bodily wisdom. The body becomes a performance, an act of presenting a certain image to the world, rather than a source of authentic experience.

The ego, born from this imaginary identification, is inherently fragile. It is built upon a foundation of illusion, a carefully constructed facade that can be easily shattered by encounters with the Real or by the overwhelming force of the Symbolic. When our imaginary identifications are challenged, when the images we have held dear are confronted with a different reality, the ego can experience significant distress. For example, a sudden illness or injury that dramatically alters one's physical appearance can be devastating, not just because of the physical discomfort, but because it undermines the entire edifice of the imaginary self. The image of oneself as healthy, strong, and attractive is disrupted, leading to a profound sense of loss and disorientation.

The mechanisms of identification are multifaceted. We identify not only with idealized images but also with others who seem to possess qualities we lack or desire. This can be a positive force, inspiring growth and aspiration. However, it can also lead to envy and resentment, particularly when the perceived perfection of others highlights our own perceived inadequacies. The constant comparison inherent in the Imaginary fuels these dynamics, creating a relentless cycle of admiration and self-criticism. The body becomes a battleground for these internal conflicts, a tangible manifestation of our perceived successes and failures in aligning ourselves with the desired image.

The phantom limb phenomenon, a curious and often distressing experience, offers a potent illustration of the Imaginary body's power. Even after the physical amputation of a limb, the individual may continue to feel the presence of that limb, experiencing sensations ranging from itching to intense pain. This is not a delusion in the psychotic sense, but rather a testament to the enduring power of the imaginary representation of the body. The brain continues to hold the image of the complete body, and the absence of the physical limb creates a disconnect between this ingrained image and the altered corporeal reality. The sensations, though originating from a non-existent limb, are intensely real to the individual, highlighting how deeply our sense of embodiment is tied to the visual and imagined form of our body.

In this Imaginary dimension, the body is often experienced as a foreign object, something to be controlled, manipulated, and perfected according to external ideals. The lived experience of bodily existence – the warmth of the sun on the skin, the ache of tired muscles, the rhythm of breathing – can be overshadowed by the relentless pursuit of an idealized visual representation. This disconnect is not merely a superficial concern; it has profound implications for our mental and physical well-being, contributing to a pervasive sense of unease, dissatisfaction, and a profound alienation from our own embodied selves. The illusion of wholeness, while initially a source of integration, can ultimately become a cage, trapping us in a perpetual cycle of striving for an image that can never truly be embodied. The body, in its raw, unmediated truth, remains elusive, masked by the shimmering veil of the Imaginary. The desire to inhabit the perfect image becomes a driving force, shaping our relationship with our physical selves in ways that are both profound and often deeply disquieting. It is within this realm that we begin to understand the seductive power of appearances and the profound impact that imagined ideals have on our lived corporeal reality. The body, as seen, as imagined, as identified with, becomes a central stage for the drama of selfhood, a drama often played out in the theatre of illusion and the relentless pursuit of an unattainable perfection. This emphasis on the visual, on the surface, can obscure the deeper, more complex realities of our embodied existence, leading to a perpetual sense of striving and often, a quiet desperation to live up to an image that is, by its very nature, an illusion.

The corporeal form, once apprehended as a mere visual construct within the Imaginary, now undergoes a profound transmutation as it enters the dominion of the Symbolic. Here, the body is no longer solely an object of identification or a canvas for idealized projections; it becomes a site inscribed with meaning, a nexus of signifiers that articulate its social and personal significance. This is the realm where language, law, and the intricate tapestry of social norms converge to shape and regulate our embodied existence, transforming the raw, lived materiality of flesh and bone into a vehicle for cultural signification. The body, in this order, is not understood in isolation but as an element within a vast semiotic network, its form and function imbued with the collective understandings and expectations of a given society.

Language, as the very architecture of the Symbolic, is instrumental in this inscription. From the moment of birth, and indeed even before, our bodies are categorized, labeled, and positioned within a pre-existing linguistic framework. The pronouncement of a name, the assignment of a gender, the categorization of race or ethnicity – these are all linguistic acts that immediately attach a web of social meanings to the physical person. These terms are not neutral descriptors; they carry with them a history of cultural associations, expectations, and often, prejudices. A body designated "male" is immediately subject to a different set of linguistic cues and social scripts than one designated "female," regardless of the individual's lived experience. These linguistic markers are the first threads in the symbolic tapestry that begins to define and constrain the body.

Consider the pervasive influence of gendered language. The very vocabulary we employ shapes our understanding of what it means to inhabit a particular gender. Terms like "masculine" and "feminine" are not merely adjectives but carry with them a dense constellation of connotations related to behavior, appearance, emotional expression, and social roles. The boy who is told he is "acting like a girl" receives a symbolic reprimand, an injunction to conform his behavior to the prescribed symbolic representation of his gender. Similarly, the girl praised for being "gentle" or "nurturing" is being reinforced in her adherence to a specific symbolic script. These linguistic reinforcements, repeated from infancy, mold the individual's self-perception and their interaction with the world, subtly but powerfully dictating how their body should be presented and inhabited. The body thus becomes a living embodiment of these symbolic distinctions, a physical manifestation of the social categories we have internalized through language.

Beyond gender, the Symbolic order dictates other significant corporeal norms. Social status, for instance, is often communicated through subtle, and not-so-subtle, bodily cues that are learned and understood within a given culture. The way one carries oneself – posture, gait, gestures – can signal education, class, or social standing. The adoption of certain fashions, the adherence to particular grooming habits, even the dialect one speaks, all serve as signifiers within the Symbolic, contributing to the construction of the body as a marker of social position. The sumptuary laws of historical periods, which dictated what clothing and adornments could be worn by different social strata, are a stark and explicit example of how the Symbolic order has directly regulated the corporeal presentation of the body to signify rank and privilege. While such laws may no longer be in effect in many contemporary societies, the underlying principle of the body as a signifier of social hierarchy persists, albeit often through more nuanced and less overt mechanisms. The individual learns to "perform" their social role through their bodily comportment, their movements, and their presentation, all guided by the invisible hand of the Symbolic.

The imposition of legal structures further solidifies the Symbolic body. Laws pertaining to public decency, for example, dictate what parts of the body can be exposed and in what contexts. These laws are not based on inherent biological necessity but on socially constructed notions of what is considered acceptable or offensive. The legal framework thus actively shapes the way bodies are clothed, presented, and perceived in public spaces. Similarly, laws regarding bodily autonomy, such as those concerning consent, are deeply intertwined with the Symbolic understanding of the body as belonging to an individual, capable of making choices and subject to certain rights and protections. These legal frameworks are not merely external constraints; they become internalized, shaping our sense of what is permissible and what is not, and influencing our self-regulation of bodily behavior. The body, in the eyes of the law, is a subject with certain rights and responsibilities, a legal entity that is recognized and regulated through the language and structures of the legal system.

The realm of acceptable bodily expression is also heavily policed by the Symbolic order. The acceptable ways to move, to express emotion, to interact physically with others are all subject to cultural scripting. A public display of intense grief or raucous laughter might be deemed inappropriate in some contexts, while celebrated in others. The permissible range of physical touch between individuals, beyond intimate relationships, is also governed by unspoken symbolic rules. These norms are learned through observation, imitation, and explicit instruction, and their transgression can lead to social disapproval, ostracism, or even more formal sanctions. The body, therefore, becomes a site where social anxieties and expectations are played out, where conformity to symbolic dictates is rewarded and deviation is punished.

Furthermore, the Symbolic order provides the framework through which we understand and regulate our own internal bodily experiences. While the Imaginary might fixate on the visual appearance of health, the Symbolic provides the language and categories through which we interpret illness. Symptoms are not just raw sensations; they are categorized as "fever," "pain," "nausea," each carrying a set of associated meanings and prescribed actions. The medical profession, a powerful institution within the Symbolic order, plays a crucial role in defining and classifying bodily states, transforming lived experience into diagnostic categories and treatment protocols. The body, when it deviates from the symbolic norm of health, becomes a site of medical intervention, subject to the expert interpretations and regulations of the Symbolic.

The concept of "proper" bodily comportment is also deeply ingrained through the Symbolic. This encompasses everything from table manners to the way one addresses superiors. These are not innate behaviors but learned performances that signify adherence to the social order. The child who is taught to "sit up straight" or "not to slouch" is not just being corrected for poor posture; they are being initiated into the symbolic language of respect and deference. The body is trained to express these social values, becoming a readable text for those who understand its symbolic grammar.

The pervasive influence of the Symbolic order on the body can also lead to a sense of alienation. When the internalized symbolic scripts about how one "should" look, feel, or behave clash with one's lived reality, a profound disconnect can emerge. An individual might feel their body is inadequate because it does not conform to the symbolic ideals of beauty, strength, or youth that are constantly disseminated through media and cultural narratives. This internal conflict, born from the tension between the lived body and the symbolic representation of the ideal body, can manifest in various forms of distress, from body dissatisfaction to more severe psychological conditions. The body, in this scenario, is experienced as a site of failure, a constant reminder of one's inability to fully inhabit the symbolic ideal.

Moreover, the Symbolic order is inherently hierarchical. The meanings attached to certain bodily presentations are often imbued with value judgments that privilege some over others. For example, certain body types might be associated with desirability, intelligence, or competence, while others are linked to laziness, ignorance, or unattractiveness. These symbolic associations, often rooted in historical power dynamics and social prejudices, can have profound and lasting impacts on individuals' lives, influencing their opportunities, their self-esteem, and their overall well-being. The body, in this sense, becomes a battleground for social ideologies, where dominant symbolic meanings can marginalize and devalue certain corporeal realities.

The imposition of the Symbolic order on the body is a continuous process, beginning in infancy and persisting throughout life. It is through the internalization of language, social norms, and legal structures that our raw corporeal existence is transformed into a meaningful and socially legible entity. This process is not without its complexities and its costs, as the symbolic dictates can both enable social cohesion and impose significant constraints on individual expression and lived experience. The body, as a product of the Symbolic, is thus an intricate interplay of biological materiality and socio-linguistic signification, a testament to the profound ways in which our cultural environment shapes even our most fundamental sense of self. The very notion of a "natural" body is a myth, as all corporeal existence is, to some degree, mediated and structured by the Symbolic order. It is through this order that we learn to navigate the social world, to understand our place within it, and to present ourselves in ways that are deemed acceptable and meaningful by our peers. The body, in its symbolic dimension, is a constant negotiation between the internal promptings of our lived experience and the external demands of the socio-linguistic matrix into which we are born.

The Real body, that irreducible kernel of being, stands as a stark counterpoint to the meticulously constructed corporeal forms of the Imaginary and the Symbolic orders. It is the raw, unmediated flux of sensation, the undeniable thrum of existence before it is filtered through representation or categorized by language. This is the realm of pure experience, the visceral encountering of the world and oneself, unburdened by meaning or interpretation. Think of the blinding flash of a sudden pain, so intense that it obliterates thought, leaving only the stark, undeniable fact of suffering. Or the primal jolt of fear, a purely physiological response that bypasses cognitive appraisal, seizing the body in its unyielding grip. These are moments when the Real asserts itself, a stark reminder of our fundamental embodiment, a materiality that precedes and, at times, overwhelms our symbolic grasp.

This dimension of the Real is intimately connected to the phenomena that lie at the edges of our lived experience, those events and states that fundamentally challenge our capacity for comprehension and articulation. Trauma, in particular, serves as a potent gateway to the Real. A traumatic event, by its very nature, is an experience that defies narrative, an intrusion of overwhelming force that fractures the continuity of subjective time and space. The mind struggles to integrate such an experience into its existing symbolic framework, leaving behind a psychic wound that echoes with the unrepresentable horror of its origin. The body, too, bears the indelible imprint of trauma, not merely as a site of injury, but as a repository of a terror that resists verbalization. The phantom limb pain, the involuntary tremors, the hypervigilance – these are not simply symptoms; they are eruptions of the Real, the body's insistent, unsymbolized memory of a violation that language cannot fully contain. The individual may recount the events of the trauma, but the raw, overwhelming sensation, the sheer terror of that moment, remains stubbornly elusive, a ghost in the machine of representation.

Death, too, stands as a monumental portal to the Real. It is the ultimate limit of our symbolic universe, the point beyond which our narratives, our identifications, our very sense of self, cease to have purchase. While we may develop elaborate symbolic rituals, philosophical discourses, and religious beliefs surrounding death, these are ultimately attempts to contain and make sense of an experience that, in its essence, is the undoing of all sense. The physical cessation of life, the literal disintegration of the organic form, is a stark and irrefutable datum of the Real. It is the ultimate confrontation with finitude, with the unceremonious end of the organism, a materiality that returns to the earth, unburdened by the ego's grand narratives or the Symbolic order's intricate web of meaning. The fear of death is not simply an intellectual apprehension of non-existence; it is a visceral, bodily dread of this ultimate dissolution, a primal recognition of our inherent vulnerability to the irreversible processes of decay and annihilation. The cadaver, in its stark, silent presence, is a potent symbol of the Real – a body stripped of its symbolic accoutrements, its social roles, its personal history, reduced to its bare, undeniable materiality.

The Real body is also the site of

jouissance, a Lacanian concept that denotes a radical, often excessive, form of pleasure or enjoyment that transcends the ordinary economy of desire and satisfaction. It is an intensity that can be both exhilarating and terrifying, a surplus that strains the Symbolic and Imaginary apparatuses that seek to regulate and contain it. Imagine the ecstatic abandon of a dancer lost in the rhythm, the body moving with an energy that seems to emanate from a source beyond conscious control. Or the overwhelming sensation of profound sexual climax, a moment where the boundaries of the self dissolve in a wave of pure, unmediated sensation. These experiences, while often interpreted through symbolic lenses, possess a raw, uncontainable quality that points to the Real. This *jouissance* is not simply pleasure; it is a surplus, an excess that spills over the boundaries of what can be comfortably assimilated into our symbolic understanding of self and pleasure. It can be a source of profound creativity and vitality, but it also carries the potential for disintegration, for a loss of self that can be both liberating and deeply unsettling. The pursuit of *jouissance* can lead individuals to push the boundaries of their physical and psychological limits, seeking those intense moments that affirm their existence in the most visceral way possible, even at the risk of self-destruction.

This dimension of the Real is also where we encounter the sheer contingency of our existence, the uncomfortable truth that our bodies are not eternal, not entirely under our control, and subject to the whims of chance and biological processes. The unexpected illness, the sudden accident, the inevitable aging process – these are all manifestations of a bodily reality that is fundamentally fragile and subject to forces beyond our symbolic mastery. The body's susceptibility to disease, its eventual decay, its proneness to injury, all point to an underlying materiality that is inherently vulnerable. We strive to impose order through medicine, through healthy lifestyles, through symbolic representations of perpetual youth and vitality, but the Real persists, a persistent reminder of our inherent mortality and the precariousness of our embodied existence. The organ transplant, for instance, while a triumph of medical technology, also highlights the precariousness of our biological selves. A vital organ can fail, requiring replacement, underscoring that the body is not a seamless, self-sufficient entity but a complex, often vulnerable, machine susceptible to breakdown.

The Real body, in its resistance to full symbolization, also reveals the limitations of language and representation. We can describe the sensation of hunger, but we can never truly convey the raw, gnawing emptiness of it to someone who has not experienced it. We can speak of the color red, but the subjective experience of seeing red, the qualia of it, remains stubbornly private and beyond linguistic capture. This is the fundamental gap that Lacan identifies between the signifier and the signified, a gap that is most keenly felt when we attempt to articulate the raw, immediate experiences of the Real. The more we attempt to translate these experiences into language, the more we inevitably flatten them, tame them, and abstract them, losing something of their original intensity and immediacy. The attempt to describe a profound, ineffable feeling of loss, for example, often results in a series of approximations, of metaphors and similes that, while evocative, can never fully capture the precise shade of that unique desolation. The words themselves become a kind of symbolic gauze, softening the sharp edges of the Real experience.

Consider the artistic impulse to represent the body. While art can powerfully evoke emotions and ideas associated with the body, it always remains a representation, a symbolic rendering. A painting of a starving child can elicit empathy and understanding, but it cannot replicate the visceral agony of starvation. A sculpture of a powerful physique can inspire admiration, but it cannot transmit the raw sensation of muscular exertion. The artist works within the symbolic order, using its tools – color, line, form, narrative – to create an echo of the Real, a resonating impression that invites the viewer to engage with their own embodied experience. Yet, the object of art, however potent, is not the thing itself. It is a signifier pointing towards a signified that ultimately eludes its grasp. The more a culture attempts to codify and represent the body, whether through idealized artistic canons, medical diagrams, or fashion trends, the more it risks obscuring the Real, the unpredictable, uncontainable materiality that lies beneath the surface of these symbolic constructions.

Furthermore, the Real manifests in bodily states that defy easy categorization or control, those moments when the body seems to act independently of our will or our symbolic understanding. Sleepwalking, for instance, is a state where the body moves and interacts with the environment in ways that are utterly opaque to the conscious, symbolic self. The dreamer acts out scenarios, navigates spaces, and performs actions that are alien to their waking identity, revealing a dimension of the body that operates outside the usual channels of conscious control and symbolic integration. These nocturnal journeys into the Real can be both bewildering and strangely potent, hinting at subterranean currents of desire and anxiety that find expression when the Symbolic order is temporarily suspended. Similarly, the involuntary spasms of a seizure, the uncontrollable weeping of deep grief, or the visceral revulsion to certain stimuli, all represent instances where the body's responses erupt with an autonomy that resists immediate symbolic explanation. They are primal reactions that bypass the deliberative faculties, asserting their power as fundamental bodily truths.

The Real body is also the locus of a profound unknowing. We may understand the biological mechanisms of our bodies with increasing scientific precision, but the subjective experience of inhabiting a body remains, in many ways, a mystery. We can analyze the neurochemical processes of emotion, but we cannot fully explain

why a particular melody can evoke a cascade of nostalgic memories, or *why* the scent of rain on dry earth can stir a deep, inexplicable sense of peace. These are experiences that arise from the complex interplay of our embodied selves and our environment, a nexus where the Real stubbornly resists a complete rational dissection. Our lived experience of the body is always in excess of what science can measure or language can articulate. It is a domain of intuition, of feeling, of a bodily wisdom that often operates beneath the threshold of conscious awareness.

The struggle with the Real is an ongoing aspect of the human condition. We are creatures who crave meaning, who seek to impose order and narrative onto the flux of existence. Yet, we are also embodied beings, tethered to a materiality that is, at times, unruly, inexplicable, and ultimately, finite. The Symbolic order provides us with the tools to navigate the social world, to communicate, to build communities, and to construct a coherent sense of self. The Imaginary allows us to dream, to idealize, to create visions of what we might become. But the Real is the ever-present undertow, the reminder of what lies beyond our comprehension, beyond our control, beyond the comforting illusions we construct. It is in the moments when these frameworks falter, when the body asserts its raw, unyielding presence, that we are brought face to face with the fundamental truths of our embodied existence – our vulnerability, our finitude, and the ultimate inscrutability of being alive. To acknowledge the Real body is to embrace a certain humility, a recognition that there are dimensions of our existence that will always elude our full grasp, that will always retain an element of mystery and irreducible materiality. It is in this confrontation with the limits of our knowing, with the stark presence of what cannot be fully captured, that we may begin to approach a more authentic understanding of ourselves as embodied beings, irrevocably shaped by the encounter with that which lies beyond the comforting reach of language and representation. The Real body is not merely a biological entity; it is the persistent whisper of the unrepresentable, the fundamental contingency that underpins our every moment of existence, a testament to the profound mysteries that reside within our very flesh and bone.

The intricate dance between the Imaginary, the Symbolic, and the Real is not a static arrangement but a perpetual, dynamic interplay that forms the very foundation of our psychic functioning. It is within this ceaseless negotiation that the contours of our embodied experience are etched, that our desires find their elusive targets, and that the enigmatic phenomenon of symptoms arises. To speak of psychic life is, in essence, to speak of this complex, interwoven fabric, where the threads of fantasy, language, and irreducible materiality are perpetually being woven and rewoven. The body, far from being a simple biological vessel, becomes the very stage upon which this tripartite drama unfolds, its sensations, pains, and pleasures registering the ongoing tensions and resolutions between these fundamental dimensions of being.

Consider, for a moment, the formation of a psychological symptom. It is rarely a simple cause-and-effect phenomenon, but rather a knot, a point of fixation, where the Imaginary, Symbolic, and Real have become entangled in a particularly problematic way.

A phobia, for instance, is a classic illustration of this intricate dynamic. The Imaginary dimension might conjure a terrifying, exaggerated image of the feared object – a spider that is not just large, but monstrous, its legs impossibly numerous and sharp, its eyes burning with malevolent intent. This phantasm, born from primal anxieties and perhaps fuelled by a childhood narrative (itself a symbolic construct), is then powerfully linked to a specific object in the Real. This link, however, is not a direct one. The Real spider, in its actual biological existence, is often less formidable than its Imaginary counterpart. The crucial element is the Symbolic imbuation of the object with overwhelming danger. Language, or the lack thereof, plays a critical role. The child might be told, in stark, absolute terms, that "spiders are deadly," a Symbolic pronouncement that, when internalized, imbues the arachnid with a terrifying significance that far outweighs its objective reality. The resulting phobic response – the overwhelming panic, the physical revulsion, the desperate need to escape – is a manifestation of the Real body reacting to this potent, albeit distorted, concatenation of Imaginary fantasy and Symbolic threat. The symptom, in this case, is the unbearable eruption of this unresolved entanglement, a psychic shorthand for a conflict that the individual cannot otherwise process.

The negotiation of desire is another arena where the interplay of these three orders is profoundly evident. Our desires are never purely biological urges; they are always shaped, mediated, and often distorted by the Imaginary and the Symbolic. We might feel a basic biological drive for nourishment, but what we desire to eat, how we desire to eat it, and when we feel justified in satisfying that hunger are all heavily influenced by our Imaginary ideals and the Symbolic codes of our culture. The allure of a particular brand of chocolate, for example, is not solely based on its taste. It is often tied to Imaginary fantasies of indulgence, of reward, of a particular lifestyle projected onto the product through advertising – a sophisticated weaving of Symbolic language and Imaginary imagery. The Symbolic order dictates the social acceptability of certain desires, the language we use to express them, and the rituals we employ to fulfill them. The Real, in this context, can be understood as the inevitable limit, the point where desire encounters the unyielding facts of our embodiment, our circumstances, and our mortality. The satisfaction of desire is often fleeting, a temporary arrest of the ceasular pursuit, and the return of a new desire or the intensified yearning for what remains unattainable points to the constant movement and tension between these dimensions.

Trauma offers a particularly stark and devastating illustration of how disruptions in this tripartite interplay can lead to profound psychological distress and somatic manifestations. When a traumatic event occurs, it is often an overwhelming intrusion of the Real that shatters the protective buffers of the Imaginary and the Symbolic. The sheer horror of the event, its suddenness, its violation of our fundamental sense of safety, can be so potent that it exceeds our capacity to symbolize it. The language we possess, the narratives we have constructed, prove utterly inadequate to contain the experience. The Symbolic order, which usually provides meaning and coherence, is fractured. The Imaginary, which might normally offer avenues for fantasy and escape, is overwhelmed by the terrifying reality. The result is a psychic wound where the Real, in its raw, unrepresentable intensity, remains trapped, unable to be processed through meaning-making.

This unresolved Real then exerts a persistent, disruptive influence on the individual's psychic functioning. The symptom becomes a way for the unsymbolized Real to make itself known, a jagged eruption from beneath the surface of what can be articulated. This can manifest in a variety of ways, often as somatic symptoms that defy conventional medical explanation. Consider the phenomenon of dissociation, where a person may feel detached from their body, as if observing themselves from the outside. This can be understood as a radical defense mechanism, an attempt to distance the Symbolic self from the overwhelming Real experience that is imprinted on the body. The body, in this instance, becomes a site of unbearable truth, and dissociation is a desperate attempt to escape its unbearable reality.

Furthermore, the Real body, having been invaded by an experience that cannot be symbolically integrated, can become a source of chronic, inexplicable pain or physical distress. This is not to say that such pain is "imaginary" in the colloquial sense of being unreal; rather, it signifies the way in which the Real, unmediated by Symbolic understanding, can become a persistent, physical burden. The body remembers the trauma in a way that bypasses narrative and meaning, expressing it through physical suffering. This can take the form of hypervigilance, where the body is in a perpetual state of alert, ready to flee from a danger that may no longer be present but is indelibly imprinted on the nervous system – a Real bodily memory of threat. It can also manifest as flashbacks, where fragments of the traumatic experience, often sensory in nature (a sound, a smell, a fleeting image), erupt into the present, re-traumatizing the individual and demonstrating the persistent intrusion of the unsymbolized Real.

The constant negotiation between these dimensions is therefore not merely an academic concept; it is the very engine of our psychological lives. When this negotiation is fluid and adaptive, we experience a sense of coherence, of agency, and of well-being. Our Imaginary fantasies enrich our lives without overwhelming us, our Symbolic representations allow us to connect and communicate effectively, and our engagement with the Real, while challenging, is ultimately integrated into our understanding of ourselves and the world. However, when the balance is disrupted, when the Real overwhelms the Symbolic and Imaginary, or when the Symbolic becomes so rigid that it stifles Imaginary exploration or denies the Real, then psychic distress inevitably arises.

The concept of

jouissance, as explored in relation to the Real body, further illuminates this dynamic. This excessive, uncontainable enjoyment, this surplus of sensation that strains the Symbolic and Imaginary apparatuses, highlights the inherent tension between the body's raw materiality and our attempts to regulate and understand it. When *jouissance* is experienced, it can feel like a direct encounter with the Real – a moment of intense, perhaps overwhelming, pleasure or even pain that transcends ordinary categories of desire and satisfaction. The Symbolic order often struggles to contain or even acknowledge such intensity, tending to reduce it to more manageable concepts of pleasure or ecstasy. The Imaginary might then attempt to idealize or reframe this experience, turning it into a fantasy of ultimate fulfillment.

However, the disruptive potential of

jouissance lies precisely in its resistance to such containment. An individual seeking to repeatedly access this intensity, perhaps through extreme sports, risky behaviors, or even certain forms of artistic expression, might be driven by a desire to affirm their existence in the face of its ultimate finitude – a confrontation with the Real. The very act of pushing the boundaries of the body and psyche can be seen as an attempt to provoke a powerful encounter with the Real, an encounter that, while exhilarating, also carries the inherent risk of disintegration, of losing oneself in the excess. The Symbolic and Imaginary frameworks, which normally provide a sense of self and stability, can be strained to their breaking point when confronted with the raw, untamed force of *jouissance*. The resulting psychic functioning might appear as obsessive pursuit, self-destructive tendencies, or a profound sense of unease that arises from the unresolvable tension between the desire for this intense encounter with the Real and the need for the Symbolic and Imaginary structures that sustain a coherent sense of self.

The formation of neurotic symptoms, for example, can be understood as a compromise formation, a way of both expressing and containing a repressed desire or a traumatic memory that stems from the interplay of these dimensions. A compulsive ritual, such as excessive handwashing, might be an attempt to symbolically cleanse oneself of a perceived contamination (a manifestation of the Real), driven by an underlying Imaginary fantasy of impurity, and sanctioned by a rigid Symbolic rule that dictates cleanliness above all else. The ritual provides a temporary, albeit insufficient, resolution to the underlying psychic tension, but it also perpetuates the entanglement of the Imaginary, Symbolic, and Real, creating a cycle of distress. The symptom, in this sense, is a signal of the ongoing struggle to integrate these disparate dimensions of experience.

The very process of psychoanalytic treatment can be viewed as an endeavor to re-establish a more fluid and adaptive interplay between the Imaginary, Symbolic, and Real. Through the analytic process, the patient is encouraged to give voice to their Imaginary fantasies, to explore the Symbolic meanings they have assigned to their experiences, and to confront the intrusions of the Real that have disrupted their psychic equilibrium. The transference, where the patient unconsciously re-enacts past relational patterns with the analyst, provides a unique space for this renegotiation. The analyst, as a figure in the Symbolic order, can help the patient to deconstruct distorted Imaginary projections and to reframe traumatic encounters with the Real. By providing a safe and consistent Symbolic environment, the analyst allows the patient to explore the raw emotions and sensations of the Real without being completely overwhelmed. The goal is not to eliminate the Real, or to deny the power of the Imaginary or Symbolic, but to foster a more harmonious and integrated relationship between them, allowing for a more coherent and less symptom-laden psychic functioning.

The body-psyche relationship, therefore, is not a duality but a continuum, a unified field of experience where the material and the psychological are inextricably linked. The Imaginary provides the dreams and desires that color our embodied existence, the Symbolic lends structure and meaning to our bodily experiences and social interactions, and the Real is the irreducible foundation, the raw, unfiltered encounter with existence itself, which ultimately shapes and limits both our fantasies and our symbols. When this interplay is harmonious, our embodiment is a source of vitality and connection. When it is fractured, the body becomes a site of profound suffering, a testament to the enduring power of those dimensions that lie beyond our immediate grasp and understanding. The journey of psychic health, in essence, is a continuous process of navigating this complex, ever-shifting terrain, of learning to live with the inherent tensions and paradoxes that arise from being both a creature of fantasy and language, and an organism irrevocably bound to the stark, unyielding reality of our embodied existence. The symptoms we develop, the desires we pursue, and the very way we experience our bodies are all profound indicators of this ongoing, vital negotiation.

Chapter 8: Trauma and the Embodied Scar

The indelible mark of trauma is not confined to the realm of conscious memory or abstract psychological distress; it is profoundly etched into the very fabric of our physical being. When an event overwhelms our capacity to process it through language and narrative, when the sheer force of the experience shatters our existing frameworks of understanding, it leaves behind a visceral imprint. This is not to say that the mind shuts down entirely, but rather that a part of the experience, a raw, unmediated residue, becomes lodged within the body. The body, in essence, becomes a living archive, a repository for memories that the conscious mind may struggle to access or articulate. These somatic memories are not mere echoes; they are often active, disruptive presences that can manifest years, even decades, after the initial trauma.

Consider the phenomenon of phantom limb pain, an intense sensation of pain in an appendage that has been amputated. While there is no longer a physical limb, the neural pathways that once registered sensation and pain in that area remain active, often rewired by the traumatic severing. This provides a potent, albeit metaphorical, illustration of how the body can continue to "remember" and react to a traumatic event long after the external circumstances have ceased. In the case of psychological trauma, the "amputation" is not of a physical limb, but of the capacity to integrate the experience into a coherent sense of self and narrative. The neural pathways associated with fear, threat, and distress can become hyper-sensitized, their activity triggered by stimuli that bear even a tangential resemblance to the original trauma. This creates a state of chronic hypervigilance, where the body is perpetually on alert, anticipating danger that may no longer be present in the external environment, but is very much alive within the nervous system.

This somatic memory can manifest in myriad ways, often presenting as physical ailments that elude conventional medical diagnosis. Chronic pain syndromes, unexplained fatigue, digestive disturbances, respiratory issues, and even certain autoimmune conditions have been linked to the lingering effects of unprocessed trauma. These are not "made up" symptoms; they are the body's direct, non-verbal communication of an overwhelming experience that has not been adequately symbolized or integrated. The body is speaking a language of sensation, of physiological dysregulation, a language that often bypasses the intellect and the capacity for verbal expression. For instance, a survivor of childhood abuse might experience persistent, gnawing stomach pains. Medical investigations may reveal no organic cause, yet the pain remains a constant, debilitating presence. This somatic symptom can be understood as the body's way of holding onto the terror and violation of the original experience, a physical manifestation of an emotional wound that has not healed. The stomach, a site of vulnerability and digestion, becomes a conduit for the unexpressed anguish.

The concept of a "flashback" offers another compelling insight into trauma's bodily imprint. While often associated with visual or auditory hallucinations, flashbacks are fundamentally sensory experiences. They are not simply reliving a memory; they are a re-experiencing of the physiological and emotional state of the traumatic event. A survivor of a car accident might suddenly be flooded with the smell of gasoline, the screech of tires, the visceral lurch of their stomach, and the overwhelming surge of adrenaline, even when sitting safely in their living room. These sensory fragments are potent because they bypass symbolic processing and directly access the body's stored response. The nervous system is reactivated, releasing stress hormones and triggering a cascade of physical sensations that mirror the original trauma. This re-enactment can be terrifying, leaving the individual feeling as if they are reliving the event in real-time, reinforcing the sense of danger and helplessness.

The process of dissociation, a common response to trauma, further underscores the body's role in remembering. Dissociation can range from mild detachment from one's surroundings to a profound disconnection from one's own body, identity, and memories. In severe forms, individuals may experience "fugue states" where they travel to unfamiliar places with no memory of how they got there, or exhibit "dissociative identity disorder," where distinct personality states emerge. From a somatic perspective, dissociation can be seen as a drastic attempt by the body-mind to create distance from unbearable physical and emotional sensations. The body remembers the overwhelming threat, and to survive, the individual essentially "leaves" their body, creating a schism between consciousness and embodied experience. This is a survival mechanism, a way to compartmentalize an experience so horrific that it cannot be held within a single, unified sense of self. The body, however, continues to hold the imprint, even if the conscious mind is disengaged.

The impact of trauma on the autonomic nervous system is a critical area of understanding. Trauma, particularly when it is chronic or occurs during developmental periods, can lead to a state of dysregulation in the sympathetic (fight-or-flight) and parasympathetic (rest-and-digest) nervous systems. The body can become stuck in a state of chronic arousal, constantly on edge, or conversely, it can shut down into a state of hypo-arousal, characterized by exhaustion and emotional numbing. This dysregulation is not a conscious choice; it is a physiological adaptation to a perceived, persistent threat. The body learns that vigilance is necessary for survival, and this learned response can persist even when the external environment is safe. This leads to a wide range of somatic symptoms, including sleep disturbances, anxiety, panic attacks, a weakened immune system, and a heightened sensitivity to stress. The body is literally wired for danger, even when the danger has long passed.

Furthermore, the very way we experience our bodies can be altered by trauma. A sense of embodiment, of feeling grounded and connected to one's physical self, can be severely compromised. Survivors may feel a sense of alienation from their bodies, viewing them as betraying, dangerous, or simply foreign. This can manifest as a reluctance to engage in physical activities, a heightened awareness of bodily sensations that are interpreted as threatening, or a generalized feeling of being unsafe in one's own skin. The body, which should be a source of grounding and comfort, becomes a site of chronic anxiety and vulnerability. This can have profound implications for relationships, self-esteem, and overall well-being, as the individual struggles to inhabit their physical form with a sense of safety and belonging.

The work of healing trauma, therefore, must necessarily involve the body. Traditional talk therapy, while valuable for processing memories and developing coping strategies, may not be sufficient on its own. Somatic therapies, such as Somatic Experiencing, EMDR (Eye Movement Desensitization and Reprocessing), and trauma-informed yoga, focus on releasing the stored energy of trauma from the body. These approaches work with the body's innate capacity for self-regulation and healing. By gently guiding individuals to reconnect with their bodily sensations, to track the subtle physiological responses associated with traumatic memories, and to develop new, more adaptive physiological responses, these therapies aim to re-regulate the nervous system and release the grip of somatic trauma. The goal is not to erase the memory, but to help the body integrate the experience in a way that no longer triggers a state of overwhelming threat.

The body's capacity for resilience is remarkable, but when faced with overwhelming adversity, it can bear scars that are not visible to the naked eye. These are the scars of altered physiological states, of hyper-sensitized neural pathways, of a nervous system that has learned to live in a state of perpetual alert. Understanding trauma's imprint on the body is crucial for comprehensive healing. It acknowledges that the trauma is not just a story, but a lived, felt experience that continues to resonate within the physical self. It recognizes that the body remembers, and in remembering, it communicates the depth of the wound and the urgent need for a healing that embraces the totality of the individual – mind, body, and spirit. The journey back to wholeness often begins with listening to what the body has been silently, and sometimes screamingly, trying to tell us. It is a testament to the enduring interconnectedness of our psychic and somatic lives, a profound reminder that when we speak of trauma, we are speaking of a wound that permeates every aspect of our being. The body, in its silent suffering and its potential for recovery, holds a vital key to understanding and overcoming the devastating legacy of traumatic experience.

When the unbearable weight of a traumatic event crushes the capacity for immediate integration, the intricate dance between mind and body can falter, leading to a profound and often disorienting state known as dissociation. This is not a deliberate act of will, but a desperate, albeit unconscious, strategy for survival. The sheer magnitude of the threat, the overwhelming intensity of fear and helplessness, can create a psychic chasm, a separation so deep that the individual effectively splits off from their own experience. It is as if the organism, faced with an onslaught it cannot process or endure, opts to divide its consciousness, to disengage from the immediate, unbearable reality. This division can manifest in a spectrum of experiences, each bearing the hallmark of disconnection.

At its milder end, dissociation might present as a generalized feeling of unreality, a sense that the world around has become muted, dreamlike, or even staged. The colours might seem less vibrant, sounds more distant, and the flow of time could feel distorted – either slowing to a crawl or accelerating at an alarming pace. This sense of derealization is akin to viewing life through a thick pane of glass, observing events unfold without truly participating in them. The individual might feel like a spectator to their own life, detached from the unfolding narrative. They can describe conversations happening around them, but the emotional resonance, the visceral connection to the unfolding present, is absent. This detachment serves as a protective buffer, a way to distance oneself from the immediate emotional pain and terror. The raw, unfiltered reality of the trauma is too much to bear, so the mind creates a subtle but significant distance, allowing the individual to endure without being completely annihilated by the experience.

More intensely, dissociation can manifest as depersonalization, a profound sense of alienation from oneself. The individual may feel as though they are no longer inhabiting their own body, observing their actions and thoughts from an external vantage point. Their limbs might feel heavy and unresponsive, or conversely, eerily light and disconnected, as if they belong to someone else. The voice they hear speaking might sound unfamiliar, the gestures they make feel alien. This is not a metaphorical feeling of being "out of sorts"; it is a deeply unsettling perceptual distortion where the very sense of self, the anchor of embodied identity, becomes fractured. They might look in the mirror and not entirely recognize the reflection, or feel a chilling disconnect between their internal sense of being and the physical form they occupy. This can be particularly terrifying when it occurs during moments of stress or perceived danger, as the fundamental ground of one's own existence feels compromised. The body, once the familiar vessel of self, transforms into an object that is observed rather than inhabited.

Amnesia, in its various forms, is another powerful manifestation of dissociative fragmentation. This can range from forgetting specific details of the traumatic event to experiencing larger gaps in memory, periods of time where consciousness seems to have simply vanished. This forgetting is not a passive failing of recall; it is an active defense mechanism. The mind, in its attempt to protect itself from the overwhelming pain and horror of the trauma, essentially locks away the memories, rendering them inaccessible to conscious awareness. These forgotten experiences, however, do not simply disappear. They often lie dormant, influencing behaviour and emotional states in subtle, unconscious ways. The individual might find themselves inexplicably drawn to certain situations, or reacting with intense fear to seemingly innocuous triggers, without understanding the underlying cause rooted in their forgotten past. The amnesia creates a void, a blank space where an experience should be, but the echo of that void can still be felt.

The feeling of detachment from one's own body is a particularly salient aspect of trauma-related dissociation. The body, which should be a source of grounding and a conduit for experiencing the world, can become a site of profound alienation. Survivors may describe their bodies as feeling numb, as if they are wrapped in cotton wool, or as if the sensations are not their own. Pain might be perceived as distant, pleasure as unattainable. This somatic disconnection is a direct consequence of the body's response to overwhelming threat. When the system is overloaded, the capacity to process sensory input accurately and coherently can break down. The body, in its effort to shield the individual from unbearable suffering, can effectively shut down its ability to transmit certain sensations, creating a chasm between the conscious mind and the physical self. This can lead to a profound sense of isolation, a feeling of being trapped within a shell that no longer feels like home.

Consider the phenomenological experience of this bodily disconnection. A survivor of severe physical assault might describe their legs as feeling like they are no longer attached to them, especially when attempting to walk. The sensation of their feet hitting the ground might be dulled, the proprioceptive feedback that normally informs them of their body's position in space becomes unreliable. They might report feeling a constant, low-grade tremor that they cannot consciously control, or conversely, a profound stillness that feels unnatural, a kind of internal paralysis. Even simple acts like touching their own skin can feel strange, as if they are interacting with an object rather than their own embodied self. This alienation can extend to a profound distrust of the body, viewing it as a betrayer, a source of weakness or vulnerability that failed to protect them. The physical sensations that should be cues for navigating the world become sources of confusion and anxiety. The body, so intricately woven into the fabric of identity and experience, becomes a stranger.

This fragmentation of the self, this psychic and somatic schism, is a testament to the astonishing adaptive capacity of the human psyche under duress. Dissociation is not a sign of weakness, but a powerful, albeit maladaptive, survival mechanism. It is the mind's and body's attempt to compartmentalize an experience that is too immense, too horrific, to be integrated into a coherent sense of self. The trauma shatters the illusion of safety and predictability, and in its wake, the individual is left to contend with a fractured reality. The body becomes a vessel carrying the weight of unintegrated experience, a silent witness to events that the conscious mind has actively disengaged from. This disconnection, while offering a temporary reprieve, creates its own set of challenges, leaving the individual feeling adrift, disconnected from themselves, from others, and from the world around them. The journey of healing, therefore, must involve not only the processing of memories and emotions but also the arduous and delicate work of re-integrating the fragmented self, of bridging the chasm between the mind that fled and the body that remained, holding its silent, embodied trauma. The goal is not to erase the dissociative response, but to understand its purpose, to acknowledge its survival value, and ultimately, to help the individual gradually and safely re-inhabit their body and their life, bringing the scattered pieces of their experience back into a coherent and embodied whole. This process requires patience, compassion, and a deep respect for the complex ways in which trauma can reshape our very perception of reality and our sense of self. The feeling of being disconnected from one's body can also manifest as a profound emptiness or hollowness, as if there is a void where vitality and sensation should reside. Survivors might describe feeling like a ghost, or like they are made of air, lacking substance and presence. This can impact their ability to feel pleasure, connection, or even basic physical needs like hunger or fatigue, as these somatic signals are either dulled or entirely absent. The body becomes an alien landscape, populated by phantom sensations or, more often, by a profound lack of felt experience. The vibrant spectrum of human sensation is reduced to a muted grey, or worse, a chilling void. This can lead to a pervasive sense of anhedonia, the inability to experience joy or pleasure, as the very capacity to feel deeply is compromised. The world loses its colour, its texture, its engaging dynamism, becoming instead a flat, uninteresting panorama viewed from a detached distance. The social interactions that should provide warmth and belonging can feel like performances, where the individual is playing a role rather than authentically participating. The lack of genuine embodied connection can lead to profound loneliness, even when surrounded by others. The body, intended as a means of connection to the external world and to one's internal landscape, becomes a barrier.

The phenomenon of emotional numbing, a common consequence of trauma-induced dissociation, further illustrates this disconnection. While the body might be physically present, the capacity to experience and express emotions is significantly impaired. Joy, sadness, anger, fear – the rich tapestry of human affect – can become inaccessible. This is not to say that emotions are absent, but rather that they are experienced in a muted, distant, or even entirely absent way. The individual might intellectually understand that they "should" feel something in a particular situation, but the actual felt experience is missing. This can lead to a sense of emptiness, a feeling of being emotionally dead or hollow. This emotional anaesthesia is a protective mechanism, preventing the re-experiencing of the overwhelming emotions associated with the trauma. However, it also isolates the individual from the full spectrum of human experience and can make genuine connection with others incredibly difficult. Without the ability to feel, to empathize, or to express a full range of emotions, relationships can become superficial and unsatisfying. The body, in its suppressed emotional state, becomes a silent observer of a life that is being lived but not fully felt.

This state of emotional detachment can also manifest as a difficulty in forming and maintaining relationships. When one feels disconnected from their own body and emotions, it becomes challenging to connect with the emotions and experiences of others. The subtle cues of non-verbal communication, the shared empathic responses that underpin healthy relationships, can be missed or misinterpreted. The individual might appear aloof, indifferent, or detached, leading others to feel shut out or confused. This can create a vicious cycle, where the isolation caused by dissociation further reinforces the sense of being disconnected and alone. The fear of intimacy can also be a significant factor, as close emotional connection might inadvertently trigger memories or sensations associated with the trauma, leading to a defensive retreat into the dissociative state. The body, unable to express or process emotional distress, becomes a barrier to authentic human connection, leaving the individual feeling adrift in a sea of emotional isolation.

Furthermore, the dissociation from the body can lead to a neglect of its needs. Without a clear sense of embodied presence, basic self-care can fall by the wayside. Eating, sleeping, hygiene – these fundamental aspects of well-being can be overlooked or performed mechanically, without the accompanying sense of self-nurturing. The body, no longer perceived as a living, feeling entity, becomes an object that needs to be managed, or worse, a burden to be endured. This can lead to a deterioration of physical health, exacerbating existing vulnerabilities and creating new ones. The neglect of the body is a direct reflection of the psychic disconnection, a symptom of a deeper alienation from oneself. The body, starved of attention and care, can begin to protest through illness or chronic pain, even if the conscious mind remains largely detached from these somatic experiences.

The experience of depersonalization can also extend to a distortion of self-perception in relation to time and space. The individual might feel as though they are outside of their own timeline, observing their past, present, and future from a distance. Events that occurred years ago might feel as if they happened yesterday, while recent events might feel like they are from a distant past. This temporal disorientation further contributes to the sense of unreality and fragmentation. Similarly, spatial perceptions can be altered. The individual might feel as though they are floating, or that the ground beneath them is unstable. The familiar contours of their environment might seem distorted or foreign, adding to the overall sense of unease and detachment. This disorientation serves to underscore the profound disruption of the individual's sense of continuity and coherence. The very framework through which we understand our existence – time, space, and self – has been fundamentally shaken by the trauma.

In some instances, the dissociative fragmentation can be so severe that it impacts the sense of personal agency and control. The individual may feel that they are not the author of their own actions, that their body is moving or speaking on its own accord, without their conscious direction. This can be a deeply frightening experience, as it undermines the fundamental belief in one's own capacity to act in the world. It is as if the reins of control have been handed over to an unknown force, leaving the individual a passive observer of their own life. This loss of agency is directly linked to the dissociation from the embodied self, as the body is the primary instrument through which we exercise our will and intention in the world. When the connection between intention and action is severed, the sense of being an active participant in one's life is profoundly diminished.

The re-integration of these fragmented aspects of the self is a central challenge in trauma recovery. It requires a gradual and careful process of re-establishing a connection with the body, with emotions, and with the narrative of one's life. This often involves therapeutic approaches that focus on somatic awareness, emotional regulation, and the gentle exploration of traumatic memories in a safe and contained environment. The aim is not to force the individual to re-experience the overwhelming aspects of the trauma, but rather to help them to gradually reclaim the parts of themselves that were disowned or fragmented in the service of survival. It is about helping the individual to find their way back home, back into their own skin, and to reclaim their sense of embodied presence and agency in the world. The journey of healing is, in essence, a journey of re-membering – not just the traumatic events, but the fragmented pieces of the self, bringing them back together into a coherent and integrated whole. This is a process that demands immense courage, but it is a journey that holds the promise of profound healing and the reclaiming of a full and embodied life. The body, so long a site of alienation and fear, can gradually transform into a source of strength, resilience, and connection.

The shadow of trauma extends far beyond the well-documented landscape of Post-Traumatic Stress Disorder. While the hypervigilance, intrusive memories, and avoidance behaviours characteristic of PTSD are crucial to recognize, they represent only a portion of the profound and often insidious ways a traumatic experience can imprint itself upon the body. The body, far from being a mere spectator to psychic distress, becomes an active participant, a canvas upon which the unspeakable is etched. When the mind, in its desperate bid for survival, compartmentalizes or dissociates, the physical organism often shoulders the burden of what cannot be consciously processed or expressed. This leads to a constellation of somatic symptoms that can emerge long after the immediate danger has passed, presenting as chronic pain, debilitating fatigue, and even the dysregulation of internal bodily systems, sometimes culminating in the development of autoimmune disorders. These are not psychosomatic in the pejorative sense, as if the symptoms are "imagined" or "less real" than those directly linked to the trauma narrative. Instead, they are deeply real physical manifestations of an overwhelmed biological system, the body's enduring attempt to contain, communicate, or discharge the energy of an unbearable experience.

Consider the chronic pain that can plague survivors. This pain is often diffuse, migrating, or seemingly unexplainable by conventional medical diagnoses. It can be a constant, dull ache, a searing, sharp agony, or a sensation of deep bruising that never fully subsides. This is not merely a psychological complaint; it is a tangible experience of suffering. The body, having experienced an overwhelming threat, can become sensitized, its pain pathways hyperactive. The nervous system, perpetually on alert, misinterprets even benign stimuli as dangerous, triggering alarm signals that manifest as pain. Imagine a soldier who, after a harrowing combat experience, finds themselves unable to shake off a persistent ache in their shoulders, a phantom burden of the weight they carried, both literally and metaphorically, during their deployment. This pain isn't a conscious choice; it's a somatic echo of the immense physical and emotional strain endured. It becomes a language the body speaks when words fail, a constant reminder of a reality that was too much to bear. This persistent physical discomfort can lead to a pervasive sense of being unwell, a depletion of energy that goes beyond mere tiredness.

Fatigue, in its most extreme forms, is another pervasive somatic consequence of trauma. This is not the fleeting tiredness after a long day's work, but a profound, bone-deep exhaustion that no amount of rest seems to alleviate. The body's energy reserves are continuously depleted by the sustained activation of the stress response. The constant state of alarm, the hypervigilance, the emotional hyper-arousal, and the underlying physiological changes that accompany these states demand an enormous amount of energy. This leaves the individual feeling constantly drained, struggling with basic daily tasks, and experiencing a significant reduction in their capacity to engage with life. This chronic fatigue can feel like wading through thick mud, where every movement requires immense effort. It can lead to social withdrawal, as the energy required for interaction becomes insurmountable, further isolating the individual and reinforcing the impact of the trauma. The body is, in essence, running on fumes, its systems chronically taxed by the lingering effects of an overwhelming threat.

The body's internal regulatory systems can also be profoundly disrupted by trauma. The intricate balance of hormones, the functioning of the immune system, and the delicate processes of digestion are all susceptible to the long-term effects of chronic stress. This dysregulation can manifest in a variety of ways, including gastrointestinal disturbances, such as Irritable Bowel Syndrome (IBS), inflammatory bowel disease (IBD), or persistent nausea and digestive discomfort. The gut, often referred to as the "second brain," is highly sensitive to stress and emotional states. When the body is in a perpetual state of alarm, blood flow is diverted away from the digestive system, and the delicate balance of gut bacteria can be disrupted, leading to a cascade of physical symptoms. Imagine the churning, unpredictable discomfort experienced by someone who has survived a severe physical violation, where their very sense of bodily autonomy was violated. The internal landscape can become as chaotic and unpredictable as the external threat they faced.

Furthermore, trauma can contribute to the development or exacerbation of autoimmune disorders. In these conditions, the immune system, which is designed to protect the body from foreign invaders, mistakenly attacks the body's own healthy tissues. The chronic stress and inflammation associated with trauma can dysregulate the immune system, making it more prone to such misdirected attacks. Conditions like rheumatoid arthritis, lupus, Hashimoto's thyroiditis, and multiple sclerosis have been increasingly linked to histories of adverse childhood experiences and other forms of trauma. The body's internal defense mechanisms, meant to preserve life, become weaponized against itself, a tragic testament to the enduring power of unresolved trauma. The body, in its desperate attempt to protect itself from perceived external threats, turns inward, attacking its own cells and tissues, a profound embodiment of internal conflict.

The concept of the body's persistent state of alarm is central to understanding these somatic symptoms. When trauma occurs, the body's primitive survival mechanisms are activated. The amygdala, the brain's threat detection center, becomes highly sensitized. The sympathetic nervous system, responsible for the "fight-or-flight" response, is perpetually triggered, leading to a cascade of physiological changes: increased heart rate, elevated blood pressure, rapid breathing, and the release of stress hormones like cortisol and adrenaline. Even after the immediate danger has passed, this system can remain in a state of hyper-arousal, making the individual hypersensitive to perceived threats. This chronic activation of the stress response wears down the body, contributing to fatigue, pain, and a general sense of being unwell. It's as if the body is constantly bracing for impact, even when the storm has long since passed. This constant tension can manifest physically as muscle rigidity, headaches, and a general feeling of being on edge, both physically and emotionally.

Consider the subtle ways this alarm state can manifest. A sudden loud noise, a slammed door, or even a perceived critical tone of voice can trigger a full-blown physiological response – a racing heart, a surge of adrenaline, a desperate urge to flee or freeze. This response is often disproportionate to the actual stimulus, a sign that the alarm system is malfunctioning, stuck in a loop of perceived danger. This can make navigating everyday life incredibly challenging, as unexpected stimuli are constantly interpreted as threats. The world becomes a minefield, and the individual is perpetually on guard, expending enormous amounts of energy simply to maintain a semblance of equilibrium. This constant state of alert leaves little room for relaxation, pleasure, or spontaneity, contributing further to the pervasive sense of exhaustion and malaise.

The body's attempt to contain or express unbearable affect also plays a significant role. When emotions are too overwhelming to be processed consciously, they can become somatized. This is particularly true for emotions that are deemed unacceptable or dangerous, such as intense anger, profound grief, or overwhelming fear. These emotions, denied conscious expression, can find a somatic outlet. The body becomes a vessel for what the mind cannot or will not acknowledge. Think of the individual who, after experiencing a devastating loss, develops a chronic cough that has no apparent medical cause. The cough might be the body's way of expelling the unshed tears, the unspoken grief, a physical manifestation of a choked-back emotional storm. Similarly, suppressed rage can manifest as chronic muscle tension, migraines, or even digestive problems. The body is, in these instances, attempting to communicate distress that has been locked away from conscious awareness.

This somatization can be incredibly subtle, leading individuals and even medical professionals to overlook the connection to trauma. A persistent rash, unexplained back pain, or a tremor that comes and goes might all be expressions of deeply buried emotional pain. The body, in its wisdom, finds a way to signal that something is deeply wrong, even if the conscious mind is unaware of the source of the distress. This highlights the interconnectedness of mind and body; they are not separate entities but rather integral parts of a unified whole. When one part is wounded, the other inevitably bears the impact. The somatic symptoms are not a failure of the body, but a testament to its resilience and its persistent attempt to communicate and heal, even in the face of profound psychic injury.

The sensory overload associated with trauma can also contribute to somatic symptoms. Traumatic events are often characterized by an overwhelming intensity of sensory input – sights, sounds, smells, textures, and bodily sensations that are too intense to be processed. The body, in its effort to manage this overload, can become dysregulated. This can lead to heightened sensitivity to stimuli in the environment, such as bright lights, loud noises, or certain textures, which can trigger anxiety and physical discomfort. Conversely, the body might also develop a numbing or a blunting of sensory perception as a protective mechanism, leading to a reduced capacity to feel pleasure or even basic bodily sensations like hunger or touch. This sensory dysregulation further contributes to the feeling of being disconnected from one's body and from the world. Imagine someone who, after experiencing a fire, becomes extremely sensitive to the smell of smoke, even at faint levels, experiencing physiological distress like nausea and shortness of breath. Their body has become a highly sensitive alarm system, forever marked by the intensity of the original sensory assault.

These somatic manifestations are not a sign of weakness or a character flaw. They are the body's intelligent, albeit often maladaptive, response to overwhelming circumstances. They are the scars that remain, etched not just on the psyche, but on the very fabric of the physical organism. Recognizing these symptoms as valid and real consequences of trauma is the first step towards healing. It requires a shift in perspective, moving beyond a purely mind-centered view of trauma to embrace a more holistic understanding of its impact on the entire person, body and mind inextricably linked. The body's enduring message of distress, conveyed through pain, fatigue, and physical illness, is a call for attention, a plea for integration, and an invitation to embark on the challenging but ultimately rewarding journey of embodied healing. This journey involves acknowledging the physical manifestations of trauma not as separate ailments, but as integral parts of the trauma narrative, deserving of the same compassion and therapeutic attention as any psychological symptom. It is about helping the individual to reclaim their body, to understand its language of distress, and to facilitate its return to a state of balance and well-being, transforming the embodied scar from a source of perpetual pain into a testament to survival and resilience.

The traumatic event, in its rawest essence, operates as an irruption of the Real, a concept that, drawing from Lacanian psychoanalysis, signifies that which fundamentally resists the full embrace of language and symbolic representation. It is the brute fact of an experience that shatters the pre-existing framework of meaning, leaving the subject disoriented and fundamentally altered. This "Real" of trauma is not a narrative to be told, not a sequence of events to be neatly filed away within the Symbolic order – the vast, interconnected system of language, culture, and social norms that structures our understanding of the world. Instead, it is a raw, undifferentiated encounter with a reality that is utterly devoid of meaning, a rupture in the fabric of existence itself.

Within this framework, the body becomes the primary, often the only, site where this unspeakable Real can be encountered. When the mind recoils from the unbearable intensity of the traumatic moment, when the capacity to process and integrate the experience into a coherent psychic narrative collapses, the physical organism bears the brunt of this unmediated reality. The sensory impact of trauma – the searing heat of fire, the jarring vibration of an explosion, the crushing pressure of physical violation, the overwhelming visual of horrific scenes, the cacophony of screams and terror – these are primal data that precede and often overwhelm any attempt at symbolic ordering. They are the pure, unadulterated sensations that bypass the filters of understanding and lodge themselves directly in the flesh, in the nervous system, in the very cellular memory of the organism.

The inherent difficulty in articulating the experience of trauma, even for those who have undergone extensive therapy, stems precisely from this encounter with the Real. How does one speak of that which, by its very nature, defies speech? How does one translate the visceral terror of a moment where the self felt utterly annihilated, not through metaphor or narrative, but through the raw, unmediated impact of sensory experience? The language available to us is woven from the threads of the Symbolic order, an order that trauma has fundamentally disrupted. To attempt to speak of trauma is often to grasp at words that feel hollow, inadequate, like trying to capture lightning in a jar. The words exist, but they fail to convey the searing intensity, the sheer physicality of the encounter.

Consider the sheer sensory onslaught that can accompany a traumatic event. It is not merely the

idea of danger, but the overwhelming surge of stimuli that floods the system. The stench of burning flesh, the piercing shriek of metal tearing, the blinding flash of light followed by absolute darkness, the feeling of being submerged in an icy grip, the taste of blood in the mouth – these are not simply events to be recalled; they are physical realities that register on a deep, pre-linguistic level. These raw sensory impressions lodge themselves within the body, bypassed by the Symbolic. They become the unacknowledged residue of the trauma, a persistent echo of a moment when the world, and the self within it, ceased to make sense.

The body, therefore, becomes the repository of what cannot be assimilated into the Symbolic order. It is where the raw, undigested fragments of the Real reside. The unspeakable is not merely a psychological burden; it is a somatic reality. The physical sensations that arise from trauma – the tremors, the sudden inexplicable pains, the autonomic nervous system's relentless alarms – are not metaphors for psychological distress. They are the direct, unmediated expression of a reality that has overwhelmed the Symbolic capacity of the individual. The body, in its rawest form, becomes the locus where this irreducible Real is encountered, a stark reminder of what lies beyond the reach of language.

This raw sensory impact is crucial. It is not the

meaning of the event, but its brute sensory force that bypasses the usual channels of psychological processing. Imagine the instantaneous, visceral terror of a near-death experience. It is not the contemplation of mortality, but the sudden, overwhelming flood of sensory input – the rushing blood, the constricted airways, the distorted visual field – that defines the experience at its most primal. This unmediated sensory data becomes lodged in the nervous system, a testament to the fact that some experiences are too potent, too immediate, to be adequately translated into narrative or conceptual understanding. They exist, rather, as a kind of somatic imprint, a direct inscription of the Real onto the body.

The Symbolic order, with its intricate web of meanings and connections, is the very structure that trauma shatters. When an individual experiences trauma, this established order, which allows us to navigate the world with a sense of coherence and predictability, breaks down. The Symbolic fails to provide a framework for understanding what has happened. The event is too extreme, too illogical, too devoid of any discernible meaning within the existing system. It is precisely this inability of the Symbolic to contain the experience that makes it so profoundly destabilizing. The subject is left adrift, dispossessed of the very tools that allow for understanding and integration.

The body, then, becomes the terrain upon which this breakdown is enacted. It is where the raw fragments of the Real, the sensory data that have resisted symbolic integration, find their lodging. These fragments are not abstract ideas; they are physical sensations, visceral reactions, autonomic responses. The trembling hand, the racing heart, the inexplicable ache – these are the physical manifestations of the Real's intrusion. They are the body's attempt, often futile, to bear witness to an experience that the Symbolic order cannot accommodate.

The unspeakable nature of trauma is inextricably linked to this encounter with the Real. It is unspeakable not because the individual is unwilling to speak, but because the very experience exceeds the capacity of language to capture its essence. The raw, unfiltered sensory data of the traumatic event resists the neat categorization and narrative construction that language typically provides. It is a brute fact that registers directly on the nervous system, bypassing the cognitive and symbolic processing that would normally render an experience intelligible.

For example, a survivor of a violent assault may recall flashes of sensory detail – the glint of metal, the specific texture of the attacker's clothing, the precise scent in the air – that remain vivid and potent, yet they struggle to weave these fragments into a coherent narrative of what happened to them. These sensory impressions are the remnants of the Real, stubbornly present, resisting the ordering force of language. They are the building blocks of an experience that defies symbolic assimilation. The body, in its vulnerability and its direct connection to the sensory world, becomes the archive of these unspeakable fragments, holding the raw data of the Real long after the event has passed.

This is why the body becomes the locus of the unresolved. When the Symbolic order collapses, when the signifying chain is broken, the impact of the Real is felt most acutely in the soma. The body is the primal canvas upon which the unmediated horror of the traumatic event is inscribed. It bears the imprint of that which could not be processed, could not be named, could not be integrated into the conscious self. The raw sensory data, stripped of any interpretative framework, becomes a persistent presence, a somatic echo of a reality that shattered the subject's coherence. The physical symptoms that emerge are not simply secondary manifestations of psychological distress; they are the direct, embodied testimony of an encounter with the Real that has left an indelible scar on the very fabric of the organism. The body, in its unadorned physicality, becomes the most faithful, albeit agonizing, witness to that which lies beyond the pale of language.

The arduous journey of healing embodied trauma is not a swift erasure of pain, but a profound process of integration, a testament to the resilience of the human spirit etched not just in the mind, but in the very sinews of the body. Having explored the ways in which trauma inscribes itself upon our physical being, creating an "embodied scar," we now turn towards the delicate and potent work of transforming that scar, not into an invisible wound, but into a mark of survival, a testament to the enduring capacity for life even in the face of profound violation. This is not about forgetting, but about remembering in a way that reclaims agency and fosters wholeness.

Therapeutic approaches that acknowledge and honor the body's role in trauma are paramount in this integrative phase. Traditional talk therapies, while invaluable for processing narrative and meaning, can sometimes fall short when the primary impact of trauma has been somatic. The memory is not just in the story, but in the tightening of the chest, the phantom ache, the involuntary flinch. Therefore, a crucial evolution in trauma treatment has been the integration of somatic awareness into psychodynamic frameworks. This means that the therapist is attuned not only to the words spoken, but to the subtlest shifts in posture, breath, and muscle tension. The body's wisdom, often bypassed in the initial shock of trauma, becomes an essential guide in the healing process. Therapies like Sensorimotor Psychotherapy, Somatic Experiencing, and EMDR (Eye Movement Desensitization and Reprocessing), with its focus on bilateral stimulation, all recognize that the nervous system holds the imprint of traumatic events and that regulation of the autonomic nervous system is a critical component of healing.

The therapeutic dialogue, in these contexts, expands beyond recounting events to exploring the

felt sense of those events. When a survivor speaks of a terrifying moment, the therapist might gently inquire, "Where do you feel that in your body right now?" or "What does that sensation tell you?" This is not an invitation to re-traumatize, but to bring a present-moment, embodied awareness to the lingering effects of past trauma. By noticing these sensations in a safe, contained therapeutic space, with a compassionate witness, the body can begin to discharge the trapped energy of the traumatic response. The fight-or-flight or freeze responses, which may have been chronically activated or perpetually suppressed, can start to find their natural rhythm of activation and release. This is often experienced as subtle but profound shifts: a loosening in the shoulders, a deeper breath, a sense of grounding in the chair. These are not mere physiological changes; they are the body's way of signaling that it is beginning to feel safe enough to process what it has held captive for so long.

Integration, in this context, does not mean returning to a pre-trauma state of being. That is a romantic impossibility; the self is irrevocably changed by such profound experiences. Instead, integration is about weaving the fragmented pieces of the self, including the somatic echoes of trauma, into a new, coherent whole. It is about creating a narrative that encompasses the experience of suffering without letting it define the entirety of one's existence. This involves developing a new symbolic meaning for the embodied scar. It is no longer solely a symbol of violation and helplessness, but can become a marker of resilience, a testament to the strength required to survive and continue living.

The process of finding new symbolic meanings is deeply personal and often unfolds gradually. For some, the scar might represent an embodied understanding of vulnerability, fostering greater empathy and compassion for themselves and others. For others, it may become a potent reminder of their own inner fortitude, a quiet acknowledgment of the immense strength they possess for having endured what they did. This shift in symbolic meaning is not a conscious, intellectual decision, but a felt sense that emerges through the integration process. It is the difference between being haunted by the past and being informed by it. The embodied scar, once a source of relentless pain and a barrier to connection, can begin to signify a profound depth of human experience, a testament to the capacity for survival and, ultimately, for healing.

Consider the individual who, after experiencing a profound loss that manifested as chronic, debilitating pain, begins to engage in mindful movement practices. Initially, the pain flares with any physical exertion, a visceral reminder of the emptiness left behind. The body is a tight, guarded fortress. Through consistent, gentle exploration, guided by a therapist and possibly a movement specialist, the individual learns to differentiate between the original wound and the protective bracing that has become habitual. They begin to notice subtle shifts in the sensation, perhaps a fleeting moment of release in the musculature, or a brief period where the pain recedes from a roaring fire to a dull ember. These small victories, seemingly insignificant in the grand scheme of suffering, are monumental in the context of embodied healing. They are the initial cracks in the fortress, allowing in the light of possibility.

The therapeutic relationship itself plays a vital role in this integrative work. The therapist offers a consistent, attuned presence, creating a "secure base" from which the individual can explore the often-frightening landscape of their embodied trauma. This relational safety is crucial. Trauma often shatters the sense of trust in others and in the world; the therapeutic relationship provides an opportunity to rebuild that trust in a controlled, supportive environment. The therapist's ability to remain calm and present, even when the client is experiencing intense emotional or physical distress, helps to regulate the client's nervous system. This co-regulation is a powerful catalyst for healing, allowing the client to gradually learn that they can tolerate difficult sensations and emotions without being overwhelmed.

The concept of reclaiming bodily integrity is central to this phase. Trauma, particularly when it involves violation, can lead to a profound sense of dissociation from one's own body, a feeling of being imprisoned within a flesh that feels alien or untrustworthy. Healing involves a slow, deliberate process of re-inhabitation, of coming home to one's physical self. This might involve simple practices such as consciously noticing the contact of one's feet on the ground, feeling the weight of one's body in a chair, or savoring the taste and texture of food. These grounding techniques are not about escaping the pain, but about anchoring oneself in the present moment, in a body that is alive and capable of experiencing sensations beyond the trauma.

Furthermore, the integration of the embodied scar involves a shift from a fragmented experience of self to a more unified one. Trauma can lead to a sense of the self being shattered into pieces, with the traumatic memory existing as a separate, intrusive entity. Healing aims to bring these pieces back together, not by erasing the trauma, but by integrating its impact into the larger tapestry of one's life story. This means acknowledging the pain, the fear, and the loss, but also recognizing the strength, the resilience, and the survival that emerged from it. The scar remains, but it is no longer the dominant feature. It becomes part of a larger, more complex, and ultimately more beautiful whole.

This transformative process can be visualized as the body's own remarkable capacity for healing. A physical wound, after it has been cleaned and stitched, leaves a scar. This scar is not a return to the pristine skin of before, but it is a sign that the body has done its work, has closed the wound, and has created a new structure that allows for continued function. The scar may be a different texture or color, but it is also a testament to the body's ability to mend. In a similar way, the embodied scar of trauma, when tended to with care and intention, can become a mark of resilience. It signifies that the deepest wounds have been addressed, that the body has found a way to contain and integrate the experience, and that life, in its persistent and vital force, continues.

The language we use to describe this process is also important. Rather than speaking of "getting over" trauma, which implies a complete eradication, we focus on "integrating" or "transforming" it. This acknowledges that the experience leaves an indelible mark, but that this mark can evolve. The embodied scar ceases to be a raw, open wound and becomes a more healed, though still present, reminder of a significant life event. It is a testament to the fact that the individual has faced the unimaginable and has not only survived but has found pathways towards a more embodied and integrated sense of self. This journey is not linear, and it requires patience, self-compassion, and often, the skilled guidance of those who understand the intricate connection between mind, body, and spirit in the face of profound adversity. The ultimate aim is not to eliminate the scar, but to understand its texture, its history, and its place within the larger narrative of a life that has been deeply impacted, but not ultimately defined, by trauma.

Chapter 9: The Body, Control, and Power Dynamics

The human psyche, in its intricate dance with the world, often seeks an anchor, a tangible point of reference around which to build a sense of self and stability. For many, this anchor is found within the confines of their own physical being. The body, with its undeniable presence and its capacity for both pleasure and pain, becomes a primary canvas upon which individuals project their deepest desires for order, predictability, and meaning. This pursuit of control over the body is not a monolithic phenomenon; it is a complex interplay of internal psychic dynamics and the pervasive influences of the external world. It is a deeply personal struggle, a constant negotiation between the self and its physical vessel, driven by an often unconscious yearning to tame the unruly currents of existence.

At the heart of this drive for bodily control lies the fundamental human need to manage anxiety. The world outside can often feel chaotic, unpredictable, and overwhelming. In the face of this external turbulence, the body offers a seemingly more manageable domain. By imposing strictures on what one eats, how one exercises, or how one presents oneself physically, individuals can create an illusion of mastery. This can be a subtle, almost imperceptible process, a quiet insistence on routine and discipline. For instance, the ritualistic adherence to a highly restrictive diet, while ostensibly about health or aesthetics, can also serve as a powerful mechanism for warding off feelings of helplessness. Each carefully measured portion, each calorie counted, becomes a small victory against the larger uncertainties of life. The act of meticulously controlling caloric intake can provide a sense of agency, a feeling that at least this one aspect of one's existence is firmly within one's grasp, even when other areas feel like they are slipping away. This control can manifest in obsessive tendencies, where the individual's thoughts become consumed by dietary minutiae, exercise schedules, or the precise contours of their physical form. The body, in this context, transforms from a source of lived experience into a project, an object to be sculpted, refined, and ultimately, mastered.

Furthermore, the body serves as a potent instrument for asserting identity. In a world where external labels and societal roles can feel both constricting and fleeting, the physical self offers a more immediate and seemingly immutable form of self-definition. The choices an individual makes about their body – from clothing and hairstyle to cosmetic modifications and physical conditioning – become outward declarations of who they are, or perhaps more accurately, who they aspire to be. This is particularly evident in adolescent development, a period characterized by a heightened awareness of the self and a fervent search for belonging. The adolescent's fascination with trends in fashion, their engagement in intense physical activities, or their preoccupation with perceived physical flaws are all part of a complex process of defining their boundaries and asserting their individuality. The body becomes a declaration: "This is me. This is what I stand for." This can extend to subcultures and movements that coalesce around particular aesthetic or physical ideals, offering individuals a sense of community and shared identity through the deliberate shaping and presentation of their bodies.

The external landscape plays an equally significant role in shaping our relationship with our bodies. Societal pressures, particularly those related to beauty standards and health regimes, exert a relentless influence. From the glossy pages of magazines to the curated perfection of social media feeds, individuals are bombarded with idealized images of physical attractiveness and well-being. These external benchmarks create a constant, often unspoken, pressure to conform. The pursuit of the "ideal" body becomes an aspirational goal, a pathway to social acceptance, romantic success, and even perceived happiness. This can lead to an internalization of these standards, where individuals begin to police their own bodies with an intensity that rivals any external critic. The desire to fit in, to be deemed attractive, or to project an image of robust health can drive individuals to engage in extreme measures, often at the expense of their own physical and psychological well-being. The constant comparison with idealized images can foster deep-seated feelings of inadequacy, fueling a cycle of striving and often, disappointment.

Consider the prevalence of diet culture, a pervasive force that often masquerades as benevolent advice. The myriad of diets, the "miracle" weight-loss products, and the emphasis on achieving a certain number on the scale all contribute to a narrative where the body is seen as something to be perpetually "fixed" or "improved." This relentless pursuit of an often unattainable ideal can lead to disordered eating patterns, excessive exercise, and a profound disconnect from the body's natural cues of hunger and satiety. The body becomes a battleground, a site where the individual wages war against their own perceived imperfections, driven by the external imperative to conform. The psychological toll of this constant struggle can be immense, leading to feelings of shame, guilt, and a pervasive sense of not being "good enough."

Similarly, the relentless promotion of rigorous fitness regimes and the glorification of peak physical performance can create an environment where a less-than-perfectly sculpted physique is seen as a sign of weakness or a lack of self-discipline. While the benefits of exercise are undeniable, the societal obsession with achieving a certain aesthetic through athleticism can push individuals beyond healthy boundaries. The pursuit of the "six-pack abs," the marathon runner's lean physique, or the bodybuilder's sculpted musculature can become all-consuming goals, often eclipsing the joy of movement and the intrinsic rewards of physical activity. The body, in this context, is not just a vehicle for experiencing life, but a testament to one's dedication, willpower, and adherence to a prevailing cultural ideal.

This desire for control often stems from a deep-seated fear of vulnerability. The body, in its very nature, is susceptible to illness, injury, and the inevitable process of aging. These inherent vulnerabilities can be deeply unsettling, triggering existential anxieties about mortality and helplessness. By imposing control over the body's appearance, its functions, and its impulses, individuals attempt to create a buffer against these fears. A body that is meticulously maintained, that adheres to strict regimens, and that appears to be in perfect working order can serve as a psychological defense against the perceived chaos of the natural world and the inevitability of decline. The obsession with youthfulness, for instance, is a prime example of this desire to exert control over the inexorable march of time. Anti-aging treatments, cosmetic surgery, and the relentless pursuit of a youthful appearance are all attempts to outwardly defy the body's natural aging process, a manifestation of the deep-seated human wish to remain in control even in the face of biological inevitability.

The internal psychic landscape also contributes significantly to this drive for bodily control. For individuals who have experienced early life adversity, trauma, or neglect, the body can become a repository of unresolved emotional pain. In such cases, the attempt to control the physical form can be a way of reenacting a sense of agency that was denied in earlier experiences. If one felt powerless as a child, the ability to dictate one's diet, exercise regimen, or even one's physical appearance can offer a profound sense of reclaiming that lost power. This can manifest as a meticulous attention to detail, a rigid adherence to rules, and a fierce resistance to any perceived deviation from the established order. The body, in this scenario, becomes a meticulously managed fortress, designed to keep out not only external threats but also the internal turmoil that threatens to breach its defenses.

The body can also be a stage upon which individuals perform their identity, particularly in situations where genuine self-expression has been suppressed. For those who have been forced to conform to societal expectations or to conceal aspects of their true selves, their physical presentation can become a carefully constructed facade. The way one dresses, the way one moves, the very tone of one's voice can be meticulously calibrated to present a desired image, an image that may bear little resemblance to the inner reality. This performative aspect of bodily control is often driven by a fear of judgment and rejection. If revealing one's true self is perceived as dangerous or unacceptable, then the creation of a controlled, palatable exterior becomes a matter of survival. This can lead to a profound sense of alienation from one's own body, as it is experienced not as a site of authentic selfhood, but as a costume, a tool for navigating a world that feels hostile to genuine expression.

The concept of "health" itself can become a domain for intense control. While a focus on well-being is generally positive, for some, the pursuit of optimal health can morph into an obsessive preoccupation. This is often referred to as "orthorexia nervosa," an unhealthy fixation on "eating pure" or "healthy" foods. Individuals with orthorexia may meticulously plan their meals, avoid entire food groups deemed unhealthy, and experience significant anxiety when confronted with foods that do not meet their stringent criteria. The body, in this context, is not just cared for; it is worshipped, and its perceived purity becomes a measure of one's moral character and self-worth. The pursuit of health becomes a rigid ideology, a set of rules that must be adhered to at all costs, even at the expense of social engagement, pleasure, and psychological well-being. The body, once a source of vitality, becomes a site of constant vigilance and anxiety.

The desire for control over the body can also be intimately linked to the management of shame. For individuals who carry deep-seated feelings of shame, often stemming from past experiences of abuse, humiliation, or societal stigma, the body can become a focal point for their self-criticism. They may perceive their physical form as inherently flawed or undesirable, a visible manifestation of their perceived inadequacy. The attempt to control the body – through dieting, exercise, or cosmetic procedures – can be a desperate effort to erase these perceived flaws and, in doing so, to eradicate the shame they embody. This is a tragically misguided endeavor, as the underlying shame is not truly addressed by external changes. Instead, the focus on physical perfection can become a way of avoiding the more difficult work of confronting and healing the wounded self. The body becomes a distraction, a substitute for the essential inner work required to dismantle the architecture of shame.

Moreover, the control exerted over the body can be a way of navigating difficult emotional terrain. When emotions are overwhelming or difficult to process, individuals may unconsciously divert their attention to the more tangible realm of the physical. Instead of acknowledging feelings of sadness, anger, or fear, they might focus on the sensation of hunger, the discomfort of muscle fatigue, or the perceived imperfection of their skin. This displacement of emotional distress onto the physical can be a form of self-soothing, albeit an unhealthy one. By focusing on a manageable physical complaint, the individual can temporarily escape the overwhelming tide of their emotions. However, this strategy ultimately prevents genuine emotional processing and can lead to a chronic disconnect from one's inner emotional life. The body, in this instance, becomes a proxy for unspoken feelings, a silent testament to the emotional pain that remains unaddressed.

The intensity of this drive for bodily control is often exacerbated by cultural narratives that equate physical perfection with success and happiness. We are encouraged to believe that if we can just achieve the "right" body – the slim waist, the toned muscles, the flawless complexion – then all our problems will disappear, and we will finally be worthy of love and acceptance. This deeply ingrained societal message can create a profound sense of internal pressure, leading individuals to embark on arduous and often unsustainable journeys of self-modification. The body becomes an object of relentless self-scrutiny, a constant reminder of perceived shortcomings. Every perceived flaw, every deviation from the idealized norm, can be interpreted as a personal failure, reinforcing feelings of inadequacy and fueling the desire for greater control.

The act of dieting, for example, is not merely about caloric restriction; it is often imbued with moral significance. Certain foods are labeled "good" or "bad," and individuals who adhere to restrictive diets are often praised for their discipline and willpower. Conversely, those who struggle to maintain such diets may experience feelings of guilt and shame, reinforcing the idea that their lack of control over their eating habits is a reflection of a deeper moral failing. This moralization of food and body shape creates a powerful incentive to maintain an appearance of strict control, even when it is detrimental to one's health and well-being. The body becomes a public display of one's perceived moral fortitude.

The influence of social media has amplified these pressures exponentially. The curated and often digitally altered images that proliferate online create an illusion of effortless perfection, fostering a culture of comparison and inadequacy. Individuals constantly compare their own lived realities to these idealized representations, leading to increased body dissatisfaction and a heightened drive to achieve an unattainable standard. The very accessibility of these images means that the pressure to conform is no longer confined to magazines or television screens; it is a constant presence, accessible at one's fingertips. This can lead to a pervasive sense of needing to "perform" a certain way with one's body, even in private, as the internalised gaze of the online world becomes a constant companion.

Ultimately, the body becomes an object of control because it is the most immediate and tangible aspect of our existence. It is the vessel through which we experience the world, the locus of our sensations, and the outward manifestation of our inner selves. In a life that can often feel fraught with uncertainty and unpredictability, the ability to exert some degree of dominion over this physical form offers a powerful, albeit often illusory, sense of mastery. The personal struggle for bodily control, therefore, is not simply about aesthetics or health; it is a profound psychological endeavor, a deeply human attempt to impose order, meaning, and a sense of self onto the ever-shifting landscape of existence. It is a testament to our innate drive to navigate the complexities of life by attempting to tame the most intimate territory we possess: our own bodies. This intimate territory, however, often becomes a site of profound internal conflict, where the desire for control clashes with the body's own wisdom and the inherent vulnerabilities of the human condition. The quest for mastery can, paradoxically, lead to a deeper sense of disconnect and dissatisfaction, a continuous striving that never quite reaches its intended destination of peace and self-acceptance.

The intricate dance between the self and its corporeal shell is a profound theater of power, where the individual's will grapples with the body's intrinsic nature, and where the whispers of external forces often drown out the body's own innate wisdom. This power dynamic is not a singular entity but a multifaceted phenomenon, a constant negotiation between internal drives and external impositions. We witness the self, in its earnest, and sometimes desperate, pursuit of control, wield a formidable power over its own physical being. This power can manifest in the disciplined adherence to stringent regimens – the meticulous calorie counting that extends beyond mere sustenance into a form of psychic fortification, or the punishing exercise routines that push the body to its perceived limits, not for the joy of movement, but as a testament to willpower.

Consider the phenomenon of self-starvation, a stark and tragic illustration of internal power over the body. Here, the conscious mind, driven by a complex amalgam of perceived flaws, societal pressures, and internal anxieties, exerts an almost absolute dominion over the body's most fundamental need: nourishment. The gnawing hunger pangs, the physical weakness, the very survival instincts of the organism are overridden by a potent psychological mandate. This is not simply about dieting; it is a profound assertion of control, a declaration that the self can dictate even the most basic biological imperatives. The body, in this context, becomes an enemy to be subdued, its needs disregarded in service of an abstract ideal. The power here is wielded by the ego, attempting to master the id's primal drives, often with devastating consequences for the physical vessel. The individual, in their relentless pursuit of a phantom perfection, can become a tyrant to their own flesh, their power a weapon turned inward.

Conversely, this internal power can manifest as excessive exercise, a relentless dedication to sculpting, toning, and perfecting the physical form. While exercise is often lauded as a cornerstone of health, when it becomes an obsession, it reveals another facet of this internal power struggle. The body is pushed beyond its capacity for repair and recovery, driven by an insatiable need for a certain aesthetic or a fear of perceived physical decline. The pain of overexertion, the exhaustion, the potential for injury are all willingly endured, a testament to the self's capacity to impose its will upon the body. This can be an attempt to ward off the anxieties of aging, to outrun the biological clock, or to achieve a state of physical perfection that is seen as the ultimate symbol of self-mastery. The body, in this instance, is not a partner in well-being but a project, an object to be relentlessly honed and improved, an endless work in progress dictated by the internal architect.

Yet, this internal dominion is rarely a solitary affair. The individual's relationship with their body is inextricably intertwined with the broader currents of power that flow through society. External forces, often insidious and pervasive, exert their influence, shaping not only our perceptions of our bodies but also the very ways in which we seek to control them. These forces are legion, ranging from the subtle, pervasive influence of cultural norms to the overt, institutionalized power of medical and political structures. They often converge, creating a complex web of expectations and demands that can lead individuals to internalize these external pressures, transforming them into the agents of their own subjugation.

Societal norms, particularly those surrounding beauty and health, are potent architects of our bodily self-perception and the subsequent drive for control. The idealized images that saturate our media landscape – the impossibly slender figures, the taut skin, the chiseled musculature – are not mere aesthetic preferences; they are powerful directives that shape our understanding of what constitutes a desirable or acceptable body. These external benchmarks become internalized, transforming into a constant, often unspoken, pressure to conform. The relentless bombardment of these images fosters a culture of comparison, where individuals perpetually measure themselves against unattainable standards, leading to widespread body dissatisfaction. This dissatisfaction, in turn, fuels the pursuit of control, as individuals attempt to mold their bodies into conformity with these external ideals, believing that such conformity will grant them social acceptance, romantic desirability, and ultimately, happiness. The power here is seductive; it promises belonging and validation, but it often demands a sacrifice of individuality and self-acceptance.

The medical establishment, while ostensibly dedicated to health and well-being, can also exert a significant influence on the power dynamics surrounding the body. The discourse of health, particularly in contemporary Western societies, is often framed in terms of risk, prevention, and optimization. This can lead to an excessive focus on quantifiable metrics – cholesterol levels, body mass index, blood pressure – that can overshadow the more holistic experience of well-being. For individuals prone to anxiety or a need for control, the medical realm can become a fertile ground for their efforts. They may engage in obsessive health-monitoring behaviors, adhering rigidly to prescribed diets and exercise regimens, and experiencing significant distress when their bodies deviate from these medicalized ideals. The body, in this context, is viewed as a collection of biological systems to be managed and optimized, a machine that requires constant maintenance and vigilant oversight. The power of medical knowledge, while often beneficial, can inadvertently create a framework where the body is perceived as inherently fragile and prone to malfunction, necessitating a constant state of control to ward off disease and ensure longevity.

Political regimes, particularly those with authoritarian tendencies, can exercise a more direct and overt form of power over individuals' bodies. In such contexts, the body can be policed, regulated, and even exploited for the state's purposes. This can manifest in a variety of ways, from controlling reproductive rights and dictating population policies to enforcing specific physical standards for citizens or soldiers. The body becomes a site of state control, its autonomy and integrity compromised in service of nationalistic agendas, ideological purity, or economic objectives. For instance, regimes that prioritize military strength might promote rigorous physical training and a particular body type for their citizens, while others might enforce strict population controls through reproductive policies. In these scenarios, the individual's power over their own body is severely curtailed, replaced by the overarching power of the state. The body is no longer a personal domain but a public asset, subject to the dictates of a larger political entity.

The intersection of these internal and external forces creates a complex and often fraught relationship with our physical selves. The self, driven by a desire for control, may adopt the very standards and expectations imposed by external forces, thus becoming an agent of their subjugation. For example, an individual might internalize the societal ideal of thinness to such an extent that they engage in disordered eating, believing that this extreme form of control over their body will lead to self-acceptance and happiness. Here, the internal drive for mastery aligns perfectly with the external pressures, creating a powerful feedback loop that reinforces the pursuit of an often unhealthy or unattainable ideal. The body becomes a battleground where the individual's internal landscape of desires and anxieties clashes with the external landscape of societal expectations and institutional dictates.

This constant interplay between internal and external pressures can lead to a profound sense of alienation from one's own body. When the body is perceived primarily as an object to be controlled, perfected, and defended against perceived threats – be they internal impulses or external judgments – it can cease to be experienced as a source of lived experience, pleasure, or authentic connection. Instead, it becomes a source of anxiety, a site of constant vigilance, and a reminder of perceived shortcomings. The body's natural signals – hunger, fatigue, pleasure, pain – can be suppressed or misinterpreted in the service of maintaining a façade of control. This disconnect can manifest in various ways, from a diminished capacity for emotional attunement to a struggle to experience genuine physical intimacy. The body, which should be a conduit for experiencing the world and one's own inner life, becomes a barrier, a source of perpetual struggle.

Furthermore, the very concept of "health" can be co-opted and weaponized by these power dynamics. While the pursuit of good health is a laudable goal, the relentless emphasis on optimal physical condition can create an environment where any deviation is seen as a failure. This is particularly evident in the rise of "wellness culture," which often promotes a highly prescriptive and often costly approach to health, emphasizing specific diets, exercise regimens, and even expensive supplements. For individuals already struggling with a need for control, this culture can provide a seemingly legitimate framework for their obsessions. The pursuit of "optimal" health can morph into an all-consuming endeavor, leaving little room for spontaneity, pleasure, or the acceptance of natural human variation. The body becomes a project of constant improvement, a testament to one's commitment to a particular set of health-related doctrines, often dictated by external authorities or prevailing trends. The power here is subtle, cloaked in the language of self-care and longevity, yet it can lead to a profound sense of inadequacy and a constant striving for an ever-receding horizon of perfect health.

The internalization of external pressures is particularly evident in the way bodies are scrutinized and judged based on race, gender, and socioeconomic status. Societal ideals of beauty and health are often implicitly or explicitly rooted in a dominant cultural framework, which can render bodies that do not conform to this standard as less desirable or even pathological. For example, dominant beauty standards often valorize lighter skin tones, specific body shapes, and Eurocentric features, leading to the marginalization and stigmatization of bodies that deviate from these norms. This external judgment can then be internalized, leading individuals to experience shame and inadequacy regarding their own physical characteristics. The pursuit of control over the body, in such cases, can become an attempt to assimilate to the dominant standard, to shed the markers of difference that invite scrutiny and judgment. The power dynamics here are deeply political, revealing how bodies are not simply personal possessions but are also sites where broader social hierarchies and power structures are enacted and reinforced.

The influence of economic forces also plays a significant role in shaping our relationship with our bodies and the power dynamics at play. The multi-billion dollar industries of diet, fitness, and cosmetic surgery thrive on the insecurities and desires that are often amplified by societal pressures. These industries actively promote products and services that promise transformation, improvement, and the attainment of idealized physical forms. They create a market for bodily control, capitalizing on the belief that physical perfection is attainable through consumption. This commercialization of bodily control can further entrench the idea that the body is an object to be manipulated and improved upon, rather than an integral part of one's lived experience. The power here is economic; it thrives on the perpetual dissatisfaction with the status quo, encouraging a continuous cycle of striving and consumption in the pursuit of an elusive ideal.

Moreover, the history of medicine and science itself has often been imbued with a paternalistic and controlling gaze towards the body, particularly the bodies of marginalized groups. For centuries, medical discourse has pathologized or pathologized differences, framing deviations from a presumed norm as evidence of disease or moral failing. This historical legacy continues to influence contemporary understandings of health and illness, contributing to a climate where the body is often viewed with suspicion and subjected to rigorous surveillance. The power of medical authority, when wielded without a critical awareness of its historical biases, can reinforce the idea that individuals are incapable of understanding or governing their own bodies, and that external experts are necessary to maintain them in a state of "proper" functioning.

The struggle for bodily autonomy is thus a complex and ongoing one, a constant negotiation between the individual's desire for self-determination and the myriad of internal and external forces that seek to exert power over their physical being. The body, in this intricate interplay, becomes a terrain of struggle, a site where competing agendas are played out, and where the very definition of selfhood is often contested. Understanding these power dynamics is crucial, not to condemn the pursuit of self-improvement or health, but to critically examine the motivations behind it and to recognize the potential for both empowerment and subjugation that lies within our relationship with our bodies. It is about acknowledging that the desire for control, while deeply human, can become a double-edged sword, capable of both liberation and profound constraint, depending on the forces that shape and direct it. The body, therefore, is not merely a passive vessel, but an active participant in these power dynamics, its resilience, its needs, and its inherent wisdom often overlooked in the relentless pursuit of external validation and internalized ideals. The ongoing challenge lies in reclaiming the body not as an object to be mastered, but as a source of authentic experience, a partner in living, and a fundamental aspect of one's embodied self.

Dieting, for many, is not simply a matter of caloric intake or nutrient balance; it is a deeply psychological undertaking, a battlefield upon which the individual wages war against perceived imperfections, seeking to sculpt not just their physique, but their very sense of self. The seemingly innocuous act of choosing what to eat, or more often, what *not* to eat, becomes an arena for the enactment of profound internal conflicts. In the relentless pursuit of an idealized body, the individual often imbues their dietary choices with an almost moral weight, viewing adherence to a strict regimen as a testament to discipline, willpower, and ultimately, worthiness. This is where the psychoanalytic perspective offers a crucial lens, revealing how the conscious, often pragmatic, goal of weight loss or healthier eating can mask a deeper, unconscious yearning for control and perfection. The body, in this narrative, is not merely a biological entity requiring sustenance; it is a project, a canvas upon which the individual attempts to paint a more desirable self.

The allure of the perfect body, amplified by relentless media portrayals and societal pressures, creates an internalized ideal that can become both a beacon and a torment. When this ideal is perceived as unattainable through ordinary means, or when the individual grapples with a fundamental sense of inadequacy, the stringent discipline of dieting can offer a seductive pathway to perceived mastery. Each forbidden indulgence, each deviation from the prescribed menu, becomes a perceived failure, a confirmation of inherent flaws, thereby fueling the compulsion to double down, to be even more rigorous, even more restrictive. The body's natural signals of hunger and satiety, its innate wisdom honed over millennia of evolution, are often overridden by the dictates of an internalized, often harsh, externalized authority. This authority, shaped by a complex interplay of societal norms, personal anxieties, and a deep-seated desire for external validation, transforms food from a source of nourishment and pleasure into an enemy to be subdued or a reward to be earned through arduous self-denial.

Consider the phenomenon of the "clean eating" movement, which, while often rooted in genuine desires for health, can readily morph into a form of orthorexia nervosa – an unhealthy obsession with eating "pure" or "healthy" food. Here, the pursuit of perfection extends beyond mere calorie restriction to encompass an intricate web of rules and regulations about food quality, origin, and preparation. The individual meticulously scrutinizes labels, avoids entire food groups deemed "toxic," and experiences significant anxiety, guilt, or even panic when faced with foods that do not conform to their rigid standards. This is not simply about making informed choices; it is about constructing a fortress of dietary purity that serves as a proxy for psychic order and moral superiority. The body, in this context, becomes a shrine to be protected from any perceived contamination, and adherence to the dietary dogma becomes a ritualistic act of self-purification, offering a fleeting sense of control in an otherwise chaotic world. The power lies in the ability to meticulously curate one's intake, a powerful assertion of control over a fundamental aspect of existence, which can be deeply reassuring for those who feel powerless in other domains of their lives.

This internal quest for perfection often manifests in an idealized relationship with the concept of "health." Health, in this framing, is not simply the absence of disease but a state of perpetual optimization, a constant striving for peak physical and mental condition. This can lead to an obsessive focus on quantifiable metrics – exercise duration, macronutrient ratios, sleep patterns, even heart rate variability – all meticulously tracked and analyzed. The body becomes an object of intense scrutiny, its deviations from the optimal norm interpreted as failures requiring immediate intervention. This is particularly evident in the rise of the "wellness industry," which bombards individuals with prescriptive advice, often expensive and exclusive, promising a pathway to ultimate health and vitality. For those with a pre-existing tendency towards obsessive behavior or a need for control, this industry provides a seemingly legitimate and socially sanctioned outlet for their psychological needs. The pursuit of health transforms into a demanding, all-consuming endeavor, where spontaneity and pleasure are often sacrificed at the altar of an ever-receding horizon of perfect well-being.

The act of exercise, too, can become a powerful tool in this unconscious pursuit of perfection and control. While regular physical activity is undeniably beneficial, it can, for some, escalate into compulsive behaviors that mirror the patterns seen in disordered eating. The gym becomes a sanctuary, a place where the individual can exert their will, sculpt their form, and escape the anxieties of everyday life. However, when exercise becomes an obligation rather than a joy, when it is driven by guilt, fear of weight gain, or a desperate need to burn off perceived transgressions, it reveals the underlying power dynamics at play. The body is pushed beyond its limits, injury is courted or ignored, and rest is seen as a sign of weakness. This relentless dedication to physical exertion is not about fostering well-being but about achieving a state of physical perfection that serves as a bulwark against feelings of inadequacy and a tangible demonstration of self-mastery.

This obsession with the physical form can also be deeply intertwined with a fear of aging and mortality. In a culture that valorizes youth and physical vitality, the visible signs of aging – wrinkles, gray hair, a less toned physique – can be perceived as markers of decline and loss of control. The rigorous dieting and exercise regimens become a desperate attempt to defy the natural process of aging, to reclaim a youthful appearance and the perceived power that accompanies it. The body, once again, is treated as an adversary to be battled, its natural transformations resisted with every calorie counted and every mile run. This fight against the inevitable can lead to a profound sense of internal conflict, as the individual struggles to reconcile their desire for eternal youth with the reality of their biological limitations. The power they seek is the power to halt time, to remain forever in a state of idealized physical perfection, a Sisyphean task that often leads to exhaustion and disillusionment.

The psychoanalytic understanding of these behaviors highlights the role of the ego in its relentless drive for control. The ego, seeking to manage anxieties and establish a sense of order, can seize upon the tangible reality of the body as a primary target for its efforts. By exerting absolute control over diet and exercise, the individual can create a false sense of mastery over their internal world. This is particularly potent when other aspects of life feel chaotic or beyond their influence. The body, in this sense, becomes a proxy for the self, and its perceived imperfections or deviations are seen as reflections of personal failings. Conversely, achieving a desired physique or adhering perfectly to a regimen is interpreted as a triumph of will, a validation of one's strength and discipline. This internal narrative, however, can perpetuate a cycle of seeking external validation for internally driven goals, creating a dependency on the approval of others or on the achievement of specific physical milestones.

The potential for these practices to become pathological is significant. When the pursuit of perfection through diet and exercise consumes an individual's thoughts, dominates their social interactions, and interferes with their daily functioning, it crosses the threshold from healthy habit to disordered behavior. This can manifest in a range of conditions, from anorexia nervosa and bulimia nervosa to obsessive-compulsive disorder and body dysmorphic disorder. In these instances, the body is no longer experienced as a lived, integrated part of the self, but rather as a source of intense anxiety, a problem to be solved through extreme measures. The power that these individuals seek to wield over their bodies, in its most extreme forms, ultimately leads to a profound disempowerment, as they become prisoners to their own obsessions and the relentless demands of their idealized self-image.

Furthermore, the concept of "self-love" can be distorted within this framework. While self-love should ideally involve acceptance and care for one's body as it is, it can, in the context of perfectionism, become conflated with the rigorous effort to

achieve a certain body. This creates a conditional form of self-acceptance, where love and worth are only granted upon the attainment of an idealized physical state. The message becomes, "I will love myself when I lose X pounds," or "I will be worthy when my body looks like Y." This conditional self-regard is a powerful driver of obsessive behaviors, as the individual is perpetually striving for a goal that, even when achieved, may not bring the promised peace or fulfillment, leading to a renewed search for the "next level" of perfection.

The psychoanalytic perspective also considers the role of early life experiences in shaping these adult preoccupations. For individuals who experienced early neglect, trauma, or a lack of consistent emotional attunement, the body can become a primary site for seeking the security and control that was missing in their formative years. The predictability of a strict diet or an intense exercise routine can offer a sense of order and safety that was absent during childhood. The body, in this way, becomes a refuge, a territory that the individual can meticulously manage, thereby creating a sense of stability. However, this reliance on external control, while offering temporary relief, can prevent the development of more adaptive coping mechanisms and a more integrated sense of self.

The cultural emphasis on thinness and muscularity as markers of success, desirability, and even moral virtue plays a significant role in perpetuating these cycles of dieting and obsessive exercise. These ideals are not merely aesthetic; they are deeply embedded in our social and psychological landscapes, influencing how we perceive ourselves and how we believe we ought to present ourselves to the world. The power dynamics are thus internalized: the external pressures to conform to certain body types become internal directives, driving individuals to engage in behaviors that, while seemingly aimed at self-improvement, often serve to reinforce external standards and perpetuate a culture of body dissatisfaction. The pursuit of perfection, in this context, becomes a societal mandate, a performance of self that is constantly judged and evaluated against a shifting, often unattainable, ideal.

Ultimately, the allure of dieting and obsessive exercise lies in their promise of ultimate control and perfection. They offer a seemingly tangible pathway to mastering oneself, to becoming the idealized version of who one believes they should be. However, from a psychoanalytic standpoint, these practices often represent a complex psychological defense mechanism, a way of managing underlying anxieties, insecurities, and a fear of imperfection. While the outward goal may be health or appearance, the deeper, unconscious motivations are often rooted in a profound yearning for order, self-worth, and a sense of agency in a world that can often feel overwhelming and unpredictable. The body, in this relentless pursuit, becomes the battleground for these internal struggles, a testament to the intricate and often fraught relationship between the self and its physical manifestation. The challenge, then, is to recognize these patterns, to question the idealized benchmarks we have internalized, and to cultivate a more compassionate and accepting relationship with our bodies, one that prioritizes genuine well-being over the elusive and often destructive pursuit of perfection.

The body, so often envisioned as a passive recipient of societal dictates or a battleground for internal conflict, possesses a profound and often underestimated capacity for resistance. It is not merely a vessel to be molded, disciplined, or perfected according to external or internalized ideals; it is a dynamic, expressive entity capable of asserting its own presence, its own will, and its own unique narrative. This capacity for agency, for actively pushing back against subjugation, resides within the very physicality of our being. When dominant narratives seek to homogenize, to pathologize, or to render certain bodies invisible, the embodied individual can become a potent site of dissent. This resistance is not always overt or politically charged in the conventional sense, though it certainly can be. It can manifest in the quiet refusal to conform, in the subtle subversion of expectations, or in the bold reclamation of a body that has been deemed "other."

Consider, for instance, the profound act of protest that takes place on the streets, in public squares, and across digital landscapes. When individuals gather, their bodies become living manifestos. The collective presence of bodies—differing in size, shape, age, ethnicity, ability, and gender expression—disrupts the illusion of a singular, normative ideal. A protest march, a sit-in, a silent vigil – these are not just gatherings of people; they are demonstrations of embodied dissent. Each raised fist, each banner held aloft, each voice that cries out in unison, is a physical declaration that the status quo is unacceptable. The very act of occupying space, of demanding to be seen and heard through one's physical presence, is a powerful assertion of bodily autonomy. It says, "I am here, I exist, and my existence, in its fullness, matters." This is particularly potent for marginalized groups whose bodies have historically been policed, controlled, and devalued. For a Black woman to occupy a space of power, for a transgender person to move through the world with unapologetic visibility, for a disabled individual to demand full access and participation – these are acts of profound bodily resistance that challenge deeply ingrained systems of oppression. They force a confrontation with the dominant narratives that have sought to define and limit these bodies. The physicality of their presence becomes undeniable, a testament to their right to exist and to thrive, rather than merely to endure.

Artistic expression offers another rich vein of bodily resistance. From dance and performance art to visual arts and literature, artists have consistently used the body as a medium to explore, critique, and subvert societal norms. Performance artists, in particular, often place their own bodies at the epicenter of their work, pushing boundaries and challenging viewers' perceptions. Think of Marina Abramović's intense performances, where her body endures extreme physical and emotional states, confronting themes of pain, endurance, and the very nature of human connection. Her work, while often deeply personal, resonates universally by tapping into primal aspects of the embodied experience. These performances are not about achieving an idealized aesthetic; they are about exploring the raw, unvarnished reality of being in a body, and in doing so, they resist the sanitization and objectification that often characterize cultural representations of the body.

Similarly, dancers have long used their physicality to tell stories, to evoke emotions, and to express defiance. A choreographer might deliberately employ movements that eschew traditional notions of grace or beauty, opting instead for gestures that convey struggle, anger, or vulnerability. The contorted posture, the jarring rhythm, the raw energy—these elements can serve to disrupt expectations and to highlight the complexities of the human experience that often lie beyond the polished facade. Choreographers who work with dancers of diverse bodies, challenging conventional ideals of athleticism and form, are also engaged in a form of resistance. They demonstrate that beauty and expressiveness are not confined to a narrow set of physical attributes, thereby broadening the cultural understanding of what it means to have a body.

The literary and visual arts also provide platforms for asserting bodily agency. Writers can craft narratives that center the experiences of individuals whose bodies have been marginalized, giving voice to their struggles and triumphs. By vividly portraying the lived reality of these bodies, writers challenge the stereotypes and biases that often surround them. They invite readers to empathize with characters whose physical experiences may differ vastly from their own, fostering a deeper understanding and appreciation for the diversity of human embodiment. Visual artists, too, can use their canvases and sculptures to reimagine the body, creating representations that defy prevailing beauty standards or that celebrate the unique characteristics of marginalized bodies. A portrait of an aging woman that emphasizes her wisdom and resilience, rather than her wrinkles, is an act of resistance against a culture obsessed with eternal youth. A sculpture that celebrates the curves and textures of a larger body challenges the pervasive thin ideal.

The concept of reclaiming marginalized bodies is a cornerstone of this embodied resistance. For too long, certain bodies have been subjected to scrutiny, judgment, and even shame. Think of the historical demonization of Black bodies, the pathologization of bodies with disabilities, the policing of LGBTQ+ bodies, or the societal disdain for bodies that do not conform to patriarchal beauty standards. Reclaiming these bodies is an active process of divestment from external judgment and an investment in self-acceptance and self-definition. It involves challenging the internalized oppressions that have taken root and cultivating a sense of pride and belonging in one's physical form. This can manifest in a variety of ways, from embracing one's natural hair texture or body shape, to proudly displaying scars or prosthetics, to advocating for inclusive representation in media and popular culture.

The fat acceptance movement, for instance, is a powerful example of bodily reclamation. It challenges the deeply ingrained societal belief that fatness is inherently unhealthy, undesirable, and a moral failing. Through activism, personal storytelling, and the creation of fat-positive communities, individuals are asserting their right to exist with dignity and joy, regardless of their size. They are demonstrating that bodies come in all shapes and sizes, and that health and well-being are not synonymous with thinness. This movement actively resists the diet industry, the medical establishment's often discriminatory attitudes towards larger bodies, and the pervasive cultural narrative that equates thinness with virtue. The act of a fat person confidently wearing clothing that celebrates their body, or advocating for fat liberation, is a direct challenge to these oppressive systems.

Similarly, the disability rights movement has long centered the concept of bodily autonomy and resistance against ableism. Rather than viewing disability as a deficit to be cured or overcome, the movement emphasizes the social model of disability, which posits that societal barriers and attitudes are the primary obstacles faced by disabled individuals. Reclaiming disabled bodies involves challenging the medical gaze that often reduces disabled individuals to their conditions, and instead recognizing their full humanity, their agency, and their unique contributions. This can involve advocating for accessibility, demanding equal opportunities, and celebrating the diverse experiences of disabled people. The visibility of disabled individuals in public life, refusing to be confined to the periphery, is an essential act of resistance that challenges the ableist assumption that their bodies are somehow less capable or less worthy of full participation in society.

The queer community has also offered profound examples of bodily resistance, challenging heteronormative and cisnormative expectations about bodies, relationships, and gender expression. From the early days of the LGBTQ+ rights movement, which involved the very visible act of taking up space and demanding recognition, to contemporary forms of gender non-conformity and the celebration of diverse sexualities, queer bodies have consistently pushed against the boundaries of societal norms. The act of self-expression through fashion, makeup, and body modification by queer individuals can be a radical assertion of identity in a world that often seeks to categorize and control. The reclamation of language and the creation of new forms of kinship and family further highlight the power of embodied experiences to forge new ways of being.

Even within seemingly mundane aspects of life, the body can be a site of subtle yet significant resistance. The decision to engage in practices that are not aimed at self-improvement or external validation, but rather at genuine self-care and pleasure, can be a form of rebellion against a culture that demands constant optimization. This might involve savoring a meal without guilt, moving one's body in a way that feels joyful rather than obligatory, or simply resting when needed, without apology. These acts, while quiet, represent a turning away from the relentless pursuit of an idealized self and a turning towards an acceptance of the body as it is, in its present moment. It is a refusal to constantly be at war with oneself, and an embrace of a more peaceful coexistence.

The act of mourning, too, can be a powerful expression of bodily agency, especially in the face of systemic violence or loss. When a community gathers to mourn a victim of police brutality, for instance, their collective grief, expressed through tears, embraces, and vigils, is a testament to the value of the life that was lost. This embodied expression of sorrow is a refusal to let the victim be erased or forgotten, and a powerful statement against the forces that caused their death. The shared physical experience of grief can be a source of strength and solidarity, and it can galvanize action.

Ultimately, the body's capacity for resistance and agency lies in its inherent aliveness, its capacity for expression, and its undeniable presence. It is through our bodies that we interact with the world, that we feel, that we act, and that we connect with others. When these bodies are subjected to oppressive forces, whether they be external political structures, internalized societal narratives, or personal anxieties, the assertion of bodily autonomy becomes an act of profound liberation. It is a testament to the enduring human spirit's ability to find freedom and to express dissent, even within the confines of physical form. The body, in its resistance, becomes not just a site of struggle, but a declaration of selfhood, a vibrant assertion of existence in a world that too often seeks to silence and control it. This intrinsic power of the embodied self to defy, to express, and to reclaim is a vital aspect of what it means to be human, a constant reminder that even in the face of overwhelming power dynamics, agency is always, in some form, possible. The body, therefore, is not merely an object to be controlled, but a subject capable of immense power, a locus of resistance that can, and does, shape our individual and collective realities.

The anorectic body, a landscape sculpted by deprivation, stands as a stark and often misunderstood testament to the human will's desperate grasp for control. It is here, in the extreme manifestation of bodily regulation, that we can observe the profound and often tragic interplay between an individual's internal world and their external physical reality. Anorexia Nervosa, in its most severe presentations, transforms the body into a battleground, a canvas upon which an individual attempts to redraw the lines of their existence when the broader strokes of life feel utterly unmanageable. The act of restricting food intake, of meticulously weighing and measuring every morsel, of obsessively monitoring weight and shape, transcends mere dietary choice. It becomes a survival mechanism, a distorted but potent strategy for navigating a psychic terrain that feels treacherous and overwhelming.

In the face of experiences that threaten to obliterate a sense of self—whether rooted in trauma, profound loss, familial dysfunction, or crushing societal pressures—the individual may find themselves utterly powerless. The external world may seem a chaotic and unpredictable force, incapable of being influenced or understood. In such dire circumstances, the body emerges as the last bastion of agency, the only domain over which an individual can exert absolute authority. By meticulously controlling what goes into their body and how their body is perceived, they create an illusion of mastery. This is not control born of strength, but rather a desperate assertion of will born from profound vulnerability. The emaciated form, the gaunt features, the skeletal frame—these are not the accidental byproducts of a diet gone awry; they are the deliberate, albeit often unconscious, outcomes of a life-or-death struggle for self-determination. The stark visual of the anorectic body, stripped bare of its vitality, becomes a potent symbol of this internal war. It is a physical manifestation of a desperate plea for order in the face of internal disarray, a silent scream echoing the profound disconnect between the self and a world that feels too large, too complex, and too threatening to engage with.

The very act of starvation becomes a form of communication, a visceral language spoken by a body pushed to its limits. When words fail, when emotions are too overwhelming to articulate, when the self feels fragmented and lost, the body steps in to tell the story. The shrinking frame signifies a withdrawal from a world that is perceived as hostile or intrusive. The constant hunger, the gnawing emptiness, becomes a tangible reminder of one's existence, a persistent echo in the void of inner turmoil. This self-imposed deprivation, paradoxically, can generate a sense of power. The individual may feel an intense pride in their ability to resist the primal urges of hunger, to defy the biological imperative for nourishment. This perceived strength, however, is a fragile construct, built upon the foundation of profound suffering. The body, once a source of experience and connection, becomes a tool for self-punishment and self-protection, a paradoxically nurturing prison.

Consider the profound psychological experience of an individual who feels perpetually unheard or unseen. Their opinions dismissed, their needs invalidated, their very existence treated as secondary to the needs and desires of others, they may internalize a deep sense of worthlessness. The world, in its apparent indifference, offers no solace, no recognition. It is in this psychic wasteland that the anorectic impulse can take root. By making their body the absolute focus of their existence, by dedicating all their energy to its reduction and control, they ensure that they are, at the very least, a presence that cannot be ignored. The extreme thinness becomes a signal, a beacon meant to attract attention, to elicit concern, even if the individual fears or rejects the very help that such attention might bring. The emaciated body is a monument to their struggle, a silent testament to their existence, a desperate attempt to force the world to acknowledge their pain. The self-starvation, in this context, is not about self-destruction for its own sake, but rather a desperate attempt at self-preservation through extreme self-regulation. It is a cry for agency in a life that feels characterized by helplessness. The body, in its skeletal fragility, becomes the sole, tangible proof of their being.

The meticulous rituals that surround food intake in anorexia nervosa—the weighing of portions, the avoidance of certain textures or colors, the complex calculations of calorie expenditure—are not merely symptoms of an eating disorder; they are the very architecture of a controlled existence. These rituals provide a sense of structure and predictability in a life that otherwise feels chaotic and overwhelming. Each adhered-to rule, each successfully resisted urge to eat, reinforces the individual's belief that they are capable of exerting control. This can be profoundly seductive, offering a temporary respite from the anxiety and fear that permeate their inner world. The rigid adherence to these rules can create a false sense of security, a feeling of being anchored in a turbulent sea. The anorectic body, therefore, becomes a manifestation of this meticulously crafted internal order, a physical representation of the psychological boundaries that the individual has erected to protect themselves from perceived threats.

The aesthetic of extreme thinness, often fetishized and promoted by certain cultural narratives, can also play a complex role in the development and maintenance of anorexia nervosa. When an individual is bombarded with images and messages that equate thinness with desirability, success, and happiness, the pursuit of extreme leanness can become intertwined with deeply held aspirations for self-worth. For someone already struggling with feelings of inadequacy, the promise of achieving an idealized body can seem like a pathway to acceptance and belonging. The anorectic body, in this context, can be seen as an attempt to embody these aspirational ideals, a desperate effort to conform to a perceived standard of perfection. This pursuit, however, is a dangerous illusion, as it leads to a state of physical and emotional deterioration rather than fulfillment. The stark visual of the emaciated body serves as a grim reminder of this distorted aspiration, a body that has been sacrificed on the altar of an unattainable and often harmful ideal. The obsession with controlling the body's appearance and size becomes a proxy for controlling one's destiny, an attempt to manifest an idealized self in the absence of a more authentic connection to one's own needs and desires.

Furthermore, the social isolation that often accompanies severe anorexia nervosa can paradoxically reinforce the individual's sense of control. As the disorder progresses, social interactions can become increasingly difficult. The physical toll of starvation may lead to fatigue and weakness, making it challenging to engage in social activities. Moreover, the individual may actively withdraw from social situations, fearing that their eating habits will be discovered or judged. This withdrawal, while isolating, can also serve to further entrench the individual's reliance on their internal world and their control over their body. The anorectic body becomes a private sanctuary, a space where the rules are clear and the outcomes are predictable, free from the complexities and potential judgments of the external world. The lack of external validation, which might otherwise challenge the disordered thinking, is thus circumvented by a self-imposed withdrawal that strengthens the anorectic narrative. The individual becomes trapped in a cycle where the perceived need for control leads to isolation, which in turn intensifies the perceived need for control.

The psychological underpinnings of anorexia nervosa often involve a deep-seated fear of not being good enough, of being inherently flawed. The desire to control one's body, to achieve an impossible standard of perfection, can be a way of attempting to compensate for these perceived deficiencies. By meticulously shaping their body into a desired form, individuals may believe they are eradicating their flaws and becoming worthy of love and acceptance. The emaciated body, in this sense, is an attempt to sculpt oneself into an ideal, to erase the parts of oneself that are deemed unacceptable. This is a tragically misguided endeavor, as it ultimately leads to the destruction of the very self it aims to perfect. The starkness of the anorectic body becomes a visual metaphor for this internal process of self-erasure, a body stripped down to its barest essentials in a desperate bid for self-acceptance. The absence of physical substance mirrors the absence of self-acceptance, a void that is desperately, and destructively, being filled by an obsession with external form.

In some instances, the development of anorexia nervosa can be linked to early experiences of trauma or abuse, where the individual's body was violated or controlled by an external aggressor. In such cases, regaining control over one's own body becomes a paramount concern, a way of reclaiming agency that was violently taken away. The act of restricting food and manipulating body weight can be seen as a defiant assertion of autonomy, a declaration that one's body is no longer a site of violation but a territory under one's own sovereign command. The emaciated body, therefore, can symbolize a profound resistance to past trauma, a desperate effort to rebuild a sense of safety and power by creating an impenetrable physical boundary. It is a body that has been weaponized, not against others, but against the perceived vulnerabilities and threats that lie within and without. The stark visual of such a body is a testament to its own survival, a survivor that has literally consumed itself in an effort to escape being consumed by others. The very act of taking away the body's sustenance becomes a way of reinforcing its claim to ownership, a radical act of self-possession in the face of overwhelming violation.

The paradox of anorexia nervosa lies in the fact that the extreme control exerted over the body ultimately leads to a profound loss of control. As the body deteriorates, it becomes increasingly difficult to function, and the individual becomes dependent on others for care. The meticulously constructed edifice of self-regulation begins to crumble under the weight of its own physical demands. Yet, the psychological grip of control remains, making it incredibly challenging to relinquish the behaviors that have become so deeply ingrained. The emaciated body, once a symbol of power, becomes a prison, a constant reminder of the disorder's insidious hold. The visual starkness of this body is not merely an aesthetic; it is a profound indicator of the psychological distress and the desperate coping mechanisms that have led to such a devastating outcome. It is a body that has been reduced, not to a healthier state, but to a state of extreme vulnerability, a direct consequence of an attempt to achieve an illusion of strength and control through deprivation. The visual representation of this extreme thinness is a powerful, albeit tragic, illustration of how the psyche can manifest its deepest anxieties and its most desperate attempts at self-preservation through the physical form. The anorectic body is a chilling emblem of control as survival, where the self, in its profound distress, attempts to navigate overwhelming circumstances by meticulously dismantling its own physical being, thereby creating a distorted sense of mastery over an otherwise uncontrollable existence.

Chapter 10: Sexuality, Gender, and the Embodied Subject

The narrative of human sexuality, as conventionally understood, often begins its dramatic arc with the tempestuous winds of puberty, a period characterized by the burgeoning of distinct genital drives and the maturation of the reproductive system. This popular conception, while understandable in its focus on the observable transformations of adolescence, risks casting a long shadow over the earliest, yet arguably most foundational, chapters of our sexual lives. It is precisely this oversight that psychoanalysis, particularly through the lens of Freudian thought, seeks to rectify. The idea of infantile sexuality is not a suggestion that infants possess a fully formed, socially codified sexual identity akin to that of an adult. Rather, it is a radical proposition: that the capacity for pleasure, the drive towards gratification, and the nascent forms of desire are woven into the very fabric of our being from the moment of birth, intimately tied to the sensory and motor experiences of our bodies. The infant's world, unburdened by the complex social and moral strictures that later shape our understanding of sexuality, is a realm of pure, unadulterated sensation. The mouth that nurses, the skin that is caressed, the anus that expels waste—these are not merely conduits for survival, but potent sources of erogenous pleasure. This is the essence of what Freud termed "polymorphous perversity," a concept that speaks to the boundless and undifferentiated nature of early desire. The infant is not yet confined by the rigid binaries of "sexual" and "non-sexual," nor is its pleasure limited to specific anatomical regions. Instead, the entire body, in its myriad interactions with the environment and with caregivers, becomes a landscape of potential erotic exploration.

The act of sucking, for instance, far from being solely about the ingestion of nourishment, is a primal scene of oral gratification. The rhythmic movement of the tongue, the stimulation of the lips, the sensation of fullness and subsequent release—these all contribute to a profound sense of pleasure that is intrinsically tied to the body. This early experience lays the groundwork for a vast array of later desires and behaviors, from the simple enjoyment of food and drink to more complex oral fixations that can manifest in adulthood. Similarly, the exploration of the anal region, often associated with the developmental stage of toilet training, is imbued with significant erotic potential. The tension and release associated with defecation, the tactile sensations of the region, and the caregiver's reactions to these bodily functions all contribute to the infant's developing understanding of pleasure and control. These early experiences, while seemingly mundane, are the building blocks of our embodied subjectivity. They teach us that our bodies are capable of generating pleasurable sensations, and they initiate a lifelong process of seeking out and organizing these experiences. The infant's body, therefore, is not a passive vessel waiting to be populated by adult desires; it is an active participant in the very construction of its sexual self.

The concept of the erogenous zone is crucial in understanding this early sexualization of the body. These are areas of the skin or mucous membranes that, when stimulated, can evoke feelings of pleasure or arousal. For the infant, these zones are not fixed or exclusively genital. They are fluid, responsive to the environment, and deeply intertwined with the infant's interactions with its primary caregivers. The gentle caress of a cheek, the warmth of a hug, the playful tickling of the feet—all these can become potent sources of erotic stimulation. This early sensitivity of the skin, for example, establishes a fundamental connection between touch and pleasure, a connection that will continue to shape our experiences of intimacy and desire throughout our lives. The infant's capacity to derive pleasure from these diffuse bodily sensations is what allows for the development of a rich and varied inner world, a world where the boundaries between the physical and the psychological, the instinctual and the emotional, are far more porous than they will be in adulthood. This primal plasticity of desire, this "polymorphous perversity," is not a deviation from the norm; it is the very foundation upon which later, more differentiated forms of sexuality are built.

The infant's world is one of immediate gratification and intense sensory experience. When an infant is hungry, the sensation is overwhelming, and the relief that comes with feeding is profoundly pleasurable. This early association between need and satisfaction, between discomfort and relief, is a fundamental learning experience that is imbued with erotic undertones. The nipple against the tongue, the warmth of milk, the feeling of satiation—these are all powerful sensory inputs that contribute to the infant's burgeoning sense of pleasure. This is not yet sexuality in the adult sense, with its complex emotional and social dimensions, but it is the raw, unadulterated material from which adult sexuality will eventually emerge. The infant is, in essence, a pleasure-seeking organism, and its early interactions with the world are largely guided by this fundamental drive. The body, in its very earliest manifestations, is an instrument of pleasure, a site where the foundations of desire are laid.

Consider the ways in which an infant learns about its own body and the bodies of others through touch. The gentle stroking of an arm, the playful patting of a back, the intimate closeness of being held—these tactile experiences are not merely comforting; they are also formative in a sexual sense. They establish a sense of bodily awareness and create a positive association with physical contact. This early exposure to pleasurable touch helps to shape the infant's developing sense of self and its capacity for intimacy. It teaches the infant that its body is a source of pleasure and that connection with others can be deeply satisfying. This groundwork is essential for the development of a healthy and fulfilling sexual life in adulthood. Without these early experiences of positive, pleasure-infused touch, individuals may struggle with issues of intimacy, body image, and sexual satisfaction later in life. The infant's body, therefore, is a highly sensitive and responsive entity, actively engaged in a process of self-discovery and pleasure-seeking from its very first moments of life.

The development of the "embodied subject" is intrinsically linked to these early experiences of infantile sexuality. The subject, the sense of self, is not born fully formed but is gradually constructed through a continuous interplay between the body's drives, its sensory experiences, and its interactions with the external world. For the infant, the body is the primary site of experience. It is through the body that the infant interacts with its environment, seeks pleasure, and learns about itself and others. The oral stage, for example, is not just about feeding; it is also about the infant's exploration of its mouth as a source of pleasure and its initial understanding of separation and connection through the act of nursing. The anal stage, often associated with the development of control and autonomy through toilet training, is also a period of intense sensory exploration and the establishment of boundaries. These early stages, characterized by their focus on specific erogenous zones and their associated drives, are critical in shaping the individual's sense of self as an embodied being with desires and needs.

The polymorphous nature of infantile sexuality means that the infant is not yet driven by a singular, genital imperative. Instead, its desires are diffuse, readily shifting from one source of pleasure to another. This fluidity is a crucial aspect of early development, allowing the infant to explore a wide range of sensory experiences and to develop a rich and varied repertoire of responses. As the individual matures, these diffuse desires gradually become more organized and focused, eventually leading to the development of adult sexual expression. However, the traces of this early polymorphousness remain, influencing our fantasies, our attractions, and our capacity for pleasure throughout our lives. The ability to find pleasure in a variety of contexts, to experience desire in ways that are not strictly genital, can be seen as a legacy of this early phase of development.

The process of individuation, of becoming a distinct self, is deeply intertwined with the exploration of bodily sensations and the pursuit of pleasure. The infant's early experiences of pleasure, whether from feeding, touch, or expulsion, help to create a sense of the body as a distinct and valuable entity. As the infant learns to differentiate its own body from the bodies of others, and as it begins to understand its own capacity for sensation and action, a sense of self begins to emerge. This nascent self is fundamentally an embodied self, grounded in the physical experiences of the world.

The satisfaction of the infant's needs, particularly those related to comfort and nourishment, provides a crucial sense of security and reinforces the idea that the body is a source of both vulnerability and pleasure.

Moreover, the caregiver's response to the infant's bodily expressions plays a significant role in shaping the infant's understanding of sexuality. When a caregiver responds to an infant's cries with comfort and affection, or when they engage in playful, affectionate touch, they are not only meeting the infant's needs but also imbuing the infant's bodily experiences with positive emotional valence. This early association between the body, pleasure, and loving connection is a vital component in the formation of a healthy sense of self and a secure attachment. Conversely, neglectful or punitive responses to the infant's bodily expressions can lead to a more conflicted relationship with one's own body and with sexuality. The infant's body, therefore, is not an isolated biological entity but is deeply embedded within a relational matrix, where its experiences of pleasure and its developing sense of self are profoundly shaped by the responses of others.

The very act of self-soothing, whether through thumb-sucking or other repetitive movements, is an early manifestation of the body's inherent drive to generate pleasure and maintain a sense of equilibrium. These seemingly simple behaviors are, in fact, sophisticated strategies for managing internal states of discomfort and for experiencing a sense of agency over one's own body. The infant, through these actions, learns that its body can be a source of comfort and that it possesses the capacity to regulate its own experience. This early sense of bodily autonomy, however primitive, is a crucial step in the development of a robust sense of self. It lays the groundwork for later expressions of assertiveness, self-care, and the ability to set boundaries in relationships. The infant's body, from its earliest moments, is a dynamic and active participant in its own development, driven by an innate capacity for seeking and generating pleasure.

The persistence of infantile sexuality into adulthood is not about retaining the exact form of infant desires, but rather about recognizing the enduring influence of these early experiences on our later psychic development and sexual expression. The ways in which we learned to seek pleasure, to manage discomfort, and to relate to our own bodies in infancy continue to shape our adult patterns of desire, intimacy, and even our understanding of what it means to be a sexual being. The "polymorphous" capacity for pleasure, for instance, can be reawakened in adult life through various forms of intimacy and exploration, demonstrating that the early foundations of our sexuality remain a vibrant and influential part of our embodied selves. The body, therefore, is not merely a biological container but a living archive of our developmental journey, a testament to the profound and lasting impact of our earliest encounters with pleasure and the world.

The body, far from being a pre-social, neutral entity, becomes a primary canvas upon which the intricate artwork of gender is painted. It is through the lens of the Symbolic order – the vast, interwoven tapestry of language, social structures, and cultural narratives – that raw biological sex begins its transformative journey into the complex, multifaceted phenomenon we understand as gender. This process is not a gentle unfolding of an inherent truth, but a powerful act of inscription, where societal expectations, ingrained beliefs, and historical narratives are literally etched onto the flesh, dictating how bodies are perceived, categorized, and ultimately, how individuals are expected to inhabit them. The very language we use to describe bodies, the ways we discuss reproduction, and the archetypal stories we tell about men and women all contribute to a pervasive cultural script that assigns meaning and value to biological differences, forging a powerful connection between the physical and the social. This is where the biological fact of sex is imbued with layers of cultural signification, becoming the bedrock upon which gender identity and expression are subsequently built.

From the moment of birth, even before a child possesses the capacity for self-awareness or abstract thought, the process of gendering begins. The infant's body, already a site of profound sensory experience as we've seen, is immediately subjected to the gaze of the Symbolic order. The cry is interpreted through a gendered lens; the way the infant is held, dressed, and spoken to carries implicit messages about who they are expected to become. Pink blankets for one, blue for another; dolls for some, toy cars for others – these are not merely benign choices but the initial strokes of a brush, initiating a process of differentiation that will profoundly shape the individual's developing sense of self. The biological attributes of sex – the presence or absence of specific genitalia, the hormonal profiles – become the perceived foundation for a whole edifice of social roles, behaviors, and personality traits. This is a powerful alchemy, where biological material is transmuted into social identity, often with little regard for the individual's lived experience or innate inclinations. The body, therefore, is not passively received but actively interpreted and molded by the surrounding culture, becoming the site where predefined notions of masculinity and femininity are made manifest.

This inscription of gender onto the body is rarely a seamless or unproblematic affair. The lived, embodied experience of an individual often clashes with the rigid expectations imposed by the Symbolic order. The body, with its inherent drives, its capacity for unexpected sensations, and its unique trajectory of development, may not always conform to the neat categories of masculine or feminine that society has prescribed. This can lead to profound internal conflict, a sense of dissonance between who one feels oneself to be and who one is expected to be. The body, intended by the Symbolic to be a straightforward signifier of a particular gender, can become a source of confusion, anxiety, and even rebellion when its lived reality diverges from its prescribed meaning. This tension highlights the artificiality of the gender binary, revealing how it forces diverse human experiences into pre-established molds, often causing distress and alienation for those who do not fit neatly within its confines.

The concept of "performing" gender becomes crucial here. Judith Butler's influential work on gender performativity suggests that gender is not something we

are, but something we *do*. It is a series of repeated actions, gestures, and stylistic choices that, over time, create the illusion of a stable, inherent gender identity. The body, in this framework, is the stage upon which these performances are enacted. The way one walks, talks, dresses, and interacts with others are all part of a continuous, often unconscious, performance of gender. These performances are not necessarily conscious acts of deception but are deeply ingrained habits, learned from observing and imitating those around us. We learn to "do" masculinity or femininity through a constant process of social mirroring and reinforcement. The body, therefore, is not merely a passive recipient of gender but an active participant in its continuous construction and reproduction.

Consider, for instance, the subtle yet profound differences in how men and women are often encouraged to occupy space. Men are frequently encouraged to spread out, to take up more room, their bodies signaling a sense of dominance and assertion. Women, conversely, are often socialized to be more contained, their posture and movements suggesting a desire to be less conspicuous, to be more accommodating. These are not inherent biological imperatives but learned performances, deeply embedded in our cultural understanding of gender. The body becomes the tool through which these performances are executed, and the consistent repetition of these performances reinforces the societal illusion of essential gender differences. The blush that spreads across a woman's cheek when complimented, the firm handshake of a man – these are all micro-performances that contribute to the larger narrative of gender being enacted on and through the body.

Furthermore, the Symbolic order dictates not only how we perform gender but also how we

perceive gender in others. Our eyes are trained to seek out cues – the pitch of a voice, the length of hair, the curve of a hip – that confirm our pre-existing notions of masculinity and femininity. When these cues align with our expectations, we readily categorize an individual. However, when they diverge, or when an individual blurs these expected markers, it can create a sense of unease or confusion. This underscores how deeply ingrained our gendered perceptions are, and how the Symbolic order has shaped our very way of seeing and interpreting the world, particularly in relation to the bodies we encounter. The body becomes a site of constant negotiation, where the individual's lived experience and the societal gaze converge, often with significant psychic consequences.

The power of the Symbolic order to shape our understanding of the body and gender is further evident in the historical and cultural variations of gender expression. What is considered masculine or feminine in one culture or era may be radically different in another. The elaborate headdresses worn by some indigenous men, the acceptance of female warriors in ancient societies, or the fluid gender roles observed in some non-Western cultures all challenge the notion of a universal, biologically determined gender. These variations demonstrate that gender is not simply a reflection of biological sex but a socially constructed phenomenon, heavily influenced by the prevailing Symbolic order. The body, while physically present, is interpreted through a lens that is constantly being reframed by cultural evolution and shifting social norms.

The psychological impact of this inscription of gender onto the body can be profound. When an individual's internal sense of self, their "gender core," does not align with the gender assigned to them at birth based on their physical characteristics, it can lead to significant distress. This is the experience of gender dysphoria, where the body itself can feel like a source of profound discomfort or alienation because it does not accurately reflect one's internal gender identity. In such cases, the body, intended by the Symbolic order to be a clear signifier of a particular gender, becomes a source of profound disconnect. The performative aspect of gender takes on a new urgency, as individuals seek to align their external presentation with their internal sense of self, often through social, medical, or personal transitions. This highlights the fundamental human need for congruence between one's internal experience and one's external presentation, and the potential suffering that arises when this congruence is disrupted by the impositions of the Symbolic.

Moreover, the Symbolic order not only dictates gender roles but also influences our very perception of embodiment. It shapes what it means to have a "male" body or a "female" body, imbuing these physical forms with specific qualities, capabilities, and limitations. For example, societal narratives often associate strength, rationality, and dominance with the male body, while associating nurturance, emotion, and passivity with the female body. These are not objective truths about biology but cultural interpretations that have become deeply ingrained. The body becomes a battleground where these competing narratives are played out, and individuals are pressured to embody these archetypes, often to the detriment of their own unique capacities and desires. The concept of "body image" itself is a product of this Symbolic inscription, as we internalize societal ideals of beauty and desirability that are often heavily gendered.

The experience of shame and judgment can also be intimately tied to the body's relationship with the Symbolic order's gendered expectations. Bodies that deviate from the norm – whether in terms of size, shape, appearance, or expression – can be subjected to intense scrutiny and condemnation. This is particularly true for those who transgress the boundaries of the gender binary. The pressure to conform to a specific gender presentation can be immense, leading individuals to suppress aspects of their true selves and to feel deeply insecure about their embodied existence. The body, in these instances, becomes a source of vulnerability, exposed to the harsh judgments of a society that has rigidly defined what it means to inhabit a particular gender.

Psychoanalytically, the construction of gender on the body can be understood as a process that begins in early childhood, interwoven with the development of the ego and the internalization of parental and societal injunctions. The infant's initial polymorphous pleasures, as we've discussed, are gradually differentiated and channeled through the emerging structures of language and social expectation. The phallus, in Lacanian thought, serves as a crucial signifier, not necessarily referring to the anatomical penis, but to a position within the Symbolic order that represents desire and difference. The inscription of this phallic signifier onto the body, through a process of identification and differentiation, plays a significant role in the formation of both masculine and feminine subjectivities. Boys are often encouraged to identify with the phallic position, while girls are understood in relation to its perceived absence or difference. This symbolic operation, enacted upon the physical body, profoundly shapes an individual's later experience of their sexuality and gender.

The Symbolic order's influence is so pervasive that it can even shape our most intimate, visceral experiences of our own bodies. The feeling of being "masculine" or "feminine" is not merely an abstract thought but a felt sense, a proprioceptive awareness that has been shaped by years of social conditioning. We learn to feel our bodies in gendered ways. The way one experiences arousal, the way one feels desire, the way one perceives physical intimacy – all of these can be influenced by the prevailing cultural narratives about gender. The body becomes a conduit for these symbolic meanings, and our subjective experience of embodiment is thus deeply intertwined with the language and social structures that define gender.

The concept of "gender embodiment" thus refers to the complex interplay between our biological sex, our psychological gender identity, and the social and cultural forces that shape how we understand and experience our bodies as gendered beings. It acknowledges that gender is not simply a matter of outward appearance or a set of behaviors, but a deeply internalized sense of self that is inextricably linked to our physical existence. The body is not a mere biological substrate upon which gender is superimposed; rather, it is an active participant in the creation and expression of gender, constantly negotiating its own reality with the demands and expectations of the Symbolic order. This negotiation can be a source of profound self-discovery and affirmation for some, while for others, it can represent a lifelong struggle to reconcile their lived embodied experience with the restrictive mandates of gender.

The continuing evolution of our understanding of gender, particularly the growing visibility and acceptance of transgender and non-binary identities, challenges the very foundations of the traditional Symbolic order. These identities highlight the limitations of a binary system that attempts to rigidly categorize bodies and experiences. They underscore the idea that gender is a spectrum, a deeply personal and fluid aspect of human experience that cannot be fully contained by rigid, socially imposed definitions. The body, in these evolving understandings, is recognized not as a fixed determinant of gender but as a site of potentiality, a physical form that can be expressed and inhabited in a myriad of ways, in alignment with an individual's authentic gender identity. This recognition is a crucial step in dismantling the oppressive structures of the Symbolic order and allowing for a more inclusive and authentic expression of gender on and through the body.

The body, in its lived reality, is also a vibrant theater of the mind, a space where the phantasmatic reigns supreme, shaping our desires and informing our erotic experiences. We are not merely biological machines driven by instinct; we are beings who navigate the world through a rich tapestry of imagination, a realm where the unspoken desires, the half-formed longings, and the deeply etched psychological landscapes converge to create a potent, often invisible, influence on our embodied sexuality. This is the domain of the Imaginary order, that crucial dimension of our psyche where images, fantasies, and illusions take flight, weaving themselves into the very fabric of our sexual being.

Within this phantasmatic realm, the body becomes a malleable entity, capable of transforming into idealized forms, archetypal figures, or even monstrous embodiments that serve as catalysts for arousal. These are not mere idle daydreams; they are active, often recurring, mental constructs that imbue our sexual encounters, both real and imagined, with a unique charge. Think of the ubiquitous presence of idealized bodies in popular culture – the sculpted physiques, the impossibly flawless skin, the perfect proportions. These images, absorbed and internalized, become part of our personal phantasmatic repertoire. They are not necessarily meant to be attained in reality, but rather to serve as potent signifiers of desirability, fueling our own erotic fantasies and shaping our internal landscape of what constitutes an exciting or fulfilling sexual experience. The body, therefore, is not simply the biological instrument of sex; it is also the canvas upon which a thousand imagined bodies are painted, each carrying its own unique erotic potential.

The process of erotic fantasy is deeply intertwined with the concept of the "phantasmatic body." This refers to the imaginary representation of a body that is not necessarily our own, or a distorted, idealized, or even monstrous version of our own body. These phantasmatic bodies can be the object of our desire, the vehicle through which we experience pleasure, or the projection of our deepest, sometimes most transgressive, sexual impulses. For instance, one might fantasize about being with a person whose body possesses attributes that are entirely different from those they typically find attractive in reality. This is not a contradiction, but rather a testament to the boundless capacity of the imagination to conjure forms that stir the erotic spirit. The phantasmatic body can be a muscular, powerful figure offering protection and dominance, or it can be a fragile, vulnerable form that evokes tenderness and a desire to nurture. It can be a stranger with an unknown face, or a familiar figure imbued with new, alluring qualities. Each of these imagined forms carries its own specific erotic charge, resonating with different aspects of our psyche and our sexual history.

Furthermore, these phantasmatic bodies are not static. They are dynamic, fluid entities that can evolve and transform within our fantasies. The idealized lover might shift in appearance, the powerful protector might reveal a hidden gentleness, or the vulnerable figure might suddenly exude an unexpected strength. This fluidity allows our fantasies to remain fresh and engaging, constantly offering new avenues for exploration and arousal. The Imaginary order, in this sense, is a vital component of our sexual vitality, preventing our erotic lives from becoming stagnant or predictable. It is the wellspring of novelty, the generator of excitement, and the architect of many of our most profound sexual experiences.

The role of transgression in erotic fantasy is also significant. Often, our deepest desires involve scenarios that would be considered taboo or unacceptable in the everyday world. These might involve power dynamics, forbidden relationships, or explorations of sexuality that push the boundaries of social norms. The phantasmatic realm provides a safe space to explore these transgressions without real-world consequences. Here, the body can be imagined in roles that are antithetical to our waking personas – the submissive can fantasize about dominance, the conventionally moral individual can explore darker impulses, and those who feel constrained by societal expectations can revel in imagined freedom. These fantasies are not necessarily an indication of a desire to act them out in reality, but rather a way of processing, understanding, and even integrating these potent, often unsettling, aspects of our own sexuality. The phantasmatic body becomes the vessel for these explorations, allowing us to embody and experience these forbidden desires in the privacy of our minds.

Consider, for example, the common fantasy of being pursued by a mysterious stranger. This phantasmatic scenario often involves a heightened sense of anticipation, an exploration of the unknown, and a focus on the sheer physical presence of the imagined pursuer. The body of this stranger, often more so than their personality or history, becomes the focal point of arousal. It is the implied power, the raw sexuality, or the sheer otherness of this imagined form that ignites the desire. The body here is not an individual with a name and a life, but a potent symbol of erotic possibility, a vessel of raw, unmediated attraction. This allows for a level of intensity and freedom that might be difficult to replicate in a real-world encounter, where the complexities of personality and social context can temper the pure, unadulterated charge of desire.

Similarly, fantasies involving power dynamics – whether of dominance or submission – are deeply rooted in the Imaginary. The phantasmatic body can be imagined in extreme states of vulnerability or control. The imagined submission might involve a surrender of agency, a release from responsibility, and a focus on the sheer physicality of the experience. The imagined dominance might involve the wielding of power, the assertion of control, and the experience of being in a position of ultimate authority. These fantasies allow individuals to explore the limits of their own desires and to experience aspects of themselves that might be suppressed in their daily lives. The body in these fantasies becomes a tool for exploring these extreme states, capable of both enduring and inflicting intense sensation.

The role of fantasy in sexual identity negotiation is also profound. For individuals exploring their sexuality, particularly during adolescence or when questioning their identity, fantasies can serve as a crucial laboratory. They provide a space to experiment with different desires, attractions, and embodiments without the pressure of external judgment. A person questioning their sexual orientation might find themselves fantasizing about individuals of genders they had not previously considered. These fantasies, while not definitive, can offer valuable insights into their developing sexual identity. The phantasmatic body becomes a mirror, reflecting back different possibilities and helping the individual to construct a sense of self that aligns with their deepest attractions.

The cultural landscape plays a significant role in shaping these phantasmatic bodies and scenarios. Media, literature, art, and even casual conversations all contribute to a shared reservoir of imagery and narratives that influence our individual fantasies. We absorb tropes of romantic heroes and heroines, images of sexual prowess, and stories of forbidden love. These external influences are then filtered through our personal experiences, our individual histories, and our unique psychological makeup, giving rise to a personalized phantasmatic world. What might be a common erotic trope in one culture can be entirely alien in another, highlighting the deeply ingrained nature of these symbolic representations in our sexual imaginaries.

The concept of the "perfect lover" is a classic example of a phantasmatic construct. This idealized figure often embodies a confluence of desirable traits – physical attractiveness, emotional availability, sexual skill, and a deep understanding of the individual's needs and desires. While the pursuit of such a perfect partner might be a romantic ideal, in reality, such a singular embodiment is unlikely. However, the fantasy of this perfect lover fuels desire, sets expectations, and can motivate individuals to seek out relationships that approximate this ideal. The phantasmatic body of the perfect lover is often composed of fragments of past loves, idealized media portrayals, and deeply held personal longings.

The Imaginary order also allows for the exploration of fears and anxieties surrounding sexuality. Fantasies can sometimes involve scenarios that are frightening or unsettling, reflecting underlying concerns about intimacy, vulnerability, or loss of control. For instance, fantasies of being overwhelmed, exposed, or rejected can arise from deep-seated anxieties about sexual performance or relational dynamics. However, by confronting these fears in the safe space of fantasy, individuals can begin to process and potentially neutralize them. The phantasmatic body in these instances can represent the embodiment of these fears, allowing for a controlled encounter with what is perceived as dangerous or threatening.

Moreover, the act of sexual arousal itself is often a complex interplay between the real and the imagined. A touch, a scent, a glance can trigger a cascade of phantasmatic associations, transforming a simple sensory input into a potent catalyst for desire. The brain, drawing on a vast library of stored images and emotional experiences, constructs a narrative, populates it with phantasmatic bodies, and imbues it with erotic significance. This is why two individuals can have the same physical experience, yet one might be intensely aroused while the other remains unmoved. The difference lies in the richness and resonance of their individual Imaginary orders. The body, in this context, becomes a sensitive receiver, attuned to both external stimuli and the internal landscape of desire.

The development of a unique sexual identity is, therefore, deeply indebted to the creative and exploratory power of the Imaginary.

It is through the constant formation and reformation of phantasmatic bodies and scenarios that individuals come to understand their own desires, their attractions, and their place within the spectrum of human sexuality. The body, in its imagined possibilities, becomes a powerful tool for self-discovery, allowing for a continuous negotiation between the biological realities of sex and the boundless, often surprising, landscapes of the erotic imagination. This is a testament to the fact that our sexuality is not solely dictated by biology or social conditioning, but is also an art form, continuously sculpted and refined within the vibrant, often surreal, realm of our inner world.

The body, as we have come to understand it through the lens of psychoanalysis, is a far more complex entity than a mere biological apparatus. It is a locus where the Imaginary, with its rich tapestry of images and fantasies, and the Symbolic, the realm of language and law, converge and interact. Yet, within this intricate weaving, there remains an elusive thread, an irreducible element that defies complete capture by either system. This is where we encounter Lacan's concept of the Real, particularly as it pertains to sexual difference. The biological fact of sex – the presence of specific genitalia, chromosomes, and hormones – is the raw material upon which our symbolic and imaginary understandings of masculinity and femininity are built. However, this biological substratum is never simply that; it is immediately interpreted, mediated, and ultimately transformed by the symbolic order and our individual imaginary constructions.

Sexual difference, from this perspective, is not a simple binary, a clear-cut division into two distinct and opposing categories. Instead, it is marked by an inherent ambiguity, a persistent remainder that resists definitive categorization. Language, the very tool we use to understand and articulate the world, is inherently inadequate to fully grasp the totality of sexual difference. We can speak of male and female, of masculine and feminine, but these terms, while crucial for social functioning and identity formation, are ultimately signifiers that point to something beyond themselves. They are attempts to chart the contours of a terrain that is fundamentally fluid and ineffable. The Real, in this context, represents that which is outside the Symbolic and the Imaginary, that which cannot be fully symbolized or imagined. It is the raw, unmediated encounter with a dimension of existence that constantly strains against the frameworks we erect to comprehend it.

Lacan's schema often posits that the male subject, in his relation to the phallus (as a signifier of lack and desire), is subjected to the Law of the Father, which attempts to impose a universal, albeit incomplete, order. However, this order is not absolute, and even within the male position, there is a recognition of a fundamental lack that drives desire. The female subject, on the other hand, is described as not being "wholly contained" by this phallic logic. Her jouissance, her particular mode of enjoyment, is often understood as being "supplementary" or "non-all," meaning it cannot be fully accounted for within the universalizing phallic equation. This does not imply a deficiency, but rather an access to a different order of being, a connection to a form of jouissance that escapes the totalizing grasp of the Symbolic. This "non-all" aspect is precisely where the Real asserts itself most powerfully in relation to sexual difference. It is the part of the feminine that cannot be reduced to a definition, that remains mysterious and unbound.

The mystery of sexual difference, therefore, is not a deficit in our understanding or a failure of language, but rather an intrinsic characteristic of its very nature. We can observe biological differences, we can construct social roles and gender identities, but the profound essence of what it means to be sexually distinct, to embody a particular sexed being, eludes complete articulation. The Real is the space of this irreducible mystery. It is the silent affirmation that no matter how much we symbolize, no matter how many images we conjure, there will always be an element of sexual difference that remains fundamentally unknowable, untamed, and outside our complete comprehension. This unknowability is not a void to be feared, but rather a generative force that fuels desire, sparks curiosity, and underscores the profound otherness that is intrinsic to human existence.

The body, in its ultimate unknowability, becomes the very stage upon which this drama of sexual difference plays out. We experience our bodies as real, as tangible entities, yet their subjective experience, their inner reality, is forever mediated by our symbolic and imaginary frameworks. The biological sex we are assigned at birth is a starting point, but it is not a fixed destiny. It is through our interactions with the Symbolic and Imaginary orders that we come to inhabit our bodies as sexed beings. However, the Real reminds us that there is a dimension to our embodied existence that transcends these categories. The sensation of touch, the flush of desire, the pang of loss – these are visceral experiences that can be described, but their raw, immediate quality, their pure being-in-the-world, is something that the Symbolic and Imaginary can only approximate.

Consider the experience of embodiment itself. While we can anatomically describe a body, and we can develop complex social and cultural understandings of what it means to inhabit that body as a man or a woman, there remains a subjective core that resists such precise mapping. The feeling of embodiment, the internal sense of being in a particular body, is not something that can be fully captured by language or visual representation. It is a lived reality that is simultaneously concrete and elusive. This is where the Real of the body intersects with the Real of sexual difference. The body is not simply an object to be known and categorized; it is a Subject that knows itself through experience, but this knowing is always partial, always mediated.

Furthermore, the limitations of language in articulating sexual difference are evident in the very way we attempt to define it. When we try to pinpoint the essence of masculinity or femininity, we invariably fall back on cultural stereotypes, biological determinisms, or abstract philosophical concepts, none of which can fully encompass the lived reality of sexed beings. The Lacanian "non-all" for the feminine, for example, highlights this linguistic inadequacy. It suggests that the feminine, in its fullest sense, cannot be fully represented by a universal signifier. There is always something that escapes, something that remains outside the system of signification. This is not a failure of the feminine, but a testament to its unique relationship with the Real.

This inherent resistance to full capture is also true for the masculine position, though perhaps in a different way. While the masculine is often associated with the phallic function, with the attempt to impose order and meaning, it too is marked by a fundamental lack. The drive for mastery and control is, in itself, a response to an underlying sense of incompleteness. The Real, in this sense, is the shared ground of this incompletion, the reminder that all human beings, regardless of their sexed position, are fundamentally marked by a constitutive lack.

The body, then, becomes the site where this interplay between the symbolic, the imaginary, and the Real unfolds. It is through our embodied experience that we navigate the social expectations and imagined ideals associated with our sex, while simultaneously encountering the irreducible Real that lies beneath these constructions. A person might identify as a man, adopt masculine behaviors, and be recognized as such by society, yet still grapple with an internal experience of their sexed being that defies easy categorization. This internal grappling is a testament to the ongoing encounter with the Real, with that which is beyond immediate symbolization or imaginative projection.

The concept of sexual difference, therefore, is not merely about understanding the categories of male and female as distinct social or biological entities. It is about acknowledging the profound mystery at the heart of sexuation, a mystery that is rooted in the Real. This Real is not a void, but a dimension of existence that is always present, always influencing our experiences, even as it eludes our attempts to fully grasp it. It is the reminder that we are, at our core, beings of flesh and spirit, of symbol and sensation, and that within this intricate tapestry, there remains an irreducible element of the unknowable that shapes our desires, our identities, and our very experience of being in the world.

The implications of this understanding for our lived experience are significant. It suggests that a rigid adherence to predefined notions of masculinity and femininity, while perhaps providing a sense of order, can ultimately limit our access to the fuller spectrum of human experience. By acknowledging the inherent ambiguity and mystery of sexual difference, we open ourselves to a more nuanced and authentic engagement with our own sexed being. We can begin to appreciate the ways in which our bodies are not just biological facts, but sites of profound subjective experience, deeply intertwined with the Symbolic and Imaginary, yet always touching upon the elusive Real.

The "body without organs" (BwO), a concept often associated with Deleuze and Guattari but with resonance in psychoanalytic thought concerning the pre-symbolic, can be seen as a way of conceptualizing this dimension of pure materiality and potentiality that exists prior to or alongside the structured, sexed body of the Symbolic and Imaginary. While Lacan focuses on the phallus as a transcendental signifier that structures sexual difference, the idea of a "pre-oedipal" or "undifferentiated" bodily experience, where distinctions are not yet firmly established, hints at a connection to the Real. This is not to say that the Real is a primordial state of undifferentiation, but rather that it represents a fundamental aspect of existence that precedes or lies beyond the ordering principles of language and imagination.

The Real, in its relation to sexual difference, is the fundamental ambiguity that sexuation itself introduces into the human condition. We are born into a world of biological sex, but this raw fact is immediately taken up by the Symbolic and Imaginary, which impose meanings, expectations, and identities. Yet, the biological difference itself, in its most fundamental aspect, is not fully communicable or translatable into the realm of language. There is a "something more" to the biological fact of sex that escapes complete symbolic capture. This "something more" is the Real, the irreducible kernel of experience that resists being fully symbolized or imagined.

This leads to an understanding of the body as ultimately unknowable, not in the sense of being inscrutable, but in the sense that its subjective reality, its lived experience, cannot be fully objectified or articulated. We can describe the physiology of a body, we can analyze its social and cultural meanings, but the inner experience of inhabiting that body, particularly as a sexed being, remains uniquely individual and, to some extent, inaccessible to others. This inaccessibility is a direct consequence of the Real's intrusion into our embodied existence. Our bodies are the very locus of this fundamental unknowability, the material expression of a dimension that lies beyond complete comprehension.

The persistent mystery surrounding sexual difference is not a failing of human intellect or a limitation of our current understanding of biology or psychology. Rather, it is an intrinsic feature of sexual difference itself, an indication of its profound and foundational connection to the Lacanian Real. The Real is that which resists symbolization, that which cannot be fully integrated into the Symbolic order or captured by the Imaginary. It is the inherent excess, the remainder, the dimension of experience that always eludes complete articulation. In the context of sexual difference, this means that no matter how precisely we define or categorize, there will always be an element that remains outside of our conceptual grasp, a fundamental ambiguity that defines our sexed existence.

The body, in its most fundamental sense, becomes the ultimate locus of this unknowability. While we can observe biological characteristics and construct elaborate systems of gender and sexuality, the subjective experience of being embodied, particularly as a sexed subject, remains a deeply personal and, to an extent, ineffable reality. The Real ensures that there is always a dimension to our embodied existence that transcends language, imagination, and even our own conscious understanding. This encounter with the Real, with the irreducible mystery of sexual difference, is not a cause for despair, but rather a testament to the profound complexity and richness of human existence. It is within this space of mystery and incompletion that true desire, authentic self-understanding, and the potential for profound connection with the Other can emerge. The body, in its unknowable depth, serves as a constant reminder of this fundamental truth.

The way we perceive our physical selves, the intricate tapestry of images and sensations that constitute our "body image," is not a static or purely objective phenomenon. Rather, it is a dynamic and deeply personal construct, perpetually shaped by a confluence of internal psychological processes and external social influences. This internal landscape of perceived physicality holds a profound and often underestimated sway over the most intimate aspects of our lives, particularly our sexual expression. It is within this intricate interplay that we find a crucial nexus: how we *see* our bodies directly influences how we *experience* them in their sexual dimension, and consequently, how we engage with sexual desire, arousal, and fulfillment.

A pervasive undercurrent in contemporary culture is the relentless bombardment of idealized body types. From the glossy pages of magazines to the curated perfection of social media feeds, we are ceaselessly presented with images of bodies that conform to narrow, often unattainable, standards of beauty and desirability. These pervasive ideals, internalized through a process that begins in early development and continues throughout life, can become potent benchmarks against which individuals measure their own physical selves. When there is a significant discrepancy between an individual's perceived body and these internalized ideals, a cascade of psychological consequences can ensue. This gap, this feeling of not measuring up, often crystallizes into a negative body image.

The impact of a negative body image on sexual expression can be profoundly inhibiting. When individuals are preoccupied with perceived flaws, imperfections, or deviations from societal norms, their focus shifts inward, away from the potential for pleasure and connection, and towards self-scrutiny and shame. This internal monologue of criticism can hijack the natural unfolding of sexual arousal and desire. The very thought of being physically vulnerable, of exposing oneself to another, can become fraught with anxiety. The fear of judgment, whether real or imagined, can lead to a hesitiation to initiate intimacy, a reluctance to explore different sexual activities, or a general sense of withdrawal from sexual encounters. In essence, the imagined gaze of the critic within, mirroring the perceived judgment of the external world, can erect formidable barriers to sexual spontaneity and enjoyment.

Consider the subtle yet pervasive ways this can manifest. An individual who harbors deep-seated dissatisfaction with their weight might avoid certain positions during intercourse, fearing it will accentuate perceived bulges or create an unflattering silhouette. Someone acutely self-conscious about the appearance of their skin might shy away from passionate kissing or tactile exploration, worried about the texture or presence of blemishes. The fear of exposing scars, stretch marks, or other bodily variations that deviate from the idealized norm can lead to a withdrawal of affection and a suppression of physical intimacy. These are not mere superficial concerns; they are deeply rooted anxieties that can significantly diminish the quality and depth of sexual experience.

Furthermore, a negative body image can distort an individual's perception of their own desirability. They may struggle to believe that they are attractive or worthy of sexual attention, even when presented with clear evidence to the contrary from their partners. This internal deficit of self-worth can lead to a hesitant and unassertive approach to sexual relationships, where they may feel less entitled to express their desires or to seek satisfaction. The capacity for sexual pleasure is intrinsically linked to a sense of self-acceptance and embodied presence. When this foundation is undermined by persistent self-criticism, the potential for profound sexual fulfillment is significantly curtailed. It becomes a struggle to be fully present in the moment, to surrender to sensation, when one is constantly battling an internal war of self-deprecation.

Conversely, when individuals cultivate a more integrated and accepting relationship with their bodies, regardless of whether they perfectly align with external ideals, a different landscape of sexual expression emerges. This is not to advocate for a passive resignation to one's physical form, but rather for an active process of self-appreciation and embodiment. When individuals feel more at ease with their physicality, they are more likely to approach sexual intimacy with a sense of confidence and openness. This acceptance allows for a greater capacity to be present in the moment, to attune to bodily sensations, and to engage in sexual activities with less inhibition.

Embracing one's physicality in a positive way often involves a reframing of what constitutes a desirable body. It moves beyond the narrow, often manufactured, ideals of the external world and embraces the unique, lived reality of one's own body. This can involve recognizing the body's strength, its capacity for pleasure, its history, and its individual contours. When an individual can appreciate their body not as a project to be perfected, but as a vessel for experience and connection, the pathways to sexual liberation begin to open.

This liberation manifests in several crucial ways. Firstly, a positive body image fosters greater sexual confidence. This confidence translates into a willingness to explore one's own sexuality and to communicate needs and desires to a partner. It allows for greater assertiveness in initiating sexual encounters, setting boundaries, and seeking out experiences that are pleasurable and fulfilling. The fear of judgment recedes, replaced by a sense of agency and self-possession.

Secondly, an integrated acceptance of one's body enhances the capacity for sexual pleasure. When one is not preoccupied with self-critique, attention can be directed towards the rich tapestry of bodily sensations that sexual activity offers. The exploration of touch, the nuances of arousal, the crescendo of orgasm – these experiences become more vivid and accessible when the mind is not constantly engaged in a battle of self-criticism. The body, experienced as a source of pleasure rather than a source of shame, becomes a more willing and capable participant in sexual intimacy.

The connection between self-perception and sexual fulfillment is a feedback loop. A positive self-perception of one's body can lead to more satisfying sexual experiences, which in turn can reinforce that positive self-perception. Conversely, negative self-perceptions can lead to unsatisfying experiences, further solidifying those negative beliefs. Therefore, the work of cultivating a healthier body image is not merely an aesthetic pursuit; it is a fundamental aspect of fostering robust sexual well-being.

This process of integration and acceptance is deeply personal and can involve a journey of self-discovery. It may involve challenging internalized societal messages about beauty and desirability, engaging in practices that promote body awareness and appreciation (such as mindful movement, yoga, or simply spending time in nature), and cultivating self-compassion. It can also involve seeking out supportive relationships and communities where one's body is accepted and valued for its uniqueness.

Moreover, the concept of "sexual expression" itself is broadened when viewed through the lens of body image. It is not solely about the act of intercourse or specific sexual behaviors. It encompasses the entire spectrum of how an individual experiences and communicates their sexuality. This includes verbal expressions of desire, non-verbal cues of affection and attraction, the willingness to explore different forms of physical intimacy, and the ability to connect with a partner on a sensual level. When body image is positive, these forms of expression become more fluid and authentic.

The embodied subject, as we have explored, is a complex interplay of biological reality, symbolic representation, and imaginary projection. The body is the tangible ground upon which these dimensions meet, and its perceived quality profoundly influences our engagement with the world, particularly in the realm of sexuality. A negative body image often signifies a disconnect between the lived, visceral reality of the body and the idealized, often alienating, images that have been internalized. This disconnect creates a rift, a hesitation to fully inhabit one's body as a site of sexual potential.

Conversely, when an individual can bridge this gap, when they can begin to see their body not as a flawed object to be judged, but as a living, breathing, sensing entity capable of immense pleasure and connection, the possibilities for sexual expression expand exponentially. This is where the concept of "acceptance" becomes paramount. It is not about a passive embrace of whatever physical form one possesses, but an active, conscious decision to relate to one's body with kindness, curiosity, and a recognition of its inherent value.

The implications of this are far-reaching for therapeutic interventions. For individuals struggling with sexual dysfunction or dissatisfaction, exploring their relationship with their body image is often a critical component of treatment. Psychoanalytic and psychodynamic approaches can help individuals unpack the origins of negative body perceptions, trace their development through early experiences and societal conditioning, and work through the underlying anxieties and insecurities that fuel self-criticism. Cognitive Behavioral Therapy (CBT) and Acceptance and Commitment Therapy (ACT) can provide practical tools for challenging negative thought patterns, developing more self-compassionate self-talk, and committing to behaviors that promote embodiment and sexual exploration.

Ultimately, the journey towards greater sexual freedom and fulfillment is inextricably linked to the journey towards greater self-acceptance and embodied presence. When we can move beyond the relentless pursuit of an unattainable ideal and learn to appreciate the unique, complex, and beautiful reality of our own bodies, we unlock a profound capacity for sexual expression. This acceptance allows us to inhabit our bodies more fully, to engage with our desires more openly, and to experience the richness and intimacy that consensual sexual connection can offer. It is in this integrated embrace of our physicality that we find not just sexual satisfaction, but a deeper connection to ourselves and to others. The body, perceived not as a battleground of flaws, but as a source of embodied experience and pleasure, becomes the fertile ground for a vibrant and authentic sexual life. This transition from a critical gaze to an appreciative embrace is central to the embodied subject's capacity for sexual flourishing. It is the recognition that the body, in all its particularities, is not a barrier to pleasure, but its very gateway.

Chapter 11: The Analytic Dyad: Body and Mind in Dialogue

The analytic consulting room, often envisioned as a neutral, almost disembodied space for the meticulous dissection of the psyche, is in reality, a charged arena. Within its confines, two embodied beings – analyst and analysand – engage in a dance of verbal and non-verbal communication, a constant interplay where the unseen currents of emotion and meaning are carried as much by the breath, the gesture, the very stillness of the analyst, as by the spoken word. The analyst's body, therefore, is not merely a passive vessel, but an active instrument, a palpable presence that profoundly shapes the therapeutic encounter. It is a presence that must be understood not just in terms of its conscious intentionality, but also in its unconscious resonance, its capacity to evoke, to contain, and to catalyze change.

Consider the analyst's posture. A slumped, weary frame might inadvertently communicate a lack of engagement, a subconscious message of burden or disinterest, even when the analyst's mind is sharply focused. Conversely, an overly rigid, almost militaristic stance can convey an unapproachable authority, erecting a barrier rather than inviting intimacy. The ideal, of course, is a posture that signals attentiveness and openness – a relaxed yet alert presence that communicates a willingness to be present, to receive, and to engage. This physical stance is not about performing a role, but about embodying a state of being: the embodied capacity to listen, to bear witness, and to hold the weight of another's unfolding narrative. It is a subtle art, requiring a constant calibration between being fully present and allowing space for the analysand's own experience to unfold without undue influence. The analyst's body becomes a silent testament to their commitment to the analytic process, a physical manifestation of their focused attention and their attuned responsiveness.

The tone of the analyst's voice is another critical dimension of their embodied presence. It is not simply the words spoken, but

how they are spoken. A voice that is too hurried can convey anxiety or a desire to quickly move past difficult material. A voice that is too slow or monotonous can lull the analysand into a state of disengagement or even boredom. The rhythm, the pitch, the volume – all carry unconscious weight. A soft, modulated tone might be perceived as comforting and inviting, fostering a sense of safety. A sharper, more incisive tone, employed judiciously, can sometimes be necessary to break through a defensive pattern or to highlight a crucial, often avoided, aspect of the analysand's experience. The analyst's voice, in its sonic qualities, can mimic or contrast with the analysand's own emotional tone, creating a resonant echo or a subtle challenge that can be therapeutically potent. It is the melody that underpins the lyrics of the analytic discourse, capable of conveying empathy, curiosity, concern, or even a carefully calibrated distance when such is needed.

Beyond these more overt aspects of physical presentation, there are the subtler, often unconscious, bodily reactions that play a significant role. A micro-expression of surprise or discomfort, a fleeting grimace, a sudden intake of breath – these are windows into the analyst's own internal world, their immediate, unmediated response to the material being presented. While the analyst strives for a high degree of self-awareness and emotional regulation, these involuntary reactions are part of the human exchange. Crucially, it is not the occurrence of such reactions, but the analyst's capacity to recognize them, to understand their potential impact on the analysand, and to integrate them into the analytic process, that is paramount. These unconscious reverberations can sometimes serve as powerful signals, pointing to areas of intense emotional charge within the analytic field that might otherwise remain hidden. They can offer a unique form of validation to the analysand, a sense of being truly heard and felt, even at an unconscious level, or conversely, can highlight the analysand's projections onto the analyst.

The consulting room itself becomes an extension of this embodied presence. The furniture, the lighting, the temperature, the very scent of the space – all contribute to the atmosphere and can subtly influence the analytic dyad. A room that feels cluttered or chaotic can mirror a sense of internal disarray in the analysand, or perhaps even reflect an unresolved aspect of the analyst's own internal environment. A room that is too stark and impersonal might feel unwelcoming and hinder the development of a secure relational base. The analyst's careful curation of this space is itself an act of embodied communication, an unconscious expression of their therapeutic intention. It is the physical container for the psychological container, and both are vital. The weight of objects, the texture of fabrics, the way light falls – these can all contribute to the sense of safety, containment, and the capacity for introspection.

The concept of embodiment for the analyst also extends to their own personal history and how it unconsciously informs their presence. Every analyst, regardless of their training, brings their own lived experiences, their own relational patterns, their own internal landscape into the consulting room. This is not to suggest that the analytic session is about the analyst's personal journey, but rather that the analyst's self-awareness and ongoing personal work are essential for understanding how their own embodied presence might be unconsciously shaping the transference and countertransference dynamics. For example, an analyst who carries unresolved grief might be unconsciously more attuned to moments of loss in the analysand's narrative, or conversely, might unconsciously shy away from such material. Similarly, an analyst with a history of feeling unheard might be particularly sensitive to moments when the analysand feels invalidated.

This is where the concept of countertransference becomes deeply intertwined with the analyst's embodied experience. The analyst's involuntary emotional and psychological reactions to the analysand are not simply abstract phenomena; they are often experienced somatically. A tightening in the chest, a knot in the stomach, a feeling of agitation – these bodily sensations can be crucial signposts, alerting the analyst to the unconscious dynamics at play. To dismiss these somatic signals as mere personal issues or distractions would be to miss a vital avenue of understanding. Instead, the analyst must learn to use their own embodied reactions as data, to reflect upon what in the analysand's material, or in the relational field, might be eliciting these responses. This is not about acting out these feelings, but about using them as a form of sensitive attunement to the analysand's inner world, and to the intricate relational matrix that is being co-created.

The analyst's deliberate choice in how they manage their own physical needs within the session also speaks to their embodied presence. Whether it is a quiet sip of water, a brief adjustment of position, or the subtle act of consulting a clock, these moments, when handled with discretion and integrated into the flow, can serve important functions. They demonstrate that the analyst is a living, breathing human being, not an automaton, and can, in certain contexts, even normalize the expression of basic human needs. However, if these actions become excessive or disruptive, they can undermine the sense of containment and focus, pulling the analysand's attention away from their own internal work and onto the analyst's perceived discomfort or distraction. The art lies in a seamless integration, where the analyst's embodied needs are managed in a way that supports, rather than detracts from, the analytic process.

Furthermore, the analyst's capacity for somatic attunement can be particularly crucial when working with analysands who struggle to verbalize their experiences or who present with somatic symptoms that are not easily explained by conventional medical frameworks. In such cases, the analyst's own felt sense of the analysand's emotional state, their ability to perceive subtle shifts in bodily tension or energy, can provide invaluable insights. This is not about diagnostically interpreting bodily symptoms from a purely physical perspective, but about understanding how the body is expressing a psychological reality. The analyst's embodied presence becomes a responsive, sensitive instrument that can pick up on these non-verbal cues and help the analysand to make connections between their physical sensations and their emotional lives.

The concept of 'analytic space' itself is thus not merely a conceptual construct, but a physically embodied one. It is the space co-created by the two individuals, a shared environment imbued with the history of their interactions, the projections and identifications that have been enacted, and the subtle influences of their embodied states. The analyst's awareness of their own body – its sensations, its tensions, its unconscious impulses – becomes a critical tool in understanding the dynamics of this shared space. By attending to their own embodied reactions, analysts can gain deeper insights into the transference and countertransference, the unconscious communication that flows between them, and the unique relational field that is being constructed session by session. This heightened somatic awareness allows the analyst to be more fully present, more deeply attuned, and ultimately, more effective in facilitating the analysand's journey of self-discovery and healing. The analyst's body, in its stillness and its subtle responsiveness, becomes a sanctuary for the unfolding of the analysand's deepest truths.

The patient's body in the consulting room is a canvas upon which the unarticulated is painted, a living testament to an inner reality that often evades the direct reach of language. While the primary mode of analytic work is indeed verbal, the analyst's attention is never solely focused on the spoken word. Instead, it is directed towards the entire organism of the patient, recognizing that the body is a repository of experience, a silent narrator of the self. Every fidget, every sigh, every posture adopted upon entering the room, offers a glimpse into the patient's internal landscape. These are not merely incidental details to be overlooked in the pursuit of a coherent narrative, but rather potent expressions that carry significant psychological weight.

Consider the subtle language of posture. A patient who enters the room and immediately collapses onto the couch, their shoulders hunched as if carrying an invisible burden, is communicating far more than their physical fatigue. This slump might speak of a lifelong habit of self-effacement, of feeling perpetually weighed down by expectations or responsibilities, or of an unconscious belief that they are too insignificant to occupy space fully. Conversely, a patient who sits rigidly on the edge of their chair, their body taut, as if ready for immediate flight, might be signaling profound anxiety, a deep-seated fear of being trapped, or a hypervigilance born from past traumas. Their physical stillness is not a sign of calm, but of an intense, held-in tension. The analyst observes these stances not to judge, but to understand the underlying emotional states and relational patterns they represent. The way a patient chooses to inhabit the physical space of the consulting room—whether they sprawl expansedly or shrink into themselves—is an immediate, non-verbal statement about their sense of self-worth, their perceived safety, and their capacity for connection.

Gestures, too, are part of this embodied discourse. A patient who habitually wrings their hands might be expressing a generalized anxiety, a nervous energy that cannot find an outlet. This gesture can also represent an unconscious attempt to "wash away" guilt or shame, or a desperate, internalized plea for help. The restless tapping of a foot, the constant touching of the face or hair, the way one's gaze darts around the room, avoiding eye contact—all these are communicative acts. They can signify impatience, a desire to escape the intensity of the analytic encounter, a difficulty in focusing, or a deep-seated discomfort with vulnerability. When a patient repeatedly touches their throat, it might be a somatic expression of an inability to speak their truth, to swallow their words, or to express anger. A hand pressed to the stomach could point to feelings of unease, nausea related to emotional distress, or a visceral reaction to something that feels indigestible within the analytic process. The analyst learns to read these somatic cues as a form of pre-verbal communication, a way for the patient's unconscious to signal what their conscious mind may be unable or unwilling to articulate.

Somatic complaints, even when presented as purely medical issues, often carry a potent psychological charge. Headaches that appear with predictable regularity before difficult sessions, digestive disturbances that flare up during periods of intense emotional processing, or chronic back pain that seems to worsen when the patient feels unsupported—these physical symptoms are frequently the body's way of participating in the analytic dialogue. The body can bear witness to emotional pain that the psyche has managed to dissociate or repress. A patient with a history of childhood neglect might develop a pervasive feeling of coldness, a phantom chill that no amount of external warmth can alleviate, symbolizing the absence of emotional warmth in their formative years. Another might experience a tightness in their chest, a physical manifestation of suppressed grief or an overwhelming sense of being constricted by their circumstances. The analyst's role is not to pathologize these physical symptoms but to explore their potential symbolic meaning within the context of the patient's life and the transference-countertransference dynamics of the session. They are often the somatic echoes of psychological distress, a language of suffering that bypasses conscious defenses.

The patient's engagement with their own body—or lack thereof—is also deeply informative. A patient who seems disconnected from their physical sensations, who describes their body as a mere vehicle for their thoughts or a source of annoyance, may be struggling with issues of embodiment, self-acceptance, or the integration of mind and body. This disconnection can stem from a history of trauma where the body became a site of violation, leading to a desperate need to disown it. Conversely, a patient who is hyper-aware of every sensation, meticulously detailing every twinge and ache, might be using their body as a way to avoid engaging with more abstract or emotionally threatening aspects of their inner world. The analyst must navigate this delicate terrain, helping the patient to find a more balanced and integrated relationship with their embodied self, a self where physical sensations are not ignored but are understood as integral to their overall experience.

The very act of speaking itself is an embodied process, and the way a patient speaks can reveal a great deal. The pace of their speech, the fluctuations in their voice's volume and pitch, their breathing patterns—these are all somatic elements that contribute to the narrative. A breathy, shallow respiration might indicate anxiety or a fear of fully expressing oneself. A voice that cracks or falters when discussing certain topics can signal underlying emotional pain or vulnerability. A staccato, rushed delivery might suggest a frantic attempt to outrun difficult emotions, while a slow, monotonous tone could mask underlying depression or a sense of detachment. The analyst listens not just to the content of the words but to the music of their delivery, recognizing that the body is always singing its own song beneath the surface of conscious thought.

Furthermore, the patient's relationship with the physical objects and boundaries of the consulting room can offer symbolic insights. How they interact with the furniture, whether they cross boundaries by touching the analyst's belongings, or how they manage the physical space around them—all can reflect their interpersonal style, their level of impulse control, and their capacity to respect relational limits. For instance, a patient who consistently encroaches on the analyst's personal space might be unconsciously seeking a closeness they never experienced, or struggling with boundaries in all their relationships. Conversely, someone who remains rigidly within a designated area, as if afraid to trespass, might be demonstrating a profound fear of intimacy or an ingrained deference to authority.

The analyst's attunement to these bodily manifestations is not about becoming a diagnostician of physical symptoms, but about understanding the symbolic language of the body within the unique context of the analytic relationship. It is about recognizing that the patient's physical presentation is an integral part of the transference, a way in which past relational patterns are being reenacted in the present. The patient might be unconsciously treating the analyst as a parental figure who was dismissive of their physical needs, leading to a somatic presentation of distress that mirrors past experiences. Or, the patient might be projecting onto the analyst their own disowned aspects of embodiment, leading to an unconscious belief that the analyst is overly critical or intrusive regarding their physicality.

The patient's body, therefore, becomes a co-conspirator in the analytic work, offering encrypted messages that, when deciphered with empathy and curiosity, can unlock deeper levels of understanding. The analyst's capacity to hold this multi-layered communication—the verbal and the non-verbal, the conscious and the unconscious, the psychological and the somatic—is what allows for the profound transformations that can occur within the analytic process. The patient's body is not just the vessel for their suffering; it is also a vital pathway to their healing, a testament to the intricate and often paradoxical ways in which the mind and body are inextricably linked in the human experience. The consulting room, in this light, is not merely a space for conversation but a living, breathing arena where the totality of the patient's being—mind, body, and soul—is invited to participate in the arduous yet ultimately rewarding work of self-discovery. The analyst, by attending to the patient's embodied presence, honors this holistic reality, recognizing that true insight often arises when the silent language of the body is finally heard.

The analyst's inner world is not a sterile, detached observatory; it is a dynamic and responsive ecosystem, intimately entwined with the patient's. This is particularly evident when we consider the phenomenon of somatic countertransference. Here, the analyst, attuned to the patient's unspoken distress, begins to experience physical sensations, discomforts, or even symptoms that seem to arise from, or directly mirror, the patient's own unconscious material. This is not a conscious projection, nor is it simply an empathic resonance; it is a visceral, bodily response that can serve as a profound diagnostic indicator, offering the analyst a direct, somatic understanding of the patient's internal landscape, a language spoken not in words, but in flesh and bone.

Imagine a patient who has been recounting a history of profound emotional neglect in childhood, a narrative laced with an almost palpable sense of emptiness. As they speak, the analyst might find themselves suddenly experiencing a chilling sensation, a feeling of deep internal cold that no amount of thermostat adjustment can dispel. This is not the analyst's own coldness, nor is it a mere intellectual understanding of the patient's emotional deprivation; it is a somatic echo of that very lack, a physical manifestation of the patient's long-held emotional starvation, now resonating within the analyst's own body. The patient's internal void has, in a sense, found a temporary, embodied home within the analyst. This somatic experience, when recognized and understood, can illuminate the depth of the patient's suffering in a way that words alone might fail to convey. It provides a raw, unmediated insight into the lived reality of the patient's inner world, a testimony to the fact that psychological pain often finds its most eloquent expression in the physical realm.

Consider another scenario: a patient grappling with intense, suppressed rage, a rage that has been meticulously walled off for years to maintain a semblance of composure. As the patient describes a seemingly minor interpersonal slight with a carefully controlled, almost brittle calm, the analyst might suddenly feel a surge of heat rising in their chest, a tightening in their jaw, or an inexplicable urge to clench their fists. These are not necessarily projections of the analyst's own anger, but rather the bodily discharge of the patient's own contained fury, channeled, however unconsciously, through the relational field. The analyst, acting as a somatic conduit, experiences the physical manifestation of a tension that the patient is unable to express or even consciously acknowledge. This somatic countertransference becomes a crucial signal: the patient's calm exterior belies a storm of unexpressed emotion, and the analyst's physical reactions provide an internal alarm bell, urging a deeper exploration of the patient's buried aggression or resentment. The analyst's ability to tolerate these bodily disturbances, to sit with the discomfort without immediate dismissal or intellectualization, is paramount. It is within this space of embodied awareness that the most potent therapeutic insights can emerge.

The analyst's own physiological responses can also offer clues to the patient's relational patterns. A patient who, from the outset of therapy, triggers a sense of physical constriction or suffocation in the analyst might be unconsciously recreating the experience of being overwhelmed or controlled by a significant figure from their past. The analyst's tightening chest or difficulty breathing becomes a somatic reenactment of the patient's own early experiences of relational suffocation or invasive presence. Similarly, if a patient consistently elicits feelings of nausea or unease in the analyst, it may point to the patient's own internal experience of something being "indigestible" in their life – perhaps a traumatic memory, a deeply held shame, or a painful truth they are struggling to process. The analyst's stomach churns, not because of something they ate, but because the patient's internal turmoil has found a somatic resonance within them. This allows the analyst to understand, on a felt sense level, the visceral nature of the patient's distress.

This phenomenon highlights the profound interconnectedness within the analytic dyad. The patient is not merely a separate entity presenting a problem to be solved; they are part of a dynamic relational field, and their unconscious material can profoundly impact the analyst's own physiological state. This is not a sign of weakness or a failure of containment on the analyst's part, but rather an indication of their sensitivity and attunement to the patient's inner world. It is a testament to the deeply embodied nature of human experience, where psychological states are invariably accompanied by physiological correlates. The analyst's body, in this context, becomes an organ of perception, a sophisticated instrument that registers the subtle vibrations of the patient's unconscious.

The challenge for the analyst lies in discerning the origins of these somatic sensations. Is this a manifestation of the patient's material, or is it a response to the analyst's own personal history, current life stressors, or transference reactions to the patient? This requires a rigorous process of self-reflection and supervision. The analyst must cultivate a keen awareness of their own bodily responses, learning to differentiate between a general somatic tension and a specific sensation that seems uniquely linked to the patient's narrative or the dynamics of the session. This often involves a detailed exploration of the timing and quality of the sensation: When did it arise? What was the patient talking about at that moment? What was the nature of the transference and countertransference patterns emerging in the room?

For instance, a patient who presents with a chronic sense of fatigue and malaise might, over time, evoke a similar weariness in the analyst, even when the patient is describing seemingly neutral events. This could signify that the patient's fatigue is not merely a symptom, but a pervasive aspect of their identity, a way of being in the world that they unconsciously transmit. The analyst's own energy levels may dip, reflecting the patient's deep-seated depletion. Conversely, a patient who expresses a great deal of nervous energy and restlessness might induce a state of heightened alertness or even agitation in the analyst. This somatic mirroring allows the analyst to grasp, at a visceral level, the sheer burden of the patient's internal agitation.

The interpretation of somatic countertransference requires a delicate balance. It is not about directly informing the patient, "I feel nauseous because you have unexpressed shame." Such a revelation could be overwhelming for the patient and might inadvertently burden them with the analyst's own internal experience. Instead, the analyst uses these somatic insights to deepen their understanding of the patient's unconscious processes, guiding their verbal interventions and the overall direction of the therapy. The somatic experience serves as a rich source of hypotheses, informing the analyst's sense of what might be going on beneath the surface. It allows them to approach certain themes with greater sensitivity or to gently probe areas that the patient seems to be unconsciously avoiding.

For example, if the analyst experiences a recurring pain in their shoulder when the patient discusses their relationship with their dominant mother, it might suggest that the patient unconsciously experiences their mother's influence as a heavy, constricting burden, a weight that they carry physically. The analyst can then explore this somatic metaphor, perhaps asking, "When you describe your mother's expectations, what does that feel like in your body?" or "It seems as though there's a heaviness associated with that part of your life." This opens up a pathway for the patient to connect their emotional experience with their physical sensations, fostering a more integrated understanding of their internal world.

The analyst's capacity to tolerate and work with somatic countertransference is a critical factor in therapeutic progress. When the analyst is able to remain present with these bodily reactions, to investigate them without defensiveness, they not only gain crucial diagnostic information but also provide a model for the patient of how to be with difficult or uncomfortable internal states. The patient learns, by observing the analyst's contained and curious response to their own embodied expressions, that their physical sensations are not necessarily something to be feared or suppressed, but rather a valuable source of information about their inner life. This can be particularly transformative for patients who have a history of having their physical or emotional distress dismissed or invalidated. The analyst's embodied presence validates the patient's experience on a fundamental level.

Furthermore, somatic countertransference can illuminate the nature of the transference itself. If a patient is unconsciously reenacting a past relational dynamic where their physical needs were ignored, the analyst might experience a subtle, persistent ache or discomfort that is easily overlooked, mirroring the patient's own suppressed physical suffering. If the patient is unconsciously seeking a nurturing, bodily comfort that was absent in their early life, the analyst might experience a feeling of warmth or fullness, a sense of being physically attuned to the patient's needs. These somatic manifestations of transference allow the analyst to understand the patient's relational world not just through the lens of their narrative, but through the felt sense of their embodied interactions.

The consulting room, therefore, becomes a space where the analyst's own body is a sensitive seismograph, registering the tremors of the patient's psychic landscape. This requires the analyst to be deeply embodied themselves, to cultivate a sophisticated interoceptive awareness, and to engage in ongoing self-exploration and supervision. It is a demanding but essential aspect of the analytic work, one that underscores the fundamental truth that the mind and body are not separate entities, but rather inextricably intertwined facets of a single, unified organism. When the analyst can attune to the somatic echoes of the patient's distress within their own being, they are not merely observing from a distance; they are participating in a profoundly embodied dialogue, facilitating a deeper and more holistic form of healing. This visceral connection, when skillfully navigated, can unlock pathways to understanding and integration that verbal communication alone might never reach, making the analyst's own embodied experience a powerful, albeit often silent, partner in the therapeutic journey. The analyst, by allowing their own body to respond, witnesses and validates the patient's embodied reality, offering a potent form of empathic resonance that transcends mere intellectual understanding. It is in this shared somatic space that the deepest transformations can begin to take root.

The analyst's task, then, is to become a translator of this primal, non-verbal discourse. It is a task that requires not just intellectual acumen but a profound attunement to the symbolic life of the body. The consulting room transforms into a crucible of interpretation, a space where the raw physicality of the patient's experience is meticulously examined, not as mere biological noise, but as a deeply meaningful, albeit often unconscious, language. This is a process of moving from the felt sense of somatic distress to its symbolic signification, enabling the patient to weave together the disparate threads of their being into a coherent narrative of self.

Consider a patient who, when discussing a perceived betrayal by a trusted friend, experiences a sudden, sharp pain in their left arm. The initial, instinctive reaction might be to dismiss it as a physical anomaly, a minor ache unrelated to the psychological narrative. However, for the analyst attuned to the body's symbolic repertoire, this pain becomes a potent signal. The left side of the body is often associated with the feminine, the receptive, the past, and the unconscious. A betrayal, particularly one involving trust, can manifest as a piercing wound, a physical manifestation of the rupture in the relational bond. The analyst's role is to gently guide the patient towards exploring this somatic experience in relation to their narrative. It is not about an immediate pronouncement: "This pain represents your wounded trust in women." Instead, it involves a nuanced inquiry. "When you describe this happening, what do you notice in your arm? Does it feel sharp, or dull? Does it remind you of anything?"

The interpretive process, therefore, is not a one-way imposition of meaning by the analyst. It is a collaborative excavation, a joint effort to decipher the symbolic grammar of the body. The patient's bodily language, whether in the form of a persistent headache during periods of intense self-criticism, a knot in the stomach when facing a difficult decision, or a tightness in the chest when recalling a traumatic event, serves as a rich source of hypotheses. The analyst listens not just to the words, but to the pauses, the intonations, the subtle shifts in posture, the involuntary gestures. These are all part of the somatic narrative, contributing to the overall message the body is attempting to convey.

For instance, a patient with a history of childhood sexual abuse might present with a constellation of seemingly unrelated physical complaints: chronic fatigue, digestive issues, and a pervasive sense of being "unclean." These are not merely the unfortunate sequelae of trauma; they are the body's eloquent, albeit deeply disquieting, language. The fatigue can represent a profound depletion of vital energy, a sense of being drained by the internal burden of the trauma. The digestive problems can symbolize the inability to "digest" or process the traumatic experience, leading to a feeling of internal toxicity. And the persistent feeling of uncleanness speaks directly to the shame and violation that often accompany such abuse, a sense that the very self has been tainted. The analyst, recognizing these somatic patterns as symbolic expressions of the trauma, can begin to explore them with the patient, not as isolated symptoms, but as interconnected facets of a deeply wounded psyche.

The consulting room becomes a stage where these embodied dramas unfold. The analyst observes how the patient holds their body. Is there a rigid guarding of the torso, suggesting a defense against emotional vulnerability? Are the shoulders hunched, conveying a sense of carrying an immense weight? Does the patient avoid eye contact, their gaze fixed on the floor as if to avoid confronting something painful? These postures are not accidental; they are the physical manifestation of the patient's internal state, their unconscious attempts to manage overwhelming emotions and experiences. The analyst's task is to help the patient become aware of these embodied patterns, to understand their origins, and ultimately, to release the holding patterns that keep them trapped.

Let's consider a patient who, when discussing their demanding boss, unconsciously begins to tap their foot with increasing intensity. This seemingly innocuous gesture can be a powerful indicator of suppressed agitation, of a desire to flee from an uncomfortable situation, or of an unexpressed impulse to assert themselves. The analyst might note this tapping and, at an opportune moment, inquire, "I notice your foot tapping. What is that like for you right now?" This gentle intervention can open a door to understanding the patient's underlying feelings of frustration, powerlessness, or even aggression that they are struggling to consciously acknowledge or express. The foot tapping is not just a physical tic; it is a message from the unconscious, a bodily translation of an unmet need or an unarticulated emotion.

The process of translating bodily language also involves attending to the more subtle, often fleeting, somatic sensations that arise during therapy. A patient describing a moment of profound loneliness might evoke a fleeting sensation of coldness in the analyst's fingertips. A patient recounting a childhood humiliation might trigger a tightening in the analyst's throat. These experiences, often dismissed as personal quirks or external stimuli, are, in fact, crucial data points. They represent a form of embodied empathy, a resonance that allows the analyst to grasp the patient's internal world on a visceral level. The analyst's ability to recognize these sensations as potentially connected to the patient's material, to hold them in awareness without immediate judgment, and to then explore their potential meaning, is central to the interpretive task.

The integration of fragmented parts of the self is a central aim of psychotherapy, and the body plays a crucial role in this process. When traumatic experiences occur, they can shatter the sense of self, leading to dissociation, where different aspects of the experience – the emotions, the physical sensations, the thoughts – become compartmentalized and inaccessible to conscious awareness. The body, however, often retains a memory of these fragmented experiences, expressing them through physical symptoms, chronic pain, or a pervasive sense of bodily unease. The analyst's work, in this context, is to help the patient re-connect with these disowned parts of themselves, to bring them back into conscious awareness, and to integrate them into a more cohesive sense of self. This might involve helping the patient to slowly, and safely, access the physical sensations associated with a traumatic memory, to bear witness to them, and to gradually imbue them with meaning.

For example, a patient who experienced a severe accident might develop chronic back pain. While medical explanations may be sought, the pain might also symbolize the immense burden they carry, the feeling of being "broken" or damaged, or the physical manifestation of a repressed emotional struggle. The analyst can work with this pain not just as a medical issue, but as a symbolic expression of the patient's inner state. Through careful exploration, the patient might begin to associate the pain with the feeling of carrying immense guilt or responsibility, or with the shock and trauma of the accident itself. As they begin to understand and process the emotional components connected to the pain, the physical sensation itself may begin to shift and transform.

The consulting room, then, is not just a space for verbal exchange; it is a somatic arena. The analyst's capacity to observe, interpret, and work with the patient's bodily language is as vital as their ability to interpret verbal communication. This requires a sophisticated understanding of the body's symbolic potential, a deep respect for the non-verbal aspects of human experience, and a willingness to engage with the patient's embodied reality. It involves recognizing that the body is not merely a vessel for the mind, but an active participant in the unfolding drama of psychic life, a repository of memory, emotion, and meaning.

The interpretation of bodily language is a delicate dance between the known and the unknown, between the explicit and the implicit. The analyst does not possess a pre-established lexicon of bodily symbols that can be applied universally. Rather, the meaning of a particular bodily expression is often unique to the individual patient, shaped by their personal history, their cultural background, and the specific dynamics of their life. Therefore, the analyst's interpretive process is always tentative, always open to revision, and always grounded in the patient's subjective experience. It is about posing questions, offering tentative hypotheses, and inviting the patient to explore the connections between their bodily sensations and their emotional and psychological world.

Consider a patient who, when discussing their mother, repeatedly touches their own throat, as if experiencing a constriction. This gesture, seemingly small and perhaps unconscious, can be a powerful indicator of unspoken emotions. It might suggest that the patient feels unable to express themselves freely in relation to their mother, that they are holding back words, or that they feel suffocated by the maternal relationship. The analyst, observing this gesture, might gently inquire, "I notice you touching your throat when you speak of your mother. What happens in your throat at those moments? Is it a tightness, a dryness, or something else?" This opens a pathway for the patient to explore the physical manifestation of their unspoken feelings, bridging the gap between bodily sensation and emotional experience.

The ultimate goal of translating bodily language is to empower the patient with a greater understanding of themselves. When patients can recognize that their physical symptoms are not random afflictions but rather meaningful expressions of their inner world, they gain a new sense of agency. They begin to see their bodies not as adversaries to be managed or silenced, but as allies, providing valuable information about their emotional well-being. This shift in perspective can be profoundly liberating, enabling them to engage with their suffering in a more integrated and less fragmented way. The consulting room, in this light, becomes a space where the patient learns to listen to their body, to trust its messages, and to use this embodied wisdom to navigate their life with greater insight and resilience.

This process of translation also involves helping the patient to tolerate and even embrace the discomfort that often accompanies the exploration of bodily sensations. Many patients have learned to suppress or ignore their physical signals, associating them with pain, anxiety, or vulnerability. The analyst's role is to create a safe and containing environment where these sensations can be approached with curiosity rather than fear. By modeling a non-judgmental and accepting attitude towards their own bodily experiences, the analyst helps the patient to do the same. This, in turn, can facilitate the release of held-in tension and the integration of disowned emotional material.

The analyst's own embodied presence is a crucial factor in this interpretive process. The analyst who is attuned to their own bodily sensations, who can tolerate the discomfort that arises from working with challenging material, provides a powerful model for the patient. When the analyst can remain calm and present while experiencing somatic countertransference, they convey a message of safety and possibility to the patient. They demonstrate that it is possible to be with difficult feelings, both physical and emotional, without being overwhelmed. This embodied attunement fosters a deeper sense of trust and connection within the analytic dyad, creating a foundation for genuine transformation.

Furthermore, the analyst must be mindful of the cultural and historical context of bodily expression. What is considered a normative bodily response in one culture may be interpreted differently in another. The analyst's awareness of these variations is essential to avoid misinterpretations and to ensure that their interpretive efforts are culturally sensitive and respectful. The language of the body, while universal in its fundamental human expression, is also shaped by the specific social and cultural landscapes in which individuals live.

In essence, the analyst's task of translating bodily language is a sophisticated and multifaceted endeavor. It requires a deep understanding of symbolic processes, a keen awareness of the non-verbal dimensions of human experience, and a commitment to working collaboratively with the patient. By deciphering the body's eloquent, albeit often cryptic, messages, the analyst helps the patient to move from fragmentation to integration, from disowned sensation to conscious understanding, and ultimately, towards a more profound and embodied sense of self. The consulting room, with its carefully calibrated atmosphere of safety and curiosity, becomes the fertile ground where this vital work of translation and integration can flourish, allowing the patient to reclaim their bodies as sources of wisdom and resilience.

The therapeutic endeavor, at its heart, is a profound journey towards integration, a weaving together of the disparate threads of human experience into a coherent and resilient tapestry of self. When this journey involves the realm of embodied suffering, the consulting room transforms into a sacred space where the body's silent eloquence is not just heard, but understood and welcomed. This final subsection of our exploration into the analytic dyad's engagement with the body focuses on the ultimate aim: the transition from a state of fragmented, physically expressed distress to a state of psychic integration, where mind and body are no longer at odds but are experienced as deeply interconnected facets of a unified whole. It is a movement from experiencing suffering as a purely somatic burden to recognizing its profound psychic underpinnings, thereby reclaiming the body not as a site of alien torment, but as a source of vital information and embodied wisdom.

Consider, for instance, the patient who arrives with a persistent, dull ache in their shoulders that has plagued them for years. Medical investigations have yielded no definitive physical cause, leaving them feeling frustrated and dismissed, as if their pain is somehow imaginary or exaggerated. Within the analytic space, this chronic shoulder tension becomes an invitation to explore. As the patient recounts the relentless pressures of their work life, the weight of unspoken resentments towards a demanding family, or the crushing burden of unfulfilled expectations, the analyst gently guides their attention to the physical sensation. "What does that weight in your shoulders feel like?" the analyst might inquire, "Is it a heaviness, a tightness, a constant pressure? And when you describe these feelings of being overwhelmed, where do you feel that most intensely?" Through this careful, iterative process of linking verbal narrative with somatic experience, the patient begins to realize that their shoulders are not merely holding tension; they are embodying a profound, accumulated sense of responsibility and strain that they have unconsciously carried. The ache is not a symptom of a broken bone or inflamed tissue; it is the physical echo of an overwhelming psychic load, a testament to the mind's intricate capacity to manifest its burdens through the body. The integration begins here, not with the eradication of the ache, but with its re-contextualization. The patient starts to see the pain not as an arbitrary affliction, but as a meaningful communication from their inner world, a signal that something in their psychic life requires attention, release, or a fundamental shift in perspective.

This journey from embodied suffering to psychic integration is a testament to the body's inherent capacity for symbolic expression. Trauma, in particular, can fragment the self, often leading to a profound disconnect between physical sensations and conscious awareness. A patient who endured a childhood of emotional neglect might experience pervasive feelings of emptiness, manifesting as a hollow sensation in their chest, accompanied by a persistent chill that no amount of warm clothing can alleviate. In the consulting room, as they begin to articulate the profound loneliness of their early years, the analyst might notice their tendency to hug themselves, or to draw inward, as if seeking to contain a void. "When you speak of feeling so alone as a child, what do you feel happening inside you, in your chest?" the analyst might ask. The patient might then describe that chilling emptiness, that sense of being an insubstantial presence. The analyst can then gently propose a connection: "It's as if that feeling of emptiness, that sense of not being truly present or acknowledged in your childhood, has found a home in your chest, a place where it's felt constantly." This is not about definitively stating, "Your emptiness is the pain in your chest," but rather offering a hypothesis, an invitation to explore. As the patient engages with this embodied representation of their emotional void, the experience of emptiness may begin to shift. It may become less of an amorphous, terrifying abyss and more of a tangible, albeit painful, sensation that can be held, examined, and eventually, understood. The coldness might lessen, or the hollowness might transform into a more accessible feeling of sadness or grief, emotions that can be processed and integrated, rather than a disavowed sensation that festers unseen and unfelt.

The process of integration is not about negating the physical reality of symptoms, but about expanding the patient's understanding of their origins and meanings. For the patient experiencing chronic digestive issues, such as bloating or discomfort, that have no clear medical etiology, the analytic process can illuminate the symbolic resonance of these bodily disturbances. When these symptoms arise during discussions of difficult family dynamics, of feeling "swallowed up" by others' needs, or of an inability to "digest" unwelcome truths, the analyst can help the patient to connect these experiences. "When you talk about your mother's constant demands, and how you feel you have to give in, what happens in your stomach?" the analyst might inquire. The patient might report a familiar sense of churning or a heavy, constricting sensation. The analyst could then offer, "It sounds as if your stomach is holding onto some of that feeling of being overwhelmed, of not being able to process or let go of what feels too difficult to accept." By acknowledging the body's role in holding these unprocessed emotional experiences, the patient begins to dismantle the wall between their physical discomfort and their psychic life. They learn that their digestive system is not simply a malfunctioning organ, but a sensitive barometer of their emotional landscape. This recognition empowers them to address the underlying emotional issues, which in turn can lead to a modulation of the physical symptoms, not through suppression, but through resolution.

The therapeutic dialogue, in this regard, becomes a potent force for re-establishing a sense of embodied wholeness. Many individuals who have experienced trauma or profound emotional deprivation learn to dissociate from their bodies, viewing them as sources of pain, shame, or betrayal. Their physical selves become alien territory, a realm to be ignored, controlled, or medicalized away. The analyst's role is to gently reintroduce the patient to their embodied existence, fostering a sense of curiosity and acceptance towards physical sensations. When a patient describes a racing heart during moments of anxiety, the analyst can invite them to explore that sensation without judgment. "What does that rapid heartbeat feel like?" they might ask. "Is it a tremor, a pounding, a fluttering? And what thoughts or images come to mind as you feel it?" This is not an attempt to stop the heart from racing, but to understand the narrative that the racing heart is part of. By bearing witness to these bodily signals, and by finding a safe space to explore them, the patient begins to dismantle the dissociation. The racing heart, once a terrifying signal of impending doom, can gradually be understood as an understandable physiological response to perceived threat, a part of the body's alarm system rather than an intrinsic flaw. This process of conscious engagement with bodily sensations facilitates their integration into the patient's overall sense of self, transforming them from alien intrusions into understandable components of their lived experience.

The integration of the body into the psychic landscape also involves acknowledging and working with the subtle, often unconscious, ways in which the body communicates its needs and distress. Consider a patient who, when discussing their intense fear of failure, begins to unconsciously clench their jaw. This seemingly minor physical manifestation is a potent indicator of suppressed aggression, of a desperate attempt to hold back an outburst, or of a deep-seated defiance against perceived external pressures. The analyst, attuned to these micro-expressions of embodied struggle, might observe this jaw-clenching and, at an appropriate moment, inquire, "As you speak of this fear of not measuring up, I notice a tension in your jaw. What is that like for you in that moment?" This gentle inquiry can open up a dialogue about the patient's internal struggle, their fear of expressing anger or assertiveness, and their tendency to internalize conflict. By bringing conscious awareness to this embodied defense, the patient can begin to understand its purpose and its cost. They may then be able to explore alternative ways of managing their fear of failure, perhaps by learning to express their anger or assertiveness in healthier ways, thereby releasing the habitual jaw-clenching. This is a crucial step towards integration, as it allows the patient to reclaim these suppressed impulses and to channel them constructively, rather than allowing them to manifest as unbidden physical tension.

The culmination of this therapeutic process lies in the patient's capacity to experience themselves as a unified whole, where the mind and body are not seen as separate entities engaged in a perpetual battle, but as interdependent and complementary aspects of their being. This integration is marked by a shift from a purely symptomatic focus to a holistic understanding of their experiences.

The patient who once presented with a litany of seemingly unrelated physical ailments, each a puzzle piece disconnected from the larger picture, begins to perceive the underlying patterns, the unifying narrative that connects their bodily sensations to their emotional life, their relational histories, and their core beliefs about themselves and the world. This is not a sudden revelation, but a gradual unfolding, a dawning realization that their physical symptoms are not arbitrary punishments, but eloquent messengers, carrying vital information about their inner state.

For example, a patient who has a history of relational ruptures, manifesting as recurring episodes of dizziness or a feeling of unsteadiness, begins to understand how these physical sensations mirror the emotional instability they have experienced in their relationships. When discussing a recent breakup, they might report a familiar sense of lightheadedness, and the analyst can then help them to explore this connection: "That feeling of unsteadiness, it seems to echo the way you've described feeling when relationships have fallen apart, a sense of your world tilting or losing its footing. Is there a way in which that physical sensation is a memory, or a continuation, of that emotional experience?" As the patient begins to acknowledge this connection, the dizziness may not disappear overnight, but its meaning transforms. It ceases to be a baffling physical malfunction and becomes a tangible representation of their vulnerability to loss and their deeply ingrained patterns of experiencing emotional upheaval. With this understanding, the patient gains a new perspective, enabling them to approach future relational challenges with a greater capacity for emotional regulation and a more grounded sense of self. They learn that their body, far from being a traitor, is an invaluable guide, offering direct access to the emotional truths that might otherwise remain hidden.

This journey towards embodied integration also involves developing a more compassionate and accepting relationship with one's physical self. For many, the body has been a source of shame, a site of perceived inadequacy, or a constant reminder of past traumas. The analytic process, by fostering a non-judgmental and curious stance towards all aspects of the patient's experience, including their physical sensations, provides a corrective emotional experience. The analyst's ability to remain present and attentive when the patient describes painful or uncomfortable bodily states serves as a model for self-compassion. As the patient learns to listen to their body with kindness, to acknowledge its messages without self-recrimination, they begin to dismantle the internal conflict that has fueled their suffering. The body, once an object of fear or disdain, gradually transforms into a partner in healing, a source of resilience and wisdom.

Ultimately, the goal of moving from embodied suffering to psychic integration is to foster a sense of authentic selfhood, a state of being where one's internal world and external manifestations are in greater harmony. This is not a state of perfection, but a dynamic process of ongoing attunement and adjustment. It is about living with a more profound awareness of the intricate interplay between mind and body, recognizing that each informs and influences the other. The consulting room, in this final phase of the analytic work, becomes a space where the patient learns to inhabit their body fully, to trust its wisdom, and to integrate its messages into a richer, more cohesive, and more resilient sense of who they are. The physical aches, the visceral discomforts, the subtle bodily tensions – once perceived as mere burdens – are recognized as integral parts of a complex and deeply human narrative, a narrative that, when fully understood and embraced, leads to a profound and embodied sense of wholeness.

Chapter 12: The Body in Trauma and Its Aftermath

The body, once a sanctuary, can become a battlefield after trauma. The echoes of danger, though the immediate threat has long since receded, can reverberate through the nervous system, leaving it perpetually on edge. This state, known as hypervigilance, is not a conscious choice or a character flaw; it is a deeply ingrained physiological response, a testament to the body's relentless effort to protect itself from perceived ongoing threats. Imagine a soldier returning from combat, their senses still finely tuned to the crack of a branch that might be a gunshot, the sudden slamming of a door that could be an explosion. This hyper-alertness, while adaptive in a war zone, becomes a constant torment in peacetime, an uninvited guest that disrupts sleep, shatters peace, and renders ordinary life a minefield of potential triggers. The civilian experiencing trauma can be equally, if not more, profoundly affected. The child who endured prolonged abuse might find themselves constantly scanning their environment, their gaze darting towards exits, their posture tense, perpetually ready to flee or defend, even in the perceived safety of their own home. This vigilance, etched into their nervous system, can manifest as an almost involuntary jumpiness, a reaction to sounds and movements that others might barely register. A dropped dish, a car backfiring, a sudden shadow – all can send a jolt of adrenaline through their system, triggering a cascade of physiological responses that mimic the original traumatic event.

This persistent state of alarm is characterized by a heightened sensitivity to stimuli. The world becomes a place of amplified noises, sharper lights, and more intense sensations. The capacity for subtle emotional perception can be dulled, replaced by a broad-stroke awareness of danger. This is because the brain, trapped in a loop of threat detection, prioritizes survival over nuanced processing. The amygdala, the brain's primal alarm system, remains on high alert, sending out constant signals of danger, while the prefrontal cortex, responsible for executive functions like reasoning and impulse control, struggles to regain its footing. The result is a nervous system that is over-aroused, easily triggered, and slow to return to a state of calm. This can make it incredibly difficult for individuals to relax, to feel safe, or to connect with others. Even in moments of apparent tranquility, a subterranean hum of anxiety persists, a low-grade thrum of unease that can escalate into full-blown panic at the slightest provocation. This can lead to a pervasive sense of dread, a feeling that something terrible is always about to happen, even when there is no discernible reason for it.

The body's persistent alarm system also impacts sleep, a fundamental restorative process that becomes a battleground for those with trauma histories. The hypervigilant mind, still on guard for threats, can interpret normal bodily sensations during sleep – a shift in breathing, a sudden noise from outside – as evidence of danger. This can lead to frequent awakenings, nightmares, and a general inability to achieve deep, restful sleep. The body, deprived of its essential repair time, becomes increasingly fragile, exacerbating other symptoms of trauma. This chronic sleep deprivation can lead to a host of physical and psychological difficulties, including impaired cognitive function, mood disturbances, and an increased susceptibility to illness. The individual might feel perpetually exhausted, their energy reserves depleted, their capacity to cope with daily stressors significantly diminished. The simple act of trying to fall asleep can become a source of intense anxiety, as the fear of nightmares or the inability to find peace looms large.

Beyond the heightened startle response and sleep disturbances, hypervigilance can also manifest as a constellation of unexplained physical ailments. The constant tension and stress can lead to chronic muscle pain, headaches, digestive problems, and a host of other somatic complaints. These are not imagined symptoms; they are the very real physical manifestations of a nervous system under siege. The body, unable to discharge the pent-up energy of the fight-or-flight response, finds other ways to express its distress. Imagine a pressure cooker, its lid held down tightly, the steam building within. Eventually, something has to give. In the case of trauma survivors, it is often the body that bears the brunt of this internal pressure. These physical symptoms can be incredibly distressing and confusing, especially when medical professionals are unable to find a clear physiological cause. This can lead to feelings of frustration, isolation, and a sense that one's own body is betraying them. The body, instead of being a source of comfort and grounding, becomes a site of chronic discomfort and mystery.

This chronic state of arousal fundamentally alters the body's baseline functioning. The sympathetic nervous system, responsible for the fight-or-flight response, becomes chronically activated, while the parasympathetic nervous system, which promotes relaxation and digestion, struggles to engage. This imbalance can lead to a wide range of physical problems, including cardiovascular issues, weakened immune function, and an increased risk of chronic diseases. The body is essentially stuck in a state of emergency, constantly expending energy and resources to prepare for threats that are no longer present. This leaves the individual feeling depleted and vulnerable, their ability to thrive severely compromised. The sense of safety within one's own skin is shattered. The body, which should be a familiar and trusted home, becomes a place of constant unease, a territory where danger lurks just beneath the surface. Every sensation, every internal shift, can be interpreted as a warning signal, amplifying the sense of being unsafe and out of control.

The concept of "somatic reactivity" further illuminates the body's persistent alarm. It refers to the exaggerated and often disproportionate physical responses that can occur even to seemingly innocuous stimuli, once a person has experienced trauma. A sudden loud noise, for instance, might trigger not just a jump, but a full-blown panic attack, complete with heart palpitations, shortness of breath, and a feeling of impending doom. This is because the traumatic experience has created a deeply ingrained association between certain stimuli and intense fear. The nervous system has learned to interpret these cues as signals of danger, bypassing rational thought and launching into a full-blown survival response. This can be profoundly disorienting and embarrassing for the individual, as their physical reactions seem out of proportion to the external situation. They may feel ashamed of their inability to control their responses, further exacerbating their feelings of distress and isolation. This exaggerated reactivity can make navigating everyday life incredibly challenging. Simple social interactions can become fraught with anxiety, as the individual constantly worries about being triggered by unexpected events or stimuli.

Furthermore, this heightened reactivity can extend to emotional experiences as well. The body's inability to fully process the initial trauma can lead to a backlog of unprocessed emotions, which can then erupt unexpectedly. A minor disagreement might escalate into a furious outburst, or a fleeting moment of sadness might plunge the individual into a deep depression. These intense emotional swings are often rooted in the body's dysregulated nervous system. The body is carrying the weight of past experiences, and when these experiences are touched upon, even indirectly, the body's alarm system is activated, leading to an overwhelming emotional response. This can make it difficult for individuals to regulate their emotions, leading to impulsive behaviors, strained relationships, and a pervasive sense of being out of control. They might feel like their emotions are too big to handle, and that they are constantly at the mercy of their own internal storms.

The lingering effects of trauma can make the body feel like an unreliable informant, a source of distress rather than a guide. The fight-or-flight response, designed to be a temporary, life-saving mechanism, can become a chronic state of being. This means that the body is perpetually primed for action, but often without a clear target or an appropriate outlet. This can lead to a restless energy, an internal agitation that makes it difficult to settle down or to find peace. The body may feel tense, coiled, and ready to spring, even in situations where there is no perceived threat. This constant state of readiness can be exhausting, depleting the individual's energy reserves and contributing to feelings of burnout and overwhelm. The body, in its attempt to protect the self, inadvertently becomes a source of persistent suffering.

This dysregulation can also impact the gut-brain axis, leading to a host of gastrointestinal issues such as irritable bowel syndrome (IBS), nausea, and changes in appetite. The constant activation of the stress response diverts resources away from digestion, and the heightened emotional state can directly influence gut motility and sensitivity. The stomach and intestines, highly sensitive to emotional cues, become a direct reflection of the nervous system's distress. An individual might experience a churning sensation in their stomach when feeling anxious, or a complete loss of appetite when feeling overwhelmed by fear. This physical discomfort can further amplify the emotional distress, creating a vicious cycle of anxiety and physical symptoms. The body's distress signals become increasingly insistent, a constant reminder of the underlying trauma.

The sense of safety within one's own skin is perhaps the most profound casualty of hypervigilance and somatic reactivity. For the traumatized individual, the body is no longer a reliable anchor in the world, but a source of vulnerability. The feeling of being grounded, of being present in one's own physical form, is elusive. Instead, there is a sense of being disconnected, of being a passenger in a body that is hijacked by fear and past experiences. This disconnect can manifest as dissociation, a state where one feels detached from their body or their surroundings. The world might seem dreamlike, unreal, or distant. The physical sensations that signal danger – a racing heart, a tight chest – can be so overwhelming that the mind attempts to escape the experience altogether. This is a survival mechanism, a way for the individual to cope with unbearable distress, but it further erodes the sense of embodied wholeness and safety.

This persistent alarm state means that the body's natural ability to regulate itself is compromised. The finely tuned balance between activation and rest, between sympathetic and parasympathetic nervous system dominance, is disrupted. The body is perpetually in "on" mode, even when there is no need for it. This chronic activation can lead to physical exhaustion, a profound sense of depletion, and an increased susceptibility to illness. The body's resources are constantly being mobilized for a threat that is not present, leaving it unable to perform its essential restorative functions. The individual may feel as though they are constantly running on fumes, their reserves depleted, their capacity to cope with even minor stressors severely diminished. This feeling of being perpetually on the brink of collapse is a hallmark of the trauma-informed, hypervigilant body. The very systems designed to keep us alive have become architects of our suffering, a cruel irony that underscores the complex and devastating legacy of trauma.

The profound disconnect experienced in hypervigilance and somatic reactivity can, in its most extreme forms, fracture the very sense of a cohesive self. Dissociative disorders represent a stark and harrowing testament to how deeply trauma can undermine the integration of our internal world, particularly our relationship with our own bodies. Where previously we've explored the body's heightened alert state and its propensity for disproportionate reactions, here we delve into the existential rupture that occurs when the body becomes less a home and more a fractured vessel, a space where the self struggles to find stable ground. This is not merely a matter of feeling uneasy in one's skin; it is a fundamental disruption of embodied identity, a profound fragmentation that can leave individuals feeling like strangers to themselves.

The concept of an "imaginary envelope," a psychoanalytic idea that describes the boundary between the self and the external world, and the feeling of being contained within one's own physical form, is severely compromised in dissociative disorders. For individuals who have endured overwhelming trauma, particularly during developmental stages when identity and self-cohesion are still forming, this sense of an intact, unified self can shatter. The body, instead of serving as a consistent anchor, becomes a site of radical division. Consciousness, memory, identity, and perception, which normally work in concert to create a seamless experience of being, become sundered. This dissociation is not a wilful act of separation; it is an involuntary survival mechanism, a desperate attempt by the psyche to escape unbearable pain and terror by fragmenting the experience, pushing unbearable aspects into inaccessible psychic spaces.

The phenomenology of dissociation is vast and varied, but a common thread is the profound sense of unreality or detachment. An individual might describe feeling as if they are watching themselves from a distance, an observer in their own life, with their body acting as a puppet controlled by unseen strings. This depersonalization, the feeling of being detached from oneself, can extend to a profound alienation from one's physical sensations. What should be familiar cues – the warmth of the sun on the skin, the ache of tired muscles, the pang of hunger – can feel distant, muted, or entirely absent. The body might feel numb, as if it is not truly theirs, a vessel that houses a consciousness detached from its physical shell. Conversely, some may experience an amplification of bodily sensations, but without the capacity to integrate them into a coherent sense of self, leading to overwhelming and terrifying visceral experiences that further alienate them from their own embodiment.

This fragmentation can manifest in profound memory gaps. Traumatic events are often the most intensely remembered, yet in dissociative disorders, large chunks of time, particularly surrounding the trauma, can be inaccessible. This amnesia is not simply forgetting; it is a psychic wall erected to protect the self from the overwhelming emotional and sensory data of the traumatic experience. When these memories do surface, they may do so as intrusive flashbacks, experienced with the full sensory and emotional intensity of the original event, but often without the narrative context that would allow for integration. This can lead to a terrifying sense of temporal dislocation, where past and present blur, and the individual feels perpetually re-traumatized. The body, still holding the physiological imprint of the trauma, may react as if the danger is immediate, even when the conscious mind has no clear recollection of the triggering event.

Identity itself can become fractured, a constellation of disconnected selves or parts. This is most evident in Dissociative Identity Disorder (DID), formerly known as Multiple Personality Disorder, where distinct personality states, or "alters," emerge to manage different aspects of the individual's experience, particularly the overwhelming trauma. Each alter may have its own name, history, and characteristics, and may even experience the world differently through the same physical body. The body, in this context, becomes a shared, often contested, territory for these different internal entities. Transitions between alters can be disorienting, marked by sudden shifts in consciousness, behavior, and even physical sensation. The body might exhibit different postures, vocal inflections, or even experience different somatic complaints depending on which part is in control. The continuity of self, so fundamental to our everyday experience, is profoundly disrupted.

Even in less extreme dissociative disorders, such as Dissociative Disorder Not Otherwise Specified (DDNOS) or specific types of depersonalization/derealization disorder, the sense of a unified self is undermined. An individual might experience periods of "zoning out," where they become unaware of their surroundings and their own actions for a period of time. They might find themselves in a different location with no memory of how they got there, or realize they have been performing tasks automatically, without conscious awareness. This "highway hypnosis" of the dissociative state underscores the fragility of conscious control and the capacity for the self to fragment and operate on autopilot when overwhelmed. The body continues to function, but the conscious, integrated "I" is temporarily absent, a stark illustration of a self that is not fully embodied.

The body can also become a repository for dissociated emotions and sensations. When an individual cannot consciously process or express feelings of terror, rage, or despair, these raw emotional energies can become lodged within the physical form. This can lead to a range of inexplicable physical symptoms, from chronic pain and fatigue to digestive distress and sensory disturbances that defy medical explanation. These are not psychosomatic in the sense of being "all in the head"; they are the somatic expressions of psychic pain that has been compartmentalized. The body is literally carrying the burden of what the mind cannot bear to acknowledge. This physical manifestation of dissociation can create a loop of suffering, where the physical discomfort further fuels the sense of being unwell and disconnected, reinforcing the idea that the body is a source of distress rather than a grounding presence.

The concept of "introjection," where external experiences and relationships are internalized, can be particularly relevant here. In the context of severe trauma, especially interpersonal trauma like abuse or neglect, the perpetrator's actions and the victim's response can become deeply woven into the fabric of the victim's self. This can lead to a profound sense of self-blame, guilt, and a feeling of being inherently damaged or "wrong." The body might carry the imprint of this internalized violation, leading to a self-perception of being "dirty," "unlovable," or fundamentally flawed. This internalized sense of defect can be so powerful that it feels like an intrinsic part of one's being, further contributing to the fragmentation of a healthy, integrated self. The body, once a site of potential self-expression and connection, becomes a symbol of shame and perceived brokenness.

The struggle for integration in dissociative disorders is a monumental one. It involves the arduous process of gradually re-connecting the fragmented parts of the self, reclaiming dissociated memories and emotions, and re-establishing a sense of coherence and continuity. This often involves working with the body, helping individuals to become more present in their physical sensations and to learn to tolerate the often overwhelming feelings that have been disavowed. Techniques that focus on grounding, mindfulness, and somatic experiencing can be crucial in helping individuals to gently re-inhabit their bodies and to begin to trust them as a source of information and support, rather than as a source of terror or alienation.

The therapeutic journey for those with dissociative disorders is one of piecing together a shattered mosaic. It requires immense patience, courage, and a deep understanding of the intricate ways in which the psyche and body respond to overwhelming adversity. The fragmented self, once a desperate measure for survival, can, with careful and sustained therapeutic effort, begin to knit itself back together, allowing for a more unified and embodied experience of life. The body, no longer a battleground of internal division, can gradually transform into a more integrated and grounded home for the self. This transformation is not about erasing the past, but about creating a new narrative, one where the body and self are no longer defined by fragmentation, but by resilience and the potential for wholeness. The journey from a fractured existence to one of embodied integrity is a testament to the human capacity for healing, even in the face of unimaginable suffering. It highlights how deeply our sense of self is intertwined with our physical presence, and how the trauma that severs this connection can lead to the most profound forms of internal estrangement. The body, in these extreme dissociative states, becomes the physical stage upon which the drama of psychic survival unfolds, a silent witness to the desperate measures the psyche takes to endure when faced with unbearable reality. The challenge for therapy is to help the individual reclaim this stage, to transform it from a place of exile into a space of belonging, where the self can finally reside in its own skin with a sense of peace and coherence.

The body, a seemingly solid and immutable entity, can harbor secrets, carrying within its very cells the indelible marks of experiences that the conscious mind may have long since buried. When trauma strikes, particularly when it is prolonged, pervasive, or experienced during critical developmental windows, the body's systems are not merely witnesses; they become active participants in a desperate bid for survival. This participation, however, often comes at a profound cost, a cost that can manifest not just as immediate distress or the hypervigilant state we've previously discussed, but as a slow, insidious unraveling into chronic illness. This is not a simple case of "mind over matter," but rather a complex interplay where the unresolved psychic narrative of trauma literally rewrites the body's biological story, transforming it into a repository of unexpressed pain and a testament to a story that has yet to find its ending.

Consider the physiological cascade that trauma unleashes. The sympathetic nervous system, the body's alarm system, is designed for short-term emergencies. It floods the system with cortisol and adrenaline, preparing us to fight or flee. But when the threat is continuous, when escape is impossible, or when the trauma is a lingering shadow, this alarm system can become chronically activated. This state of perpetual readiness, known as allostatic load, puts an immense strain on every organ system. The cardiovascular system works overtime, leading to hypertension and increased risk of heart disease. The immune system, initially primed for acute stress, can become dysregulated, either overreacting and promoting inflammation, or suppressing itself, leaving the body vulnerable to infection. The digestive system, so sensitive to emotional states, can become a source of chronic discomfort, from irritable bowel syndrome to more serious inflammatory conditions. The endocrine system, responsible for hormonal balance, can become profoundly disrupted, impacting everything from metabolism to mood. In essence, the body, trapped in a cycle of perceived danger, begins to break down under the relentless pressure.

This persistent physiological dysregulation, however, is more than just a biological consequence of stress; it is deeply intertwined with the

narrative of the trauma. When traumatic memories are too overwhelming to be consciously processed and integrated, they don't simply disappear. Instead, they can become fragmented, replaying in the background of consciousness as intrusive thoughts, nightmares, or somatic sensations. The body, in its attempt to cope, might develop its own language of distress, a non-verbal expression of the unspeakable. Chronic pain, for example, can be understood not just as a physical sensation but as a persistent echo of past terror, rage, or helplessness that has found no other outlet. The body becomes the canvas upon which this unresolved narrative is painted, a somatic metaphor for emotional wounds that have refused to heal.

The concept of the body as an "unresolved narrative" suggests that chronic illnesses can be viewed as embodied stories of trauma that have not yet reached their conclusion. Imagine a person who experienced profound neglect and emotional abandonment in childhood. While they might develop coping mechanisms and even achieve external success in adulthood, the core wound of feeling unseen, unheard, and unloved can remain deeply embedded. The body, perpetually seeking the safety and nurturance it never received, might manifest this unmet need through chronic fatigue, autoimmune disorders, or digestive issues that reflect a fundamental struggle to nourish and sustain oneself. The illness becomes a somatic testament to a childhood story of scarcity and longing that has never been fully acknowledged or repaired.

Furthermore, the dissociation that can accompany severe trauma can play a crucial role in the development of chronic illness. If certain emotional states—such as rage, grief, or fear—become too dangerous to acknowledge, they can be pushed out of conscious awareness. However, these disavowed emotions don't vanish; they can become lodged in the body, manifesting as physical symptoms. A person who suppressed their anger for years might develop chronic inflammatory conditions, the repressed rage finding an outlet in the body's inflammatory response. Similarly, profound grief that could not be expressed might manifest as debilitating fatigue or a compromised immune system, the body literally carrying the weight of unmourned loss. The illness, in these instances, becomes a physical embodiment of a psychic reality that remains unarticulated.

The body's systems, when under prolonged duress, can also lose their capacity for flexible self-regulation. This loss of homeostasis can lead to conditions where the body's own defenses turn against it, as seen in autoimmune diseases. Here, the immune system, designed to protect, begins to attack healthy tissues. This can be metaphorically linked to a self that has been so deeply wounded by external forces that it has internalized the aggression, turning its protective mechanisms inward. The body is no longer distinguishing between friend and foe, mirroring a psyche that has lost its boundaries and its capacity for self-compassion, a direct consequence of an unresolved narrative of violation.

Consider the profound impact of intergenerational trauma. The narrative of suffering can be passed down through families, not just through stories and behaviors, but through epigenetic changes that alter gene expression and stress response. A grandchild, who never directly experienced the original trauma, may still inherit a body that is primed for a state of alert, more susceptible to chronic stress-related illnesses. This suggests that the "unresolved narrative" can extend beyond the individual, becoming a generational legacy held within the very biological makeup of descendants. The body, in this context, becomes a living archive of ancestral pain.

The very nature of chronic illness often involves a long, drawn-out struggle, a relentless battle against an insidious enemy. This mirrors the experience of prolonged trauma, where the individual feels trapped, powerless, and constantly under siege. The persistent physical symptoms can become a form of re-traumatization, a daily reminder of vulnerability and suffering. When medical interventions prove insufficient or temporary, the sense of hopelessness and despair can deepen, further entrenching the belief that the body is fundamentally broken, a site of perpetual distress. This creates a vicious cycle where the physical symptoms exacerbate psychological distress, which in turn amplifies the physiological response, perpetuating the chronic illness.

The inability to fully articulate the traumatic experience can lead to a profound sense of isolation. When the body is constantly sending signals of distress, but these signals cannot be translated into coherent words or understood by others, the individual can feel like an alien in their own skin. The illness becomes a barrier to connection, further reinforcing the feeling of being fundamentally flawed and unlovable. This disconnection from others can amplify the sense of internal disconnection, solidifying the body as a site of suffering rather than a source of comfort or strength. The unresolved narrative, in its silence, becomes an all-consuming presence, defining the individual's existence through the lens of perpetual physical and emotional pain.

The body's capacity for resilience is immense, but even the most robust systems have their limits. Chronic illness, in this light, is not a sign of personal failure, but a testament to the body's prolonged and arduous struggle to contain and process experiences that exceed its adaptive capacity. It is the somatic manifestation of a story that has been forcibly interrupted, a narrative that demands to be heard and understood, even if it speaks through the language of disease. The challenge for healing lies not only in managing the physical symptoms but in helping the individual to access and eventually resolve the underlying psychic narrative that their body is so desperately trying to express. This involves creating a safe space where the story can be told, the emotions can be felt, and the body can begin to release the burden it has carried for so long, finally moving towards integration and wholeness.

The preceding chapters have laid bare the profound ways trauma can fracture our sense of self, leaving the body not as a sanctuary, but as a landscape scarred by an unresolved past. We've explored how the physiological echoes of survival responses can morph into chronic conditions, how the unexpressed narrative of suffering can become embedded in our very tissues, and how dissociation can alienate us from our physical being. The body, once a vehicle for experiencing life, can transform into a repository of fear, a source of persistent distress, and a physical testament to experiences that have overwhelmed our capacity to process them. Now, we turn our attention to the crucial work of healing: the arduous yet profoundly rewarding process of re-inhabiting this traumatized body. This is not about erasing the past, but about gently, deliberately, and with immense compassion, reclaiming a sense of presence and safety within the physical self, transforming it from a site of fragmentation and fear into a locus of stability and self-awareness.

The journey back into the body, especially one that has been a battleground of trauma, is not a simple matter of willing oneself to be present. For many, the very sensation of being alive within their skin is intrinsically linked to danger, to a hypervigilance that never truly ceases, or to a profound numbness that shields them from unbearable pain. The somatic landscape, once a source of information and connection, has become a territory to be avoided, a place where memories flicker and emotions surge unbidden, often without a clear narrative or conscious understanding. This is where therapeutic interventions specifically designed to foster a sense of embodied safety become paramount. These approaches recognize that healing cannot solely reside in the cognitive realm; it must be anchored in the here and now, in the tangible reality of physical sensation, experienced in a way that allows for regulation and integration.

One of the cornerstones of this re-inhabitation is the practice of grounding. Grounding techniques are essentially invitations to the nervous system to recognize that it is safe, in this moment, to be present in the body. They work by gently drawing attention to sensory experiences that are neutral or pleasant, anchors that can tether us to the present reality. Imagine a person who is overwhelmed by intrusive memories, their heart pounding, their breath shallow, their muscles tensed as if bracing for an imminent threat. A simple grounding exercise might involve feeling the weight of their feet on the floor. This sensation, the solid contact with the earth, can be a surprisingly powerful anchor. The instruction is not to analyze the sensation, not to judge it, but simply to notice it. To feel the texture of the floor through their socks, the pressure on their soles, the subtle shift in balance as they distribute their weight. This act of focused, non-judgmental sensory awareness interrupts the cycle of re-traumatization by redirecting the nervous system's attention to concrete, present-moment stimuli.

Another common grounding technique involves engaging with objects in the immediate environment. This might mean picking up a smooth stone, feeling its coolness, its texture, its weight in the palm of the hand. Or it could involve tracing the outline of a leaf, noticing its veins, its edges, its subtle undulations. The key is intentional, mindful engagement with the sensory properties of an external object. The mind, often racing with anxious thoughts or caught in the loop of past events, is gently guided to focus on the external, tangible world. This external focus provides a counterpoint to the internal storm, offering a brief respite and a sense of connection to something outside of the overwhelming internal experience. The repetitive, gentle nature of these exercises allows the nervous system to begin to learn that it can shift its focus, that it is not irrevocably bound to the past or to the threat response.

The practice of mindful breathing is also a fundamental grounding technique, though it requires careful guidance for those with trauma histories. For many, conscious attention to breath can trigger feelings of suffocation, panic, or a resurgence of traumatic memories associated with helplessness or restriction. Therefore, the approach must be gentle and invitational. Instead of deep, diaphragmatic breaths, which can feel too intense, a therapist might suggest simply noticing the natural rhythm of the breath. Feeling the air entering and leaving the nostrils, noticing the rise and fall of the chest or abdomen, without trying to change it. The goal is not to force a calm breath, but to become aware of the breath as it is, a constant, life-sustaining rhythm that is happening regardless of the internal chaos. This awareness can create a sense of an anchor, a steady presence amidst the turbulence. If the breath becomes too overwhelming, the invitation is to return to the sensation of the feet on the floor or the hands on a stable surface, reinforcing the idea that there are multiple points of entry back to the present.

Mindfulness, as a broader practice, extends beyond simple grounding exercises. It is about cultivating an attitude of present-moment awareness without judgment. For individuals who have experienced trauma, this often means learning to observe their internal experiences—thoughts, emotions, and bodily sensations—from a distance, as if they were clouds passing in the sky or leaves floating down a stream. This capacity for detached observation is crucial because, for many survivors, sensations and emotions are perceived as overwhelming, dangerous, and all-consuming. Mindfulness teaches that these experiences, while intense, are transient. They do not define the entirety of the self. For instance, a person might notice a tightening in their chest, a sensation often linked to anxiety or fear. Instead of immediately identifying with it ("I am anxious"), mindfulness encourages them to acknowledge it ("There is a sensation of tightness in my chest"). This subtle shift in language creates a crucial space between the experiencer and the experience, reducing the likelihood of being swept away by the emotion or sensation.

However, the application of mindfulness with trauma survivors requires specialized training. Traditional mindfulness practices, if not adapted, can inadvertently trigger a trauma response. For example, a guided meditation that instructs someone to "fully embrace" their feelings might be overwhelming for someone who has spent years dissociating from intense emotions. Trauma-informed mindfulness emphasizes pacing, titrating the exposure to difficult sensations, and always offering options for self-regulation and returning to safety. It's about building a capacity to tolerate distress, not about forcing oneself to confront unbearable feelings before one is ready. The emphasis is on building resilience, strengthening the capacity to remain present with discomfort without being overwhelmed, so that the body can gradually learn that it can contain challenging experiences.

This leads us to the realm of Somatic Experiencing (SE), a therapeutic modality developed by Dr. Peter Levine. SE is built on the understanding that trauma is not just a psychological event but a physiological one, and that the body holds the memory of the traumatic event in its nervous system. When the fight-or-flight response is activated during a traumatic event and cannot be completed, the pent-up energy gets "stuck" in the body, leading to symptoms like hypervigilance, anxiety, chronic pain, and a host of other physical manifestations we've discussed. SE aims to release this trapped survival energy by facilitating the completion of the natural defensive responses that were interrupted.

The core of SE is the process of "titration" and "pendulation." Titration involves gently bringing the client's attention to small, manageable pieces of the traumatic experience or its associated sensations, rather than overwhelming them with the entire memory at once. This could mean focusing on a subtle physical sensation—a tingling in the hands, a tightness in the jaw—that is linked, however distantly, to the trauma. The therapist guides the client to notice this sensation, to explore its qualities, and to observe how it changes. This is done in very small doses, interspersed with moments of returning to a state of felt safety, often through grounding techniques or focusing on neutral bodily sensations. This gradual exposure allows the nervous system to process the information without being re-traumatized.

Pendulation, on the other hand, involves helping the client to consciously move between the difficult, contracted, or activated states associated with trauma and states of ease, resource, or relaxation within the body. Imagine a client experiencing a surge of anxiety related to a past event. Instead of fighting the anxiety, the SE therapist might guide them to notice the anxiety in their body—perhaps as a racing heart and shallow breath. Then, they would be invited to consciously shift their attention to a part of their body that feels more neutral or even pleasant—perhaps the feeling of their feet on the ground, or a sense of warmth in their hands. The client is encouraged to "pendulate," to move back and forth between these two states: the activated state and the resource state. This process helps the nervous system to recognize that it has the capacity to shift, to move out of a state of overwhelm and into a state of relative calm. It teaches the body that it can experience distress and then return to a state of equilibrium, which is profoundly healing.

Somatic Experiencing also places a strong emphasis on "tracking" the body's subtle responses. This involves paying close attention to the client's felt sense, noticing micro-movements, shifts in posture, changes in breathing, and other unconscious physiological responses that occur as they engage with a sensation or memory. These subtle cues are seen as vital pathways to understanding how the trauma is held in the body and what is needed for its release. For example, a client might be recounting a seemingly innocuous detail, but the therapist notices a slight tremor in their hand or a fleeting change in their facial expression. The therapist might gently inquire, "What do you notice happening in your body right now as you say that?" This inquiry encourages the client to become more attuned to their own bodily wisdom, recognizing that their body is communicating vital information about their internal state.

The goal of SE is not to verbally process the narrative of the trauma, although that may eventually become possible and helpful. Instead, the focus is on renegotiating the

physiological imprint of the trauma. By allowing the body to complete its natural survival responses in a safe and contained manner, the nervous system can discharge the trapped energy. This release can manifest in various ways: involuntary trembling, sweating, a deep sigh, a release of tension, or even crying. These are not signs of regression or distress, but rather the body's natural mechanisms for releasing stored energy. The therapist's role is to witness these releases, to ensure they are contained within the client's window of tolerance, and to support the client in integrating these experiences.

Another significant aspect of re-inhabiting the body involves cultivating a sense of agency and empowerment within one's physical experience. Trauma often strips individuals of their sense of control, leaving them feeling like passive recipients of harm. Therapeutic approaches that emphasize choice and self-direction are therefore essential. In SE, for example, the client always has the agency to decide how much to engage with a particular sensation or memory. They are encouraged to say "stop" at any time, to shift their focus, or to ask for a different approach. This repeated experience of having control over their own internal process can begin to counteract the pervasive sense of helplessness that trauma often engenders.

Furthermore, the body can be understood as a source of "felt sense"—an intuitive, bodily knowing. Dr. Eugene Gendlin, who developed Focusing, described the felt sense as a "thing in a person's body which is a certain something, a... a sort of hazy, fuzzy, hard-to-describe... bodily meaning." In the context of trauma, this felt sense might be distorted or difficult to access due to dissociation or chronic activation. However, by gently guiding individuals to tune into these bodily meanings, even the subtle ones, they can begin to access a deeper wisdom and guidance system within themselves. This is not about intellectual understanding, but about a direct, embodied knowing that can inform their healing process. For example, a client might have a vague feeling of unease, a subtle clenching in their gut, when faced with a particular decision. Instead of dismissing it, a Focusing-oriented approach would encourage them to gently attend to that sensation, to ask it what it needs, and to allow it to unfold. This process can reveal underlying fears or needs that the conscious mind has not yet grasped, providing crucial information for navigating life and making choices that honor their well-being.

The journey of re-inhabiting the body is also about transforming the body from a place of shame and judgment into a source of self-compassion and acceptance. For many survivors, their bodies have become sites of intense self-criticism, burdened by the physical symptoms of trauma and the perceived flaws that accompany them. Therapeutic work can involve gently challenging these self-critical narratives. This might include exploring the origin of these beliefs, understanding how they developed as a response to trauma, and cultivating an attitude of kindness towards oneself. Practices such as self-compassion meditation, where individuals learn to offer themselves the same warmth, understanding, and acceptance they would offer a dear friend, can be profoundly transformative. This involves acknowledging one's suffering without judgment, recognizing that suffering is a part of the human experience, and actively working to be kind to oneself during difficult times.

The integration of somatic practices into trauma therapy also recognizes that the body can be a source of resilience and strength, even in the face of immense adversity. While the body may have been compromised by trauma, it has also been instrumental in survival. Acknowledging this inherent capacity for resilience can be empowering. This might involve identifying and amplifying bodily sensations of strength, stability, or comfort, even if they are fleeting or subtle. For instance, a therapist might ask a client to notice any sensations of groundedness, of being held by the chair, or of a steady rhythm in their breathing, however faint. By deliberately focusing on these positive sensations and allowing them to expand, individuals can begin to build an internal resource of safety and strength that can be called upon when needed.

Ultimately, the process of re-inhabiting the traumatized body is a testament to the profound interconnectedness of mind, body, and spirit. It is about weaving back together the fractured pieces of the self, recognizing that the body is not merely a vessel for the mind, but an integral part of our being, holding our stories, our memories, and our capacity for healing. By engaging in grounding, mindfulness, and somatic therapies, individuals can gradually learn to trust their bodies again, to feel safe within their own skin, and to transform the legacy of trauma from a source of chronic suffering into a testament to their enduring strength and resilience. This is a journey of reclaiming one's physical presence, of learning to inhabit the present moment fully, and of forging a new relationship with the self—one that is grounded, compassionate, and deeply alive. The body, once a battlefield, can become a home. It is a slow, often challenging, but ultimately profoundly hopeful path towards wholeness, where the narrative of suffering can finally find its resolution, not just in words, but in the felt sense of peace and presence within the entirety of one's being. This reclamation is not about forgetting, but about integrating, about learning to carry the story of survival without being defined by its pain. It is about rediscovering the body as a source of wisdom, comfort, and connection, a vital partner in the ongoing dance of life.

The body, once a landscape of fear and fragmentation, begins to shift. It is a slow, often imperceptible, metamorphosis, moving from the relentless grip of survival to the expansive freedom of thriving. This is the essence of embodied resilience—the profound, innate capacity of the human organism to not only endure the seismic shifts of trauma but to actively heal, adapt, and ultimately, flourish. It is a testament to the astonishing plasticity of our biological and psychological systems, a testament to the deep-seated drive towards wholeness that persists even in the face of overwhelming adversity. We have delved into the ways trauma can imprint itself upon the nervous system, freeze it in a state of perpetual alert, or disconnect it from the present moment. We have understood how the body can become a repository of unexpressed emotion, a silent witness to suffering that has bypassed conscious comprehension. Now, we celebrate the transformation, the emergent strength that arises not in spite of these experiences, but often, paradoxically, because of them.

To move from survivor to thriver is to acknowledge that the body's story is not solely one of damage, but also of endurance. The very systems that were activated to keep us alive during a traumatic event—the heightened senses, the rapid reflexes, the ability to compartmentalize overwhelming feelings—these, while problematic in their chronic activation, represent a powerful internal arsenal that facilitated survival. Resilience, in this context, is not about erasing the scars, but about learning to integrate them into a richer, more textured understanding of self. It is about recognizing that the body, having weathered such storms, holds within it an extraordinary capacity for repair, for recalibration, and for the cultivation of new ways of being. This isn't a passive unfolding; it is an active, often courageous, engagement with the self, supported by therapeutic modalities that honor the wisdom of the body.

The journey towards thriving is characterized by a deepening of felt safety within the physical self. It's about cultivating an internal environment where the body can begin to differentiate between past threats and present realities. This involves actively engaging in practices that signal to the nervous system that it is no longer in constant peril. Imagine someone who, after a period of intense hypervigilance, begins to consciously explore sensations of comfort and stability. Perhaps it's the feeling of warm water on their skin during a shower, a sensation that, when approached with mindful awareness, can speak of gentleness and care. Or it might be the simple act of sinking into a comfortable chair, allowing the support of the furniture to communicate a sense of being held. These are not merely passive experiences; they are active invitations to the nervous system to attune to safety. Each instance of experiencing benign sensation, however fleeting, becomes a brick in the foundation of a new, more secure embodied identity.

Furthermore, the development of embodied resilience involves reclaiming the body's capacity for joy and pleasure, even if these feelings are initially experienced as foreign or even suspect. For those who have endured trauma, pleasure can sometimes feel undeserved, or it can trigger a resurgence of fear—the "watchful waiting" for the other shoe to drop. Therapeutic work often involves gently guiding individuals to explore these sensations with curiosity rather than apprehension. This might involve engaging in activities that naturally evoke a sense of delight, such as listening to music that stirs the soul, savoring a delicious meal with undivided attention, or engaging in gentle, flowing movement. The intention is not to force joy, but to create fertile ground for it to emerge, to allow the body to remember and re-learn that it is capable of experiencing positive affect. This re-acquaintance with pleasure is a powerful counterpoint to the numbing or overwhelming negative affect that often characterizes the trauma response.

The concept of "resource states" becomes paramount in this transition. These are internal or external anchors of safety, strength, and well-being that an individual can access when feeling overwhelmed. For some, this might be a vivid memory of a peaceful place, the feeling of a beloved pet's fur, or the internal sensation of a stable, strong part of their body. Therapeutic interventions, particularly those rooted in somatic approaches, actively work to identify, strengthen, and integrate these resource states. The practice involves repeatedly accessing the resource, noticing the felt sense of it in the body, and then intentionally returning to that feeling before engaging with a difficult memory or sensation. This builds the capacity for self-regulation, teaching the nervous system that it has an internal capacity to return to a state of equilibrium, even amidst challenging experiences. It is like building a robust internal "home base" that can be visited at any time, offering solace and stability.

Moreover, embodied resilience is deeply intertwined with the reclamation of personal agency and self-efficacy. Trauma often strips individuals of their sense of control, leaving them feeling powerless and reactive. The process of thriving involves consciously choosing how to engage with one's body and one's experiences. This might manifest as making deliberate choices about self-care, setting boundaries that honor one's needs, or engaging in physical activities that foster a sense of strength and competence. For instance, an individual who once felt trapped by chronic pain might, through therapeutic work and consistent practice, begin to explore gentle movement that not only alleviates discomfort but also cultivates a sense of mastery over their physical experience. This shift from passive victim to active participant in one's own healing journey is a cornerstone of embodied thriving.

The transformation is also evident in how the body's inherent wisdom is accessed and honored. Instead of viewing bodily sensations as mere symptoms to be suppressed, the thriving individual learns to see them as vital communication signals. This requires a nuanced understanding, recognizing that the body holds information about both past distress and present well-being. For example, a subtle tightening in the shoulders might not immediately be interpreted as a relapse into anxiety, but rather as a signal that more support or rest is needed. This attunement to the body's subtle cues allows for a more responsive and compassionate approach to self-care, preventing the build-up of unaddressed stress and fostering a more harmonious relationship with one's physical self. It is about listening deeply to the body's whispers before they become shouts.

The body, in its resilience, also offers the potential for integration, for weaving together the fragmented pieces of the self. The dissociation that often accompanies trauma creates a chasm between the mind and the body. As healing progresses, this chasm begins to close. The memories that were once disembodied and overwhelming start to be integrated into a coherent narrative, and the physical sensations that were alien and terrifying become understood as part of a larger, albeit difficult, life experience. This integration is not about forgetting, but about re-contextualizing. The body, having borne witness to the trauma, becomes a wise elder, holding the story with a newfound sense of groundedness and perspective. It is through this embodied integration that individuals can begin to feel whole again, their past experiences present but no longer defining their every moment.

Ultimately, the transformed body, the body that has moved from survivor to thriver, is a testament to the profound capacity for hope and renewal that resides within us. It is a body that has been scarred, yes, but also a body that has been strengthened by its ordeal. It has learned to navigate turbulent internal landscapes and has emerged with a deeper appreciation for moments of peace and stability. The chronic tension may have eased, the hypervigilance may have softened, and the sense of alienation from oneself may have given way to a growing sense of embodied presence. This is not an endpoint, but an ongoing process, a continuous dance of engaging with life from a place of embodied strength and wisdom. It is the quiet power of a body that has known profound suffering and has, against all odds, learned to live fully and meaningfully once more, a living testament to the enduring power of the human spirit.

Chapter 13: The Body's Representation in Culture and Society

The human body, a vessel of immeasurable complexity and profound experience, does not exist in a vacuum. Its every nuance, from the subtlest blush of embarrassment to the most pronounced declaration of physical prowess, is constantly being interpreted, shaped, and often dictated by a vast, invisible architecture of cultural scripts. These are not written laws, but deeply ingrained narratives, societal expectations, and aesthetic ideals that permeate our lives from birth, influencing how we perceive our own physicality and how we are perceived by others. They are the unspoken directives that tell us how our bodies *should* look, *should* behave, and *should* feel, providing a framework through which we understand our own embodied existence and navigate our social world.

These cultural scripts are incredibly diverse, varying not only between distinct societies but also across different subcultures within a single nation, and even shifting over time. Consider, for instance, the wildly different ideals of beauty that have held sway throughout history and across continents. In some eras and cultures, a fuller figure was celebrated as a sign of health, prosperity, and fertility, signifying that an individual had access to ample resources. The voluptuous Venus figurines of prehistoric Europe, for example, are often interpreted as embodiments of these ancient ideals. Conversely, in other contexts, extreme thinness has been valorized, particularly in Western societies during certain periods, often linked to notions of discipline, self-control, and an aspirational, almost ethereal, aesthetic. These shifting sands of desirability mean that what is considered the pinnacle of attractiveness in one culture or time period might be viewed as unhealthy or even undesirable in another. This constant negotiation of aesthetic norms profoundly impacts an individual's self-esteem and body image, leading to internal struggles when their own physicality does not align with the prevailing cultural ideal. The pressure to conform can be immense, driving individuals to engage in extreme diets, rigorous exercise regimes, or even surgical interventions, all in an effort to align their physical form with the culturally prescribed blueprint.

Beyond mere appearance, cultural scripts also dictate a vast array of bodily behaviors. Think about the norms surrounding personal space, for example. In some cultures, it is perfectly acceptable, even expected, to stand quite close to someone during a conversation, a practice that might feel invasive and overwhelming in others. Similarly, gestures, posture, and even the ways in which we express emotions physically are all subject to cultural coding. A direct gaze might be interpreted as a sign of confidence and honesty in one culture, while in another, it could be seen as disrespectful or confrontational. The way we eat, the way we walk, the way we sit – all are imbued with meaning that is learned and internalized through our socialization. These behavioral scripts serve to regulate social interaction, ensuring a degree of predictability and order. When individuals deviate from these norms, they can be perceived as awkward, rude, or even socially deviant, even if their intentions are benign. This can lead to significant anxiety and self-consciousness, particularly in cross-cultural encounters, where the unspoken rules of embodiment are constantly being tested and negotiated.

The concept of health itself is deeply embedded within cultural narratives. While there are biological realities to health and illness, what is considered "healthy" behavior, what symptoms are deemed significant, and how illness is managed are all culturally influenced. For example, the Western emphasis on individual responsibility for health, often manifested in meticulous tracking of fitness metrics, calorie intake, and sleep patterns, is not a universal approach. In some cultures, health might be understood more holistically, as a state of balance with nature or as a communal responsibility. The willingness to seek medical intervention, the perception of pain, and the ways in which individuals express discomfort or seek solace are also shaped by cultural conditioning. The stoic endurance of pain, lauded in some contexts, might be seen as neglect in others. This cultural lens through which we view health can significantly impact an individual's self-care practices, their relationship with medical professionals, and their overall well-being. It can also create tension when individuals from different cultural backgrounds interact within healthcare systems, where differing assumptions about the body and illness can lead to misunderstandings and suboptimal care.

Furthermore, these cultural scripts extend to our understanding of bodily capabilities and limitations. What is considered a normal range of physical ability can vary dramatically. For individuals with disabilities, these cultural scripts can be particularly impactful, dictating not only societal perceptions of their capacity but also influencing the accessibility of environments and opportunities. The cultural narrative of "normalcy" often implicitly marginalizes those who deviate from a perceived physical standard, creating barriers to full participation in society. Conversely, some cultures may place a higher value on physical strength and athletic achievement, creating intense pressure on individuals to excel in these areas, sometimes to the detriment of other aspects of their development.

The internalization of these cultural scripts begins at a very young age. From the toys we are given – dolls with impossibly perfect proportions, action figures embodying physical ideals – to the stories we are told and the media we consume, we are constantly bombarded with messages about what our bodies should be like. Advertising, in particular, plays a significant role in perpetuating and reinforcing these ideals, creating a perpetual sense of inadequacy that can only be remedied by purchasing the latest product or adopting a new lifestyle. This relentless messaging can lead to a disconnect between an individual's lived experience of their body and the idealized version presented by culture. The body can become an object of constant scrutiny and self-judgment, rather than a source of grounded presence and personal experience.

The influence of these scripts is not confined to conscious thought; they deeply affect our unconscious processing of bodily sensations and experiences. A subtle ache, a momentary feeling of fatigue, or even the natural process of aging can be interpreted through the lens of cultural ideals. If aging is culturally framed as a decline into unattractiveness and infirmity, then the physical changes associated with it will likely be experienced with dread and resistance. Conversely, if a culture embraces the wisdom and dignity of age, these transitions may be met with greater acceptance and grace. The ways in which we manage bodily functions, such as menstruation, defecation, and sexuality, are also heavily regulated by cultural norms, often shrouded in taboos and shame. These aspects of our embodied existence, fundamental to human life, become sites of cultural policing, dictating what is acceptable to discuss, acknowledge, or express.

The digital age has amplified the reach and intensity of these cultural scripts. Social media platforms, with their curated feeds and emphasis on visual presentation, have created an unprecedented arena for comparison and self-surveillance. Filtered images, carefully posed photographs, and the constant showcasing of idealized bodies can create a distorted reality, making it increasingly difficult for individuals to accept their own authentic physicality. The pressure to perform a certain version of oneself online, to present a flawless and desirable image, can be exhausting and emotionally taxing, further embedding the idea that our worth is tied to our physical appearance and the approval of others. This digital landscape often exacerbates existing anxieties, leading to a sense of constant competition and a perpetual feeling of not measuring up.

Moreover, these cultural scripts are not static; they are dynamic and contested. Social movements, feminist critiques, body positivity initiatives, and diverse cultural expressions constantly challenge and re-negotiate these ingrained norms. The growing awareness of the harm caused by unrealistic beauty standards, the celebration of diverse body types, and the advocacy for inclusivity are all examples of how cultural scripts are being actively reshaped. These counter-narratives offer alternative frameworks for understanding and valuing the body, encouraging a move away from rigid ideals towards a more authentic and self-accepting relationship with our physicality. The work of reclaiming one's body from the dictates of cultural expectation is an ongoing process, requiring a conscious effort to critically examine the messages we receive and to cultivate an embodied experience that is rooted in self-compassion and personal truth, rather than societal validation. This process involves not only resisting harmful narratives but also actively seeking out and creating spaces that affirm diverse and authentic embodied experiences. It is about understanding that the body is not merely a canvas upon which cultural ideals are painted, but a vibrant, living entity with its own inherent value and wisdom, deserving of respect and care, irrespective of its alignment with prevailing societal norms. The ongoing dialogue and evolution of these cultural scripts highlight the profound interplay between individual experience and collective understanding, demonstrating that our relationship with our bodies is a continuously negotiated and socially constructed phenomenon.

The relentless barrage of imagery that constitutes modern media and art doesn't merely reflect societal ideals of the body; it actively constructs and polishes them into an almost blindingly radiant, yet frequently unobtainable, sheen. From the glossy pages of fashion magazines to the flickering screens of cinema and the curated grids of social media, we are presented with a relentless parade of bodies that embody a very specific, and often narrow, definition of perfection. This is not a passive observation; it is an active immersion into a visual language that speaks of youth, slenderness, muscularity, flawless skin, and a general aura of effortless vitality. These are the bodies that sell us products, the bodies that inhabit our dreams, and increasingly, the bodies that inform our perception of our own physical selves. The cumulative effect of this persistent exposure is the reinforcement of an "imaginary envelope" – a conceptual space where our personal, lived experience of our bodies is constantly measured against a potent, idealized external standard.

Advertising, in particular, wields an almost alchemical power in its ability to imbue products with the promise of achieving these coveted physical attributes. A simple beverage can be linked to the lithe form of a supermodel; a skincare line is presented as the key to erasing the very passage of time; a fitness program becomes the gateway to a body sculpted by gods. These advertisements rarely depict the messy, ordinary reality of human existence – the persistent effort, the occasional setbacks, the natural fluctuations of weight and skin. Instead, they offer a polished fantasy, a visual shorthand for aspirational living. The models used are often digitally enhanced, their imperfections airbrushed away, their features subtly altered to conform to a universally (or at least, widely disseminated) appealing aesthetic. This meticulous curation creates a disconnect; the viewer is shown a result, a seemingly effortless transformation, without the corresponding journey. The underlying message is insidious: "You, too, can achieve this, if only you purchase this product, adopt this lifestyle." The body, in this context, becomes a project, a work in progress, perpetually falling short of an ever-receding horizon of perfection.

Cinema and television contribute to this idealization through the deliberate casting and styling of actors. The leading lady is almost invariably slender, with clear skin and striking features. The heroic male lead possesses a physique that suggests both strength and discipline. While diversity is slowly, and often grudgingly, making inroads, the dominant archetypes remain deeply entrenched. Furthermore, the narrative itself often reinforces these ideals. Characters who embody these physical standards are often portrayed as more successful, more desirable, and more capable.

The unspoken implication is that physical attractiveness is intrinsically linked to overall worth and happiness. This is particularly impactful during formative years, when young viewers are absorbing these visual cues and internalizing them as blueprints for their own aspirations. The fantasy presented on screen can become a powerful, almost gravitational force, pulling individuals towards a standardized notion of beauty that may be entirely at odds with their unique genetic makeup and life circumstances.

Visual arts, from classical painting to contemporary sculpture, have historically engaged with the human form, but the modern era has seen a particular emphasis on the idealized body. While Renaissance artists might have celebrated a fuller, more robust physique as a symbol of health and abundance, contemporary art often mirrors the media's obsession with thinness and sculpted musculature. This is not to say that all art perpetuates these ideals; many artists actively challenge them. However, the art that achieves mainstream recognition and commercial success frequently adheres to these established aesthetic norms. Galleries and museums, acting as cultural arbiters, can inadvertently reinforce these standards by showcasing art that aligns with popular notions of beauty. Even when the intent is to provoke or critique, the visual language employed often relies on familiar tropes of the idealized body, thereby inadvertently amplifying their presence.

The digital age has, of course, amplified these trends exponentially. Social media platforms, by their very nature, are visual mediums that encourage self-presentation. Users curate their online personas, selecting the most flattering photos, applying filters that smooth skin and enhance features, and presenting a carefully constructed version of themselves. This creates a dizzying array of seemingly perfect bodies, leading to an environment of constant comparison. When we scroll through our feeds, we are inundated with images of friends, celebrities, and influencers who appear to effortlessly embody the prevailing ideals. This can foster a profound sense of inadequacy, a feeling that one's own everyday reality – with its perceived flaws and imperfections – falls woefully short. The "imaginary envelope" expands to encompass this digital realm, creating a virtual space where the pressure to conform is even more intense because the comparison is so pervasive and seemingly endless.

The concept of youthfulness is another facet of the idealized body that is relentlessly promoted. Advertising, film, and art all conspire to present youth as the ultimate state of being, equating it with beauty, energy, and desirability. Wrinkles are seen as defects to be erased, gray hairs a sign of decline, and any physical manifestation of aging is often framed as something to be combatted. This creates a pervasive fear of growing old, a cultural narrative that devalues the experiences and wisdom that often accompany age. The visual representation of older individuals in media often falls into stereotypical categories – the wise elder, the doddering grandparent, or conversely, the surprisingly youthful and glamorous retiree. The nuanced reality of aging, with its unique beauty and inherent dignity, is frequently overlooked in favor of a singular, youth-obsessed aesthetic. This relentless emphasis on perpetual youth can lead to profound anxiety for individuals as they age, fostering a sense of invisibility or obsolescence if they do not conform to the idealized image of an ageless body.

The pressure to achieve these idealized bodies is not merely a superficial concern; it has tangible psychological and physical consequences. The constant striving to attain an unattainable standard can lead to disordered eating patterns, excessive exercise, body dysmorphia, and a pervasive sense of self-loathing. The "imaginary envelope" becomes a cage, constricting an individual's sense of self and worth, tying it inextricably to their physical appearance. This can manifest in a constant preoccupation with perceived flaws, a relentless cycle of dieting and weight cycling, and a deep-seated dissatisfaction with one's own body. The message is clear: the body is a site of perpetual critique, an object to be molded and perfected according to external dictates, rather than a source of embodied experience and personal identity.

Furthermore, the universality of these idealized bodies within mainstream media and art contributes to a homogenization of beauty standards. While there is a growing movement towards celebrating diversity, the dominant cultural narrative still leans heavily on a narrow range of features and body types. This can marginalize individuals whose natural appearance deviates from these norms, leading them to feel alienated or "othered." The visual arts and media, in their power to shape perception, have a crucial role to play in either perpetuating this narrowness or actively dismantling it. When the prevailing images consistently showcase a similar type of body, it sends a powerful message about what is considered acceptable, desirable, and ultimately, "normal." This can have a profound impact on self-esteem and social inclusion for a vast number of people.

The impact of this constant exposure to idealized bodies extends beyond mere dissatisfaction; it can create a profound disconnect between the lived body and the culturally manufactured ideal. Our bodies are dynamic, changing entities, shaped by genetics, lifestyle, environment, and the simple passage of time. They are also the primary vehicles through which we interact with the world, experiencing joy, pain, pleasure, and connection. When this lived reality is constantly contrasted with an artificial, unattainable standard, it can lead to a sense of alienation from our own physical selves. We may begin to view our bodies not as partners in our experience of life, but as projects to be constantly judged and improved. The body becomes an object of external validation, its inherent worth diminished by its failure to meet the demands of the media and art landscape.

The inherent power of visual representation cannot be overstated. Images have a direct and potent impact on our emotions and perceptions, often bypassing rational thought. The repeated exposure to idealized bodies in media and art creates deeply ingrained associations between these images and desirable qualities such as happiness, success, and love. This subconscious conditioning means that even when we intellectually understand that these images are often artificial or unattainable, they still exert a powerful influence on our desires and aspirations. The "imaginary envelope" is thus not just a conceptual space; it is a deeply felt psychological reality, shaped by the visual narratives we consume daily.

Consider the subtle ways in which these ideals are reinforced. In a film scene, a character might be rewarded with romantic attention or career success immediately after a physical transformation – a diet, a new haircut, a more revealing outfit. This narrative shorthand links physical change directly to positive outcomes, reinforcing the idea that altering one's body is a prerequisite for happiness. In advertising, a product is not just sold; it is often sold alongside a lifestyle, and that lifestyle is invariably embodied by individuals who fit the prevailing aesthetic mold. These are not isolated incidents; they are recurring patterns that, over time, shape our collective understanding of what constitutes a desirable body.

The challenge lies in recognizing the constructed nature of these ideals and actively seeking out alternative representations. It requires a critical engagement with the media we consume, questioning the messages embedded within advertisements and appreciating the diverse forms that beauty and vitality can take. The art world, in particular, has the potential to be a powerful counter-force, showcasing bodies that are not merely idealized but also authentic, complex, and representative of the vast spectrum of human experience. When art moves beyond the perpetuation of narrow aesthetic standards to explore the embodied reality of different lives, it can help to broaden our understanding of what it means to have a body and to inhabit it with dignity and self-acceptance. The "imaginary envelope" can then begin to expand, making room for a more inclusive and less judgmental perception of our own physical selves and those around us. The constant negotiation between our lived bodies and the idealized versions presented to us is a defining feature of modern existence, and understanding the role of media and art in this process is crucial for fostering a healthier and more authentic relationship with our physicality.

The assertion that our bodies are merely personal vessels, solely under our individual dominion, is a profoundly misleading notion in the grand theatre of human society. In reality, the physical form serves as a potent battleground, a canvas upon which societal ideologies are painted, enforced, and at times, violently contested. This dynamic interplay, often termed 'body politics,' reveals how power operates not just through grand pronouncements or economic policies, but through the intimate, granular control and categorization of our physical selves. The body, far from being an apolitical entity, is a nexus of political struggle, a site where broader societal debates about autonomy, identity, and belonging are made manifest.

One of the most prominent arenas of body politics, and perhaps the most intensely debated, revolves around reproductive rights. The ability, or inability, of individuals to control their own reproductive capacity is intrinsically linked to their autonomy, their social standing, and their very existence as recognized members of society. Laws governing abortion, contraception, and assisted reproductive technologies are not merely administrative regulations; they are deeply political interventions into the most personal of decisions, wielding immense power over individuals, particularly women. These debates are rarely framed purely on medical grounds, but are instead saturated with moral, religious, and socio-economic ideologies that seek to define the 'proper' use and destiny of the female body. When the state, or powerful societal factions, dictate who can reproduce, when, and under what circumstances, they are enacting a profound form of social control. This control can be used to reinforce existing social hierarchies, to police particular communities, or to enforce specific moral codes. The discourse surrounding these issues often demonizes or pathologizes certain choices, framing them as threats to the social fabric, thereby justifying state intervention and limiting individual agency. The ramifications extend beyond the immediate individual, influencing family structures, economic opportunities, and intergenerational power dynamics. The very definition of personhood and citizenship can be shaped by these political battles over the body's capacity to create life.

Beyond reproduction, the pervasive influence of gender norms constitutes another critical aspect of body politics. From infancy, bodies are often assigned specific trajectories based on perceived gender, dictating everything from clothing and toys to expected behaviors and emotional expressions. These norms, deeply ingrained in cultural practices and institutions, serve to maintain a patriarchal order where certain attributes and roles are valorized for men, while others are prescribed for women. The pressure to conform to these binary expectations can be immense, leading to the marginalization, pathologization, or even criminalization of those who deviate. Transgender and gender non-conforming individuals, for instance, often face significant legal, social, and medical hurdles as a direct consequence of these rigid body politics. Their very existence challenges the established order, prompting aggressive attempts to 'correct' or erase them. The policing of gender expression, whether through societal ridicule, discriminatory policies, or outright violence, demonstrates how the body is a site for the enforcement of ideological boundaries. The construction of masculinity and femininity is not a neutral process; it is imbued with power relations that shape opportunities, perceptions, and the very sense of self.

Race, too, is inextricably linked to body politics. Historically and contemporaneously, racial categories have been constructed through physical characteristics, and these categories have been used to establish hierarchies of power, privilege, and oppression. The racialized body has been subjected to systematic control, exploitation, and violence, from the enslaved African body treated as property to the Indigenous body deemed uncivilized and in need of assimilation. Even in contemporary societies, racial profiling by law enforcement, differential access to healthcare based on race, and the media's perpetuation of stereotypes about racialized bodies all underscore the persistent political significance of race inscribed on the body. The very idea of race is a social construct, yet its physical manifestations – skin color, hair texture, facial features – have been weaponized to justify systemic discrimination. The way bodies are perceived and treated based on their racial markers reveals a deep-seated political agenda that seeks to maintain existing power structures and to deny full humanity to certain groups. This often manifests in the disproportionate criminalization of certain racial groups, the medical neglect of others, and the pervasive biases that shape how bodies are viewed and valued in society.

The regulation of public health, particularly in times of crisis, further illuminates the operation of body politics. Epidemics and pandemics, while posing genuine biological threats, also reveal how state power is exercised over bodies. Quarantine measures, vaccine mandates, and restrictions on movement are all examples of how public health concerns can be leveraged to assert control over individual bodies and collective behavior. While these measures may be framed as necessary for the common good, they often disproportionately impact marginalized communities, revealing pre-existing inequalities and power dynamics. The discourse surrounding infectious diseases can also become racialized or politicized, leading to the scapegoating of certain groups and the erosion of trust in public institutions. The control of individual bodies in the name of public health can become a slippery slope, raising crucial questions about the balance between individual liberty and collective security, and who ultimately gets to define what constitutes a 'threat' and who is deemed 'suspect'. The historical instances of states using public health as a pretext for social control are numerous, and the current global health landscape continues to be a fertile ground for observing these complex dynamics.

Furthermore, the aestheticization of the body, as discussed in earlier sections, also carries political weight. The relentless promotion of specific body types as ideal, predominantly thin, youthful, and able-bodied, serves to marginalize and devalue those who do not conform. This creates a subtle but pervasive form of social control, pressuring individuals to conform to narrow standards of appearance to gain social acceptance, professional opportunities, and even basic dignity. Bodies that are considered 'deviant' – whether due to disability, weight, age, or other factors – can be rendered invisible or subjected to stigma, limiting their participation in public life and reinforcing societal biases. The beauty industry, fashion, and media all play a role in this political project, profiting from and perpetuating these narrow ideals. The ability to dictate what is considered beautiful or desirable is a form of cultural capital that can be used to maintain existing power structures, reinforcing the idea that only certain bodies are worthy of attention, respect, and belonging.

Even seemingly innocuous aspects of daily life, such as the design of public spaces, can be imbued with body politics. The accessibility of buildings and transportation for people with disabilities, the provision of gender-neutral restrooms, and the availability of spaces for diverse forms of physical activity all reflect implicit decisions about whose bodies are accommodated and whose are marginalized. These design choices are not neutral; they are political statements that shape how individuals experience their physical environment and their place within it. The 'ableist' design of much of our built environment, for instance, implicitly prioritizes the bodies of the able-bodied, creating barriers and exclusions for those with physical impairments. Similarly, the insistence on gendered public facilities can create discomfort and even danger for transgender individuals, reinforcing the binary and rendering them 'other.'

The very act of categorizing bodies—whether by age, ability, gender, race, or health status—is a political act. These categories are not natural classifications but are social and historical constructs that have been used to assign power, privilege, and disadvantage. When bodies are sorted and labeled, they become subject to specific sets of rules, expectations, and forms of surveillance. This process of categorization can lead to the normalization of inequality, making it seem as though certain groups are inherently different or less capable, rather than the product of systemic forces. The medicalization of various bodily experiences, for example, can serve to depoliticize issues that are fundamentally rooted in social and economic inequality. Conditions that are more prevalent in marginalized communities might be framed as individual health problems rather than as symptoms of broader societal injustices.

In essence, the body is never simply a private affair. It is a locus of power, a site of struggle, and a primary means through which societal ideologies are enacted and resisted. The political dimensions of the body are woven into the very fabric of social life, from the most intimate decisions about reproduction to the broadest policies governing public health and social order. Understanding these dynamics is crucial for comprehending how power operates in society, how inequalities are perpetuated, and how individuals and communities can challenge dominant narratives and reclaim agency over their own physical beings. The battles fought over bodies—whether in courtrooms, legislative chambers, or through everyday interactions—are fundamental to the ongoing negotiation of who we are as a society and who has the right to define the contours of human existence.

The physical form, far from being a neutral vessel, becomes a deeply contested territory for those whose identities exist at the fringes of societal acceptance. For individuals belonging to marginalized groups, the body is not simply an aspect of selfhood; it is a primary site where prejudice, discrimination, and systemic oppression are acutely felt and internalized. This lived reality often shapes a profound and complex relationship with one's own corporeal being, a relationship frequently marked by experiences of shame, alienation, and objectification.

Consider the lived experience of individuals whose racial or ethnic backgrounds mark them as "other" within dominant cultural narratives. The relentless exposure to media portrayals that stereotype, demonize, or render invisible their bodies can foster a deep-seated discomfort with their own physical presence. Skin color, hair texture, or facial features, instead of being celebrated as unique markers of heritage, can become sources of insecurity, particularly when constantly juxtaposed against idealized, often ethnocentric, beauty standards. This can manifest as a desire to alter one's appearance to conform, a form of internalized oppression that seeks to erase the very characteristics that define one's identity. The fear of being perceived as "different" can lead to a constant self-surveillance, a mental burden that depletes energy and erodes self-esteem. The body, therefore, becomes a site of internal conflict, where societal judgment is internalized, creating a chasm between the self and the physical self. This is not merely about vanity; it is about the constant negotiation of visibility and acceptance in a world that often signals that certain bodies are inherently less desirable, less worthy, or even dangerous. The subtle and overt ways in which racialized bodies are policed—from street harassment to discriminatory hiring practices based on perceived appearance—reinforce the notion that their physicality is not entirely their own, but is rather subject to external judgment and control.

Similarly, the experience of disability profoundly shapes one's corporeal existence and the relationship with the body. For many, the world is not designed with their bodies in mind. Navigating a built environment that is often inaccessible – with stairs instead of ramps, narrow doorways, or public transportation that fails to accommodate mobility devices – can transform the simple act of moving through space into a Sisyphean task. This constant friction between the body and its environment breeds a sense of alienation, a feeling of being an outsider in a world that assumes a certain normative physicality. Beyond the practical challenges, societal attitudes towards disability can be deeply damaging. The gaze of others, often laden with pity, morbid curiosity, or an assumption of helplessness, can reduce the individual to their disability, stripping them of their complexity and agency. This objectification can be profoundly disempowering, fostering a sense of shame about the body's perceived limitations, even when those limitations are not as profound as perceived. The medicalization of disability can further exacerbate this, often framing the body as a problem to be fixed rather than an integrated aspect of self, leading to invasive procedures or a constant focus on perceived deficits.

For individuals whose gender identity or expression deviates from societal norms, the body can become a source of profound distress and vulnerability. Transgender and gender non-conforming individuals often experience a dissonance between their internal sense of self and the physical body they inhabit, a phenomenon known as gender dysphoria. This can lead to immense psychological suffering and a deep longing to align their physical form with their authentic gender identity. The societal and legal barriers to gender-affirming care can prolong this suffering, forcing individuals to endure bodies that feel fundamentally "wrong." Beyond dysphoria, these individuals often face intense scrutiny, judgment, and even violence directed at their bodies. Their physical presentation becomes a battleground, with cisnormative expectations dictating what is considered "acceptable." This can range from being misgendered and invalidated to facing harassment or physical assault simply for existing in a body that defies binary categorization. The policing of their bodies, whether by family, peers, or the state, can lead to profound alienation from their own physical selves, a sense of their body being constantly under siege.

The intersectionality of these identities further complicates the corporeal experience. A Black transgender woman, for instance, may face a confluence of racism, transphobia, and misogyny, each layer of oppression impacting her relationship with her body in unique and devastating ways. The stereotypes associated with her race may intersect with the prejudices against her gender identity, creating a hyper-visibility that is simultaneously dehumanizing and dangerous. The objectification she experiences might be amplified, her body subjected to a gaze that sexualizes, exoticizes, and devalues her on multiple fronts. The fear of violence, a pervasive concern for many marginalized individuals, can be particularly acute for those who embody multiple marginalized identities.

However, this narrative of shame and alienation is not the entirety of the story. In the face of pervasive societal prejudice, marginalized communities have consistently demonstrated an extraordinary capacity to reclaim their bodies, forging powerful senses of identity, belonging, and resistance through shared corporeal experiences and cultural expressions. These acts of reclamation are not simply about self-acceptance; they are often acts of defiance against systems that seek to define, control, and diminish them.

For many racialized communities, cultural traditions offer a powerful antidote to the corrosive effects of internalized oppression. The celebration of diverse skin tones, hair textures, and body shapes through art, music, dance, and storytelling can serve to re-center and validate bodies that have been historically denigrated. Consider the vibrant expressions of Black culture, where the celebration of the Black body has been a central theme in music and dance, from the empowering rhythms of hip-hop to the expressive movements of contemporary dance. These cultural forms not only provide a space for self-expression but also serve as a collective affirmation of beauty and worth, challenging dominant aesthetic norms. Similarly, Indigenous communities often maintain strong connections to their ancestral lands and traditional practices, which imbue their bodies with a sense of belonging and rootedness that transcends external judgment. The physical act of participating in traditional ceremonies, wearing cultural attire, or engaging in ancestral crafts can be profoundly grounding, reaffirming a connection to heritage and community that offers solace and strength.

The disability rights movement, for example, has been instrumental in shifting the discourse around disability from one of deficit to one of difference and pride. The concept of "crip culture" reclaims the language and experiences associated with disability, challenging the idea that disabled bodies are inherently less valuable or capable. Through art, literature, and activism, individuals with disabilities are asserting their right to self-determination, celebrating their bodies as sites of unique experiences and perspectives. The focus shifts from what the body *cannot* do to what it *can* do, and how its unique form contributes to a richer understanding of human diversity. The development of adaptive technologies and the fight for accessibility are not just practical advancements; they are acts of bodily sovereignty, enabling individuals to engage with the world on their own terms.

Within LGBTQ+ communities, the reclaiming of the body is often a vibrant and visible act of resistance. Pride parades, drag performances, and the creation of art and literature that centers queer and trans bodies are all powerful affirmations of self and community. These spaces provide an opportunity to celebrate identities and desires that have been historically suppressed, to challenge heteronormative and cisnormative expectations, and to forge connections based on shared experiences of marginalization and resilience. The reclamation of language, too, plays a crucial role. Terms that were once used as slurs are often reappropriated and imbued with new meaning, transforming them from weapons of oppression into badges of pride. The body becomes a canvas for self-expression, adorned and presented in ways that defy conventional norms, a visible declaration of authenticity and defiance.

Furthermore, the very act of collective action, of marching, protesting, and organizing, can be a profound corporeal affirmation for marginalized groups. When bodies that have been taught to shrink, to hide, or to apologize for their existence come together in a public space, united in a common cause, there is an undeniable power in that shared physicality. The synchronized chants, the banners held high, the physical presence of numbers – all these elements serve to amplify voices and assert a collective claim to space and recognition. These public displays of embodiment are not just about making demands; they are about demonstrating presence, about refusing to be rendered invisible. The shared vulnerability of exposing one's marginalized body in a public sphere, often in the face of potential hostility, is also a testament to the profound strength and solidarity that can emerge within these communities.

The cultivation of intimacy and care within marginalized communities also serves as a vital form of corporeal reclamation. In a world that often objectifies or pathologizes their bodies, the creation of spaces where bodies are accepted, cherished, and respected can be profoundly healing. This can manifest in diverse ways, from the development of supportive peer groups and community health initiatives to the simple acts of touch, affirmation, and solidarity between individuals. These practices of care reinforce the notion that their bodies are not solely sites of struggle, but also sources of pleasure, connection, and resilience. The creation of safe spaces, whether physical or digital, where individuals can share their experiences without fear of judgment or reprisal, allows for a deeper processing of trauma and a stronger affirmation of self-worth. These shared narratives, spoken and embodied, knit together the fabric of community and foster a collective sense of agency. The act of nurturing one's own body, of engaging in self-care practices that acknowledge and honor its needs, becomes a radical act in the face of systems that prioritize its exploitation or erasure. This can range from seeking out culturally competent healthcare providers to engaging in practices that bring joy and comfort, such as art, gardening, or movement that feels good.

Ultimately, the corporeality of marginalized identities is a testament to the complex and often contradictory ways in which bodies are lived and perceived within society. While the forces of oppression seek to impose shame, alienation, and control, the resilience and creativity of marginalized communities continually forge paths toward reclamation, resistance, and affirmation. The body, in this context, is not merely a passive recipient of societal norms but an active site of identity formation, a source of profound personal meaning, and a potent symbol of collective struggle and triumph. The ongoing negotiation of the body's representation within culture and society is, therefore, intimately tied to the ongoing struggle for liberation and equality, where the affirmation of one's embodied self is a fundamental act of self-determination and political agency. The very act of speaking one's truth about embodied experiences, of sharing stories that challenge dominant narratives, is a powerful contribution to this ongoing dialogue. It is through these embodied acts of resistance and reclamation that the definition of what it means to be human is broadened, challenged, and ultimately, enriched.

The pervasive narratives that shape our understanding of the body, often etched by the chisel of culture and society, can feel like unyielding fortresses. We are bombarded with ideals, with prescriptions of what a body *should* be, how it *should* function, and how it *should* be presented. These messages, insidious in their ubiquity, can create a profound disconnect between our lived corporeal experience and an imposed, often unattainable, ideal. Yet, within this seemingly inescapable framework, lies the potent and deeply personal act of reclamation. It is a journey back to the self, a conscious disentanglement from the external dictates that have, perhaps unconsciously, sculpted our relationship with our own physicality. This journey is not about rejecting the body, but about re-inhabiting it with a renewed sense of agency and authenticity. It's about shifting from a passive reception of societal mandates to an active, discerning engagement with what it truly means to be embodied, in all its glorious imperfection.

This process begins with a critical awakening, a conscious turning of the gaze upon the very messages we have absorbed. It necessitates a willingness to deconstruct the inherited ideals of beauty, health, ability, and desirability that have been presented as universal truths. We must ask ourselves: Whose interests do these ideals serve? Who benefits from the homogenization of bodies, from the policing of flesh into predefined molds? This is not a call to nihilism, but to a discerning appraisal. It is about recognizing that the "perfect" body portrayed in media, the "healthy" lifestyle espoused by influencers, the "normal" functioning presented by medical professionals, are often filtered through specific cultural lenses, laden with economic, social, and political biases. This critical engagement allows us to peel back the layers of imposed meaning and begin to discern the whispers of our own embodied truth. It's about understanding that the pressure to conform is not an inherent flaw in our own bodies, but a reflection of societal anxieties and power structures. The realization that these ideals are, in fact, constructs, can be incredibly liberating. It opens up the possibility that our own unique physical reality is not a deviation from the norm, but a valid and valuable expression of human diversity.

Embracing diversity in body types and lived experiences is a crucial step in this reclamation. It requires actively seeking out and celebrating the myriad forms that human bodies take, moving beyond the narrow confines of what is typically valorized. This might involve consciously consuming media that features a wider spectrum of ages, sizes, ethnicities, abilities, and gender expressions. It could mean supporting artists, writers, and creators who challenge conventional aesthetics and offer authentic representations of embodiment. Beyond passive consumption, it involves actively seeking out communities and individuals who embody this diversity and learning from their lived experiences. These encounters can be profoundly transformative, offering glimpses into bodies and lives that defy the dominant narrative, demonstrating resilience, beauty, and worth in ways that are unexpected and deeply moving. It's about recognizing that the stories of bodies that have been marginalized – the plus-size dancer, the elderly athlete, the disabled artist, the gender-nonconforming activist – are not exceptions to the rule, but vital threads in the rich tapestry of human existence. Their stories expand our understanding of what is possible, what is beautiful, and what is inherently valuable about the physical self.

Cultivating a profound sense of self-acceptance and bodily integrity is the bedrock upon which a liberated embodied existence is built. This is not a superficial "liking" of one's appearance, but a deeper, more foundational acceptance of the body as it is, in this moment. It involves extending compassion and kindness to ourselves, recognizing that our bodies are constantly navigating the world, bearing witness to our lives, and deserve our respect and care. This practice can manifest in numerous ways. It might involve a conscious effort to challenge negative self-talk, replacing critical inner monologues with affirmations of self-worth. It could involve engaging in practices that nurture the body, not as a means to an end (e.g., achieving a certain aesthetic), but as an act of self-love in itself. This might include mindful movement that feels good, nourishing foods that energize and sustain, adequate rest, and the creation of spaces for relaxation and rejuvenation. It's about shifting the focus from external validation to internal appreciation. When we can stand before a mirror and acknowledge our physical form with a sense of peace, rather than judgment, we have taken a significant step towards reclaiming our bodies. This acceptance is not a static destination, but an ongoing practice, a gentle, persistent dialogue with the self.

This reclamation also involves re-evaluating our relationship with physical sensations and experiences. Our bodies are constantly communicating with us through aches, pains, pleasures, and discomforts. Often, in our pursuit of external ideals, we learn to ignore, suppress, or pathologize these signals. To reclaim the body is to become a more attentive listener, to attune ourselves to the subtle language of our physicality. This might involve developing a greater awareness of how certain foods make us feel, how different types of movement impact our energy levels, or how stress manifests in our physical being. It is about developing an intuitive understanding of our own unique bodily needs and responding to them with care. This might mean pushing back against the urge to "power through" exhaustion, or recognizing and honoring moments of pain as signals that require attention rather than something to be endured in silence. It's about moving from a mechanistic view of the body – as a machine to be optimized – to an organic understanding, one that acknowledges its inherent wisdom and cyclical nature.

The journey towards a more liberated embodied existence is intrinsically linked to an ongoing process of unlearning. We must actively unlearn the shame that has been associated with certain body parts, functions, or variations. For example, the societal discomfort surrounding menstruation, aging, or bodily fluids often leads to a sense of secrecy and shame. Reclaiming the body involves dismantling these taboos, acknowledging these experiences as natural and human, and fostering open conversations that normalize and destigmatize them. This unlearning extends to our understanding of health and illness. Rather than viewing the body solely through a medicalized lens, we can begin to integrate a holistic perspective that considers the interplay of physical, emotional, social, and environmental factors in our well-being. This might involve questioning the over-medicalization of certain conditions or recognizing the limitations of purely symptom-based approaches to health. It is about embracing a more nuanced and empowering understanding of our own health and vitality.

Furthermore, reclaiming the body involves asserting our right to bodily autonomy in every sphere of life. This is particularly crucial for individuals whose bodies have been historically controlled or violated. It means drawing clear boundaries regarding touch, personal space, and how our bodies are discussed or depicted. It involves advocating for our reproductive rights, making informed decisions about medical treatments, and resisting any form of coercion or manipulation that seeks to dictate how we inhabit our physical selves. Bodily autonomy is not just a legal or political concept; it is a deeply personal affirmation of our inherent right to self-determination. It is the fundamental recognition that our bodies are our own, and that we are the ultimate authorities on how they are cared for, presented, and experienced. This can involve challenging societal norms that dictate how women should dress, how bodies of color should behave in public, or how individuals with disabilities should present themselves. It is about claiming ownership of our physical presence and refusing to allow external forces to define or diminish it.

The cultivation of mindful embodiment practices can serve as powerful tools in this reclamation process. Practices such as yoga, Tai Chi, Qigong, or even simple conscious breathing exercises can help individuals reconnect with their bodies in a non-judgmental way. These practices encourage an awareness of the present moment, fostering a deeper appreciation for the physical sensations, movements, and rhythms of one's body. By focusing on the breath, on the feeling of the ground beneath one's feet, or on the gentle stretching of muscles, individuals can begin to observe their bodies with curiosity and kindness, rather than criticism. These practices can help to release stored tension, improve body awareness, and cultivate a sense of inner peace. They offer a sanctuary within the self, a space where the body is not a project to be perfected, but a source of wisdom and strength to be discovered and honored. The emphasis shifts from achieving a specific pose or mastering a complex technique to simply

being present within one's own skin. This presence fosters a sense of groundedness, making it easier to resist the pull of external pressures and remain centered in one's own authentic experience.

The narrative of reclamation is also one of intentional community building. Creating spaces where bodies are accepted and celebrated in their diversity is essential. This can be achieved through support groups, shared artistic endeavors, or simply through fostering authentic connections with others who are on a similar journey. When we find ourselves in community with those who understand and validate our embodied experiences, the burden of alienation often lessens, replaced by a sense of belonging and shared strength. These communities can serve as vital sources of affirmation, offering encouragement, perspective, and a collective voice to challenge dominant narratives. They provide a mirror in which we can see our own diverse beauty reflected, reinforcing the understanding that our bodies are not aberrations, but variations within a rich spectrum of human experience. Sharing stories within these communities—stories of struggle, resilience, joy, and self-discovery—can be incredibly powerful, weaving a collective narrative of embodied liberation.

Ultimately, the path towards a more liberated embodied existence is not a destination but an ongoing evolution. It is a continuous process of questioning, learning, accepting, and asserting. It requires courage to stand in our own authentic physicality, even when it deviates from societal expectations. It demands a commitment to self-compassion, recognizing that this reclamation is a deeply personal and often challenging undertaking. By consciously engaging with these principles – critical appraisal of cultural messages, embracing diversity, cultivating self-acceptance, listening to our bodies, unlearning shame, asserting autonomy, practicing mindful embodiment, and building supportive communities – we can begin to dismantle the external constraints that have shaped our relationship with our bodies. We can move towards a state where our physicality is not a source of anxiety or a battleground for societal approval, but a deeply respected and cherished aspect of our integrated selves, a foundation for a more authentic and fulfilling life. This is the essence of reclaiming the body: to inhabit it fully, with grace, power, and an unwavering sense of self-possession. It is an invitation to experience the world, and ourselves, from a place of embodied truth.

Chapter 14: Transference and the Embodied Analyst-Analysand Relationship

In the intimate theatre of the consulting room, a peculiar alchemy often takes place, one that transcends the explicit dialogue and conscious intentions of both analyst and analysand. It is here, within the carefully constructed container of the therapeutic space, that the echoes of past relationships, long-buried emotional currents, and ingrained patterns of relating are not merely remembered, but *re-enacted*. This phenomenon, central to the psychoanalytic endeavor, is known as transference. It is the unconscious projection of feelings, desires, expectations, and anxieties from significant past relationships onto the analyst, who, by virtue of their role, becomes the unwitting recipient of these spectral visitors from the analysand's inner world.

Imagine, for a moment, a patient named Eleanor, who, from her very first session, finds herself perpetually seeking the analyst's approval. Her sentences are laced with tentative questions, her posture a subtle plea for validation, and any perceived critique, however gentle, triggers a disproportionate sense of shame and panic. This is not simply a manifestation of anxiety about the therapeutic process; it is, in large part, the ghost of her relationship with her mother, a woman whose love was conditional, whose praise was scarce, and whose disapproval loomed large, shaping Eleanor's nascent sense of self-worth. The analyst, in this scenario, is not perceived as the neutral, objective professional they strive to be, but as a potential source of that same elusive, conditional affection. Every nod, every attentive silence, every carefully chosen word is filtered through the lens of this deeply ingrained relational template. Eleanor doesn't consciously think, "My mother never approved of me, so I must earn this analyst's approval at all costs." Instead, the feeling of inadequacy, the desperate yearning for affirmation, and the pervasive fear of rejection simply

are, manifesting in her interactions with the analyst as if the past were a present and immediate reality.

This is the essence of transference: it is an unconscious repetition. The consulting room becomes a stage, not for a historical reenactment, but for a living, breathing manifestation of the analysand's most fundamental relational experiences. The analyst, in turn, is cast in a role that is not entirely of their own making, a role dictated by the script written by the analysand's unconscious. This projection is not limited to negative feelings or conflicts. It can encompass idealizations, intense desires, fears of abandonment, or even the relentless pursuit of rescue. The analyst might be seen as a perfect, all-knowing healer, a stern judge, a rejecting figure, or a nurturing parent, depending on the specific constellations of past experiences being replayed. The depth and pervasiveness of these deeply ingrained patterns are crucial to understanding the power of transference. These are not fleeting impressions; they are the very architecture of the analysand's internal world, the deeply worn grooves through which their emotions and expectations flow.

Consider, too, the case of David, who, despite a history of successful professional relationships, finds himself in frequent, escalating conflicts with his analyst. He is quick to interpret the analyst's interventions as attacks, his silences as judgment, and any attempt to explore his defensive maneuvers as an attempt to undermine him. What lies beneath this pattern? It is likely the echo of his tumultuous relationship with his father, a man who was authoritarian, dismissive of David's opinions, and prone to explosive anger. The analyst's office, intended as a safe space for exploration, becomes, in David's unconscious perception, a battleground, mirroring the very dynamics that made him feel threatened and invalidated in his formative years. He is not consciously trying to provoke the analyst or sabotage his own therapy; rather, he is unconsciously driven to recreate the familiar, albeit painful, dynamic, seeking, perhaps, to finally master it or gain the recognition he never received. The intensity of his reactions, often disproportionate to the analyst's actual words or actions, is a clear indicator that something more profound is at play than a simple misunderstanding.

The beauty, and indeed the therapeutic leverage, of transference lies in this very re-enactment. The consulting room offers a unique opportunity to observe these deeply ingrained patterns in vivo, in a safe and contained environment. Instead of merely talking about past relationships, the analysand is, in a sense,

reliving them with the analyst. This provides an unparalleled window into the unconscious, allowing the analyst to understand not just what the analysand says, but how they relate, how they feel, and how they make others feel. It's akin to watching a play unfold, where the characters and the drama are drawn directly from the analysand's inner life, and the analyst, while a participant, also holds the director's chair, capable of pausing the action, reflecting on the script, and guiding the exploration.

This dynamic is not a deliberate choice by the analysand; it is an unconscious imperative. The patterns of attachment, the ways of seeking comfort, the strategies for managing distress, and the internalized representations of self and other, formed in early life, are deeply ingrained. They are not easily discarded or consciously altered. When new relationships are formed, these pre-existing blueprints are automatically activated, shaping how the new individual is perceived and how the relationship unfolds. The analyst, in their role as a consistent, responsive, and non-judgmental figure, becomes an ideal – and often unavoidable – canvas for these projections. The very qualities that make the therapeutic relationship conducive to healing – its consistency, its focus on the analysand, its relative freedom from the demands of everyday life – also make it a potent site for transference.

For instance, an analysand who experienced neglect in childhood might unconsciously feel that the analyst is withholding attention or care, even when the analyst is actively engaged. They might interpret the analyst's scheduled breaks as abandonment or the focus on other patients as a sign of personal insignificance. Conversely, an analysand who experienced overly intrusive parenting might find themselves feeling smothered by the analyst's attentiveness, interpreting genuine care as an attempt to control or overwhelm them. These are not rational judgments; they are the direct, affective experiences of an unconscious internal world being projected onto the present. The analyst's responses, whether perceived as critical, nurturing, dismissive, or seductive, are not always received as intended, but as confirmations of these deeply held, often archaic, beliefs about relationships and the self.

The process of working through transference is, therefore, central to analytic change. It involves the analyst helping the analysand to recognize that their feelings and reactions towards the analyst are not solely a reflection of the present reality, but also a manifestation of past experiences. This recognition, often achieved through careful interpretation and exploration of the analysand's affective responses, allows for a critical re-evaluation of these ingrained patterns. It is about understanding

why a particular stimulus evokes a specific reaction, *where* that reaction originated, and *how* it is currently impacting their relationships, including the therapeutic one. This insight is not merely intellectual; it is accompanied by a significant emotional release and a modification of the unconscious relational template. As the analysand gains insight into the origins of their transference reactions, they can begin to disentangle the past from the present, freeing themselves from the compulsion to repeat old patterns.

This disentanglement is a gradual process, and the consulting room serves as the laboratory for this work. The analyst, attuned to the subtle shifts in the analysand's demeanor, tone of voice, and narrative, can begin to identify the underlying dynamics at play. When an analysand expresses frustration with the analyst's perceived slowness, for example, the analyst might not defensively assert their efficiency, but rather explore the feeling of impatience. They might ask, "What is it about this slowness that feels so unbearable? Does it remind you of anyone or any situation where you felt you had to wait for something important?" This gentle inquiry invites the analysand to connect the present experience to past ones, to see how the dynamic with the analyst is an echo of a more significant, formative experience.

The deeply ingrained nature of these patterns cannot be overstated. They are not superficial habits that can be easily changed with a conscious decision. They are woven into the fabric of the personality, formed through years of interaction and experience. These patterns represent the analysand's best attempts, however maladaptive they may seem now, to navigate the world and their relationships based on the information and emotional resources available to them at the time. They are, in a sense, survival mechanisms that have become rigid and limiting. The consulting room provides a unique space where these mechanisms can be safely examined, understood, and, ultimately, loosened. The analyst's consistent presence and their ability to tolerate the analysand's projections without retaliating or becoming overwhelmed are critical to this process.

Consider the intensity of the feelings that can arise in transference. A seemingly minor comment from the analyst might trigger a wave of rage, or a moment of shared laughter might be imbued with an intense, almost romantic, significance. These powerful emotional responses are not necessarily indicators of the analyst's skill or lack thereof, but rather evidence of the depth and potency of the unconscious material being activated. The analyst's task is not to judge these feelings but to understand them as valuable data, clues to the analysand's inner world. By exploring these intense emotional reactions, the analyst and analysand can uncover the root of these powerful affect states, leading to a profound understanding of the analysand's emotional landscape.

The concept of transference is not static; it is a dynamic and ever-evolving aspect of the therapeutic relationship. As the analysis progresses, the transference itself may shift and change, reflecting new insights and the analysand's developing capacity to relate in different ways. Initially, the transference might be dominated by a powerful idealization or a fierce resistance. As the analysand begins to trust the process and the analyst, the transference may evolve to include more nuanced feelings, such as disappointment, anger, or even ambivalence. The analyst's capacity to navigate these shifts, to remain present and responsive to the evolving transference, is crucial for the therapeutic work. It is this very fluidity of transference that allows for ongoing exploration and growth.

Furthermore, transference is not always straightforward or easily identifiable. It can be subtle, manifesting in the analysand's choice of words, their body language, or even in what they

don't say. The analyst must be highly attuned to these nuances, piecing together fragments of communication to understand the underlying relational dynamics. A repeated theme in the analysand's narratives about friends or family might, in fact, be a disguised representation of their feelings towards the analyst. The analyst's skill lies in recognizing these patterns and gently bringing them to the analysand's attention, not as a definitive pronouncement, but as a tentative exploration: "I notice that you've spoken several times about feeling unheard in your relationships. I wonder if that feeling might be present for you here, in our sessions?"

The consulting room, therefore, is more than just a place for conversation; it is a unique relational environment where the past is brought to life, not as a historical document, but as a living, breathing force. The analyst's ability to recognize, understand, and work with transference is paramount to the success of the analytic process. It is through this careful navigation of the unconscious repetitions, the projected feelings, and the re-enacted patterns that the analysand can achieve a deeper understanding of themselves and, ultimately, find freedom from the limitations of their past. The deeply ingrained nature of these patterns means that this process is rarely a linear or simple one, but it is precisely within this complex interplay of past and present, unconscious and conscious, that profound transformation can occur.

The analytic consulting room, often perceived as a sanctuary for verbal exploration, is in reality a stage where the body itself becomes a profound theatre of transference. Beyond the spoken word, beyond the carefully articulated narratives, the analysand's physical being speaks a language of its own, a visceral testament to the unconscious projections and relational imprints that shape their experience. The body, in its palpable presence, is not merely a vessel for the mind; it is an active participant, a crucial indicator of the transference dynamics at play, offering a rich and often untamed source of interpretive material for the analyst.

Consider the subtle, yet telling, shifts in posture that can betray underlying feelings. An analysand who unconsciously perceives the analyst as an authority figure, perhaps mirroring a stern or critical parent, might adopt a hunched, defensive stance. Shoulders rounded, gaze averted, they present a physical embodiment of submission or fear, even while their words might express a desire for assertiveness or independence. This physical tension, this involuntary contraction of the body, is not a conscious choice to appear subservient; it is a somatic manifestation of an internalized relational blueprint. The analyst's every utterance, every perceived nuance of expression, can be unconsciously translated into a threat or a judgment, prompting a physical bracing against anticipated criticism or rejection. Conversely, an analysand who unconsciously idealizes the analyst, viewing them as a benevolent, all-knowing figure, might lean forward eagerly, eyes wide with anticipation, their body radiating a hopeful dependency. This physical engagement, while seemingly a sign of genuine interest, can also be an embodied plea for validation and rescue, a physical mirroring of an infantile yearning for an idealized caregiver. The analyst becomes the embodiment of all that is hoped for, and the body's posture reflects this hopeful, yet potentially overwhelming, investment.

The language of gestures and micro-expressions can also serve as potent conduits for transference. A hand unconsciously clenched at the side, a foot tapping with restless energy, a fleeting frown that crosses the brow before being quickly suppressed – these are not random bodily movements. They are often involuntary somatic expressions of unconscious emotional states, amplified by the specific relational context of the therapy room. For an analysand who struggles with feelings of aggression or hostility towards an authority figure, these gestures might manifest as subtle signs of defiance or irritation, a physical acting out of impulses that cannot be consciously expressed. The analyst, attuned to these non-verbal cues, can begin to discern the undercurrents of the analysand's emotional landscape, recognizing that a restless leg might not simply indicate boredom, but a visceral struggle with contained anger or a desperate urge to escape an overwhelming internal or external situation. Similarly, the repeated self-soothing gestures, such as rubbing a forearm or touching one's own neck, can signal a profound need for comfort and reassurance, a body reaching out for the soothing touch it may have lacked in early life, now projected onto the analyst's presence.

Somatic complaints, too, frequently find their roots in the fertile ground of transference. Headaches that flare up before sessions, digestive issues that manifest during particularly intense moments of exploration, or inexplicable aches and pains that seem to coincide with specific topics of discussion – these physical symptoms can be potent, albeit unconscious, expressions of emotional distress. The body, in its attempt to communicate what the mind cannot or will not articulate, becomes the site of these internal conflicts. An analysand who experienced emotional neglect might develop a recurring "emptiness" in their stomach, a physical manifestation of a pervasive feeling of being unfed emotionally. When the analyst, in their professional capacity, probes into these feelings, the somatic symptom might intensify, not necessarily because the analyst is causing harm, but because the body is re-enacting the very experience of emotional starvation and the painful awareness of unmet needs. The pain is real, the discomfort is palpable, but its origin lies in the unconscious translation of relational deficits into bodily experience. The analyst's task here is not to treat the symptom as a purely physical ailment, but to explore its symbolic meaning within the context of the transference, to understand how the body is bearing witness to the analysand's internal world.

Consider the analysand who, after a session where the analyst gently challenged a deeply held belief, experiences a sudden, sharp pain in their shoulder. This pain, while physically distressing, can be understood as a somatic representation of the immense effort involved in shifting one's internal landscape, of the body bracing against the discomfort of cognitive and emotional dissonance. It is the body's protest against change, a physical manifestation of resistance that mirrors the analysand's internal struggle. The analyst might then inquire, "I notice you're holding your shoulder quite tightly. Does this pain feel familiar in any way? Does it arise at moments when you feel your beliefs are being questioned?" This exploration can lead to the understanding that the shoulder pain is not merely an incidental physical occurrence, but a deeply symbolic expression of the analysand's fear of vulnerability and their ingrained pattern of rigidly defending their internal world, a pattern that is being activated and illuminated within the transference.

Physiological responses also play a crucial role in this embodied transference. The sudden onset of blushing, the tightening of the chest, a tremor in the hands, or even an accelerated heart rate can all be indicators of powerful, unconscious emotional currents. These are not simply conscious reactions; they are the body's autonomic nervous system responding to perceived threats or intense emotional stimuli, often triggered by the transference. For an analysand who carries a deep-seated fear of intimacy or exposure, the analyst's genuine warmth and attentiveness might inadvertently trigger a panic response, a physiological alarm bell signaling danger, even when no conscious threat exists. The body, in this instance, is reacting to the analyst not as they are, but as a figure who embodies a past experience of overwhelming closeness or scrutiny, leading to a fight-or-flight response that manifests as physical symptoms. The analyst's calm, steady presence, coupled with an exploration of these physiological sensations, can help the analysand to differentiate between the present reality and the echoes of past trauma, gradually desensitizing the body's alarm system.

The subtle shifts in breathing patterns can also offer profound insights. An analysand who feels unheard or dismissed might unconsciously hold their breath, a physical expression of their inability to find their voice or their fear of speaking out. Conversely, a sigh that escapes during a moment of perceived emotional closeness might not signify sadness, but rather a somatic release of tension, a bodily expression of relief that the anticipated danger of vulnerability has not materialized. These breathing patterns are not mere coincidences; they are the unconscious body's way of participating in the dialogue, of conveying emotional states that elude verbal articulation. An analyst observing a client who takes shallow, rapid breaths when discussing a sensitive topic might gently inquire, "I notice your breathing seems to quicken when we touch on this. What is it like in your body at those moments?" This invitation to somatic awareness can unlock a deeper understanding of the analysand's internal experience, revealing how anxiety or apprehension is physically embodied.

Even the seemingly mundane aspects of physical presence, such as fidgeting or stillness, can carry significant transference meaning. Excessive fidgeting might signal an unresolved restlessness, a body unable to settle due to underlying anxieties or an unconscious desire to escape the intensity of the therapeutic encounter. It can be a physical manifestation of a mind that is constantly racing, unable to find peace, a pattern often rooted in early experiences of instability or unpredictability. The analyst, rather than viewing this as a disruption, can explore it as a direct expression of the analysand's internal state: "You seem to be moving quite a bit today. What is happening in your body when you feel that urge to move?" This inquiry acknowledges the body's communication and opens a pathway to understanding the source of the restlessness, potentially linking it to past experiences of being unable to find a secure footing. Conversely, a profound stillness, an almost frozen quality of the body, can indicate a deeply ingrained defensive posture, a physical manifestation of the need to be invisible or to avoid any action that might provoke an adverse reaction, a pattern often seen in individuals who have experienced trauma or severe criticism.

The analyst's own body, too, becomes a crucial element in this dynamic. While the focus is often on the analysand's manifestations, the analyst's non-verbal cues – their posture, their breathing, their subtle shifts in attention – can unconsciously influence the analysand's projections. An analyst who is unconsciously anxious might exhibit a tense posture or a tendency to shift their weight, which the analysand might then perceive as disapproval or impatience. The analysand's body, in turn, is exquisitely sensitive to these subtle signals, often picking up on and reacting to them in ways that are not consciously understood. This highlights the bidirectional nature of embodied transference, where the analyst's own embodied presence can both trigger and be perceived through the lens of the analysand's transference.

Moreover, the concept of embodiment extends to the very way in which an analysand organizes their physical space within the consulting room. The distance they choose to place between themselves and the analyst, the way they arrange their body in relation to the furniture, or even the way they handle objects in the room – a pen, a tissue, a glass of water – can all be unconscious expressions of their relational patterns. An analysand who feels distrustful might unconsciously create a physical barrier, perhaps by sitting further away or by placing a bag strategically between themselves and the analyst. Conversely, an analysand who is seeking closeness might subtly shift their body closer, or their gaze might linger on the analyst's face with an intensity that suggests a desire for connection beyond the therapeutic frame. These seemingly small details are potent indicators of the internal relational world being enacted, providing the analyst with a rich tapestry of non-verbal data to integrate with the verbal narrative.

The somatic experience of emotion is a fundamental aspect of human existence, and in the therapeutic setting, these somatic manifestations become particularly salient when they intersect with transference. When an analysand describes feeling a "lump in their throat" when discussing a difficult childhood memory, or a "tightness in their chest" when feeling anxious about their progress, these are not simply metaphors. They are direct somatic experiences of emotional states that are deeply intertwined with their relational history. The analyst's role is to help the analysand to recognize these physical sensations as valid and meaningful expressions of their internal world, and to understand how these sensations are being re-activated and amplified in the transference. By acknowledging and exploring the bodily experience, the analyst can help the analysand to integrate their emotions more fully, moving from a purely intellectual understanding to a more embodied sense of self-awareness.

For instance, a patient who experienced early emotional invalidation might present with a chronic feeling of being "stuck" or "frozen" in their body. When the analyst attempts to explore their past, the patient may describe a physical sensation of immobility, as if their limbs are heavy and unresponsive. This bodily sensation is a direct echo of their early experience of having their emotions dismissed or ignored; their body learned to shut down, to become still and unexpressive, in order to survive an environment where such displays were not met with understanding or support. In the transference, this sensation of being frozen can become palpable when the analyst encourages expression or attempts to facilitate movement towards change. The analyst can then work with this, not by demanding the patient "move," but by exploring the sensation itself: "When you describe feeling frozen, what is that like in your body? Can you locate that feeling precisely? Does it feel like a protective state?" This approach honors the body's wisdom and allows the analysand to gradually understand the adaptive function of this somatic defense, and ultimately, to begin to unfreeze.

The transference, therefore, is not solely a cognitive or emotional phenomenon; it is profoundly embodied. The body, in its intricate web of sensations, movements, and physiological responses, provides a direct and often unfiltered window into the analysand's unconscious relational world. By attending to these embodied manifestations, analysts can gain a more comprehensive understanding of the transference dynamics at play, allowing for a richer, more nuanced, and ultimately, more effective therapeutic intervention. The consulting room, in this light, becomes a space where the entirety of the analysand – mind, body, and spirit – converges, offering a unique opportunity for profound healing and transformation. The analyst's capacity to hold and interpret this embodied transference is a testament to the depth and complexity of the analytic process, where every sigh, every gesture, and every somatic complaint can hold the key to unlocking the deepest layers of the self.

The analyst's inner landscape, while ostensibly a neutral and observing terrain, is far from immune to the seismic shifts initiated by the analysand's transference. Indeed, the very act of attunement, the analyst's finely honed capacity to resonate with the analysand's internal world, inevitably opens a channel through which the analysand's projected experiences can flow back. This phenomenon, known as countertransference, is not merely an intellectual understanding of the analysand's pain or distress; it is often experienced as a palpable, embodied response within the analyst themselves. These are not abstract empathic leaps but concrete, physiological and emotional reverberations that mirror, albeit in a transformed manner, the analysand's unconscious material.

Consider the analyst who, upon beginning a session with a particularly anxious analysand, finds their own chest tightening, a familiar physical precursor to panic that they themselves might experience in moments of profound distress. This is not a sign of the analyst's own pathology being triggered in an unproductive way, but rather a visceral recognition of the analysand's internal state. The analysand, perhaps wrestling with a deep-seated fear of engulfment or a crippling sense of impending doom, unconsciously projects this terror onto the analyst. The analyst, in turn, experiences a somatic echo of this projected fear, a physiological response that, if understood correctly, offers a direct ingress into the analysand's lived experience. The tightness in the chest becomes a physical language, a somatic communication from the analysand's unconscious, mediated through the analyst's own embodied response. The analyst's task is then not to dismiss this sensation as their own anxiety, but to investigate it: "I notice a similar feeling in my own chest today, a sense of... constriction, perhaps. I wonder what that might be like for you, to carry that feeling so consistently?" This inquiry, born from the analyst's embodied countertransference, transforms a potentially disruptive internal experience into a potent therapeutic tool, allowing the analysand to witness and explore their own embodied pain through the analyst's shared, yet distinct, somatic resonance.

Another common manifestation of embodied countertransference is the subtle, yet undeniable, shift in the analyst's posture or physical tension. An analysand who harbors deeply repressed anger and perceives the analyst as a safe container for this forbidden emotion might unconsciously push against this perceived boundary. This pushing, this implicit aggression, can manifest in the analyst as a subtle bracing of their own body, a tightening of the jaw, or an unconscious leaning back, a physical resistance to an imagined force. It's as if the analysand's repressed rage, projected onto the analyst, elicits a corresponding, albeit often unconscious, defensive posture in the analyst. This is not to say the analyst is inherently defensive, but rather that their body is momentarily embodying the pressure exerted by the analysand's unconscious dynamics. A skilled analyst, attuned to these internal bodily shifts, might then gently bring this to the analysand's attention: "I found myself tensing up just now, almost as if I were bracing for something. Does that feeling of resistance or bracing resonate with anything you're experiencing, either in yourself or in our interaction?" This invitation to explore the shared bodily experience can illuminate the analysand's own struggle with aggression, their fear of expressing it, and the ways in which they unconsciously test the boundaries of safety. The analyst's embodied countertransference, in this instance, serves as a relational barometer, indicating the presence and intensity of the analysand's projected affect.

The realm of physiological responses also offers fertile ground for embodied countertransference. The analyst might experience an unexpected surge of warmth, a flushed sensation, or even a sudden onset of fatigue that seems to emerge from nowhere. These are not necessarily indications of the analyst's personal issues being triggered in an overwhelming manner, but can be potent somatic reflections of the analysand's internal states. For example, an analysand who feels deeply ashamed or humiliated, and who unconsciously projects these feelings onto the analyst, might elicit a sense of warmth or even discomfort in the analyst that mimics blushing or a feeling of exposure. The analyst, rather than dismissing this as their own embarrassment, can explore it: "I'm feeling a sense of warmth, almost like a flush, as we discuss this. It makes me wonder about the feeling of exposure or perhaps shame. Is that something that's present for you as well?" This open exploration of the analyst's embodied experience can provide the analysand with a novel way of understanding their own internal world, seeing their projected emotions reflected back in a tangible, physical form. Similarly, a profound sense of weariness or lethargy that descends upon the analyst during a session could signal an analysand burdened by a pervasive sense of hopelessness or emotional exhaustion, their internal state having a draining effect on the analyst's energetic field.

Digestive disturbances, headaches, or inexplicable aches and pains can also manifest as embodied countertransference. An analysand carrying a heavy burden of unspoken grief or a relentless sense of guilt might unconsciously transmit this somatic weight to the analyst. The analyst might then experience a dull ache in their stomach, a persistent knot in their shoulders, or a throbbing headache that seems directly linked to the content of the session. These physical symptoms are not signs of illness but rather somatic translations of the analysand's internal suffering, experienced through the analyst's own embodied being. The analyst's awareness of such sensations, coupled with an understanding of their potential countertransference origins, allows for a deeper engagement with the analysand's unspoken pain. The analyst might inquire, "I've been noticing a persistent ache in my shoulders today, particularly when we've been discussing your family. Does that sensation of being weighed down, or perhaps a tension in the shoulders, feel familiar to you in any way?" This line of inquiry can unlock access to the analysand's repressed emotional burdens, offering a somatic pathway to explore feelings that may otherwise remain inaccessible.

The analyst's own breathing patterns can also become a sensitive indicator of embodied countertransference. An analysand who is struggling with suffocation, a sense of being overwhelmed by demands, or a fear of speaking their truth might, through their transference, evoke a feeling of breathlessness or restricted breathing in the analyst. The analyst might find themselves unconsciously holding their breath or taking shallow, rapid breaths, mirroring the analysand's internal struggle. This embodied resonance provides a tangible, visceral connection to the analysand's experience. The analyst, recognizing this shift in their own physiological state, might gently observe, "I'm finding it a little difficult to take a full breath at this moment, as if something is constricting. I wonder if that feeling of restricted breathing resonates with anything for you, perhaps a feeling of being unable to exhale fully or to speak freely?" This invitation can foster a deeper understanding of the analysand's internal experience of constraint or overwhelm, allowing them to see their struggle reflected in the analyst's embodied response.

Furthermore, the analyst's sensory experiences can become conduits for embodied countertransference. A sudden aversion to a particular scent, an inexplicable feeling of discomfort in a certain temperature, or a heightened sensitivity to noise could all be somatic manifestations of the analysand's internal world being projected onto the analyst. An analysand who experienced early sensory deprivation or overwhelming, chaotic sensory input might unconsciously evoke in the analyst a heightened or diminished sensory experience that mirrors their own internal landscape. For instance, an analysand who lived in a chaotic, noisy environment might unconsciously project a sense of sensory overload onto the analyst, leading to an increased sensitivity to ambient sounds or a feeling of being bombarded by stimuli. The analyst, if they become aware of this heightened sensitivity, can use it as a point of exploration: "I'm finding myself quite sensitive to the sound of the clock ticking today, more so than usual. It feels almost intrusive. I wonder if that heightened awareness of external stimuli is something you experience, or if it reminds you of anything?" This approach acknowledges the embodied nature of the analysand's experience and invites them to explore the origins of their sensory sensitivities within the transference.

The analyst's capacity to remain present and curious in the face of these embodied countertransference responses is paramount. It requires a robust sense of self-awareness, a well-developed capacity for introspection, and a continuous process of self-exploration outside of the analytic dyad. The analyst must be able to differentiate between their own pre-existing issues and the responses that are clearly being evoked by the analysand's transference. This differentiation is not always easy and requires careful attention to the nuances of the experience. Is this a familiar anxiety that I have brought into the room, or is this a novel sensation that seems directly linked to the analysand's narrative and projected affect? The analyst's own personal therapy, supervision, and ongoing training are critical in cultivating this capacity for discernment.

When embodied countertransference is not recognized or is acted out unconsciously, it can lead to significant ruptures in the therapeutic alliance. The analyst might become irritable, withdrawn, or overly eager to steer the conversation away from certain topics, all without understanding the underlying countertransference dynamics. This can result in the analysand feeling misunderstood, invalidated, or even rejected, further reinforcing their patterns of relational difficulty. For example, if an analyst, experiencing a somatic manifestation of the analysand's repressed rage as a feeling of being attacked, unconsciously withdraws or becomes overly placating, they are inadvertently enacting a familiar pattern of abandonment or avoidance for the analysand, hindering the potential for growth.

Conversely, when embodied countertransference is consciously held and explored, it becomes an invaluable source of insight. It allows the analyst to access a deeper, more intuitive understanding of the analysand's internal world, providing a powerful pathway for interpretation and therapeutic intervention. The analyst's body, in essence, becomes a finely tuned instrument, capable of registering and processing the unspoken language of the analysand's unconscious. This embodied resonance bridges the gap between intellectual understanding and lived experience, fostering a more profound and transformative therapeutic process. It allows the analyst to move beyond simply hearing the analysand's words to truly feeling and understanding the depth of their emotional and somatic reality. This shared embodied experience, when navigated with awareness and skill, can foster a unique sense of connection and attunement, paving the way for genuine healing and integration. The consulting room, therefore, is not just a space for verbal exchange, but a dynamic relational field where the analyst's embodied responses become integral to the unfolding therapeutic narrative, offering a profound testament to the interconnectedness of human experience.

The therapeutic journey is rarely a linear ascent. More often, it is a labyrinthine exploration, marked by recurring patterns, echoes of the past that reverberate in the present. Within the confines of the consulting room, these echoes coalesce into what we term transference, a powerful engine of both disruption and profound healing. But transference is not merely a mental construct, a projection of old feelings onto new figures; it is an embodied phenomenon, a deeply somatic experience that shapes the very fabric of the analytic encounter. The previous sections have laid the groundwork for understanding how the analyst's own body can become a sensitive instrument, registering the subtle, often unconscious, currents of the analysand's projected world. Now, we turn our attention to the crucial, and often challenging, process of "working through" these transference dynamics, a process where the body, far from being a passive bystander, becomes an active participant in the transformative work of therapy.

Working through transference is not a single event but a sustained process of repetition and revision. It is in the repeated enactment of old patterns, played out in the transference, that the unconscious finds its voice. The consulting room, with its predictable rhythm and contained environment, offers a unique stage for these dramas to unfold. The analysand, driven by an unconscious imperative, will inevitably, and often unwittingly, recreate familiar relational dynamics with the analyst. This might manifest as an insistence on certain narrative themes, a testing of the analyst's boundaries, or a repetition of specific emotional states that are characteristic of their early relationships. The analyst's role is not to be a passive recipient of these enactments but to serve as a conscious witness and facilitator, helping the analysand to recognize the familiar contours of these old scripts.

The body, however, is rarely a silent observer of these internal dramas. It is, in fact, a repository of deeply ingrained somatic memories, a physical embodiment of the analysand's relational history. When transference patterns emerge, they do so not just in thought and feeling, but in posture, in gesture, in the subtle tremors of a hand, in the cadence of breath, and in the myriad of unspoken physiological responses. The analysand who carries a history of neglect might unconsciously adopt a posture of withdrawal, of making themselves small, as if to avoid further abandonment. Their voice might become hesitant, their gaze averted, their breathing shallow, all signaling a deep-seated fear of being seen, of being acknowledged, lest that acknowledgment be followed by rejection.

Consider, for instance, an analysand who, in their childhood, experienced a parent who was emotionally volatile and unpredictable. This unpredictability created a constant state of hypervigilance, a bodily tension that became their default mode. In the analytic setting, this pattern can resurface. The analysand might find themselves habitually bracing their shoulders, their jaw clenched, their stomach knotted, even when the content of the session is neutral or positive. This somatic vigilance is a direct echo of their past, a bodily rehearsal of anticipating the next emotional storm. When the analyst, attuned to these subtle somatic cues, gently invites exploration, saying something like, "I notice a certain tension in your shoulders when we discuss your family. It's as if you're perpetually ready for something to happen. What does that feeling of readiness, or perhaps apprehension, feel like in your body?" the analysand is given an entry point to understand this embodied transference.

This is not simply about interpreting the analysand's words; it is about recognizing the language of their body, a language that often speaks louder and more honestly than their verbal discourse. The working through begins when the analysand, with the analyst's guidance, starts to connect these bodily sensations to the historical emotional patterns they are unconsciously recreating. The clenched jaw becomes not just a physical symptom, but a physical manifestation of an unmet need for safety and predictability. The knotted stomach represents the internalized anxiety of an unstable environment. By bringing these embodied enactments into conscious awareness, the analysand begins to loosen their grip. They learn that the tension they carry is not an inherent part of their being but a learned response, a survival mechanism that, while once necessary, now hinders their ability to form secure attachments.

The process of working through transference also involves a conscious revision of these patterns. Once the analysand can identify the somatic echoes of their past, they can begin to consciously choose a different response. In the safe container of the analytic relationship, they can experiment with softening the clenched jaw, with allowing their shoulders to relax, with taking a deeper, more expansive breath. These are not merely symbolic gestures; they are acts of embodied self-regulation. As the analysand practices these new somatic responses within the therapeutic relationship, they begin to internalize them. The consulting room becomes a laboratory for creating a new internal working model, not just of relationships, but of the self.

The analyst's role in this process is crucial. They must be able to hold the space for this repetition to occur, to tolerate the discomfort that the analysand's enactments can evoke, and to offer interpretations that are not only psychologically insightful but also somatically resonant. When the analysand expresses frustration, for example, and the analyst notices a corresponding feeling of constriction in their own chest, they can use this shared somatic experience to deepen the exploration. "I'm feeling a sense of being shut down, almost as if my breath is caught in my throat, as you express this frustration. I wonder if that feeling of being unable to express something fully, or being somehow blocked, is familiar to you?" This shared embodied experience can be profoundly validating for the analysand, who may have long felt isolated in their bodily distress.

Furthermore, the working through of transference involves a process of differentiating the past from the present. The analysand may have unconsciously projected the traits of a critical parent onto the analyst, leading to an internal experience of being constantly judged or scrutinized. This projection can manifest somatically as a feeling of being exposed, of blushing, or of a general sense of unease in their skin. The analyst's consistent, non-judgmental presence, however, can gradually help the analysand to recognize that the analyst is not, in fact, the internalized parent. This recognition can be facilitated by the analyst's ability to gently point out discrepancies between the analysand's projections and the reality of the therapeutic relationship. "I hear how intensely you fear my disapproval right now, and I notice a flush rising in my cheeks as you describe this. Yet, I also want to acknowledge that what you're fearing is not what I am experiencing or intending. Can you sense that difference, even just a little?" This invitation to notice the present reality, to feel the difference between the projected threat and the actual safety of the relationship, is a vital step in working through.

The physical space of the consulting room itself can also become a part of this working through process. The chair the analysand sits in, the arrangement of the furniture, the light filtering through the window – all these elements can become imbued with meaning and can participate in the transference. An analysand who felt confined or trapped in their home environment might unconsciously feel a sense of claustrophobia in the consulting room, their breathing becoming restricted, their desire to leave intensifying. The analyst, attuned to this somatic discomfort, can use it as a point of inquiry. "I notice you seem to be looking towards the door more frequently today, and your breathing seems a little shallow. Does this space feel confining to you in any way? Does it remind you of being stuck somewhere?" By exploring these somatic responses to the environment, the analysand can begin to understand how their past experiences of confinement are being reactivated and projected onto the present therapeutic setting.

The process of working through is also about developing a more conscious and integrated relationship with one's own body. For many individuals who have experienced trauma or chronic stress, their bodies have become sites of distress, disconnection, or even betrayal. The body may hold the unspeakable memories of abuse, the phantom pains of emotional neglect, or the chronic tension of constant vigilance. Working through transference offers an opportunity to reclaim the body, to transform it from a source of suffering into a source of wisdom and resilience. As the analysand learns to attune to their bodily sensations, to differentiate between signals of danger and signals of safety, they begin to develop a more compassionate and integrated sense of self.

This involves moving beyond purely intellectual understanding. While interpretations are vital, they are most effective when they are grounded in and validated by the analyst's embodied experience. When an analysand describes feeling numb or disconnected, and the analyst experiences a similar sense of dullness or emotional detachment in themselves, this shared somatic experience can create a powerful bridge. The analyst can then say, "I'm noticing a sense of distance myself, as if a fog has descended. I wonder if that feeling of being disconnected, of not quite being present, is something you experience often?" This approach acknowledges the analysand's internal state in a palpable way, allowing them to feel truly seen and understood on a level that transcends mere words.

The working through of transference is not about eradicating unconscious patterns entirely, for they are an intrinsic part of the human psyche. Rather, it is about transforming their impact, about loosening their compulsive grip on the individual's life. It is about developing a greater capacity for conscious choice, for self-regulation, and for forging new, more fulfilling ways of relating to oneself and to others. The somatic dimension of this work is paramount. By learning to listen to the wisdom of their bodies, to understand the language of their embodied transference, analysands can unlock deeply buried emotions, resolve long-standing conflicts, and ultimately achieve a more integrated and authentic sense of self.

The consulting room, in this light, is not just a space for verbal dialogue, but a dynamic relational field where the analyst and analysand co-create a space for embodied exploration. It is a space where the unconscious can be brought into conscious awareness, not just through narrative, but through the felt experience of the body. The repetitions of transference, once understood and consciously revised, become the very pathways to psychic restructuring. The body, once a silent witness or an unwilling carrier of past traumas, becomes an active partner in the process of healing and transformation. This is the essence of working through transference – a profound, embodied journey towards integration and freedom.

The labyrinthine journey of working through transference, as we have explored, is fundamentally an unfolding narrative of repetition, recognition, and revision. It is a process where the echoes of the past, resonating within the consulting room, are brought into conscious awareness, not as inert historical data, but as living, breathing somatic experiences. Yet, the ultimate arc of this therapeutic voyage leads us beyond the mere dissection of these patterns. It culminates in a profound transformation, a movement towards what can be termed embodied authenticity. This is not merely an intellectual grasp of one's psychological landscape, but a felt, lived experience of a self that is more integrated, flexible, and genuinely present in the world.

When the analysand, guided by the analyst's attuned presence, begins to discern the subtle somatic signatures of their ingrained relational patterns, a fundamental shift commences. The clenched jaw, the shallow breath, the averted gaze – these physical manifestations of old anxieties and defenses are no longer perceived as immutable aspects of their being. Instead, they are recognized as learned responses, as intricate, often unconscious, adaptations to past environments. This realization, deeply rooted in bodily awareness, forms the bedrock upon which authenticity can be built. The analysand starts to understand that the tightness they feel when expressing a need is not an intrinsic flaw, but a physical echo of past rejections, a bodily strategy for self-protection that has, over time, become a self-imposed cage.

This dawning awareness allows for a crucial differentiation. The embodied patterns that once dictated reactions, that automatically triggered a predictable response in interpersonal interactions, can now be consciously observed. The analysand learns to witness the impulse to retreat, to defend, to please, or to withdraw, not as an irresistible force, but as a familiar narrative playing out in their physiology. This act of witnessing, of creating a space between stimulus and response, is where genuine agency begins to blossom. It is akin to a dancer recognizing the ingrained choreography of their movement and, instead of being compelled by it, choosing to imbue each step with intention and awareness. The body, which was once a stage for automatic repetitions, becomes a site of conscious choice.

Consider, for instance, an analysand who consistently adopts a posture of self-effacement in the presence of perceived authority figures, a pattern deeply etched into their musculoskeletal system. Their shoulders slump, their gaze drops, and their voice often softens to a near whisper. This is not a conscious decision to appear subservient; it is a deeply ingrained somatic response, a physical manifestation of a lifelong belief in their own inadequacy, often rooted in early experiences of being overshadowed or diminished. Through the process of working through transference, this analysand might begin to notice the physiological sensations preceding this posture. They might feel a familiar knot in their stomach, a tightness in their throat, and a distinct pulling sensation that draws their shoulders forward. The analyst's gentle inquiry, such as, "When you speak about your boss's critique, I notice a subtle drawing inward, as if you're trying to make yourself smaller. What is that sensation like in your body, that feeling of shrinking?" can invite a deeper exploration.

As the analysand begins to connect these physical sensations to the underlying beliefs and historical experiences, the possibility for a different embodied response emerges. The consulting room, acting as a safe laboratory, provides the opportunity to practice. With the analyst's support, the analysand can experiment. They can consciously attempt to lift their chin slightly, to broaden their shoulders, to allow their breath to deepen, and to project their voice with more conviction. These are not mere superficial adjustments; they are acts of somatic rebellion against old programming. Each attempt, even if tentative, begins to rewire the neural pathways, to create new embodied habits. The feeling of discomfort that might initially accompany these novel physical expressions – the unfamiliarity of standing taller, the slight apprehension of being more visible – is itself a valuable piece of data, a signal of the old patterns being challenged.

This movement towards embodied authenticity is not about eradicating all past influences, but about integrating them in a way that allows for genuine expression. The residual traces of past defenses, the whispers of old anxieties, do not disappear entirely. Instead, they are understood within a larger, more resilient framework. The analysand learns to acknowledge these inner stirrings without being overwhelmed or dictated by them. They develop a capacity for self-compassion, recognizing that these patterns arose from a need to survive, and that their persistence, while now problematic, was once a testament to their resourcefulness. This nuanced acceptance is a hallmark of authenticity; it is not about achieving a state of perfect, unblemished selfhood, but about embracing the complex, multifaceted reality of one's lived experience.

The analyst's role in this final stage of working through transference is to facilitate this unfolding authenticity. It involves a delicate balance of acknowledging the analysand's lived reality – the felt experience of their present state – while also holding the vision of their potential for genuine connection. This might mean, for example, that an analysand who has habitually expressed anger through passive aggression, manifesting as a subtle withdrawal of warmth or a passive resistance that is palpable in their stiffening posture and averted eyes, begins to experiment with more direct, yet still contained, expressions of their feelings. The analyst might observe, "I notice that when you feel frustrated, there's a distinct stillness that comes over you, a sort of freezing. It's as if all movement, all expression, stops. Can we explore what that stillness feels like, and what it might be holding back?"

As the analysand begins to articulate these held-back emotions, perhaps feeling a tremor in their voice or a clenching in their gut as they do so, the analyst's validation is crucial. It is not simply saying, "It's okay to be angry," but acknowledging the embodied reality of that anger. "I can sense the energy building within you, a palpable tension in your chest. It's as if you are holding back a powerful force. It is understandable that you would want to protect yourself from unleashing such intensity." This validation allows the analysand to inhabit their emotions more fully, to understand them as signals rather than as threats. The consulting room becomes a space where these potent, often feared, emotions can be explored and expressed in a way that is both safe and ultimately liberating.

Authenticity, in this context, is profoundly embodied. It is the congruence between one's inner experience and one's outer expression, facilitated by a body that is no longer a site of rigid defenses but a fluid, responsive instrument of self. When the analysand can move beyond the compulsive repetition of old relational scripts, they begin to inhabit their bodies in a new way. They become more attuned to their own needs, more able to set boundaries, and more capable of genuine intimacy. The physical manifestations of their inner world – their posture, their gestures, their vocalizations – become more aligned with their authentic feelings and intentions.

Consider an analysand who, after years of relational trauma, has developed a profound distrust of intimacy, manifesting as a physical recoil at any perceived closeness, a tightening of their diaphragm, and a shallow, rapid breathing pattern that signals an impending escape. The working through of transference, in this instance, involves not just understanding the psychological reasons for this distrust, but also actively re-patterning the body's response. The analyst might, with great care and attunement, invite the analysand to notice the physical sensations of closeness. "As we sit here, sharing this quiet space, I notice your breath seems to quicken. There's a subtle tension that seems to rise in your shoulders. What is happening in your body as we simply *are* together in this way?"

As the analysand gradually learns to tolerate these sensations, to recognize that closeness does not inevitably lead to danger, their body begins to adapt. The diaphragm can relax, the breath can deepen, and the shoulders can soften. This is not about suppressing the old fear, but about integrating it, about creating new embodied experiences that override the old ones. The physical experience of safety and connection begins to build, providing a new internal reference point. The body, once a sentinel of past threats, becomes a reservoir of present resilience and capacity for connection.

This leads to a more flexible and responsive self. The rigid binaries of "safe" versus "dangerous," "connected" versus "alone," begin to dissolve. The analysand develops a capacity to hold complexity, to recognize that relationships can be both intimate and challenging, that vulnerability can coexist with strength. This is reflected in their embodied responses, which become more nuanced and context-dependent. They are no longer compelled to react with the same automatic intensity to every interpersonal situation. They can pause, sense into their body, and choose a response that is more aligned with their current reality and their authentic desires.

The shift from repetition to embodied authenticity is not a sudden eureka moment, but a gradual unfolding. It is the accumulation of small moments of embodied awareness, of conscious choice, and of courageous self-expression. It is the journey from a self that is a prisoner of its past to a self that is a sovereign agent of its present and future. The analyst, throughout this process, serves as a mirror, a guide, and a safe harbor, reflecting back the analysand's own emerging authenticity, validating their struggles, and celebrating their victories, however small they may seem.

Ultimately, the successful working through of transference leads to a profound sense of liberation. The analysand discovers that their body, far from being a source of unbidden, intrusive reactions, can become a source of wisdom, intuition, and genuine connection. They learn to listen to its signals, to trust its innate intelligence, and to express themselves with an integrity that is deeply rooted in their embodied experience. The consulting room, which may have once felt like a space of intense scrutiny or uncomfortable repetition, transforms into a sanctuary where the self, in all its complexity, can be fully and authentically present. This embodied authenticity is not merely the absence of symptoms, but the vibrant presence of a self that is alive, responsive, and capable of forging genuine connections in the world. It is the flowering of the therapeutic journey, a testament to the power of the analyst-analysand relationship to facilitate a deep and lasting transformation, one felt and lived within the very fabric of the body. This signifies a profound shift, not just in the analysand's internal world, but in the very way they inhabit their existence, moving from a state of reactive repetition to one of conscious, embodied presence. The body, once a landscape of ingrained patterns and projections, becomes the canvas upon which a new narrative of authentic selfhood is painted, stroke by gentle, deliberate stroke.

Chapter 15: From Suffering to Signification: The Integrated Self

The body, often experienced as a landscape of torment, a visceral canvas upon which distress is writ large, is, in its deepest sense, a profound reservoir of symbolic meaning. Our journey through the labyrinthine corridors of suffering, as traced in these pages, is ultimately a movement towards deciphering these potent, often unspoken, languages of the flesh. What begins as a constellation of raw, undifferentiated pain – a tightness in the chest that steals breath, a knot in the stomach that paralyves action, a tremor in the hands that betrays fear – gradually, with attunement and exploration, begins to yield its secrets. These initial, confusing manifestations, so often perceived as mere symptoms, are in fact the nascent stirrings of a more articulate self, the first whispers of a narrative struggling to emerge from the depths of lived experience.

The transformation of physical distress into a symbolic language is not a passive occurrence; it is an active, alchemical process. It is the profound realization that the body, in its myriad presentations of discomfort, is not simply a vessel of random affliction, but a meticulously crafted text, awaiting interpretation. The tightness that constricts the throat when confronted with an injustice, for instance, is not merely a physiological response to stress. It is a symbol, a potent, embodied representation of a suppressed voice, of words left unsaid that carry the weight of past indignities. Similarly, the inexplicable fatigue that plagues an individual might not be a sign of physical exhaustion alone, but a corporeal metaphor for emotional depletion, a body's way of signaling a profound need for rest and replenishment that has been denied for too long.

This reframing of symptom as symbol is the linchpin of the integrated self. When the analysand, guided by the analyst's compassionate inquiry, begins to approach their physical discomfort not with dread or avoidance, but with curiosity and an openness to meaning, a fundamental shift occurs. The pain is no longer an enemy to be vanquished, but a messenger to be understood. The trembling hand, once a source of shame and a prompt for immediate concealment, can be seen as a physical expression of an intense internal emotional charge, a bodily attempt to discharge an overwhelming psychic energy. By acknowledging the tremor, by tracing its origins to a specific emotional context, the analysand begins to imbue it with meaning, transforming it from a chaotic symptom into a coherent symbol of their internal state.

Consider the individual who experiences chronic, debilitating headaches. For years, these may have been dismissed as mere physical ailments, treated with medication that offers only temporary respite. However, through the lens of symbolic interpretation, these headaches might begin to reveal themselves as manifestations of an overwhelming burden of responsibility, a psychic pressure that the mind, unable to bear directly, has displaced onto the physical body. The throbbing pain becomes a symbol of the relentless demands and expectations that the individual feels compelled to carry, a physical ache mirroring the emotional weight of a life lived under constant duress. The process then becomes one of not just seeking pain relief, but of understanding what that pain

represents. What are the "weights" being carried? What are the "demands" that cause this internal pressure?

This reframing is not an intellectual exercise alone; it is a deeply felt, embodied transformation. The body itself begins to speak a new language, one of coherence and intentionality, rather than one of chaos and brute force. The suffering, which was once a formless, overwhelming entity, begins to coalesce into specific, recognizable patterns. These patterns, once understood, can then be worked with, integrated, and ultimately, transformed. The raw grief that manifests as a pervasive physical ache throughout the body, for example, can, through the process of symbolic articulation, begin to take on more defined forms. It might be expressed as a tightness in the chest that symbolizes a longing for lost connection, or a heavy sensation in the limbs that represents the felt difficulty of moving forward in life without the presence of the loved one.

The transformation from symptom to symbol is intrinsically linked to the development of self-awareness and agency. When the body's signals are understood as meaningful communications, rather than as random disturbances, the individual gains a new capacity to respond. The constricted breath, previously experienced as an inexplicable panic attack, might, upon symbolic deciphering, be understood as the body's protest against a situation that feels suffocating or violating. This understanding opens the door for a deliberate shift in behavior: the individual might not be able to eliminate the situation immediately, but they can begin to communicate their distress more clearly, to seek support, or to create small pockets of breathing room for themselves. The symptom, once a paralyzing force, becomes an impetus for informed action.

This journey from suffering to signification is a testament to the inherent wisdom of the body. It is a process that honors the body's capacity to hold and to express what the conscious mind may struggle to articulate. The unspoken trauma, the unresolved grief, the deeply buried fears – these do not simply disappear. They find a voice within the physical form, manifesting as a vocabulary of physical sensations and dis-eases. The task of psychoanalysis, in this context, is to become fluent in this body language, to help the analysand translate these often-painful expressions into a language of understanding, integration, and ultimately, empowerment.

Consider the child who, in the absence of verbal capacity to express their distress, develops a chronic skin condition. This eczema, burning and inflamed, is not a random biological event. It is a potent symbol of an internal state of agitated vulnerability, a body's cry for comfort and protection in an environment that may feel harsh or overwhelming. The scratching, the redness, the discomfort – these are all part of a non-verbal narrative of feeling exposed and raw. When this is understood, the focus shifts from merely treating the skin to addressing the underlying emotional landscape, to creating an environment of safety and responsiveness that can help the body to heal itself, not just symptomatically, but fundamentally.

The symbolic language of the body is as rich and varied as human experience itself. It encompasses not only pain and distress, but also joy and vitality. When the body begins to express itself in a new, more integrated way, it is not simply the absence of suffering that is experienced, but the presence of something profoundly positive. A freed breath, for instance, is not just the absence of constriction;

it is the palpable sensation of expansion, of life force flowing unimpeded. A relaxed posture, beyond the mere release of muscular tension, can symbolize a newfound sense of ease and belonging in the world, an embodied freedom from constant vigilance.

The transformation of suffering into symbol is, therefore, a generative process. It is the fertile ground from which a more integrated and authentic self can emerge. The pain that was once a source of isolation and confusion becomes a bridge to deeper understanding, both of oneself and of others. By learning to read the body's symbolic communications, we unlock a more profound level of self-knowledge, one that is grounded in the lived reality of our physical being. This is where the true work of healing lies: not in erasing the past or denying the pain, but in weaving it into the fabric of a more meaningful present, in transforming the language of suffering into the eloquent prose of a fully realized self.

This transition is not about achieving a state of perfect health or the eradication of all physical discomfort. Rather, it is about developing a more nuanced and compassionate relationship with one's own body, understanding its messages, and responding to them with greater awareness and intention. The body's journey from raw symptom to eloquent symbol is, in essence, the journey of the self towards greater wholeness and integration. It is the profound recognition that within our physical experiences lie the keys to unlocking our deepest truths, to understanding the narratives that shape us, and to ultimately, living a life that is not only less burdened by suffering, but richer in meaning and authentic expression. The body, in its capacity to symbolize, becomes the ultimate storyteller, and in learning to listen, we learn to author our own lives with greater wisdom and grace.

The exploration of suffering's transformation into signification culminates in the essential task of integrating the psychic and the corporeal. For too long, Western thought, and indeed, many therapeutic modalities, have operated under a Cartesian dualism, a fundamental separation of mind and body. This schism, while perhaps offering a convenient intellectual framework, ultimately proves detrimental to the holistic development of the self. Our journey through the nuanced landscape of distress has demonstrated that this separation is not merely an abstract philosophical debate, but a lived reality that contributes to our sense of fragmentation and alienation. The body, often cast as the unwitting receptacle of the mind's anxieties, or conversely, the mind perceived as a detached overseer of the body's biological functions, exists in a constant, intricate dialogue. To truly achieve a state of integrated being, this dialogue must be recognized, honored, and fostered. The psychic and the corporeal are not opposing forces vying for dominance, nor are they distinct entities to be reconciled through a forced, artificial alliance. Instead, they are two indispensable facets of a single, unified organism, each informing and shaping the other in an ongoing dance of existence.

The profound entanglement of our mental and physical states is not a theoretical construct; it is an observable phenomenon in the everyday lives of individuals. Consider the subtle yet pervasive ways in which emotional states manifest physically. A prolonged period of anxiety can lead to chronic muscle tension, digestive disturbances, or a compromised immune system. Conversely, physical illness or injury can profoundly impact our mood, leading to feelings of depression, irritability, or a loss of motivation. These are not isolated incidents, but rather consistent indicators of an intrinsic interconnectedness. When these connections are ignored, when the physical is treated as merely a biological machine separate from the emotional and psychological realms, healing becomes superficial, and the underlying patterns of distress persist. The psychosomatic experience, once a perplexing mystery, begins to reveal itself as a testament to this profound unity. It is the body's eloquent, albeit often uncomfortable, way of communicating deeply held emotional truths that may not yet have found their way into conscious awareness or verbal expression. The migraine that strikes after a particularly stressful week, the rash that flares up during periods of intense emotional turmoil, the persistent fatigue that follows a significant loss – these are not aberrations, but rather legible inscriptions on the body's surface, bearing witness to the intricate interplay between our inner world and our physical form.

This inherent unity of the psychic and the corporeal is not a new revelation; it is a truth that has been recognized in various traditions throughout history, often lost in the scientific and philosophical currents of modernity. Ancient healing practices frequently understood illness as a manifestation of an imbalance in the whole person – mind, body, and spirit. The modern emphasis on treating symptoms in isolation, whether through pharmaceuticals or purely physical interventions, often overlooks the fertile ground where psychological distress takes root and manifests physically. The reductionist approach, while effective in managing certain acute conditions, can inadvertently reinforce the sense of a divided self. It perpetuates the idea that a problem is either "in the head" or "in the body," when in reality, it is often a phenomenon that spans both domains. The body's capacity to bear witness to our psychic burdens is immense, and when we begin to listen to its language, we unlock a deeper, more resonant pathway to healing. The discomfort, the pain, the peculiar sensations that arise are not arbitrary afflictions but rather potent metaphors, embodied expressions of our internal landscape.

The integration of the psychic and the corporeal is, therefore, not merely an optional add-on to therapeutic work, but its very cornerstone. When we approach the body not as a separate entity, but as an intrinsic part of our lived experience, capable of holding and communicating our deepest emotional truths, a profound shift occurs. This shift allows us to move beyond the mere management of symptoms towards a more profound understanding and transformation of the underlying causes of suffering. Consider, for instance, the individual who experiences chronic back pain. While physical therapy and pain medication might offer some relief, true resolution may lie in exploring the emotional burdens they are literally carrying. Is the pain a manifestation of unspoken responsibilities, of a weight too heavy to bear, or perhaps a refusal to move forward in a certain direction? When the body's signals are interpreted not as mere physiological malfunctions but as symbolic expressions of our psychic lives, we gain a crucial vantage point. The pain becomes a messenger, urging us to examine the unseen forces that are impacting our well-being.

This process of integration is deeply embodied. It is not an intellectual exercise of acknowledging the mind-body connection, but a visceral experience of feeling it, of living it. It involves cultivating a greater attunement to the body's subtle cues, learning to decipher its non-verbal language. This might involve practices such as mindful movement, body-based psychotherapies, or simply the dedicated practice of bringing a curious and compassionate awareness to physical sensations as they arise. When the analysand begins to explore a physical symptom with the same depth of inquiry as they would a recurring dream or a persistent thought pattern, the boundaries between the psychic and the corporeal begin to dissolve. The tightness in the chest that accompanies fear is not just an unpleasant sensation; it is the body's palpable manifestation of a constricted spirit, a feeling of being overwhelmed or trapped. By attending to this sensation, by exploring its contours and its context, we begin to understand not just the physical feeling, but the emotional narrative it represents.

The illusion of separation is a powerful one, reinforced by societal norms and often by the very language we use to describe our experiences. We speak of "having" a body as if it were an accessory, separate from our true selves. We talk about "overcoming" physical limitations, implying that the body is an obstacle to be conquered rather than an integral part of who we are. This linguistic dichotomy subtly perpetuates the sense of fragmentation. True integration, however, involves embracing the body as an essential component of our identity, recognizing its wisdom, its vulnerability, and its profound capacity for expression. It means acknowledging that our physical experiences are not separate from our emotional lives, but rather are deeply interwoven, each influencing and shaping the other in a continuous feedback loop. The body is not a passive recipient of experience; it is an active participant, a co-creator of our reality.

When the psychic and the corporeal are integrated, a sense of groundedness and wholeness emerges. The individual feels more present in their own skin, more connected to their lived reality. The fragmentation that often characterizes suffering begins to recede, replaced by a more cohesive sense of self. This is not to say that physical discomfort or emotional pain disappears entirely, for these are inherent aspects of the human condition. Rather, the

relationship to these experiences transforms. The suffering is no longer a disembodied torment or a purely physical affliction, but a meaningful part of one's narrative, understood through the lens of an integrated self. The tension in the shoulders, for example, might be recognized not just as a physical knot, but as a symbol of the burdens of responsibility that the individual feels compelled to carry. This recognition does not magically erase the tension, but it imbues it with meaning, allowing for a more conscious and intentional response.

The process of integrating the psychic and the corporeal is a dynamic and ongoing one, a continuous negotiation between our internal states and our physical embodiment. It requires patience, curiosity, and a willingness to explore the often-uncomfortable territories where mind and body meet. It challenges the deeply ingrained notion that the body is merely a vehicle for the mind, and instead, elevates it to its rightful place as a fundamental locus of meaning and experience. When we acknowledge that our physical sensations are not random occurrences but are deeply connected to our emotional and psychological lives, we begin to unlock a more profound level of self-understanding. The pain, the pleasure, the discomfort, the ease – all become part of a rich and complex tapestry of human experience, where the psychic and the corporeal are inextricably bound.

Furthermore, this integration fosters a greater capacity for resilience and adaptation. When we are attuned to the body's signals, we are better equipped to recognize early signs of distress and to intervene before they escalate into overwhelming crises. The subtle tightening in the jaw, the faint tremor in the hands, the slight shift in posture – these can all be early indicators of rising emotional tension. By noticing these signals and understanding their potential meaning, we can employ coping strategies, seek support, or make necessary adjustments to our environment or our behavior, thereby preventing a cascade of more severe physical and psychological symptoms. The body, in this sense, becomes a sophisticated early warning system, providing us with invaluable information about our internal state and our relationship with the external world.

The false dichotomy between mind and body can lead to a sense of disembodiment, where individuals feel disconnected from their physical selves, as if observing their lives from a distance. This disembodiment can manifest as a lack of vitality, a feeling of being out of touch with one's own sensations, and a difficulty in experiencing genuine pleasure or connection. The work of integration, therefore, is also the work of re-embodiment, of reclaiming one's physical presence and experiencing the world through a fully integrated sensory and emotional apparatus. It is about learning to inhabit one's body fully, to feel its aliveness, its capacity for sensation, and its inherent wisdom. This re-embodiment is crucial for fostering a sense of agency and for living a life that is rich in sensory experience and grounded in the present moment.

The body holds the history of our experiences in a way that the conscious mind sometimes struggles to articulate. Unprocessed emotions, past traumas, and deeply ingrained patterns of relating can all leave their mark on our physical being. These imprints are not merely memories stored in the brain; they are often felt sensations, habitual tensions, and chronic physical ailments that serve as a somatic archive of our lives. The integration of the psychic and the corporeal involves not only deciphering these somatic inscriptions but also working with them to facilitate release and transformation. This might involve techniques that help to gently release stored tension, to process buried emotions held within the body, or to develop new, more adaptive physical responses to old triggers.

Ultimately, the achievement of an integrated self is a testament to the profound interconnectedness of all aspects of our being. It is the realization that the psychic and the corporeal are not distinct entities to be reconciled, but rather are two sides of the same coin, each essential for the full expression of life. When this integration is realized, the individual experiences a sense of authenticity and wholeness that transcends mere symptom relief. They are better able to navigate the complexities of life with greater awareness, resilience, and a deeper appreciation for the richness and wisdom of their embodied existence. The journey from suffering to signification, when viewed through the lens of psychic-corporeal integration, becomes a path toward a more vibrant, meaningful, and fully realized life, where the body's wisdom is honored and its language is understood. This is the essence of becoming truly whole: not the absence of challenges, but the capacity to meet them from a place of unified strength and profound self-knowing.

Language, that intricate tapestry woven from thought, emotion, and intention, acts as the crucial bridge between the raw, visceral reality of our bodily sensations and the conceptual, narrative self. Without it, the body's eloquent, silent pronouncements would remain trapped in the realm of the ineffable, a perpetual echo in the chambers of our being, inaccessible to conscious understanding or deliberate integration. The journey from suffering to signification is, in many ways, a linguistic excavation, a patient and often arduous process of unearthing meaning from the fertile, yet sometimes forbidding, terrain of our embodied existence. It is through the act of naming, of articulating, that we begin to move beyond mere subjective experience towards a shared, comprehensible reality, and more importantly, towards a coherent internal landscape.

Consider the individual grappling with a persistent, unexplained ache in their limbs, a subtle tremor that belies their outward composure, or a pervasive sense of unease that settles in their gut. These are not simply physiological occurrences; they are potential carriers of meaning, somatic whispers from the deep unconscious. Yet, until these sensations find their way into the realm of language, they remain largely unintegrated. The body speaks in a language of pressure, of heat, of constriction, of vibration – a rich lexicon of the Real that precedes and often dwarfs our verbal capacities. This pre-linguistic communication is potent, capable of conveying the weight of unspoken anxieties, the phantom pains of past wounds, or the burgeoning desires that have yet to find conscious form. However, without the intermediary of language, this communication can feel overwhelming, chaotic, and ultimately, alienating. It is akin to receiving a complex message in a foreign tongue, one feels the intensity of its delivery, the urgency of its import, but the precise content remains elusive, fostering frustration and a sense of helplessness.

The therapeutic encounter, in its most profound manifestations, is an arena where this linguistic translation takes place. The analyst, through careful attunement and gentle inquiry, helps the analysand to bridge the gap between the felt sense and the spoken word. It is not merely about assigning a label to a symptom, but about co-creating a narrative that imbues the physical experience with meaning. For example, a patient who reports a chronic tightness in their chest might initially describe it simply as "discomfort." Through a process of exploration, however, this discomfort might begin to unravel, revealing itself as a physical manifestation of suppressed grief, of a felt sense of being unable to breathe freely in the face of overwhelming loss. The language used to describe this sensation evolves from a generic descriptor to a more specific, emotionally resonant articulation: "It feels like a heavy stone is pressing down, preventing me from exhaling completely," or "It's a suffocating sensation, as if the air itself is too thick to pass through." Each of these linguistic formulations, while still rooted in the embodied experience, begins to paint a more detailed and nuanced picture, offering a pathway towards understanding and eventual integration.

This process of linguistic translation is fundamental to moving from the raw, unmediated experience of suffering – the overwhelming surge of pain or anxiety – to a more symbolic representation. The Symbolic order, as understood in psychoanalytic theory, is the realm of language, culture, and social norms, the very structure that allows us to organize and make sense of our experiences. When suffering remains purely within the Real – the traumatic event, the overwhelming sensation – it can be devastatingly uncontainable. Language, however, allows us to "symbolize" this experience, to give it form and structure, to contain it within a narrative. This does not diminish the pain or erase the trauma, but it transforms it from an all-consuming force into something that can be processed, understood, and ultimately, integrated into the fabric of one's life. The body's silent screams are given a voice, and in that voice lies the potential for healing.

The power of articulation extends beyond the clinical setting, shaping our understanding of ourselves and our interactions with the world. When we can articulate our embodied experiences, we not only gain insight but also foster connection. Sharing a physical sensation with another, translating the internal into the external through words, can create a sense of validation and shared humanity. A friend who says, "I know exactly what you mean; I get that same knot in my stomach when I'm about to give a presentation," offers not just empathy but a linguistic resonance that affirms the reality of the other's embodied experience. This mutual recognition through language is a powerful force against isolation, reminding us that our internal struggles, even when expressed through the body, are part of a larger human tapestry.

Furthermore, language acts as a crucial tool in understanding and processing desire. The body is a site of profound desire, of urges, of longings that often precede conscious thought. These desires can be complex, sometimes contradictory, and at times, deeply unsettling. The ability to articulate these desires, to name them and explore their nuances, is essential for navigating them constructively. Without language, desire can feel like an untamed force, leading to impulsive actions, guilt, or a pervasive sense of unfulfillment. The act of verbalizing a desire, of bringing it into the light of conscious awareness through language, allows for a more considered approach. It opens up possibilities for understanding the origins of that desire, its potential implications, and how it aligns with one's broader sense of self. This is not about suppressing desire, but about engaging with it in a conscious, integrated manner, a process made possible by the capacity for linguistic expression.

Trauma, in particular, highlights the indispensable role of language in embodied understanding. Traumatic experiences often overwhelm our capacity to process them, leaving behind fragmented memories, somatic echoes, and emotional dysregulation. The body becomes a repository of this unprocessed trauma, manifesting as flashbacks, hypervigilance, or chronic physical symptoms. The journey of healing from trauma necessarily involves the arduous but vital work of linguistic articulation. It is through carefully guided narrative reconstruction, through finding words to describe what was once unspeakable, that individuals can begin to process the event, to integrate it into their life story, and to reclaim their sense of self. This is not about reliving the trauma in a destructive way, but about weaving it into a coherent narrative, giving it a place within one's life without allowing it to define one's entire existence. The terror of the moment, the helplessness, the violation – these unspeakable horrors are transformed, through language, into a testament to survival, a story of resilience.

The language we use to describe our bodies and our experiences also shapes our embodied understanding. If we habitually refer to our bodies as "weak," "flawed," or "unreliable," we internalize these linguistic judgments, creating a self-fulfilling prophecy of discomfort and disconnection. Conversely, cultivating a language of appreciation, of curiosity, and of acceptance towards our physical selves can foster a more positive and integrated embodied experience. This involves not just the external words we use, but the internal monologue, the self-talk that accompanies our embodied existence. The shift from "I hate my aching back" to "My back is telling me it needs rest and care" is a subtle yet profound linguistic transformation that opens the door to a more compassionate and responsive relationship with one's body.

Within the therapeutic space, the concept of "talking cure" finds its deepest resonance. It is not merely the act of speaking, but the specific quality of that speech – its honesty, its vulnerability, its willingness to explore the uncomfortable – that facilitates healing. The analyst acts as a linguistic mirror, reflecting back the analysand's words, their intonations, their silences, with an attentiveness that allows for new layers of meaning to emerge. This is where the raw Real of sensation begins its ascent into the Symbolic. A sigh, a choked sob, a tremor in the voice – these are all non-verbal cues that language can then begin to unpack. The analyst might inquire, "What does that sound feel like in your body?" or "When you say you feel 'empty,' where do you notice that emptiness?" These questions invite the analysand to translate the embodied experience into more precise linguistic terms, transforming vague discomfort into a rich tapestry of sensation and emotion.

The process of integration, therefore, is deeply intertwined with linguistic fluency – not necessarily in terms of vocabulary, but in the capacity to articulate one's internal world. This includes the ability to recognize and name subtle shifts in bodily sensation, to connect these sensations to emotional states, and to weave these connections into a coherent narrative of one's life. It is the capacity to say, "When I feel that familiar tension in my shoulders, I know it's because I'm feeling overwhelmed by my responsibilities," or

"The lightness I feel after talking about my hopes and dreams is a physical sensation of freedom." These are not just observations; they are articulations of an integrated self, where the mind and body are in communication, and that communication is made comprehensible through language.

The written word also plays a significant role in this process of embodied understanding. Journaling, for instance, can be a powerful tool for individuals to explore their physical sensations and emotional experiences in a private, self-directed way. By writing about a recurring pain, a disturbing dream, or a moment of intense anxiety, individuals can begin to identify patterns, trace connections, and gain insight into the underlying causes of their distress. The act of putting pen to paper, or fingers to keyboard, forces a degree of organization and clarity that may be difficult to achieve through spoken word alone. The written word provides a tangible record, a physical manifestation of one's internal landscape, which can be revisited, analyzed, and used as a basis for further exploration, whether in therapy or in personal reflection. This externalization of the internal can be particularly helpful when emotions are too overwhelming or too diffuse to be grasped through immediate introspection.

Moreover, literature itself, as a form of collective linguistic expression, can offer profound insights into embodied understanding. The way authors describe physical sensations, emotional turmoil, and the intricate interplay between the inner and outer worlds can resonate deeply with our own experiences. Reading a passage that vividly captures the feeling of grief as a physical weight, or the exhilaration of love as a bodily effervescence, can not only validate our own sensations but also expand our linguistic repertoire for describing them. These literary encounters act as a form of vicarious embodied experience, allowing us to explore different dimensions of human existence through the lens of language, enriching our own understanding of what it means to be fully embodied. It is through these shared linguistic explorations that we come to recognize the universality of certain bodily experiences, even as we appreciate their unique manifestation in each individual.

The challenge lies in the fact that language, while powerful, can also be limiting. It is a tool that attempts to capture the vastness of lived experience, and inevitably, some aspects will always elude precise articulation. The Real, in its raw intensity, often exists beyond the reach of words. However, the endeavor to use language to approximate, to gesture towards, these ineffable experiences is precisely what allows for the transformation from suffering to signification. It is the persistent effort to find the right words, the most evocative metaphors, the most resonant descriptions, that marks the journey towards an integrated self. The moments when language falters, when we struggle to find the words to express the depth of our feeling or the intensity of our sensation, are not necessarily failures, but rather points of contact with the limits of the Symbolic, reminding us of the profound depth of our embodied existence.

In essence, language serves as the architect of our embodied understanding. It is the scaffolding upon which we build meaning from the raw materials of sensation and emotion. Without this linguistic framework, the body's experiences might remain a chaotic jumble, a source of confusion and distress. But with the careful, deliberate, and often courageous application of language – spoken, written, or interpreted – we can begin to construct a coherent narrative of our embodied lives. This narrative, rich with the textures of physical sensation and the nuances of emotional experience, becomes the foundation of an integrated self, a self that can not only suffer but also understand, articulate, and ultimately, thrive. The journey from the visceral to the symbolic is a testament to the human capacity to make meaning, a process deeply rooted in our ability to communicate the incommunicable, to translate the whispers of the body into the resonant language of the soul.

The journey toward an integrated self, one that has moved from the raw immediacy of suffering to the nuanced terrain of signification, opens a crucial vista: the practice of a more humane engagement with ourselves and, by extension, with the world. This is not merely an academic or therapeutic achievement, a conceptual understanding to be filed away, but a fundamental shift in how we inhabit our own skin and relate to the lived realities of others. To truly integrate the complexities of our embodied existence—the whispers of desire, the echoes of past wounds, the persistent hum of bodily needs, the sharp edges of conflict—is to cultivate a deeper wellspring of self-compassion. This compassion arises not from a place of indulgence or self-pity, but from a profound, embodied understanding of shared human vulnerability.

When we have grappled with the difficult task of translating inarticulate physical distress into discernible meaning, when we have acknowledged the body as a site of not just sensation but of profound communication, we begin to recognize the universality of such struggles. The ache in the lower back that speaks of unspoken burdens, the tightening in the chest that signals a stifled protest, the gnawing anxiety in the gut that points to an unacknowledged threat—these are not isolated anomalies. They are variations on a theme, the somatic language of a creature attempting to navigate the often treacherous currents of life. By painstakingly deciphering our own bodily narratives, we gain an intuitive, felt sense of how others might be wrestling with similar internal dialogues, even if their somatic expressions differ. This recognition is the bedrock of empathy. It moves beyond a mere intellectual acknowledgment of another's pain and enters the realm of felt solidarity, a quiet knowing that "I, too, have known such whispers, such burdens, such storms within."

This nuanced understanding of our own embodied experience also liberates us from the tyranny of unattainable perfection. The integrated self acknowledges that the body, while a source of wisdom and resilience, is also susceptible to illness, fatigue, and the inevitable limitations of its physical form. To embrace our embodiment is to accept this inherent fragility, to recognize that moments of weakness, of pain, or of "unproductive" stillness are not failures of character but essential aspects of the human condition. When we can extend this acceptance to ourselves, when we can offer a gentle hand to our own weary limbs or a soothing word to our anxious heart, we create an inner sanctuary. This sanctuary, built not on denial but on honest, compassionate acknowledgment, becomes the launching pad for extending that same grace outward.

Consider the individual who has, through dedicated inner work, come to understand a recurring pattern of conflict in their relationships. Perhaps a tendency to withdraw when feeling overwhelmed, or conversely, to lash out defensively. This understanding, forged through the hard-won integration of past hurts and present reactions, allows for a different response. Instead of self-recrimination ("Why can't I just be normal?" or "I always mess things up"), there emerges a more humane appraisal: "This is how my body and mind react when I feel threatened. It's an old pattern, born of past experiences. How can I, with compassion for this part of me, choose a different path now?" This internal dialogue, imbued with self-compassion, is transformative. It disentangles the behavior from the core identity, creating space for change without the corrosive weight of shame.

This cultivated self-compassion naturally extends to our interactions with others. When we witness someone struggling—whether with visible illness, emotional distress, or social awkwardness—our immediate, almost instinctual response is often shaped by our own internal landscape of self-judgment or self-acceptance. If we are accustomed to berating ourselves for perceived flaws, we are more likely to judge others harshly for theirs. Conversely, if we have learned to approach our own vulnerabilities with kindness, we are better equipped to meet the vulnerabilities of others with understanding and non-judgment. We recognize the shared human propensity for error, for pain, for getting lost in the labyrinth of our own internal worlds. This recognition fosters patience, encourages listening, and opens the door to genuine connection.

Furthermore, the human experience is inextricably linked with the negotiation of desire. From the most primal urges to the most sophisticated aspirations, desire is a constant, dynamic force. An integrated self understands that desire is not inherently good or bad, but a natural, often complex, aspect of being alive. We learn to observe our desires without immediate identification, to acknowledge their presence without necessarily being driven by them. This involves recognizing that desires can be fleeting, contradictory, and sometimes even at odds with our deeply held values. The process of integrating this understanding means learning to sit with the discomfort of unfulfilled longing, to differentiate between healthy aspirations and destructive obsessions, and to appreciate the richness that desire brings to life without allowing it to dictate our every action.

This nuanced engagement with desire is crucial for ethical conduct. When we are aware of the potent, often irrational, pull of our own desires—for power, for pleasure, for validation—we become more sensitive to how these same forces might be impelling others. This awareness cultivates a heightened sense of responsibility in our interactions. We are less likely to exploit another's vulnerabilities if we understand the universal allure of gratification, and more likely to respect boundaries if we recognize the innate drive for autonomy and self-preservation that underlies all beings. The ethical imperative, in this light, is not about adhering to a rigid set of external rules, but about cultivating an internal ethical compass guided by a profound respect for the complexity of sentient experience, a respect born of intimate self-knowledge.

The very act of living in a physical body—our embodiment—is a source of both profound connection and potential alienation. We are grounded in our physical existence, experiencing the world through sensory input, through the rhythms of breathing and digestion, through the limitations and capacities of our flesh. Yet, societal pressures, cultural conditioning, and personal experiences can lead us to dissociate from our bodies, to view them as mere vehicles for the mind, or worse, as sources of shame and inadequacy. The integrated self, having navigated the path from suffering to signification, reclaims the body not as an object to be managed or controlled, but as a living, breathing, speaking partner in the journey of existence. This reclamation involves listening to its wisdom, honoring its needs, and recognizing its inherent dignity.

When we embrace our embodiment with kindness, we begin to perceive the embodiment of others with a similar sense of shared reality. We understand that every person is navigating the world within a unique physical vessel, with its own history of joys, pains, and limitations. This perspective fosters a deeper connection, transcending superficial differences. The way someone moves, their posture, their gestures—these are all expressions of their embodied experience, and when viewed through a lens of compassion informed by our own embodied journey, they become avenues for understanding rather than grounds for judgment. This allows for a more authentic and less reactive engagement with others, fostering relationships that are built on a foundation of mutual recognition and respect for the fundamental experience of being alive in a body.

The challenge, of course, is that this path is not linear. The integrated self is not a static endpoint but a dynamic process, a continuous unfolding of greater awareness and more compassionate engagement. There will be moments when old patterns resurface, when the body's whispers become clamors, when the weight of suffering threatens to eclipse signification. In these moments, the lessons learned are not forgotten but become resources. The ability to return to the practice of self-compassion, to revisit the process of linguistic translation, to acknowledge the inherent vulnerability without succumbing to despair—these are the hallmarks of an integrated self that is actively living a humane existence.

This proactive engagement with our inner landscape cultivates a profound sense of agency. It is the realization that while we cannot always control the circumstances of our lives or the sensations that arise within us, we can choose our response. We can choose to meet our suffering with curiosity rather than resistance, to approach our desires with wisdom rather than impulsivity, and to engage with our embodiment with respect rather than disdain. This conscious choice, repeated over time, shapes not only our internal world but also our external reality, creating ripples of compassion and understanding that extend far beyond our individual selves.

Ultimately, the reward of this arduous yet deeply rewarding inner work is a more profound and authentic connection with oneself and with the world. It is the experience of living with a sense of wholeness, where the fragmented pieces of our experience—the embodied sensations, the emotional currents, the cognitive narratives—begin to cohere into a rich and meaningful whole. This coherence allows us to move through life with greater ease, resilience, and a sense of purpose. We become more capable of experiencing joy, of navigating sorrow, and of contributing to the well-being of others in a way that is both effective and deeply humane. This is the essence of the integrated self: not a perfected being, but a being deeply engaged with the fullness of its own existence, extending that engagement outward with grace and unwavering compassion. It is the realization that our own journey from suffering to signification is a vital contribution to a more humane world, a testament to the transformative power of self-understanding and the boundless capacity for empathy.

The edifice of an integrated self, so painstakingly constructed through the arduous yet illuminating process of translating raw suffering into meaningful signification, is not a final, immutable structure. Rather, it is a dynamic, breathing entity, engaged in a perpetual dialogue with itself and with the vast, intricate tapestry of existence. This dialogue is not an afterthought, a postscript to the journey, but the very essence of its continuation. It is the ongoing, vital conversation between the conscious mind and the profound, often inarticulate, wisdom of the unconscious, a conversation that finds its most immediate and resonant expression in the body. To imagine this integration as a cessation of effort, a state of arrival, would be to misunderstand the very nature of life itself, which is a ceaseless unfolding, a constant becoming.

The body, far from being a passive vessel or a mere biological mechanism, is an active participant, a co-creator of meaning. It is the primordial language through which we first apprehend the world, and it continues to speak to us, even when our conscious awareness has drifted elsewhere. The unconscious mind, a vast reservoir of experiences, memories, archetypal patterns, and primal drives, does not operate in isolation. It communicates, it seeks expression, and its messages are often filtered, translated, and broadcast through the somatic realm. This is not a one-way transmission; it is a continuous, intricate feedback loop. Our conscious thoughts, our emotional states, our interpretations of events—all of these shape our physiological responses, influencing our posture, our breathing, our muscle tension, the very rhythm of our internal organs. Conversely, the state of our body—its aches, its comforts, its limitations, its vitality—profoundly impacts our mental and emotional landscape, influencing our mood, our cognitive function, our capacity for connection.

This understanding invites us into a lifelong practice of mindful engagement with ourselves, a continuous attunement to the subtle yet insistent language of our embodied experience. It is an invitation to cultivate a relationship of deep curiosity and unwavering kindness with our own physical presence. Consider the everyday phenomenon of a familiar ache, a persistent stiffness in the shoulder that has become a constant companion. In the past, it might have been met with frustration, a silent curse, or a desperate attempt to ignore it, a binary response that casts the body as either functioning perfectly or failing catastrophically. But now, viewed through the lens of signification, this ache is not an enemy to be vanquished but a messenger to be heard. What might this tension be communicating? Is it the residue of a long-held resentment, a physical manifestation of carrying an emotional burden that has become too heavy? Is it a signal of exhaustion, a primal call for rest and replenishment that has been consistently ignored? The process of asking these questions, of approaching the sensation with an open heart and a discerning mind, is itself an act of integration. It is the conscious self extending a hand of inquiry to the unconscious realm, seeking to understand its dispatches.

This ongoing dialogue is also about appreciating the symbolic richness of our bodily existence. Every sensation, every nuance of feeling, can be seen as a metaphor, a coded message from deeper levels of our being. A racing heart might not just be a sign of fear or excitement; it can also symbolize a yearning for something to happen, a pulse of anticipation for change. A knot in the stomach can transcend mere indigestion to represent a feeling of being trapped, of having swallowed something indigestible from our environment or our past. These are not literal translations, but interpretive possibilities, avenues of exploration. The journey of signification is not about finding a single, definitive meaning for every bodily experience, but about cultivating the capacity to hold multiple interpretations, to remain open to the fluid, ever-shifting nature of meaning itself. It is about recognizing that our bodies are living libraries, filled with stories waiting to be read, and that we are the lifelong librarians, constantly engaged in the act of annotation and interpretation.

The unconscious, in its relentless pursuit of wholeness, will continue to present us with its insights, often in veiled or symbolic forms. Dreams will persist, offering surreal landscapes and enigmatic characters that speak to our hidden desires, our unresolved conflicts, and our deepest aspirations. Intuitive flashes, those sudden bursts of knowing that seem to arise from nowhere, will continue to punctuate our awareness, guiding us, warning us, or revealing truths that lie beyond the grasp of rational thought. These are not aberrations to be suppressed or dismissed, but vital transmissions from the depths of our psyche. The integrated self, having learned the art of signification, approaches these phenomena not with alarm but with a sense of respectful engagement. It understands that these are not random occurrences but carefully curated messages, designed to facilitate our growth and to guide us toward greater authenticity. The ongoing dialogue, therefore, involves a sustained effort to remain receptive to these unconscious communications, to actively seek understanding, and to integrate their wisdom into our conscious lives.

This continuous engagement fosters a profound sense of agency, not in the sense of controlling every aspect of our experience, but in the capacity to consciously co-create our reality. When we are aware of the dynamic interplay between our inner world and our outer circumstances, we can make more informed and intentional choices. We can recognize how our habitual patterns of thought, our deeply ingrained beliefs, and our unacknowledged emotional states might be contributing to the realities we are experiencing. This awareness allows us to step out of the role of passive victim and into the position of active participant, capable of responding to life's challenges with greater wisdom and resilience. The body, in this context, becomes a sensitive barometer, providing us with real-time feedback on our alignment with our deepest intentions and values. A sense of ease and flow in the body can signal that we are on the right path, while discomfort or resistance can indicate a need for re-evaluation.

The relationship with the unconscious is, by its very nature, a lifelong process of discovery. There are no shortcuts, no definitive cures, only the continuous practice of deepening our understanding and expanding our capacity for conscious awareness. Each stage of life brings new challenges, new experiences, and new opportunities for the unconscious to communicate its messages. Childhood traumas, adolescent anxieties, adult responsibilities, the inevitable losses and transitions that mark the passage of time—all of these leave their imprint and provide fertile ground for the ongoing dialogue. The integrated self is one that embraces this lifelong journey, recognizing that growth is not a destination but a continuous unfolding, a rich and inexhaustible process of becoming.

Furthermore, the body's symbolic language is not static; it evolves and adapts as we do. What a particular sensation signifies at one point in life may carry a different nuance or weight at another. The chronic pain that once represented an overwhelming sense of helplessness might, with years of dedicated self-exploration, come to signify immense inner strength and resilience, a testament to the capacity to endure and to find meaning even in the face of adversity. The desires that once felt like urgent demands may, with maturity and a deeper understanding of self, transform into a source of creative energy and purposeful aspiration. This fluidity of meaning is a testament to the dynamic nature of the human psyche and the body's remarkable capacity for adaptation and expression.

To truly inhabit this ongoing dialogue is to embrace a profound sense of wonder at the complexity and richness of our own existence. It is to recognize that within each of us lies a universe of meaning, a vast and intricate landscape waiting to be explored. The journey from suffering to signification, therefore, is not merely about alleviating pain or resolving conflict; it is about awakening to the full spectrum of our human experience, about discovering the profound beauty and inherent wisdom that lies at the core of our being. It is about transforming existence itself into a sustained act of profound self-discovery and expression, a continuous dance of integration, where every sensation, every thought, every encounter becomes an opportunity to deepen our understanding and to live more fully, more authentically, and more compassionately.

This lifelong practice cultivates a deep and abiding appreciation for the symbolic nature of our lived reality. It is the recognition that the world around us, in its myriad forms, often mirrors our internal landscapes. The external challenges we face—the difficult relationships, the professional setbacks, the moments of profound uncertainty—can be seen not as random misfortunes, but as potent catalysts for inner growth, as external manifestations of internal dynamics seeking resolution. The integrated self learns to engage with these external situations not just on a practical level, but also as opportunities to further decipher the ongoing dialogue between their inner and outer worlds. A conflict with a colleague, for instance, might be a somatic echo of an unresolved childhood power struggle, or a manifestation of an unacknowledged fear of failure.. By approaching such situations with a lens of symbolic interpretation, informed by a deep knowledge of one's own somatic and emotional patterns, one can engage with them not only to resolve the immediate issue but also to gain deeper self-understanding. This approach transforms everyday life into a rich, symbolic text, where every interaction, every experience, offers clues to the unfolding narrative of the self.

The body, in its most primal form, is the anchor of our subjective experience, the constant, undeniable presence that grounds us in reality. Yet, our conscious minds often race ahead, seeking to escape the limitations of the physical, the perceived imperfections, the inevitable discomforts. The ongoing dialogue is, in essence, a gentle but persistent call for reunion, a plea for the mind to return to its source, to acknowledge and honor the profound wisdom held within the physical form. It is about learning to listen to the body not just when it screams in pain, but when it whispers in comfort, when it hums with vitality, when it sighs with contentment. These subtler messages are equally significant, offering insight into what nourishes us, what brings us joy, and what allows us to flourish. The integrated self cultivates an awareness of this entire spectrum of bodily communication, recognizing that both the distress and the delight of the physical realm are integral parts of the grand, ongoing conversation of being.

This continuous exploration also involves a profound shift in our relationship with time and change. The past, with its accumulated suffering and its formative experiences, is not a burden to be shed or a ghost to be exorcised, but a vital part of the narrative. The unconscious mind holds these memories, these imprints, and their influence continues to shape our present reality. The ongoing dialogue allows us to revisit these past experiences not with the raw pain of their original occurrence, but with the wisdom and perspective gained through the process of signification. It is about understanding how past wounds have shaped our present responses, and how, with conscious intention and self-compassion, we can begin to rewrite those narratives, to disentangle ourselves from the echoes of what was, and to create new possibilities for what can be. This is not about erasing the past, but about integrating its lessons, about allowing its wisdom to inform our present and to shape a more liberated future.

The concept of the "unconscious" itself can be understood not as a static entity, but as a living, breathing aspect of our psyche that is in constant flux, influenced by our experiences, our environment, and our conscious choices. This dynamic quality means that the dialogue is never truly finished. New layers of meaning will always emerge, new connections will be forged, and the journey of self-discovery will continue to unfold in unexpected and often beautiful ways. The integrated self, therefore, is characterized not by a final state of enlightenment, but by a profound capacity for continued learning, for embracing the mystery, and for engaging with life's unfolding journey with open curiosity and unwavering courage. It is the realization that the practice of becoming, of seeking meaning, and of living in dialogue with oneself is, in itself, the ultimate reward, the very essence of a life fully lived.

The ongoing dialogue, then, is a testament to the enduring human capacity for growth and transformation. It is the recognition that even in the face of immense suffering, the potential for meaning and integration always remains. This continuous exploration of the body's symbolic language, of the unconscious's rich tapestry, and of the dynamic interplay between the two, transforms our existence from a series of isolated events into a cohesive, meaningful narrative. It is a journey that promises not a cessation of struggle, but a deeper capacity to navigate it, to learn from it, and ultimately, to transcend it. The body, as the profound and ever-present messenger, invites us into this continuous conversation, offering its insights and its wisdom, guiding us toward a more integrated, more authentic, and more profoundly meaningful life. It is an invitation to participate in the ongoing miracle of self-creation, an endless process of discovery that imbues every moment with the potential for deeper understanding and richer expression.

Back Matter

This appendix is dedicated to providing supplementary resources and reflective tools for readers seeking to deepen their engagement with the concepts presented in this book. It includes:

Guided Meditations for Embodied Awareness: A series of short, guided practices designed to facilitate a more intimate connection with somatic experiences, helping to translate bodily sensations into meaningful insights.

Journaling Prompts for Signification: A curated list of prompts to encourage introspection and the active exploration of bodily signals, symbolic interpretations, and the dialogue between conscious and unconscious processes.

Recommended Reading: A bibliography of further texts that delve into psychosomatics, depth psychology, somatic experiencing, mindfulness, and related fields, offering pathways for continued learning and exploration.

Case Study Snippets (Anonymized): Brief, illustrative examples derived from clinical practice and personal reflection, showcasing the principles of signification in action across diverse human experiences.

Signification: The process of translating raw experience, particularly bodily sensation and emotional distress, into meaningful understanding and conscious awareness. It involves discerning the symbolic language of the unconscious and integrating its messages into the self.

Somatic: Pertaining to the body, especially as distinct from the mind or spirit. In this context, it refers to the physical sensations, tensions, and experiences that carry psychological meaning.

Embodied Awareness: The state of being consciously connected to and present with one's physical sensations, feelings, and bodily states, recognizing them as vital sources of information.

Archetypal Patterns: Universal, archaic patterns and images that derive from the collective unconscious and are the psychic counterparts of instincts.

Depth Psychology: A broad term for psychological theories that emphasize the unconscious and symbolic processes, such as those developed by Freud, Jung, and their successors.

Unconscious: The part of the mind of which we are not aware and from which we cannot voluntarily retrieve information. It is seen as a repository of repressed memories, instincts, and unconscious desires.

Integration: The process of bringing together disparate parts of the self—conscious and unconscious, mind and body, past and present—into a cohesive and harmonious whole.

The journey of understanding the intricate interplay between the body, the mind, and the unconscious is a path paved by the profound inquiries of countless thinkers and practitioners. This work stands on the shoulders of giants in the fields of psychoanalysis, depth psychology, somatics, and contemplative traditions. While a comprehensive list would extend far beyond the scope of this volume, key foundational texts and influential voices that have shaped the conceptual framework herein include:

Assagioli, R. (1965). Psychosynthesis: A Manual of Principles and Techniques.

Bateson, G. (1972). Steps to an Ecology of Mind.

Castaneda, C. (1968). The Teachings of Don Juan: A Yaqui Way of Knowledge.

Erikson, E. H. (1968). Identity: Youth and Crisis.

Freud, S. (1923). The Ego and the Id.

Gendlin, E. T. (1997). Focusing.

Hamer, D. (2009). The Body Keeps the Score: Brain, Mind, and Body in the Healing of Trauma.

Jung, C. G. (1959). The Archetypes and the Collective Unconscious.

Kabat-Zinn, J. (2013). Full Catastrophe Living: Using the Wisdom of Your Body and Mind to Face Stress, Pain, and Illness.

Lowen, A. (1975). Bioenergetics.

Neumann, E. (1954). The Origins and History of Consciousness.

Pierre, J. (2018). The Body Speaks Its Mind: The Somatic Approach to Healing.

Further references will include seminal works on symbolic interpretation, dream analysis, and embodied cognition.

Did you love *The Body and the Symbol: Where Desire Takes Form*? Then you should read *Psychoanalysis: The Hidden Architecture of the Mind*[1] by Deivede Eder Ferreira Psychoanalyst!

[2]

Psychoanalysis: The Hidden Architecture of the Mind is a profound journey into the symbolic structure of the human psyche.In this work, **Deivede Eder Ferreira** — psychoanalyst, philosopher, and founder of ABRAFP (The Brazilian Association of Philosophy and Psychoanalysis) — unveils how the unconscious shapes our emotions, choices, and inner conflicts.

Bridging the insights of **Freud, Jung, and Lacan**, Ferreira explores repression, desire, and the fragile architecture that sustains thought and identity. Each chapter illuminates the unseen logic

---

1. https://books2read.com/u/brJERw
2. https://books2read.com/u/brJERw

beneath human experience, transforming psychoanalysis from a theory of treatment into a philosophy of being.

Written in a clear, lyrical, and intellectually rigorous style, the book blends philosophy, psychology, and poetry. Ferreira's reflections reveal how unconscious forces guide dreams, guilt, love, and creativity — and how understanding them can lead to genuine transformation.

Within these pages, readers will discover:

The origins and evolution of psychoanalysis — from Freud's discoveries to modern thought.The central role of the unconscious and repression in shaping desire.The connection between language, symbols, and emotional life.Clinical insights that show how self-knowledge begins in listening to one's own silence.

For students, therapists, philosophers, or anyone drawn to the mysteries of the mind, **Psychoanalysis** offers both clarity and depth. It is a lantern in the labyrinth of the self — a timeless exploration of what it means to be human.

Read more at www.abrafp.org.

Also by Deivede Eder Ferreira Psychoanalyst

Psychoanalysis Series

Psychoanalysis: The Hidden Architecture of the Mind
Dreams and the Language of the Unconscious
The Body and the Symbol: Where Desire Takes Form
The Mirror of Desire: How the Unconscious Shapes Love

The Philosophers We Loved: A Fictional Collection by ABRAFP

When Plato Loved: The Tragedy of the Man Who Tried to Show the Sun
Schopenhauer, Nietzsche and La Mettrie: The Last Banquet

Standalone

Psychoanalysis

Watch for more at www.abrafp.org.

About the Author

Deivede Eder Ferreira is a psychoanalyst, philosopher, and writer recognized for uniting the precision of theory with the depth of human experience.He is the founder of **ABRAFP – The Association of Philosophy and Psychoanalysis**, established in 2008, through which he trains and inspires thinkers, students, and mental health professionals worldwide.

His works explore the intersections between psychoanalysis, philosophy, and the unconscious, restoring meaning to modern life through clarity, reflection, and poetic insight.

Read more at https://www.abrafp.org/.

www.ingramcontent.com/pod-product-compliance
Lightning Source LLC
LaVergne TN
LVHW090255210926
848480LV00001B/29